Logic of Programming and
Calculi of Discrete Design

W0192994

NATO ASI Series

Advanced Science Institutes Series

A series presenting the results of activities sponsored by the NATO Science Committee, which aims at the dissemination of advanced scientific and technological knowledge, with a view to strengthening links between scientific communities.

The Series is published by an international board of publishers in conjunction with the NATO Scientific Affairs Division

A Life Sciences	Plenum Publishing Corporation
B Physics	London and New York
C Mathematical and Physical Sciences	D. Reidel Publishing Company Dordrecht, Boston, Lancaster and Tokyo
D Behavioural and Social Sciences	Martinus Nijhoff Publishers Boston, The Hague, Dordrecht and Lancaster
E Applied Sciences	
F Computer and Systems Sciences	Springer-Verlag Berlin Heidelberg New York
G Ecological Sciences	London Paris Tokyo
H Cell Biology	

Logic of Programming and Calculi of Discrete Design

International Summer School directed by
F. L. Bauer, M. Broy, E. W. Dijkstra, C. A. R. Hoare

Edited by

Manfred Broy

Fakultät für Mathematik und Informatik, Universität Passau
Postfach 2540, 8390 Passau, Federal Republic of Germany

Springer-Verlag
Berlin Heidelberg New York London Paris Tokyo
Published in cooperation with NATO Scientific Affairs Divison

Proceedings of the NATO Advanced Study Institute on Logic of Programming and Calculi of Discrete Design held in Marktoberdorf, Federal Republic of Germany, July 29–August 10, 1986

Library of Congress Cataloging in Publication Data. NATO Advanced Study Institute on Logic of Programming and Calculi of Discrete Design (1986 : Marktoberdorf, Germany) Logic of programming and calculi of discrete design. (NATO ASI series. Series F, Computer and systems sciences ; vol. 36) "Published in cooperation with NATO Scientific Affairs Division." "Proceedings of the NATO Advanced Study Institute on Logic of Programming and Calculi of Discrete Design held in Marktoberdorf, Federal Republic of Germany, July 29–August 10, 1986"–Verso t.p. 1. Formal languages–Congresses. I. Broy, M., 1949-. II. North Atlantic Treaty Organization. Scientific Affairs Division. III. Title. IV. Series: NATO ASI series. Series F, Computer and system sciences; no. 36. QA267.3.N38 1986 005.13'1 87-20638

ISBN-13: 978-3-642-87376-8   e-ISBN-13: 978-3-642-87374-4
DOI: 10.1007/978-3-642-87374-4

This work is subject to copyright. All rights are reserved, whether the whole or part of the material is concerned, specifically the rights of translation, reprinting, re-use of illustrations, recitation, broadcasting, reproduction on microfilms or in other ways, and storage in data banks. Duplication of this publication or parts thereof is only permitted under the provisions of the German Copyright Law of September 9, 1965, in its version of June 24, 1985, and a copyright fee must always be paid. Violations fall under the prosecution act of the German Copyright Law.

© Springer-Verlag Berlin Heidelberg 1987
Softcover reprint of the hardcover 1st edition 1987

2145/3140-543210

Preface

In computing science design plays an eminently important role. By now, it is quite clear that the issue of proper design of programs within a formal calculus is one of the most interesting and most difficult parts of computing science. Many demanding problems have to be envisaged here such as notations, rules and calculi, and the study of semantic models. We are far away from comprehensive and widely accepted solutions in these areas. Discussions at the summer school have clearly shown that people have quite different perspectives and priorities with respect to these three main areas.

There is a general agreement that *notation* is very important. Here, notation is not so much used in the sense of "syntactic sugar", but rather in the sense of abstract syntax, in the sense of language constructs. Proper notation can significantly improve our understanding of the nature of the objects that we are dealing with and simplify the formal manipulation of these objects. However, influenced by educational background, habits, and schools of thought there are quite different tastes with respect to notation. The papers in these proceedings show very clearly how different those notations can be even when talking about quite similar objects.

There is also a general agreement that *rules of inference, transformation rules, and rewriting rules, forming calculi for proving and designing,* are of major interest. But here, again, people might find quite different opinions as to which forms of rules are best suited, which levels of reasoning are best suited, how formal the reasoning should be. However, it is necessary to underline once more that at least the machine needs a completely formal system when computing with information. Computation in an abstract view always means working in a deductive theory with a concrete control strategy.

Besides deductive theories, notations can refer to or express *mathematical models*, as is done, for example, in *denotational semantics*. Basically, in this way, the meaning of the considered notation is given in terms of well-known and well-understood mathematical concepts.

There was a lot of discussion within the summer school on the question "what is a mathematical or semantic model good for?" Some people argued that semantic models should not be used at all since they do not help us in formal reasoning. Other people argued that mathematical models are necessary for our understanding of deductive theories and that as an ultimate goal understanding is more important than formal manipulation. It is quite clear that the discussions within the summer school did not come to a particular conclusion in that point. I invite the reader of this volume to go through the articles and to make up his mind by himself. By doing so he may come to the conclusion that model-oriented and deduction-oriented treatments of formalisms are not competing but complementary approaches.

The individual lecture notes in this volume exhibit a wide spectrum of aspects of logic of programming and calculi of discrete design. They range from general questions of logic and design calculi to foundations of logic programming and questions of specification and verification of programs, from algebraic specifications to special design calculi for particular structures such as distributed systems, programs working with lists, or the logic of switching circuits.

Like each previous summer school in Marktoberdorf, this one also proved to be an undertaking that benefited almost more from the ideas and understanding of the participants than it did from those of the lecturers. The participants were motivated in following the lectures in a way which was hard to believe, in attending discussions, in criticizing approaches and working hard on understanding and maybe even improving the presented material. But also the lecturers gave outstanding presentations such that the summer school again became a definite highlight in our academic life.

This was complemented through the excellent organization and the perfect environment that we again found in Marktoberdorf. Therefore I would like to thank here, once more, all the people who worked hard to make this summer school a success and to prepare these fine proceedings which give an excellent overview of the state of the art.

Passau, April 1987   Manfred Broy

Table of Contents

F.L. Bauer

E.W. Dijkstra

E.C.R. Hehner

R.S. Bird

J.A. Robinson

Part I

Programming Calculi

Computation is just a special form of schematic deduction which may be called reduction. Programming, which means the formal specification of computation patterns, can therefore be viewed as the description of a schematic reduction process. In a computation certain rules are applied that help to reduce a given term to a special "normal" form. The applied rules are part of the theory underlying the basic computation structures that are also used as the basic programming structures. The set of these rules forms a programming calculus which can be used for the derivation of programs.

An Introduction to the Theory of Lists

Richard S. Bird

Programming Research Group,
University of Oxford,
11 Keble Rd.,
Oxford OX1 3QD,
United Kingdom.

Abstract

In these lectures we introduce a notation and a calculus for specifying and manipulating computable functions over lists. The calculus is used to derive efficient solutions for a number of problems, including problems in text processing. Although programming *per se* is not the main topic, we indicate briefly how these solutions can be implemented in a purely functional programming language.

Acknowledgements

Much of the theory presented in these lectures was developed in collaboration with L.G.L.T. Meertens of the Centrum voor Wiskunde en Informatica, Amsterdam. The influence of David Turner's work on the development of notation for functional programming has also been substantial. A particular debt of gratitude is owed to Phil Wadler who contributed a great deal in the way of ideas and examples. The work was supported by a grant from the Science and Engineering Research Council of Great Britain.

NATO ASI Series, Vol. F36
Logic of Programming and Calculi of Discrete Design
Edited by M. Broy
© Springer-Verlag Berlin Heidelberg 1987

1. Elementary Operations

1.1 List Notation. A *list* is a linearly ordered collection of values of the same general nature; one can talk about the first element of a list, the second element, and so on. Lists are also called *sequences*, a term more commonly found in other branches of mathematics, but there is no difference between the concepts and we shall use the two words interchangeably.

A finite list is denoted using square brackets and commas. For example, $[1, 2, 3]$ is a list of three integers and $[['b', 'y', 'e'], ['b', 'y', 'e']]$ is a list of two elements, each element being a list of characters. The empty list is written as $[\,]$ and a singleton list, containing just one element a, is written as $[a]$. In particular, $[[\,]]$ is a singleton list containing the empty list as its only element. Lists can be infinite as well as finite, but in these lectures we shall consider only finite lists.

Unlike a set, a list may contain the same value more than once. For example, $[1, 1]$ is a list of two elements, both of which happen to be 1, and is distinct from the list $[1]$ which contains only one element.

The special form $[m \ldots n]$ will be used to denote the list of integers in increasing order from m to n inclusive. If $m > n$, then $[m \ldots n] = [\,]$.

It was stated at the outset that lists are collections of values of the same general nature. What this means is that we can have lists of numbers, lists of characters, even lists of functions; but we shall never mix two distinct kinds of value in the same list. Given this restriction, the kind (or *type*) of list under consideration can be described in a simple manner. A list of numbers will be assigned the type $[Num]$ (read as: *list of Num*); a list of characters will be assigned the type $[Char]$, and so on. For example, $[[Num]]$ describes the type of lists of lists of numbers, and $[A \rightarrow B]$ describes the type of lists of functions from A to B. It is useful to extend this notation and write $[A]^+$ to denote the *non-empty* lists whose elements are of type A.

In order that the above convention for naming types should work satisfactorily, it is necessary to allow type expressions to contain *type variables*. To illustrate why, consider the empty list $[\,]$. As the empty list is empty of all conceivable values, it possesses the type $[Num]$, $[Char]$, as well as infinitely many others. The resolution of this situation is to assign $[\,]$ the type $[\alpha]$, where α is a type variable. To assert that a value has type $[\alpha]$ is to say that it has type $[A]$ for every possible type A. In this sense, the concept of a type variable is just a convenient abstraction for describing universal quantification over types. The device is also useful for describing *generic* functions. For example, the function *id*, where $id\ x = x$, possesses the type

$\alpha \to \alpha$. Further examples will be seen below.

A general comment on our typographical conventions should be made at this point. We shall use letters a, b, c, ..., at the beginning of the alphabet to denote elements of lists, and letters x, y, z at the end of the alphabet to denote the lists themselves. On some occasions we shall want to emphasise that a particular list is, in fact, a list of lists. Compound symbols xs, ys and zs will be used to denote lists which contain lists as elements. The names of functions will be written in italics, while infix operators will be written using special symbols of various kinds.

Having covered most of the special notation, we shall now introduce a small number of useful functions and operators for manipulating lists. They will be described informally: precise definitions will be given later when the necessary machinery has been developed.

1.2 Length. The length of a finite list is the number of elements it contains. We denote this operation by the operator $\#$. Thus,

$$\#[a_1, a_2, ..., a_n] = n.$$

In particular, $\#[\,] = 0$. For $m \leq n$ we have that

$$\#[m...n] = n - m + 1.$$

The type of $\#$ is given by

$$\# : [\alpha] \to Num.$$

The operator $\#$ takes a list, the nature of whose elements is irrelevant, and returns a (nonnegative, integer) number; hence the above type assignment.

1.3 Concatenation. Two lists can be concatenated together to form one longer list. This function is denoted by the operator $+\!\!\!+$ (pronounced "concatenate"). Thus,

$$[a_1, a_2, ..., a_n] +\!\!\!+ [b_1, b_2, ..., b_m] = [a_1, a_2, ..., a_n, b_1, b_2, ..., b_m].$$

In particular, we have

$$[\,] +\!\!\!+ x = x +\!\!\!+ [\,] = x$$

for all lists x, so the empty list is the *identity element* of the operator $+\!\!\!+$. Concatenation is also *associative*; we have

$$x +\!\!\!+ (y +\!\!\!+ z) = (x +\!\!\!+ y) +\!\!\!+ z$$

for all lists x, y and z.

A simple relationship between $\#$ and $\#\!\!+$ is given by the equation

$$\#(x \mathbin{+\!\!+} y) = \#x + \#y$$

for all finite lists x and y.

Finally, the type of $\mathbin{+\!\!+}$ is given by

$$\mathbin{+\!\!+} \; : [\alpha] \times [\alpha] \to [\alpha].$$

Concatenation takes a pair of lists, both of the same kind, and produces a third list, again of the same kind; hence the type assignment.

1.4 Map. The operator $*$ (pronounced "map") applies a function to each element of a list. We have

$$f * [a_1, a_2, \ldots, a_n] = [f \, a_1, f \, a_2, \ldots, f \, a_n].$$

In particular, $f\,[\,] = [\,]$. The type of $*$ is given by

$$* : (\alpha \to \beta) \times [\alpha] \to [\beta].$$

Hence, in the expression $f * x$, the first argument f is a function with type $\alpha \to \beta$, and the second argument x is a list with type $[\alpha]$. The result is a list of type $[\beta]$. These type variables can be instantiated to specific types. For example, if $even : Num \to Bool$ is the predicate which determines whether a number is even, then

$$even * [1 \ldots 4] = [false, true, false, true],$$

has type $[Bool]$. Here, $true$ and $false$ denote the two constants of type $Bool$.

As with other infix operators, the operator $*$ is allowed to appear in expressions accompanied by only one of its arguments. In particular, we can write $(f*)$ to denote the function of type $[\alpha] \to [\beta]$, where $f : \alpha \to \beta$, which takes a list and applies f to every element. By the same convention, $((f*)*)$ is a function which takes a list of lists and applies $(f*)$ to every element.

There are a number of important identities concerning $*$. First of all, $*$ distributes through $\mathbin{+\!\!+}$; for all lists x and y we have

$$f * (x \mathbin{+\!\!+} y) = (f * x) \mathbin{+\!\!+} (f * y).$$

Second, * distributes (backwards) through functional composition:

$$(f \cdot g)* = (f*) \cdot (g*).$$

We shall encounter many applications of these two identities in due course. Another rule is that if f is an injective function with inverse f^{-1}, then

$$(f*)^{-1} = (f^{-1}*).$$

1.5 Filter. The operator $\triangleleft$ (pronounced "filter") takes a predicate p and a list x and returns the list of elements of x which satisfy p. For example, we have

$$even \triangleleft [1 \ldots 10] = [2, 4, 6, 8, 10].$$

The type of $\triangleleft$ is given by

$$\triangleleft : (\alpha \rightarrow Bool) \times [\alpha] \rightarrow [\alpha].$$

Like *, the operator $\triangleleft$ distibutes through $+\!\!\!+$: for all lists x and y we have

$$p \triangleleft (x +\!\!\!+ y) = (p \triangleleft x) +\!\!\!+ (p \triangleleft y).$$

We also have the laws

$$
\begin{aligned}
p \triangleleft q \triangleleft x &= q \triangleleft p \triangleleft x \\
p \triangleleft p \triangleleft x &= p \triangleleft x \\
p \triangleleft f * x &= f * (p \cdot f) \triangleleft x,
\end{aligned}
$$

for all functions p, q and f and lists x. The first law (commutativity of filters) says that filtering a list with a (total) predicate q, and then filtering the result with a (total) predicate p, gives the same answer as first filtering with p and then with q. The second law says that $(p \triangleleft)$ is an idempotent operation. The third law (commutativity of map and filter) says that mapping with f followed by filtering with p gives the same result as first filtering with $p \cdot f$ and then mapping with f. We can also express these laws using functional composition:

$$
\begin{aligned}
(p \triangleleft) \cdot (q \triangleleft) &= (q \triangleleft) \cdot (p \triangleleft) \\
(p \triangleleft) \cdot (p \triangleleft) &= (p \triangleleft) \\
(p \triangleleft) \cdot (f*) &= (f*) \cdot ((p \cdot f) \triangleleft).
\end{aligned}
$$

1.6 Operator precedence. In addition to the above operators we have also encountered, without explicitly mentioning the fact, the operation of functional application. Functional application is denoted by just a space in formulae, and when no confusion can arise the space is sometimes omitted. Thus $f\,a$ means f "applied to" a. Application associates to the left, so that $f\,a\,b$ means $(f\,a)\,b$ and not $f\,(a\,b)$.

It is normal in mathematical notation which deploys a number of infix operators to provide certain rules of precedence and association in order to reduce the number of brackets. We shall suppose that functional application is more binding than any other operator, so $f\,x \mathbin{+\!\!+} y$ means $(f\,x) \mathbin{+\!\!+} y$ and not $f(x \mathbin{+\!\!+} y)$. It is also convenient to suppose that $\mathbin{+\!\!+}$ has a low precedence, so $f*x \mathbin{+\!\!+} g*y$ means $(f*x) \mathbin{+\!\!+} (g*y)$ and not $f*(x \mathbin{+\!\!+} g*y)$. For the other operators we shall put in brackets to clarify meaning. However, we shall assume that, in the absence of brackets, operators associate to the right in expressions. For example, $f * p \triangleleft x$ means $f * (p \triangleleft x)$ and not $(f * p) \triangleleft x$.

2. Reduction

2.1 The reduction operators. Most of the operations introduced in the first section transform lists into other lists. The reduction operators to be described in the present and following section are more general in that they can convert lists into other kinds of value as well.

The first reduction operator, written "/" and pronounced "reduce", takes an operator $\oplus$ on the left and a list x on the right. Its effect is to insert $\oplus$ between adjacent elements of x. Thus:

$$\oplus/[a_1, a_2, \ldots, a_n] = a_1 \oplus a_2 \oplus \cdots \oplus a_n.$$

For the right-hand side of this equation to be unambiguous in the absence of brackets, the operator $\oplus$ must be associative. In fact, the form $\oplus/x$ is only permitted when $\oplus$ is an associative operator, so the grouping of terms on the right is irrelevant.

In the case that the second argument of / is a singleton list $[a]$, we have from the informal description of $\oplus/$ that

$$\oplus/[a] = a.$$

Moreover, we also have

$$\oplus/(x \mathbin{+\!\!+} y) = (\oplus/x) \oplus (\oplus/y)$$

whenever x and y are non-empty lists. These two equations (the definition of / on singletons and the distributive law) are important and will be used frequently in what follows.

The informal definition of / given above does not prescribe a meaning for the expression $\oplus/[\,]$. If $\oplus$ has an identity element e, then we suppose $\oplus/[\,] = e$; otherwise $\oplus/[\,]$ is not defined. The reason for this choice is to preserve the distributive law when either x or y is the empty list. Since

$$a = \oplus/[a] = \oplus/([a] + [\,]) = (\oplus/[a]) \oplus (\oplus/[\,]) = a \oplus e,$$

and also

$$a = \oplus/[a] = \oplus/([\,] + [a]) = (\oplus/[\,]) \oplus (\oplus/[a]) = e \oplus a,$$

it follows that, if defined, $\oplus/[\,]$ must be both a left and right identity element of $\oplus$. Hence, $\oplus/[\,]$ can only be the (unique) identity element of $\oplus$.

The type of / is given by

$$/ : (\alpha \times \alpha \to \alpha) \times [\alpha] \to \alpha.$$

Thus, in the combination $\oplus/x$, the operator $\oplus$ has a type of the form $\alpha \times \alpha \to \alpha$ and x has a type of the form $[\alpha]$. The combination will then have type α.

Some simple cases of reduction, indicative of the general utility of the operator, are given in the following definitions:

$$
\begin{aligned}
sum &= +/ \\
product &= \times/ \\
flatten &= +\!\!+/ \\
all\ p &= (\wedge/) \cdot (p*) \\
some\ p &= (\vee/) \cdot (p*) \\
min &= \downarrow/ \\
max &= \uparrow/
\end{aligned}
$$

All the operators involved in these definitions are associative and all, except the last two, have identity elements. The identity element for $+$ is 0, so $sum\,[\,] = 0$; for multiplication the identity element is 1, so $product\,[\,] = 1$, and so on. The expressions $+/$ and $\times/$ correspond to the special symbols $\sum$ and $\prod$ used in other branches of mathematics. For example,

$$
\begin{aligned}
\textstyle\sum_{j=1}^{n} f_j &= +/f * [1 \ldots n] \\
\textstyle\prod_{j=1}^{n} j &= \times/[1 \ldots n].
\end{aligned}
$$

The function *flatten* takes a list of lists and concatenates them to form a single list. Since $[\,]$ is the identity element of $+\!\!+$ we have $+\!\!+/[\,] = [\,]$.

The binary operators $\wedge$ and $\vee$ denote the operations of logical conjunction and disjunction respectively. Accordingly, the function *all* takes a predicate p and a list x and returns the value *true* if all the elements of x satisfy p, and *false* otherwise. For example,

$$all\ even\ [2, 4, 6] = true.$$

The function *some* takes similar arguments p and x and returns *true* if at least one of the elements of x satisfies p, and *false* otherwise. For example,

$$some\ (= 1)\ [2, 4, 6] = false.$$

Since

$$
\begin{aligned}
a \wedge true &= true \wedge a &= a \\
a \vee false &= false \vee a &= a,
\end{aligned}
$$

it follows that $all\ p\,[\,] = true$ and $some\ p\,[\,] = false$ for all predicates p.

The operators $\uparrow$ and $\downarrow$ select the greater and lesser of their two (numerical) arguments respectively. Hence *max* selects the maximum of a list of numbers and *min* selects the minimum. These two operators are considered further below.

2.2 Fictitious values. Neither $\uparrow$ nor $\downarrow$ have identity elements in the domain of finite numbers, so both $max\,[\,]$ and $min\,[\,]$ are undefined. Despite this, it is often useful to be able to manipulate expressions involving terms of the form $\uparrow/x$ and $\downarrow/x$ without taking special precautions to ensure $x \neq [\,]$. The same holds for other operators without identity elements. Provided certain rules are observed, we can always invent a "fictitious" value to act as an identity element of a given operator. Suppose $\oplus$ is an associative operator, defined over some domain X but not possessing an identity element. Invent a new value e and adjoin it to X. Define $\oplus'$ by the rules

$$
\begin{aligned}
a \oplus' b &= b, &&\text{if } a = e \\
&= a, &&\text{if } b = e \\
&= a \oplus b, &&\text{otherwise.}
\end{aligned}
$$

The new operator $\oplus'$ is associative, has identity element e, and agrees with $\oplus$ on arguments in X. For example, we can invent fictitious values $\uparrow'/[\,]$ and $\downarrow'/[\,]$ — calling them $-\infty$ and ∞ say — and adjoin them to the domain of finite numbers. As long as no other properties of these fictitious elements are assumed, we can continue to use the undecorated operators in expressions and derivations. Care must be exercised to avoid imputing any additional laws to the new values. For example, the law

$$\downarrow/(a+)*x = a+\downarrow/x$$

is only valid when restricted to the case $x \neq [\,]$.

To give another illustration of a useful operator which has no identity element, define $\ll$ by

$$a \ll b = a.$$

Since

$$(a \ll b) \ll c = a = a \ll (b \ll c),$$

the operator $\ll$ is associative, and we can form $\ll/x$. The value of this expression is the first element of the list x. This is a useful operation and we define

$$head\ x\ =\ll/x.$$

(A similarly useful operation is

$$last\ x\ =\gg/x,$$

where $a \gg b = b$.) The operator $\ll$ does not possess an identity element. If e were an identity element, then we would have $e \ll a = a$ for all a; but since $e \ll a = e$ by the definition of $\ll$, the conclusion would be that $e = a$ for all a. If necessary, we can invent a fictitious value e and define

$$
\begin{aligned}
a \ll' b &= b, &&\text{if } a = e \\
&= a, &&\text{otherwise.}
\end{aligned}
$$

The function $\ll'$ agrees with $\ll$ on non-fictitious arguments.

2.3 Homomorphisms.

There is a close relationship between reductions and homomorphisms on sequences. By definition, a function h defined on finite lists is a homomorphism if there exists an associative operator $\oplus$ with identity element e such that $h[\,] = e$ and

$$h(x + \!\!\!+\, y) = h\,x \oplus h\,y$$

for all lists x and y. If h is not defined on the empty list, then $\oplus$ is not required to possess an identity element and the above equation is asserted for non-empty lists only.

If h is a homomorphism, then h is uniquely determined by $\oplus$ and the values of h on singleton sequences. In other words, if we define f by the equation

$$f\,a = h\,[a],$$

then h is determined by $\oplus$ and f alone. The following lemma says that every homomorphism can be expressed as the composition of a reduction and a map, and every such composition is a homomorphism.

Lemma 1 [Homomorphism Lemma]. *A function h is a homomorphism with respect to $\#$ if and only if $h = (\oplus/) \cdot (f*)$ for some operator $\oplus$ and function f.*

Proof. First, suppose $h = (\oplus/) \cdot (f*)$. Then

$$
\begin{aligned}
h\,(x \# y) &= \oplus/f*(x \# y) \\
&= \oplus/((f*x) \# (f*y)) \\
&= (\oplus/f*x) \oplus (\oplus/f*y) \\
&= h\,x \oplus h\,y,
\end{aligned}
$$

using the distributive laws for $*$ and $/$. Furthermore, if $\oplus$ has an identity element e, then

$$h\,[\,] = \oplus/f*[\,] = \oplus/[\,] = e.$$

Hence h is a homomorphism.

To prove the converse, suppose h is a homomorphism, so that

$$h\,(x \# y) = h\,x \oplus h\,y$$

for some operator $\oplus$. Define f by the equation

$$f\,a = h\,[a].$$

We show $h = (\oplus/) \cdot (f*)$ by induction on the length of sequences.

If $h\,[\,]$ is defined, then it is the identity element of $\oplus$ and so

$$h\,[\,] = \oplus/[\,] = \oplus/f*[\,].$$

If $\#x = 1$, that is, $x = [a]$ for some a, then we have

$$h\,[a] = f\,a = \oplus/[f\,a] = \oplus/f*[a],$$

using the definition of $/$ on singletons and the definition of $*$. In the case $\#x = n$, where $n > 1$, we can set $x = y \# z$, where $1 \le \#y, \#z < n$. By induction, we can suppose $h\,y = \oplus/f * y$ and $h\,z = \oplus/f * z$ and hence compute

$$
\begin{aligned}
h(y \mathbin{+\!\!+} z) &= h\,y \oplus h\,z \\
&= (\oplus/f * y) \oplus (\oplus/f * z) \\
&= \oplus/f * (y \mathbin{+\!\!+} z),
\end{aligned}
$$

using the distributive laws for $*$ and $/$ as before. This completes the proof.

2.4 Definition by homomorphisms. Many of the functions already introduced are homomorphisms. A reduction itself is a homomorphism and so is a map. We have

$$\oplus/ = (\oplus/) \cdot (id*)$$

where id is the identity function, and

$$f* = (\mathbin{+\!\!+}/) \cdot (g*)$$

where g is the function defined by $g\,a = [f\,a]$.

A filter is also a homomorphism. We have

$$p \triangleleft = (\mathbin{+\!\!+}/) \cdot (f_p*),$$

where the function f_p is defined by $f_p\,a = [a]$ if $p\,a$ and $f_p\,a = [\,]$ otherwise. This function replaces elements which satisfy p by singleton lists and others by the empty list. The filtered sequence can then be obtained by concatenating these lists together.

The length operator can be defined as the homomorphism

$$\# = (+/) \cdot (K_1*),$$

where $K_c\,a = c$ for all a. Every element of the list is therefore replaced by 1 and the result is summed to give the length.

The functions *head* and *last* are homomorphisms:

$$
\begin{aligned}
head &= (\ll/) \cdot (id*) \\
last &= (\gg/) \cdot (id*),
\end{aligned}
$$

where $a \ll b = a$ and $a \gg b = b$.

Of course, not all functions on lists are homomorphisms. One useful sufficient condition is that h is *injective*, i.e. $h(x) = h(y)$ if and only if $x = y$. If h is injective, then its inverse h^{-1} is well-defined on the range of h. Thus, if we define $\oplus$ by

$$u \oplus v = h(h^{-1}\,u \mathbin{+\!\!+} h^{-1}\,v),$$

then it follows that

$$
\begin{aligned}
h(x \mathbin{+\mkern-8mu+} y) &= h(h^{-1}(h\,x) \mathbin{+\mkern-8mu+} h^{-1}(h\,y)) \\
&= h\,x \oplus h\,y
\end{aligned}
$$

Hence h is the homomorphism $(\oplus/) \cdot (f*)$, where, as usual, $f\,a = h\,[a]$.

A simple application of this result is given by the function *reverse* which reverses the order of the elements in a list. Clearly, *reverse* is injective and is its own inverse. Hence

$$
reverse = (\oplus/) \cdot (f*),
$$

where

$$
x \oplus y = reverse(reverse\ x \mathbin{+\mkern-8mu+} reverse\ y).
$$

An informal argument, left to the reader, shows this last expression is equal to $(y \mathbin{+\mkern-8mu+} x)$. By convention, let $\oplus$ and $\widetilde{\oplus}$ be related by the equation

$$
x \mathbin{\widetilde{\oplus}} y = y \oplus x.
$$

Also, let the special symbol $\square$ denote the function which transforms values into singleton lists so that $\square a = [a]$ for all a. Then we can write

$$
reverse = (\widetilde{\mathbin{+\mkern-8mu+}}/) \cdot (\square*)
$$

We turn now to a more advanced application of the same idea.

2.5 Example: processing text. Suppose we define a *text* to be a list of characters and a *line* to be a list of characters not containing the newline character NL. These classes can be introduced as new types:

$$
\begin{aligned}
Text &= [Char] \\
Line &= [Char \setminus \{\mathrm{NL}\}].
\end{aligned}
$$

In this section we want to define a function *lines* which takes a text and returns the list of lines that make up the text. The function *lines* is an important component in many text-processing applications. It can be specified formally as the inverse of another function, *unlines* say, which inserts newline characters between adjacent lines and then concatenates the result. The definition of *unlines* is as a reduction:

$$
\begin{aligned}
unlines &= \oplus/ \\
x \oplus y &= x \mathbin{+\mkern-8mu+} [\mathrm{NL}] \mathbin{+\mkern-8mu+} y.
\end{aligned}
$$

The operator $\oplus$ does not have an identity element, so the value of $unlines\,[\,]$ is not defined. We therefore assign $unlines$ the type

$$unlines : [Line]^+ \to Text,$$

where $[X]^+$ denotes the non-empty members of $[X]$. It is easy to verify that $unlines$ is injective. This means $lines$ can be completely specified by the single equation

$$lines(\oplus/xs) = xs \tag{1}$$

for all non-empty sequences of lines xs.

Since $lines$ itself is injective, we can look for a suitable homomorphism of the form

$$lines = (\otimes/) \cdot (f*). \tag{2}$$

If we succeed, then we shall have converted an implicit specification (1) into a constructive definition (2). The synthesis is by straightforward calculation.

First we determine f. By a standard argument we have

$$f\,a = lines\,[a]$$

If a is not the newline character, then

$$lines\,[a] = lines(\oplus/[[a]]) = [[a]]$$

using the definition of $/$ on singletons and Equation (1). For $a = \text{NL}$ we have

$$
\begin{aligned}
lines\,[\text{NL}] &= lines([\,] \mathbin{+\!\!\!+} [\text{NL}] \mathbin{+\!\!\!+} [\,]) \\
&= lines([\,] \oplus [\,]) \\
&= lines((\oplus/[[\,]]) \oplus (\oplus/[[\,]])) \\
&= lines(\oplus/[[\,],[\,]]) \\
&= [[\,],[\,]],
\end{aligned}
$$

using the definition of $\oplus$ and Equation (1).

Putting these results together,

$$
\begin{aligned}
f\,a &= [[\,],[\,]], \quad \text{if } a = \text{NL}, \\
&= [[a]], \quad\ \text{otherwise.}
\end{aligned}
$$

Second, we determine $\otimes$. Since each argument of $\otimes$ is a non-empty list, we need only consider the definition of $(xs \mathbin{+\!\!\!+} [x]) \otimes ([y] \mathbin{+\!\!\!+} ys)$. Using Equations (1) and (2) and the distributive properties of $/$, we have that

$$
\begin{aligned}
(xs \mathbin{+\!\!\!+} [x]) \otimes ([y] \mathbin{+\!\!\!+} ys) &= lines(\oplus/(xs \mathbin{+\!\!\!+} [x])) \otimes lines(\oplus/([y] \mathbin{+\!\!\!+} ys)) \\
&= lines((\oplus/(xs \mathbin{+\!\!\!+} [x])) \mathbin{+\!\!\!+} \oplus /([y] \mathbin{+\!\!\!+} ys)).
\end{aligned}
$$

Now,

$$\oplus/(xs \,+\!\!+\, [x]) \;=\; (\oplus/xs) \oplus (\oplus/[x])$$
$$=\; (\oplus/xs) \,+\!\!+\, [\text{NL}] \,+\!\!+\, x,$$

and similarly

$$\oplus/([y] \,+\!\!+\, ys) = y \,+\!\!+\, [\text{NL}] \,+\!\!+\, (\oplus/ys).$$

Their concatenation is therefore

$$(\oplus/xs) \,+\!\!+\, [\text{NL}] \,+\!\!+\, x \,+\!\!+\, y \,+\!\!+\, [\text{NL}] \,+\!\!+\, (\oplus/ys)$$
$$=\; (\oplus/xs) \,+\!\!+\, [\text{NL}] \,+\!\!+\, (\oplus/[x \,+\!\!+\, y]) \,+\!\!+\, [\text{NL}] \,+\!\!+\, (\oplus/ys)$$
$$=\; (\oplus/xs) \oplus (\oplus/[x \,+\!\!+\, y]) \oplus (\oplus/ys)$$
$$=\; \oplus/(xs \,+\!\!+\, [x \,+\!\!+\, y] \,+\!\!+\, ys).$$

We conclude using Equation (1) that

$$(xs \,+\!\!+\, [x]) \otimes ([y] \,+\!\!+\, ys) \;=\; lines(\oplus/(xs \,+\!\!+\, [x \,+\!\!+\, y] \,+\!\!+\, ys))$$
$$=\; xs \,+\!\!+\, [x \,+\!\!+\, y] \,+\!\!+\, ys.$$

Note that the above derivation actually juggles with some potentially fictitious values. No meaning has been assigned to $\oplus/[\,]$, yet terms of the form $\oplus/xs$ appear in a context where the case $xs = [\,]$ is not specifically excluded. No confusion can arise because, as we have seen in §2.2, a fictitious identity element of $\oplus$ can be added to the domain of values without inconsistency.

Notice also that, unlike $\oplus$, the operator $\otimes$ does have an identity element, namely $[[\,]]$. This follows from the fact that $\oplus/[[\,]] = [\,]$, since

$$\otimes/[\,] = \otimes/(\oplus/[[\,]]) = [[\,]].$$

It is instructive to develop this example a little further to show how other text processing functions can be synthesised. Define a *word* to be a non-empty sequence of characters not containing the newline or space characters. We can define the type *Word* by the equation

$$Word = [Char \setminus \{\text{NL}, \text{SP}\}]^{+}.$$

In a similar spirit to before, we can seek a constructive definition of a function *words* for breaking a line into words. The type of words is therefore

$$words : Line \rightarrow [Word].$$

The function $unwords : [Word]^+ \rightarrow Line$ defined by

$$
\begin{aligned}
unwords &= \oplus/ \\
x \oplus y &= x + [\text{SP}] + y
\end{aligned}
$$

takes a sequence of words and concatenates them after inserting a space between adjacent words. The function $unwords$ is injective, but not surjective. For example, none of the lines $[\,]$, $[\text{SP}]$, $[\text{SP}, \text{SP}]$, . . . and so on, are in the range of $unwords$. However, if we temporarily admit the empty list as a possible word, then $unwords$ becomes surjective on the augmented domain and we can define its inverse in an exactly similar way as we have done for $unlines$. Having done this, we can now define $words$ by filtering out the empty sequences. Hence

$$
words = ((\neq [\,])\triangleleft) \cdot (\otimes/) \cdot (f*)
$$

where

$$
\begin{aligned}
f\,a &= [[\,],[\,]], \quad \text{if } a = \text{SP} \\
&= [[a]], \quad\;\; \text{otherwise}
\end{aligned}
$$

and, as before,

$$
(xs + [x]) \otimes ([y] + ys) = xs + [x + y] + ys.
$$

Note that, although $words \cdot unwords$ is the identity function on non-empty sequences of words, the function $unwords \cdot words$ is not the identity function on lines. Redundant spaces are removed between words.

Finally, to complete a logical trio of functions, we can define a *paragraph* to be a non-empty sequence of non-empty lines and seek a definition of a function *paras* which breaks a sequence of lines into paragraphs. The type *Para* can be defined by the equation

$$
Para = [Line^+]^+.
$$

We require *paras* to have type $[Line] \rightarrow [Para]$. The function *unparas*, where

$$
unparas : [Para]^+ \rightarrow [Line],
$$

is defined by

$$
\begin{aligned}
unparas &= \oplus/ \\
xs \oplus ys &= xs + [[\,]] + ys,
\end{aligned}
$$

This function takes a sequence of paragraphs and converts it to a sequence of lines by inserting a single empty line between adjacent paragraphs and concatenating the result. Like *unwords*, the function *unparas* is injective but not surjective. Again, by temporarily admitting the empty paragraph, we can make *unparas* surjective and define its inverse in the usual way. The empty sequences can then be filtered from the result.

To summarise: the types we have introduced are

$$
\begin{aligned}
Text &= [Char] \\
Line &= [Char \setminus \{\mathrm{NL}\}] \\
Word &= [Char \setminus \{\mathrm{NL}, \mathrm{SP}\}]^+ \\
Para &= [Line^+]^+
\end{aligned}
$$

The three "un-functions" are

$$
\begin{aligned}
unlines &: [Line]^+ \to Text & unlines &= \oplus_{\mathrm{NL}}/ \\
unwords &: [Word]^+ \to Line & unwords &= \oplus_{\mathrm{SP}}/ \\
unparas &: [Para]^+ \to [Line] & unparas &= \oplus_{[\,]}/
\end{aligned}
$$

Here, we have

$$
x \oplus_a y = x + [a] + y.
$$

The three inverse functions are

$$
\begin{aligned}
lines &= (\otimes/) \cdot (f_{\mathrm{NL}}*) \\
words &= ((\neq [\,]) \triangleleft) \cdot (\otimes/) \cdot (f_{\mathrm{SP}}*) \\
paras &= ((\neq [\,]) \triangleleft) \cdot (\otimes/) \cdot (f_{[\,]}*),
\end{aligned}
$$

where

$$
\begin{aligned}
f_b\, a &= [[\,],[\,]], \quad \text{if } a = b \\
&= [[a]], \qquad \text{otherwise}
\end{aligned}
$$

and

$$
(xs + [x]) \otimes ([y] + ys) = xs + [x + y] + ys.
$$

These six functions have a variety of uses. We give just two. The number of lines, words and paragraphs in a text can be counted by

$$
\begin{aligned}
countlines &= \# \cdot lines \\
countwords &= \# \cdot (+/) \cdot (words*) \cdot lines \\
countparas &= \# \cdot paras \cdot lines.
\end{aligned}
$$

Second, we can normalize a text by removing redundant empty lines between paragraphs and spaces between words. We have

$$
\begin{aligned}
normalize &= unparse \cdot parse \\
parse &= ((words*)*) \cdot paras \cdot lines \\
unparse &= unlines \cdot unparas \cdot ((unwords*)*).
\end{aligned}
$$

To *parse* a text here means to break it into lines, paragraphs and words. The type of *parse* is

$$parse : Text \rightarrow [[[Word]]]$$

For injective functions f and g we have

$$(f \cdot g)^{-1} = g^{-1} \cdot f^{-1}$$
$$(f*)^{-1} = (f^{-1}*),$$

from which it follows that *parse* is injective and the definition of *unparse* is correct.

2.6 Promotion lemmas. As simple consequences of the Homomorphism Lemma of §2.3 we can derive the following useful identities. They generalise the distributive laws of $*$, $\lhd$ and $/$.

Lemma 2 [Promotion]. *For arbitrary function f, predicate p and associative operator $\oplus$ we have:*

$$
\begin{array}{lrcl}
(*\,\text{promotion}) & (f*) \cdot (\!+\!/) &=& (\!+\!/) \cdot ((f*)*) \\
(\lhd\,\text{promotion}) & (p\,\lhd) \cdot (\!+\!/) &=& (\!+\!/) \cdot ((p\,\lhd)*) \\
(/\,\text{promotion}) & (\oplus/) \cdot (\!+\!/) &=& (\oplus/) \cdot ((\oplus/)*).
\end{array}
$$

Proof. Set $h = (f*) \cdot (\!+\!/)$. It is an easy calculation to show that

$$h\,[x] = f * x$$

and also

$$h(xs +\!\!\!+ ys) = h\,xs +\!\!\!+ h\,ys.$$

Hence h is the homomorphism $(\!+\!/) \cdot ((f*)*)$. This establishes the $*$ - promotion law. Similar reasoning establishes $/$ - promotion. Finally, to prove $\lhd$ - promotion, recall that $(p\,\lhd)$ is a homomorphism of the form $(\!+\!/)\cdot(f*)$ for a suitable function f, the definition of which is not relevant for the present proof. Using in turn, $*$ - promotion, $/$ - promotion and the distributivity of $*$ through composition, we have

$$
\begin{array}{rcl}
(p\,\lhd) \cdot (\!+\!/) &=& (\!+\!/) \cdot (f*) \cdot (\!+\!/) \\
&=& (\!+\!/) \cdot (\!+\!/) \cdot ((f*)*) \\
&=& (\!+\!/) \cdot ((\!+\!/)*) \cdot ((f*)*) \\
&=& (\!+\!/) \cdot (((\!+\!/) \cdot (f*))*) \\
&=& (\!+\!/) \cdot ((p\,\lhd)*)
\end{array}
$$

as required.

The term "promotion" is used to describe these results because they say that rather than mapping, reducing or filtering over one large sequence, one can divide the sequence into shorter ones, map, reduce or filter each of these (hence "promoting" the operation into the component sequences) and collect the outcomes. For example, consider the rule

$$(\downarrow/) \cdot (+\!\!+/) = (\downarrow/) \cdot ((\downarrow/)*).$$

In words this says the minimum of a flattened list of lists of numbers can be obtained by first minimising over each component list and then minimising over the results. If one of the component lists is empty, then its minimum will be the fictitious value ∞, but since $\infty \downarrow a = a \downarrow \infty = a$ the minimum of the minimums will only be ∞ if all the component lists are empty.

2.7 Selection and indeterminacy. We end the section with a discussion of two new operators which are mainly used with reductions.

Many problems in computation can be formulated as optimisation problems: find the cheapest, shortest, longest or perhaps the value of greatest profit in some given class of values. Such problems can be specified with the help of two new operators, $\downarrow_f$ and $\uparrow_f$. Just as $(a \downarrow b)$ selects the minimum of two numbers a and b, so $(a \downarrow_f b)$ selects either a or b according to which is smaller: $f\,a$ or $f\,b$. In the definition of $\downarrow_f$, function f has generic type $(\alpha \to Num)$. The definition of $(a \uparrow_f b)$ is analogous: it selects a or b depending on which is greater: $f\,a$ or $f\,b$ (from now on we shall ignore $\uparrow_f$ as it is treated in an exactly similar manner to $\downarrow_f$). We have

$$
\begin{aligned}
a \downarrow_f b \;&=\; a, \quad \text{if } f\,a < f\,b \\
&=\; b, \quad \text{if } f\,a > f\,b.
\end{aligned}
$$

The lacuna in this definition occurs in the case $f\,a = f\,b$. If f is an injective function on the range of values of interest, then $f\,a = f\,b$ only if $a = b$ and we can assign $(a \downarrow_f b)$ their common value. For example, $\downarrow = \downarrow_{id}$. However, in the majority of practical cases the function f is not injective. To ask for the longest or shortest sequence in a class of sequences is really an abuse of language: there may be more than one such sequence. What is meant is *some* longest or shortest sequence.

In developing constructive solutions to problems of optimisation, the under specification permitted by $\downarrow_f$ can be very useful, especially as we are not normally concerned with any other property of the result than that it minimises f. Accordingly, we shall allow expressions to contain occurrences of the operator $\downarrow_f$ when f is not an injective function. In these cases we interpret $\downarrow_f$ as standing for $\downarrow_{f'}$, where f' is some injective function — the precise nature of which we are not interested in — which respects the ordering given by f. That is, $f\,a < f\,b$ implies $f'\,a < f'\,b$. If $a \neq b$ but $f\,a = f\,b$, then either $f'\,a < f'\,b$ or $f'\,a > f'\,b$ and we do not care which. We suppose without proof that such an extension f' exists for any f (this assumption is related to the Axiom of Choice in Set theory).

When carrying out equational reasoning with $\downarrow_f$ we must be careful not to ascribe any properties to $\downarrow_f$ which are not implied by the foregoing convention. Only the following properties may be assumed:

$$
\begin{array}{lrcl}
\text{(associativity)} & a \downarrow_f (b \downarrow_f c) & = & (a \downarrow_f b) \downarrow_f c \\
\text{(idempotence)} & a \downarrow_f a & = & a \\
\text{(commutativity)} & a \downarrow_f b & = & b \downarrow_f a \\
\text{(selectivity)} & a \downarrow_f b & = & \text{either } a \text{ or } b \\
\text{(minimality)} & f(a \downarrow_f b) & = & f\,a \downarrow f\,b.
\end{array}
$$

At certain stages during the development of a constructive definition it may become appropriate to exercise a choice about the value of $(a \downarrow_f b)$ when $f\,a = f\,b$. Such a step is called a *choice* step and will be denoted by the sign $\rightsquigarrow$. For instance, if $f\,a = f\,b$ we can write

$$a \downarrow_f b \rightsquigarrow a$$

The sign $\rightsquigarrow$ can be read as "may be refined to". Taking a choice step is to be regarded as imposing a further property on the injective function f' of which f is the representative. This means that any choice step must be consistent with every previous choice step. For example, if $f(1) = f(2)$ and we decide, in some chain of reasoning, to impose the choice $1 \downarrow_f 2 \rightsquigarrow 1$, then it follows that

$$1 \downarrow_f 2 + 1 \downarrow_f 2 \rightsquigarrow 1 + 1 \downarrow_f 2 = 1 + 1 = 2.$$

However, the following reasoning is *not* valid:

$$1 \downarrow_f 2 + 1 \downarrow_f 2 \rightsquigarrow 1 + 1 \downarrow_f 2 \rightsquigarrow 1 + 2 = 3.$$

Having exercised a choice, the consequences must be followed consistently.

The major use of selection functions occurs in conjunction with reduction. For example, $\uparrow_\# / xs$ returns some longest sequence in the list of sequences xs. We shall see many examples in due course. As an extension to the minimality law we have

$$f \cdot (\downarrow_f /) = (\downarrow /) \cdot (f*).$$

For $f = \#$ this law expresses the formal equivalence of the English phrases "the length of the shortest" and "the minimum of the lengths".

3. Directed reduction and recursion

3.1 Left and right reduction We now introduce two more reduction operators: $\nleftarrow$ (pronounced "right-reduce") and $\nrightarrow$ (pronounced "left-reduce"). They are closely related to the reduction operator $/$, but each takes three arguments: an operator $\oplus$, a value e and a list x. They can be described by the equations

$$
\begin{aligned}
(\oplus \nleftarrow e)[a_1, a_2, \ldots, a_n] &= a_1 \oplus (a_2 \oplus (\cdots(a_n \oplus e))) \\
(\oplus \nrightarrow e)[a_1, a_2, \ldots, a_n] &= (((e \oplus a_1) \oplus a_2) \cdots \oplus a_n).
\end{aligned}
$$

In particular, we have

$$
\begin{aligned}
(\oplus \nleftarrow e)\,[\,] &= e \\
(\oplus \nrightarrow e)\,[\,] &= e.
\end{aligned}
$$

The operator $\oplus$ used in a left or right reduction need not be associative, so the brackets in the above equations are necessary. Indeed, the type of $\oplus$ may not even take the form $\alpha \times \alpha \to \alpha$. The types of $\nleftarrow$ and $\nrightarrow$ are given by

$$
\begin{aligned}
\nleftarrow &: ((\alpha \times \beta \to \beta) \times \beta) \to [\alpha] \to \beta \\
\nrightarrow &: ((\beta \times \alpha \to \beta) \times \beta) \to [\alpha] \to \beta.
\end{aligned}
$$

In the expression $(\oplus \nleftarrow e)x$, the operator $\oplus$ has type $\alpha \times \beta \to \beta$, the value e has type β and x has type $[\alpha]$. The expression then has type β. Analogous reasoning applies to the combination $(\oplus \nrightarrow e)x$. Note that $(\oplus \nleftarrow e)$ and $(\oplus \nrightarrow e)$ are both functions with type $[\alpha] \to \beta$.

Why do we need two more reduction operators? There are a number of answers to this question. First, the directed reductions can be regarded as "implementations" of the operator $/$ in which the order of computation is completely specified. If $\oplus$ is associative with identity e, then certainly

$$\oplus / = (\oplus \nleftarrow e) = (\oplus \nrightarrow e),$$

so undirected reductions can be expressed as directed reductions in two ways at least. In this sense, the directed reductions reflect a naive policy of sequential evaluation and can be translated directly into a suitable programming language. This point is amplified below.

The second, and more pragmatic answer is that many more functions can be described by directed reductions than by $/$. For example, the function $(f*)$ cannot be defined in terms of $/$, but we do have

$$(f*) \; = \; (\oplus\!\!\not\,[\,])$$
$$\text{where } a \oplus x = [f\,a] \mathbin{+\!\!\!+} x.$$

Furthermore, although every homomorphism can be expressed as a directed reduction (see §3.4), many functions which are not homomorphisms can be defined as directed reductions. For example, consider the function *prefix* which takes a predicate p and a list x as arguments and returns the longest initial segment of x all of whose elements satisy p (problems about segments will be discussed in §4). Thus,

$$\textit{prefix even}\,[2,4,1,8] = [2,4].$$

The function *prefix* is not a homomorphism, but we do have

$$\textit{prefix}\,p = (\oplus\!\!\not\,[\,]),$$

where

$$\begin{aligned} a \oplus x \; &= \; [a] \mathbin{+\!\!\!+} x, \quad \text{if } p\,a \\ &= \; [\,], \qquad\quad\ \text{otherwise.}\end{aligned}$$

To illustrate this definition, consider

$$\begin{aligned} \textit{prefix even}\,[2,4,1,8] \; &= \; 2 \oplus (4 \oplus (1 \oplus (8 \oplus [\,]))) \\ &= \; [2] \mathbin{+\!\!\!+} [4] \mathbin{+\!\!\!+} [\,] \\ &= \; [2,4] \end{aligned}$$

Further examples of directed reductions will be seen in due course.

3.2 Recursive characterisation.

From the informal definition of $(\oplus\!\!\not\,e)$ we have

$$\begin{aligned} (\oplus\!\!\not\,e)[\,] \; &= \; e \\ (\oplus\!\!\not\,e)([a] \mathbin{+\!\!\!+} x) \; &= \; a \oplus (\oplus\!\!\not\,e)x \end{aligned}$$

for all elements a and lists x. Since every non-empty list can be expressed uniquely in the form $[a] \mathbin{+\!\!\!+} x$, these two equations characterise the behaviour of $(\oplus\!\!\!\!/\,e)$ completely. Putting it another way, we can regard $f = (\oplus\!\!\!\!/\,e)$ as the *solution* of the recursive equations

$$
\begin{aligned}
f\,[\,] &= e \\
f\,([a] +\!\!\!+ x) &= a \oplus f\,x
\end{aligned}
$$

In these equations the value of $f\,[\,]$ is specified directly, and the value $f\,([a] +\!\!\!+ x)$ is specified in terms of a and $f\,x$. Thus f is determined incrementally from "right to left". This explains the direction of the arrow in the sign $\oplus\!\!\!\!/$. The progress of computation is essentially "recursive" (literally: to go backwards).

In the case of a left-reduction $(\oplus\!\!\!\!/\!\!\!\!\rightarrow e)$, the informal description gives

$$
\begin{aligned}
(\oplus\!\!\!\!/\!\!\!\!\rightarrow e)\,[\,] &= e \\
(\oplus\!\!\!\!/\!\!\!\!\rightarrow e)\,(x +\!\!\!+ [a]) &= (\oplus\!\!\!\!/\!\!\!\!\rightarrow e)x \oplus a
\end{aligned}
$$

for all a and x. (Recall that functional application is more binding than any other operator and so the right hand side of the last equation is read as $((\oplus\!\!\!\!/\!\!\!\!\rightarrow e)x) \oplus a$.) Hence $(\oplus\!\!\!\!/\!\!\!\!\rightarrow e)$ processes lists from "left to right". The progress of computation is therefore essentially "iterative".

We shall now show that the function $(\oplus\!\!\!\!/\!\!\!\!\rightarrow e)$ can also be characterised by the recursive equations

$$
\begin{aligned}
(\oplus\!\!\!\!/\!\!\!\!\rightarrow e)\,[\,] &= e \\
(\oplus\!\!\!\!/\!\!\!\!\rightarrow e)\,([a] +\!\!\!+ x) &= (\oplus\!\!\!\!/\!\!\!\!\rightarrow (e \oplus a))\,x.
\end{aligned}
$$

The first equation is immediate, so it is only necessary to show that the second one holds. We do this by induction on the length of x. For the empty list $[\,]$, we reason

$$
(\oplus\!\!\!\!/\!\!\!\!\rightarrow e)\,[a] = e \oplus a = (\oplus\!\!\!\!/\!\!\!\!\rightarrow (e \oplus a))[\,].
$$

For the case $x +\!\!\!+ [b]$, we reason inductively

$$
\begin{aligned}
(\oplus\!\!\!\!/\!\!\!\!\rightarrow e)([a] +\!\!\!+ (x +\!\!\!+ [b])) &= (\oplus\!\!\!\!/\!\!\!\!\rightarrow e)([a] +\!\!\!+ x +\!\!\!+ [b]) \\
&= (\oplus\!\!\!\!/\!\!\!\!\rightarrow e)([a] +\!\!\!+ x) \oplus b \\
&= (\oplus\!\!\!\!/\!\!\!\!\rightarrow (e \oplus a))\,x \oplus b \\
&= (\oplus\!\!\!\!/\!\!\!\!\rightarrow (e \oplus a))(x +\!\!\!+ [b]),
\end{aligned}
$$

using the associativity of $+\!\!\!+$ and the second defining equation for $(\oplus\!\!\!\!/\!\!\!\!\rightarrow e)$.

It follows that $f = (\oplus \not{} e)$ can be regarded as the solution of the recursive equations

$$
\begin{aligned}
f &= g\,e \\
g\,e\,[\,] &= e \\
g\,e\,([a] \mathbin{+\!\!+} x) &= g\,(e \oplus a)\,x
\end{aligned}
$$

We see therefore that both left and right reductions can be characterised by recursive equations of the same general form. In this form, a function f on lists is defined by (i) giving the value of $f\,[\,]$ directly; and (ii) specifying $f([a] \mathbin{+\!\!+} x)$ in terms of $f\,x$. Every list, of any type whatsoever, is either empty or of the form $[a] \mathbin{+\!\!+} x$ for *unique* values of a and x, so these two schemes are sufficient to characterise functions over (finite) lists. This style of recursive definition is a feature of functional programming languages (see [5] and [7]).

In functional programming the operation of concatenation is not provided as primitive. Instead, there is given a primitive operator ":" (pronounced "cons") which inserts a value into a list as a new first element. Thus, we have

$$
a : x = [a] \mathbin{+\!\!+} x.
$$

The type of ":" is given by

$$
(:) : \alpha \times [\alpha] \to [\alpha].
$$

Since

$$
[a_1, a_2, \ldots, a_n] = a_1 : (a_2 : (\ldots(a_n : [\,]))),
$$

every list, of any type whatsoever, can be constructed by inserting its elements successively into the empty list (hence the reason for the name "cons" which is an abbreviation for the word "construct").

We can define $\mathbin{+\!\!+}$ in terms of cons by

$$
x \mathbin{+\!\!+} y = (: \not{} y)x
$$

for all lists x and y. From this equation the cost of evaluating $x \mathbin{+\!\!+} y$ is proportional to the length of x, assuming a ":" operation has unit cost.

There are a number of reasons why cons is taken as the primitive operation for lists in functional programming. One is that every non-empty list can be expressed in the form (or "pattern") $a : x$ in exactly one way, so that one can define an arbitrary recursive function by a scheme based on the patterns $[\,]$ and $a : x$. On the other hand, a non-empty list can be expressed in the form $x \mathbin{+\!\!+} y$ in many ways and this can lead to ambiguity in a definition (unless, of course, the function is a homomorphism). Another reason concerns questions of efficiency to which we now briefly turn.

3.3 Efficiency considerations. With the introduction of the directed reduction operators we have begun to approach the question of what can reasonably be expected in the way of systematic computation by a machine. Although we shall not go into details of the underlying mechanisms, it is appropriate at this point to say something about the amount of time and space required to carry out the evaluation of a directed reduction. Most often, we shall solve a problem by a directed reduction and it is necessary to have some appreciation of the gains in efficiency thereby obtained.

First, let us consider a right-reduction $(\oplus \!\!\!\!\not\!/\, e)x$. If the list x has length n, then the definition of $\not\!/$ suggests that the evaluation of $(\oplus \!\!\!\!\not\!/\, e)x$ requires n applications of the operator $\oplus$. However, not every computation with a right-reduction must necessarily begin at the right hand end of the list and traverse backwards to the head. To illustrate this point, consider the function $prefix(< 3)$ which selects the longest initial segment of a list of numbers, all of whose elements are less than 3. We have $prefix(< 3) = (\oplus \!\!\!\!\not\!/\, [\,])$, where

$$
\begin{aligned}
a \oplus x &= a : x, && \text{if } a < 3 \\
&= [\,], && \text{otherwise.}
\end{aligned}
$$

Here, $a : x$ is used in preference to $[a] +\!\!+ x$. Using the recursive characterisation of $\not\!/$ as the basis, we can "unfold" the computation of $prefix(< 3)\,[1\ldots100]$ in the following way:

$$
\begin{aligned}
prefix(< 3)\,[1\ldots100] &= (\oplus \!\!\!\!\not\!/\, [\,])[1\ldots100] \\
&= 1 \oplus (\oplus \!\!\!\!\not\!/\, [\,])[2\ldots100] \\
&= 1 : (\oplus \!\!\!\!\not\!/\, [\,])[2\ldots100] \\
&= 1 : (2 \oplus (\oplus \!\!\!\!\not\!/\, [\,])[3\ldots100]) \\
&= 1 : 2 : (\oplus \!\!\!\!\not\!/\, [\,])[3\ldots100] \\
&= 1 : 2 : (3 \oplus (\oplus \!\!\!\!\not\!/\, [\,])[4\ldots100]) \\
&= 1 : 2 : [\,] \\
&= 1 : [2] \\
&= [1, 2]
\end{aligned}
$$

The length of this derivation is proportional to the length of the resulting list, *not* the length of the original list. In other words, the number of $\oplus$ operations actually carried out is 3 not 100. The crucial fact which enables the calculation to be shortened is that for $a \geq 3$ we have $a \oplus x = [\,]$ for *all* lists x. Since the value of x is not required, it need not be calculated. This strategy of symbolic evaluation combined with the policy of performing only those calculations necessary to determine the result is known as *lazy evaluation*. Lazy evaluation can be programmed into a mechanical evaluator quite easily (see [5]), though we shall not go into details.

Here is another, more dramatic example. Consider $(\ll \mathbin{+\!\!\!/} e)x$, where $a \ll b = a$. We have

$$
\begin{aligned}
(\ll \mathbin{+\!\!\!/} e)[1 \ldots 100] &= 1 \ll (\ll \mathbin{+\!\!\!/} e)[2 \ldots 100] \\
&= 1,
\end{aligned}
$$

so the computation terminates after only one step.

Now let us turn to left-reductions. The situation here is different from right-reduction in that, when processing lists from left to right, all the elements do have to be considered in order for the result to be returned. Consider, for instance, the symbolic evaluation of $(\ll \mathbin{/\!\!\!+} 0)[1,2,3]$, where $a \ll b = a$. This evaluation is based on the recursive characterisation of $\mathbin{/\!\!\!+}$ by the equations

$$
\begin{aligned}
(\oplus \mathbin{/\!\!\!+} e)[\,] &= e \\
(\oplus \mathbin{/\!\!\!+} e)(a : x) &= (\oplus \mathbin{/\!\!\!+} (e \oplus a))x
\end{aligned}
$$

For the specific example, we have:

$$
\begin{aligned}
(\ll \mathbin{/\!\!\!+} 0)[1,2,3] &= (\ll \mathbin{/\!\!\!+} (0 \ll 1))[2,3] \\
&= (\ll \mathbin{/\!\!\!+} 0)[2,3] \\
&= (\ll \mathbin{/\!\!\!+} (0 \ll 2))[3] \\
&= (\ll \mathbin{/\!\!\!+} 0)[3] \\
&= (\ll \mathbin{/\!\!\!+} (0 \ll 3))[\,] \\
&= (\ll \mathbin{/\!\!\!+} 0)[\,] \\
&= 0.
\end{aligned}
$$

In this evaluation the complete list is traversed before the answer is returned.

To summarise these observations: right-reductions can be more *time* efficient than left-reductions; this happens when values of the operator concerned do not always depend on the full evaluation of the right-hand arguments. Such an operator is said to be *non-strict* (in its right argument).

The reverse situation can occur with space efficiency. Left-reduction can be more efficent in the amount of space required to carry out the computation. Compare the evaluations of $(+ \mathbin{+\!\!\!/} 0)[1,2,3]$ and $(+ \mathbin{/\!\!\!+} 0)[1,2,3]$. For the former we have:

$$
\begin{aligned}
(+\!\not/0)[1,2,3] &= 1+(+\!\not/0)[2,3]\\
&= 1+(2+(+\!\not/0)[3])\\
&= 1+(2+(3+(+\!\not/0)[\,]))\\
&= 1+(2+(3+0))\\
&= 1+(2+3)\\
&= 1+5\\
&= 6.
\end{aligned}
$$

In this computation the sizes of the intermediate expressions grow in proportion to the length of the original list. This is an important measure because the sizes of the intermediate expressions reflect the amount of space which would have to be available to a mechanism in order to carry out the computation.

On the other hand, we can compute:

$$
\begin{aligned}
(+\!\not/0)[1,2,3] &= (+\!\not/(0+1))[2,3]\\
&= (+\!\not/1)[2,3]\\
&= (+\!\not/(1+2))[3]\\
&= (+\!\not/3)[3]\\
&= (+\!\not/(3+3))[\,]\\
&= (+\!\not/6)[\,]\\
&= 6,
\end{aligned}
$$

and the size of the intermediate expressions never grows beyond a constant amount. The inner calculations are performed as they arise: this is safe because + is a *strict* function, demanding complete evaluation of its arguments to determine the result.

In general, it is better to use right reduction when the operator concerned is non-strict and left reduction when it is strict. For example, when the operator is one of $+\!\!+$, $\wedge$, or $\vee$, we use right reduction; and when it is one of $+$, $\uparrow$, or $\downarrow$, we use left reduction.

This concludes a brief treatment of efficiency issues. In describing the symbolic evaluation of expressions, we have outlined the main method by which functional programming languages are implemented. For further details the reader should consult [5] or [7]. Since we wish to present problems, derivations and solutions at a higher level of abstraction than is provided by specific constructs in particular programming languages, it is left to informed readers to develop for themselves the connections between directed reductions and programs in conventional or functional languages.

3.4 Duality and specialisation. We state without proof two useful results concerning the relationship between the various forms of reduction.

Lemma 3 [Duality] *For all $\oplus$ and e we have*

$$(\oplus \!\not\leftarrow\! e) = (\widetilde{\oplus} \!\not\rightarrow\! e) \cdot reverse,$$

where $a \,\widetilde{\oplus}\, b = b \oplus a.$

Lemma 4 [Specialisation] *Every homomorphism can be defined as either a left or a right reduction. More precisely,*

$$(\odot/) \cdot (f*) = (\oplus \!\not\leftarrow\! e) = (\otimes \!\not\rightarrow\! e),$$

where

$$
\begin{aligned}
a \oplus b &= f\,a \odot b \\
a \otimes b &= a \odot f\,b.
\end{aligned}
$$

We give just one illustration of the specialisation lemma. Consider the function

$$lines = (\otimes/) \cdot (f*)$$

of §2.5, where

$$
\begin{aligned}
f\,a &= [[\,],[\,]], \quad \text{if } a = \text{NL} \\
&= [[a]], \qquad \text{otherwise}
\end{aligned}
$$

and

$$(xs \!+\!\!+\! [x]) \otimes ([y] \!+\!\!+\! ys) = xs \!+\!\!+\! [x \!+\!\!+\! y] \!+\!\!+\! ys.$$

Set $a \oplus xs = f\,a \otimes xs$. Since $\otimes/[\,] = [[\,]]$, we have by specialisation that

$$lines = (\oplus \!\not\leftarrow\! [[\,]]).$$

It remains to simplify the definition of $\oplus$. First, if $a = \text{NL}$, then

$$
\begin{aligned}
a \oplus (x : xs) &= f\,\text{NL} \otimes ([x] \!+\!\!+\! xs) \\
&= [[\,],[\,]] \otimes ([x] \!+\!\!+\! xs) \\
&= [[\,]] \!+\!\!+\! [[\,] \!+\!\!+\! x] \!+\!\!+\! xs \\
&= [[\,]] \!+\!\!+\! [x] \!+\!\!+\! xs \\
&= [\,] : x : xs,
\end{aligned}
$$

using the relation $a : x = [a] \!+\!\!+\! x$ and the definition of f and $\otimes$.

Second, if $a \neq \mathrm{NL}$, then

$$
\begin{aligned}
a \oplus (x : xs) &= [[a]] \otimes ([x] \mathbin{+\!\!+} xs) \\
&= [[\,] \mathbin{+\!\!+} [[a]]) \otimes ([x] \mathbin{+\!\!+} xs) \\
&= [\,] \mathbin{+\!\!+} [[a] \mathbin{+\!\!+} x] \mathbin{+\!\!+} xs \\
&= (a : x) : xs.
\end{aligned}
$$

Hence we obtain

$$
\begin{aligned}
a \oplus (x : xs) &= [\,] : x : xs, \quad \text{if } a = \mathrm{NL} \\
&= (a : x) : xs, \quad \text{otherwise.}
\end{aligned}
$$

3.5 Accumulation. We end the discussion on directed reductions by introducing another operator $\mathbin{-\!\!/\!\!/\!\!\rightarrow}$ (pronounced "accumulate") which is closely related to left-reduction. Examples of its use will feature in the next section. Like $\mathbin{-\!\!/\!\!\rightarrow}$ the operator $\mathbin{-\!\!/\!\!/\!\!\rightarrow}$ takes an operator $\oplus$, a value e and a list x as arguments. Its effect is described by the equation

$$
(\oplus \mathbin{-\!\!/\!\!/\!\!\rightarrow} e)[a_1, a_2, \ldots, a_n] = [e, e \oplus a_1, (e \oplus a_1) \oplus a_2, \ldots, ((e \oplus a_1) \cdots \oplus a_n)].
$$

The operator $\mathbin{-\!\!/\!\!/\!\!\rightarrow}$ encapsulates a common pattern of computation in which a sequence $c_0, c_1, \ldots, c_n$ is defined in terms of a given sequence $a_1, a_2, \ldots, a_n$ and a starting value e by a reccurrence relation of the form

$$
\begin{aligned}
c_0 &= e \\
c_{k+1} &= c_k \oplus a_{k+1} \quad (0 < k < n)
\end{aligned}
$$

We have

$$
[c_0, c_1, \ldots, c_n] = (\oplus \mathbin{-\!\!/\!\!/\!\!\rightarrow} e)[a_1, \ldots, a_n].
$$

For example, the list $0!, 1!, \ldots n!$ of factorial numbers can be defined by the expression

$$
(\times \mathbin{-\!\!/\!\!/\!\!\rightarrow} 1)[1 \ldots n].
$$

This expression can be evaluated more efficiently than the alternative

$$
fac * [0 \ldots n],
$$

where $fac\ k = \times / [1 \ldots k]$. The former requires just n multiplications to generate the list, while the latter requires $n(n-1)/2$ multiplications.

In general,

$$
(\oplus \mathbin{-\!\!/\!\!\rightarrow} e) = last \cdot (\oplus \mathbin{-\!\!/\!\!/\!\!\rightarrow} e),
$$

so every left-reduction can be defined in terms of an accumulation. More interesting is the fact that an accumulation can be defined as a left-reduction. We have

$$(\oplus \!\!-\!\!/\!\!\!\!\rightarrow e) = (\otimes \!\!\not\rightarrow [e]),$$

where

$$x \otimes a = x + [last \ x \oplus a].$$

This result shows why the number of $\oplus$ operations can be reduced from $O(n^2)$ to $O(n)$, where n is the length of the argument list.

Alternatively, we can characterize $\!\!-\!\!/\!\!\!\!\rightarrow$ by two recursive equations:

$$
\begin{aligned}
(\oplus \!\!-\!\!/\!\!\!\!\rightarrow e)[\,] &= [e] \\
(\oplus \!\!-\!\!/\!\!\!\!\rightarrow e)(a:x) &= [e] + (\oplus \!\!-\!\!/\!\!\!\!\rightarrow (e \oplus a))x.
\end{aligned}
$$

From the point of view of efficiency, this definition is superior to the definition as a left-reduction. Under a strategy of lazy evaluation using the recursive definition as a basis, elements of the result list can be produced before the argument list is completely traversed.

4. Segments and Partitions

4.1 Definitions. The object of the present section is to derive computationally efficient solutions for a number of problems about segments. A list y is said to be a *segment* of x if there exist u and v such that $x = u + y + v$. A list y is an *initial segment* of x if there exists a v such that $x = y + v$, and a *final segment* if there exists a u such that $x = u + y$.

The function *inits* returns the list of initial segments of a list, in increasing order of length. The function *tails* returns the list of final segments of a list, in decreasing order of length. Thus

$$
\begin{aligned}
inits[a_1, a_2, \ldots, a_n] &= [[\,], [a_1], [a_1, a_2], \ldots, [a_1, a_2, \ldots, a_n]] \\
tails[a_1, a_2, \ldots, a_n] &= [[a_1, a_2, \ldots, a_n], [a_2, a_3, \ldots, a_n], \ldots, [\,]]
\end{aligned}
$$

Since both functions are injective, they can be defined formally as homomorphisms; using the specialisation lemma, they can therefore be defined as directed reductions. We shall do this directly. Since $inits([a] + x)$ consists, in order, of $[\,]$ and the list of initial segments of x in which each element is prefixed by a, we have

$$
\begin{aligned}
inits[\,] &= [[\,]] \\
inits([a] + x) &= [[\,]] + ([a] +) * inits \ x.
\end{aligned}
$$

Solving this recursion gives

$$inits = (\oplus \nleftarrow [[\,]]),$$

where

$$a \oplus xs = [[\,]] \mathbin{+\mkern-8mu+} ([a] \mathbin{+\mkern-8mu+}) * xs.$$

Analogous reasoning gives

$$
\begin{aligned}
tails\,[\,] &= [[\,]] \\
tails(x \mathbin{+\mkern-8mu+} [a]) &= (\mathbin{+\mkern-8mu+} [a]) * tails\,x \mathbin{+\mkern-8mu+} [[\,]],
\end{aligned}
$$

and so

$$tails = (\oplus \nrightarrow [[\,]]),$$

where

$$xs \oplus a = (\mathbin{+\mkern-8mu+} [a]) * xs \mathbin{+\mkern-8mu+} [[\,]].$$

We shall make use of the recursive characterisation of *tails* below.

The following simple result, whose proof is omitted, relates the function $\mathbin{+\mkern-8mu+\mkern-8mu\to}$ to $\nrightarrow$.

Lemma 5 *For all* $\oplus$, e *and lists* x *we have*

$$(\oplus \mathbin{+\mkern-8mu+\mkern-8mu\to} e)x = (\oplus \nrightarrow e) * inits\,x.$$

The function *segs* returns a list of all segments of a given list. We shall define

$$segs\,x = \mathbin{+\mkern-8mu+}/tails * inits\,x.$$

For example,

$$segs[1,2,3] = [[\,],[1],[\,],[1,2],[2],[\,],[1,2,3],[2,3],[3],[\,]]$$

The order in which the segments appear in this list is not important for our purposes and we shall make no use of it. Notice that the empty list occurs more than once in the result.

4.2 Segment decomposition The following theorem can be used as the starting point in the derivation of efficient solutions to a number of problems about segments.

Theorem 1 [Segment Decompostion] *Suppose S and T are defined by*

$$S\,x \;=\; \oplus/f * p \triangleleft segs\,x$$
$$T\,x \;=\; \oplus/f * p \triangleleft tails\,x.$$

Then $S\,x = \oplus/T * inits\,x$.

Proof. The proof is by straightforward calculation. We have

$$
\begin{aligned}
S\,x \;&=\; \oplus/f * p \triangleleft segs\,x \\
&=\; \oplus/f * p \triangleleft (\;+\!\!+/tails * inits\,x) && (\text{defn.}\,segs) \\
&=\; \oplus/f * (\;+\!\!+/(p\triangleleft) * tails * inits\,x) && (\triangleleft\,\text{promotion}) \\
&=\; \oplus/(\;+\!\!+/(f*) * (p\triangleleft) * tails * inits\,x) && (*\,\text{promotion}) \\
&=\; \oplus/(\oplus/) * (f*) * (p\triangleleft) * tails * inits\,x && (/\,\text{promotion}) \\
&=\; \oplus/((\oplus/) \cdot (f*) \cdot (p\triangleleft) \cdot tails) * inits\,x && (*,\cdot\,\text{distrib.}) \\
&=\; \oplus/T * inits\,x && (\text{defn.}\,T)
\end{aligned}
$$

Corollary 1 *Suppose $T = (\otimes\!\!\not\rightarrow\!e)$ for some operator $\otimes$ and value e. Then*

$$S = (\oplus/) \cdot (\otimes\!\!-\!\!\!\not\rightarrow\!e).$$

Proof. Immediate, using the above relationship between $-\!\!\!\not\rightarrow$ and $\not\rightarrow$.

It follows from this corollary that if $\oplus$ and $\otimes$ have constant cost, then $S\,x$ can be computed in $O(n)$ steps, where $n = \#x$.

The following lemma gives a sufficient condition for T to be expressible as a left reduction.

Lemma 6 *Suppose $T\,x = \oplus/f * tails\,x$, where $f = (\otimes\!\!\not\rightarrow\!e)$. If $\otimes$ distributes through $\oplus$, i.e.*

$$(a \oplus b) \otimes c = (a \otimes c) \oplus (b \otimes c),$$

then $T = (\odot\!\!\not\rightarrow\!e)$, where

$$a \odot b = (a \otimes b) \oplus e.$$

Proof. It is easy to show $T\,[\,] = e$. We prove $T(x +\!\!+ [a]) = (T\,x \otimes a) \oplus e$. Solving these equations gives the required result. To establish the equation, observe that if $f = (\otimes\!\!\not\rightarrow\!e)$, then

$$f * (\;+\!\!+\,[a]) * xs = (\otimes a) * f * xs$$

for all lists (of lists) *xs*. Furthermore, if $\otimes$ distributes through $\oplus$, then

$$\oplus/(\otimes a) * xs = (\otimes a)(\oplus/xs).$$

Using these results, together with the recursive characterisation of *tails*, we can therefore compute

$$
\begin{aligned}
T(x + [a]) &= \oplus/f * tails(x + [a]) \\
&= \oplus/f * ((+[a]) * tails\ x + [[\,]]) \\
&= \oplus/((\otimes a) * f * tails\ x + [e]) \\
&= (\oplus/(\otimes a) * f * tails\ x) \oplus e \\
&= (\otimes a)(\oplus/f * tails\ x) \oplus e \\
&= (T\ x \otimes a) \oplus e.
\end{aligned}
$$

This completes the proof.

This result can be illustrated by solving a problem of Gries. The problem is to compute the minimum of the sums of all segments of a given list of positive and negative numbers: in symbols,

$$minsum\ x = \downarrow/(+/) * segs\ x.$$

Direct calculation from this expression requires $O(n^3)$ steps, where $n = \#x$. There are $O(n^2)$ segments of x and each can be summed in $O(n)$ steps. As the minimum of the sums can be computed in $O(n^2)$ steps, there are $O(n^3)$ steps in total. However, it is easy to derive a linear time algorithm. Since $(+/) = (+\!\!\not\!/0)$ and $+$ distributes through $\downarrow$, we have from the work above that

$$minsum = (\downarrow/) \cdot (\odot \!\!\not\!/ 0),$$

where $a \odot b = (a + b) \downarrow 0$.

4.3 Extremal problems. A common problem is to find some longest segment of a list satisfying a given property p. In text processing, for example, we may want to take the longest initial segment of a list of words which will fit on a line of given width. By repeating this process with the remaining words on subsequent lines, it is possible to solve the problem of formatting text. This problem will be discussed in more detail later on.

Let us consider the problem of computing the functions

$$
\begin{aligned}
S\ x &= \uparrow_\#/p \triangleleft segs\ x \\
I\ x &= \uparrow_\#/p \triangleleft inits\ x \\
T\ x &= \uparrow_\#/p \triangleleft tails\ x
\end{aligned}
$$

It will be assumed throughout that p holds for the empty list at least, so there is always a well-defined (and, indeed, unique in the case of I and T) solution for any given list x. Assuming $O(n^k)$ steps are required to determine whether p holds for a list of length n, the time required to compute $S\,x$ is $O(n^{k+2})$ steps, where $n = \#x$. Our purpose is to examine useful conditions which can be imposed on p to reduce this estimate.

We mention three such conditions. A predicate p on lists will be called *prefix-closed* if

$$p(x \mathbin{+\!\!+} y) \Rightarrow p\,x$$

for all x and y (here, $\Rightarrow$ denotes logical implication). Similarly, p is called *suffix-closed* if

$$p(x \mathbin{+\!\!+} y) \Rightarrow p\,y.$$

Finally, p is *segment-closed* if it is both prefix and suffix-closed; that is,

$$p(x \mathbin{+\!\!+} y) \Rightarrow p\,x \wedge p\,y.$$

for all x and y. The terminology is appropriate since it is easy to show that a segment-closed predicate holds for all segments of x whenever it holds for x.

Each of the three classes of predicates is closed under the operations of conjunction and disjunction. One can also show that p is prefix-closed if and only if

$$p \vartriangleleft \mathit{inits}\ x = \mathit{inits}(\uparrow_{\#} /p \vartriangleleft \mathit{inits}\ x).$$

A similar characterisation holds for suffix-closed predicates.

We now state without proof two results concerning these properties.

Lemma 7 *If p is prefix-closed, then $T = (\oplus\!\!\!\not{}\,[\,])$, where*

$$x \oplus a = \uparrow_{\#} /p \vartriangleleft \mathit{tails}(x \mathbin{+\!\!+} [a])$$

Consequently, $S = (\uparrow_{\#} /) \cdot (\oplus\!\!\!\not{}\!\!\to[\,])$.

The second part of the lemma follows from the Corollary to the Segment Decomposition Theorem. To see what this result buys in the way of increased efficiency, suppose

$$(\oplus\!\!\!\not{}\!\!\to[\,])x = [x_0, x_1, \ldots, x_n],$$

where $n = \#x$. Let $l_j = \#x_j$. To compute x_{j+1} from x_j requires p to be applied in succession to lists of lengths $l_j + 1, l_j, \ldots l_{j+1}$. If p requires $O(n^k)$ steps for a list of length n, then the jth step requires

$$\sum_{i=l_{j+1}}^{l_j+1} i^k$$

steps. Summing over j leads to the result that $S\,x$ can be computed in $O(n^{k+1})$ steps.

We give one illustration. Let *nodups x* denote the property that list x contains no repeated elements. If the only available comparison test is the test for equality, the computation of *nodups* requires $O(n^2)$ steps on a list of length n. Direct calculation of

$$\uparrow_{\#} /\, nodups \lhd segs\ x$$

therefore requires $O(n^4)$ steps. However, *nodups* is prefix-closed, so using the algorithm implicit in the above result we can bring the time down to $O(n^3)$ steps.

The next lemma shows how to decrease the time still further.

Lemma 8 *Suppose p is segment-closed, holds for all singleton sequences, and satisfies*

$$p(x +\!\!+ [a]) = p\,x \wedge q\,a\,x$$

for some suitable predicate q. Then $T = (\oplus \!\not\to [\,])$, where

$$x \oplus a = (\uparrow_{\#} /\, q\,a \lhd tails\ x) +\!\!+ [a]$$

Consequently, $S = (\uparrow_{\#} /) \cdot (\oplus \!\not\to [\,])$.

It can be shown that if q is computable in $O(n^k)$ steps, then $S\,x$ can be computed in $O(n^{k+1})$ steps.

To illustrate this result, consider the *nodups* problem again. The predicate *nodups* is segment-closed and holds for all singleton sequences. Moreover,

$$nodups(x +\!\!+ [a]) = nodups\,x \wedge all(\neq a)x$$

Since $all(\neq a)x$ can be computed in $O(n)$ steps, where $n = \#x$, we have that $\uparrow_{\#} /\, nodups \lhd segs\ x$ can be computed in $O(n^2)$ steps.

4.4 Partitions. A *partition* of a list x is a decomposition of x into non-empty segments. In symbols, xs is a partition of x if

$$+\!\!\!+/xs = x \wedge all\,(\neq [\,]) \, xs.$$

The function *parts* returns a list of all possible partitions of x. In this subsection we state without proof an important theorem for solving problems of the form

$$\downarrow_f /\, all\ p \lhd parts\ x$$

for suitable f and p. We first give two illustrations of why this problem is important in practice.

Text-formatting. Suppose x is a list of words (see §2.5 for the relevant definitions used in this example). An important problem in text processing is to format text into lines of given width m, ensuring as many words as possible are on each line (adjacent words being separated by at least one space). A list x will fill a line of width m just in the case that $m \geq \#unwords\,x$. Define

$$fits\ m\ x = m \geq \#unwords\ x.$$

The problem of formatting text can be described as an optimisation problem

$$format\ x = \downarrow_{waste} /\, all(fits\ m) \lhd parts\ x,$$

where *waste* is a suitable measure of the badness of a given way of breaking text into lines. This problem was considered in [1], where the following definitions of waste were examined:

$$
\begin{aligned}
waste1 &= (\uparrow/) \cdot (whitespace\ m*) \\
waste2 &= (+/) \cdot (whitespace\ m*),
\end{aligned}
$$

where $whitespace\ m\ x = m - \#unwords\ x.$

Sorting by merging. A list of numbers can be sorted by first partitioning the list into ordered segments (called *runs*) and then merging the runs. The function

$$runs\ x = \downarrow_\# /\, all\ ordered \lhd parts\ x$$

determines the optimal way to partition the sequence prior to merging. In fact, if $x \otimes y$ denotes the ordered list which results when x and y are merged, then

$$sort\ x = \otimes/runs\ x$$

specifies the complete sorting procedure.

For suitably restricted f and p, the problem of computing

$$\downarrow_f / all \; p \triangleleft parts \; x$$

can be solved by a "greedy" algorithm which computes the solution incrementally by taking as much of x at each stage as it can. We define

$$
\begin{aligned}
greedy \; p \; x \;\; = \;\; & [\,], && \text{if } x = [\,] \\
= \;\; & [x'] + \! + greedy \; p \; (x \setminus x'), && \text{otherwise} \\
& \text{where } x' = \uparrow_\# / p \triangleleft inits \; x
\end{aligned}
$$

For an initial segment x' of x, the value of $x \setminus x'$ is the final segment which remains when x' is removed from x. For suitable p we shall see how to compute x' quickly, so the greedy algorithm can be very efficient.

We need two conditions on f to relate the greedy algorithm to the partition problem. Say a function $f : [[\alpha]] \to Num$ is *stable* if

$$f \; xs \leq f \; ys \Rightarrow f([x] + \! + xs) \leq f([x] + \! + ys)$$

for all lists xs, ys and x.

Furthermore, say f is *greedy* if

$$f([x + \! + y + \! + z] + \! + xs) \leq f([x + \! + y] + \! + [z] + \! + xs) \leq f([x] + \! + [y + \! + z] + \! + xs)$$

for all x, y, z and xs.

One proof of the following result can be found in [1].

Theorem 2 [The Greedy Theorem for Partitions] *Suppose p is segment-closed and holds for all singletons. Suppose f is stable and greedy. Then*

$$\downarrow_f / all \; p \triangleleft parts \; x \rightsquigarrow greedy \; p \; x.$$

Notice the refinement step $\rightsquigarrow$. The theorem does not state that the greedy algorithm gives the only optimal way of partitioning x, but just one optimal way. Moreover, the conditions on f are such that knowledge of f is not required for execution of the algorithm.

Two obvious applications of the theorem are to the problems of formatting text and sorting by merging. For the first, the predicate *fits m* is segment-closed and *waste2* can be shown to satisfy the hypothesis on f. For the second, the predicate *ordered* is segment-closed and the function #

is stable and greedy. Both problems can therefore be solved by a greedy algorithm.

There remains the problem of computing

$$\uparrow_\# /p \triangleleft \mathit{inits}\ x$$

quickly, since this is crucial to the success of the greedy algorithm. We state without proof a final lemma which addresses this problem. In the statement we use the function *prefix* mentioned in §3 and a related function *take* which selects initial segments of a list with given length: *take n x* takes the initial segment of x of length n.

Lemma 9 *If p is prefix-closed and $p = q \cdot (\oplus\!\!\not\rightarrow\!e)$, then*

$$\uparrow_\# /p \triangleleft \mathit{inits}\ x = take(\#y - 1)x$$

where $y = prefix\ q\,((\oplus\!\!-\!\!/\!\!\!\!\rightarrow\!e)x)$.

To illustrate this result, recall that

$$\mathit{fits}\ m\ x = m \geq \#\mathit{unwords}\ x$$

From §2.5 we have $\# \cdot \mathit{unwords} = (\oplus/) \cdot (\#*)$, where $n \oplus m = n + m + 1$. By the specialisation lemma, we have $(\oplus/) \cdot (\#*) = (\otimes\!\!\not\rightarrow\!e)$, where e is the identity element of $\oplus$, so $e = -1$, and $n \otimes w = n + \#w + 1$. It follows that

$$\mathit{fits}\ m = (m \geq) \cdot (\otimes\!\!\not\rightarrow\!e).$$

As $(\mathit{fits}\ m)$ is prefix-closed, the lemma is applicable and reduces the cost of calculating

$$\uparrow_\# /\mathit{fits}\ m \triangleleft \mathit{inits}\ x$$

to $O(m)$ steps.

4.5 Conclusions. We hope we have shown enough of the theory of lists to convince the student of its mathematical depth and elegance, as well as its usefulness in deriving solutions to practical problems. There are many subjects we have not touched on: the theory of subsequences, permutations, arrays (lists of lists), and infinite lists to name just a few. There are other kinds of greedy theorem for other kinds of problems about lists. Even having disposed of lists, there remains trees, bags and sets for which a similar generic theory is appropriate.

References

1. Bird, R.S. Transformational programming and the paragraph problem. *Science of Computer Programming* 6 (1986) 159-189.

2. Bird, R.S. The promotion and accumulation strategies in transformational programming. *ACM. Trans. on Prog. Lang. and Systems* 6 (1984) 487-450. Addendum *Ibid* 7 (1985).

3. Bird, R.S. and Hughes, R.J.M. The alpha-beta algorithm: an exercise in program transformation. *Inf. Proc. Letters* (to appear 1986).

4. Bird, R.S. and Meertens L.G.L.T Two exercises found in a book on algorithmics. *Proc. TC2 Conference on Program Specification and Transformation*, Bad Tolz, W. Germany 1986 (to appear Springer LNCS 1986).

5. Bird, R.S. and Wadler, P. *An Introduction to Functional Programming* Prentice-Hall (to be published 1987).

6. Meertens, L.G.L.T Algorithmics - towards programming as a mathematical activity. *Proc. CWI Symp. on Mathematics and Computer Science*, CWI Monographs, North-Holland, 1 (1986) 289-334.

7. Turner, D. Recursion equations as a programming language. *Functional Programming and its Applicatons*, Cambridge University Press, Cambridge, U.K. 1982.

A heuristic explanation of Batcher's Baffler

Edsger W.Dijkstra
Dept. of Computer Sciences
University of Texas at Austin
Austin, Texas 78712-1188
USA

Abstract

Batcher's Baffler - so named by David Gries - is a sorting algortihm that is of interest because many of its "comparison-swaps" can be executed concurrently. It is also of interest because it used to be hard to explain.

This note explains Batcher's Baffler by designing it. Besides including all heuristics, it has two distinguishing features, both contributing to its clarity and brevity:

(0) the (little) theory the algorithm relies upon is dealt with in isolation;

(1) by suitable abstractions, all case analyses have been removed from the argument. (End of Abstract.)

Batcher's Baffler - so named by David Gries after K.E. Batcher, who designed it in 1968 - is a sorting algorithm. Its building block considers a set of disjoint pairs of elements, swapping each pair of values that is out of order; the pairs of the set being disjoint, they will be treated as if dealt with concurrently. Since eventually all pairs have to be in order, we are interested in theorems about sets of "comparison swaps" that maintain for some other pairs the fact that they are already in order.

We shall present the relevant lemmata graphically, in the form of directed graphs with dotted arrows and solid arrows. A dotted arrow $x \dashrightarrow y$ stands for the "comparison swap"

$$\{true\}\, x,y := x \underline{\min} y,\ x \underline{\max} y\ \{x \leq y\}.$$

A solid arrow $x \rightarrow y$ stands for the invariant relation $x \leq y$; more precisely, the graphs representing our lemmata should be read as follows: if initially the inequalities corresponding to the solid arrows hold, they are maintained by the execution of the operations corresponding to the dotted arrows (whose inequalities eventually hold as well).

 Lemma 0

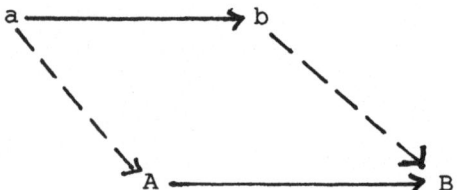

<u>Proof</u> The maximum of the four values is initially an element of the set {b,B}, hence finally equal to B; the inequality A≤B is therefore maintained. Similarly, the minimum of the four values is initially an element of the set {a,A}, hence finally equal to a; the inequality a ≤b is therefore maintained. (End of Proof.)

<u>Lemma 1</u>

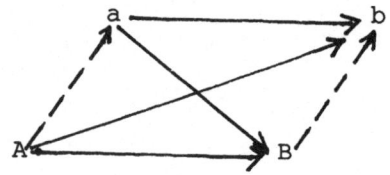

<u>Proof</u>
The four solid arrows are together equivalent to a <u>max</u> A≤b <u>min</u> B; this relation is maintained by each of the operations corresponding to the dotted arrows. (End of Proof.)

So much for the little theory we need.

```
        *                       *

            *
```

Our purpose is to sort array f(i: 0≤ i <N). For simplicity's sake, this finite array is mentally extended in both directions to infinity, i.e. with values "−∞" to its left and values "+∞" to its right (the direction from left to right being the order of increasing subscript value).

With the predicate OK being given by

$$OK.i.j \equiv f.i \leq f.j$$

our purpose is to establish relation R given by

$$R \equiv (\text{A}i :: OK.i.(i+1))$$

by rearranging the values of f(i: 0 ≤ i < N). Note that, thanks to our extension, OK.i.j trivially holds for i < 0 ∨ j ≥ N.

The algorithm manipulates array   f   only by means of the operation   Ord.i.j   with   i < j   and given by

Ord.i.j = $\underline{if}$ OK.i.j → skip | ¬ OK.i.j → swap.f.i.j $\underline{fi}$

-the swap interchanges the values of f.i and f.j -. The operation Ord.i.j establishes OK.i.j. Note that, thanks to our extension,

i < 0 ∨ j ≥ N ⇒ Ord.i.j = skip,

independently of the value of f(i: 0 ≤ i < N).

In view of R we choose as invariant P0 given by

P0 ≡   (Ai:: OK.i.(i+t)),

which is easily established since t ≥ N ⇒ P0. This choice suggests for Batcher's Baffler the form

"establish t ≥ N" {P0}
; $\underline{do}$ t ≠ 1 → "decrease t under invariance of P0"
$\underline{od}$ {R}.

The guiding principle of our development is that, once an OK relation has been established, it will be maintained, i.e. if "decrease t under invariance of P0" involves the transition from t = t' to t = t", we require

(Ai:: OK.i.(i+t")) ⇒ (Ai:: OK.i.(i+t')),

an implication whose validity requires (in view of OK's transitivity) t' to be a multiple of t". Under that constraint, the most modest decrease of t - i.e. the one that strengthens P0 as little as possible - is halving it, and we therefore propose to restrict t to powers of 2. (At this stage this proposal is tentative; its wisdom will transpire shortly.)

Explicit incorporation of the manipulations on t yields for Batcher's Baffler

t := 1; $\underline{do}$ t < N → t := 2·t $\underline{od}$ {P0 ∧ t is a power of 2}

; $\underline{do}$ t ≠ 1 → t := t/2

        ; {P1: (Ai :: OK.i.(i+2·t))}

        "restore P0"

        {P0: (Ai :: OK.i.(i + t))}

$\underline{od}$ {R}.

The rest of this note is concerned with the development of the subalgorithm for "restore P0" as specified above by its pre- and postconditions. (For this subalgorithm it is no longer relevant that t is a power of 2.)

The design of Batcher's Baffler is driven by the desire to find groups of Ord operations with disjoint argument pairs, because such Ord operations could be executed concurrently. As each Ord operation establishes the corresponding OK relation, we are invited to select from the postcondition P0 a group of OK relations with disjoint argument pairs. Such a group occurs in

P2 ≡   (**A**i: e.i: OK.i.(i+t))

if we can find a predicate e such that

(0)   e.i. ≡ ¬ e.(i+t).

There are many such predicates, all variations on the same theme; the simplest one is

(1)   e.i. ≡ (i mod 2·t) < t

Remark It is the factor of 2 in the above formula that will justify our earlier choice to restrict t to powers of 2. (End of Remark.)

In order to capture the remaining OK relations of P0 we write P0 as P2 ∧ P3, thus finding

P3 ≡   (**A**i: ¬ e.i.: OK.i.(i+t)).

Note that (0) is maintained when e is replaced by ¬e; in other words: also the OK relations occuring in P3 have disjoint argument pairs.

Using || to denote the potentially concurrent combination of statements, we have indeed

S2:{true} (|| i : e.i: Ord.i.(i+t)) {P2} and
S3:{true} (|| i : ¬e.i: Ord.i.(i+t)) {P3}.

But we cannot achieve P2 ∧P3 - i.e. P0 - by performing S2 and S3 consecutively (in some order), for in general the second one will destroy what the first one has accomplished. So we have to proceed more carefully, e.g. first establishing P2 - the choice is irrelevant, as we were free to call either polarity of the partitioning predicate e - and then establishing P3 with a repetition for which P2 is an invariant, i.e. we may expect that repetition to establish P2∧P3 under invariance of P2 ∧P4, where P4 is a suitable generalization of P3.

In order to be a suitable generalization of P3, P4 too should be composed of OK-relations with disjoint argument pairs. In view of (0) this can be achieved by replacing t in Ok.i.(i+t) by an odd multiple of t. Since the general even value has a slightly simpler form than the general odd value, we propose to rewrite   P3 -see(0)-as

P3 ≡   (**A** i: e.i: OK.(i+t).(i+2·t))

and propose for P4

P4 ≡   (**A**i: e.i: OK.(i+t).(i+v·t)) with even v,

the latter to ensure that all argument pairs in P4 are disjoint. It now stands to reason to consider

S4:   {true} (|| i : e.i: Ord.(i+t).(i+v·t)) {P4}

and to investigate under which conditions S4 maintains P2. Because   v   is even, it suffices to investigate the fate of OK.(i+v·t).(i+v·t+t) with i satisfying e.i. With its incident Ord operations it yields the picture

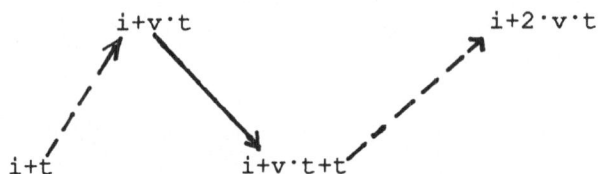

which is certainly not a lemma, but we can recognize the sequence --> → --> in Lemma 1, redrawn for the purpose:

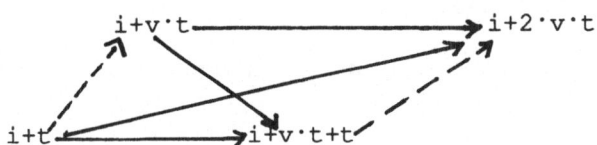

Of the three solid arrows added, the two horizontal ones -v being even!-are implied by P1. The third one is implied by P4$^V_{2·v}$. In other words, for statement S4 we have established the theorem

   {P1 ∧P2∧P4$^V_{2·v}$} S4 {P2 ∧ P4}.

Taking the invariance of P1 for the time being for granted, this theorem tells us, as

   P4 ∧ v=2 ⇒ P3,

that we can establish P3 under invariance of P2 by first establishing P4 with v equal to a sufficiently high power of 2, and then repeatedly halving v while maintaining P2 ∧P4 by executing S4.

Independently of e, P4 holds if $(v-1) \cdot t \geq N$; with e as given in (1), however, the weaker $v \cdot t \geq N$ suffices. With that choice for e (and still under the assumption of the invariance of P1) we get the following program for Batcher's Baffler.

```
|[t, v0 : int;   t, v0 := 1,1
; do t < N →t := 2·t od {P0 ∧ v0·t ≥ N}
; do t ≠1 →t,v0 := t/2, 2·v0 {P1 ∧ v0·t ≥ N}
   ; (||i: e.i: Ord.i.(i+t)) {P1 ∧ P2 ∧ v0·t ≥ N}
   ; |[ v: int; v := v0 {P1 ∧ P2 ∧ P4}
      ; do v ≠ 2 →v := v/2 {P1 ∧ P2 ∧ P4ᵛ₂·ᵥ}
          ; (|| i : e.i: Ord.(i+t).(i+v·t))
                  {P1∧ P2∧ P4}
      od {P2 ∧ P3}
   ]|{P0 ∧ v0·t ≥ N}
od{ P0 ∧ t = 1}
]|{R}.
```

We are left with the obligation to verify that P1, i.e.

$(\underline{A}i:: OK.i.(i+2 \cdot t))$

is maintained by S2 and S4. The latter two are both of the form

$(|| i: p.i: Ord.i.(i+m \cdot t))$

with p.i. ≡e.i. or p.i. ≡¬ e.i and with odd m. In

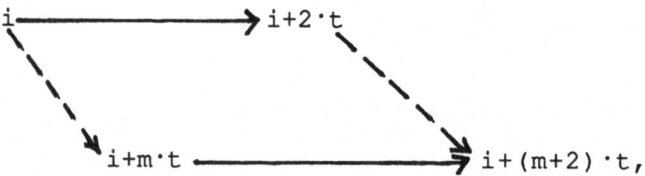

however, we recognize Lemma 0. With either choice for p, each OK relation of P1 occurs, because m is odd, in precisely one such diagram, and this settles the invariance of P1.

And this completes our derivation of Batcher's Baffler.

History and acknowledgements

We are first and foremost indebted to K.E. Batcher, who invented this algorithm in 1968. I saw it for the first time explained and proved to be correct in a manuscript by David Gries. His explanation is in two steps, dealing with "sort two-ordered" first, and then reducing the complete sorting task to repeated applications of the former; in the above I have followed his way of breaking down the invariant.

In the fall semester of 1985, my target was the derivation of programs rather than just their explanation. The leitmotiv of that course was that, in the design of a program, it often pays to develop the underlying theory first. It had been chosen because of my experience that such a theory could provide a strong heuristic guidance. Because I did not know it too well and it looked sufficiently ambitious, Batcher's Baffler was one of the examples selected as proving ground for this approach. As we did not know what would be needed, our initial theory encompassed more than the two lemmata given here.

The ATAC (=Austin Tuesday Afternoon Club) focussed its attention on the theory and the graphical notation of its lemmata; this led to a completion of the theory and an improvement of its presentation.

The ETAC (=Eindhoven Tuesday Afternoon Club) focussed its attention on the argument that led to my design and suggested several improvements. There, C.S. Scholten suggested the extension of the finite array to an infinite one; this suggestion deserves to be mentioned explicitly since it did away with the last case analyses in the argument.

Finally, an oversight - in the initialization of P4 - was pointed out to me in late December'85, when I had the privilege of presenting Batcher's Baffler to the Eindhoven Informatics Colloquium.

All these contributions are gratefully acknowledged.

PREDICATIVE METHODOLOGY

Eric C.R. Hehner
Lorene E. Gupta
Andrew J. Malton

University of Toronto

Summary

We introduce a predicative semantics of programs and show its use in programming. With it, logic errors can be detected and reported when they are made, just like syntax errors. Programming paradigms are stated precisely as theorems. The use of paradigms in larger programs is shown to be the same as the mathematician's use of theorems in the proof of larger theorems.

Introduction

To specify a mechanism, we must first decide what quantities are of concern. Whether we are specifying a watch or a waterwheel, there will be aspects that we care to be specific about and other aspects that are not directly of interest. Overspecification is a common error. For example, a specification of an auto body may say that it is to be made of aluminum, when instead the specification should state only the desired strength, weight, shape, and cost. Even if aluminum is the only material currently known to have the desired properties, it is not a desired property itself, so the decision to use aluminum belongs to the implementer.

We shall be specifying desired computer behavior, or computations. A reasonable choice of concerns might be: the result of a computation, its speed, and its expense. In this paper (as in so many others), we confine our interest to results, ignoring speed and expense. One way to express the result of a computation is as the values of some variables; these values may be thought of as the computer's memory state, or part of it, at some instant. Another way is as a sequence of values; this sequence may be thought of as communications from the computer over a period of time. Either way, the

NATO ASI Series, Vol. F36
Logic of Programming and Calculi of Discrete Design
Edited by M. Broy
© Springer-Verlag Berlin Heidelberg 1987

result will, in general, depend on supplied input data. We may express the input in ways that are similar to the expression of output: either as the values of some variables (the computer's memory state at an earlier time), or as a sequence of values (communications to the computer).

When the desired result is finite (the values of a finite number of variables or a finite sequence of communications) and the result has been achieved, then the computer may as well terminate its activity. But it is not really our business whether it does so; perhaps it does some unobservable housekeeping afterward. If the desired result includes an unending sequence of communications, then obviously the computer's activity cannot end. We may sometimes infer something about termination or nontermination from a specification, but to speak of it directly would be overspecification. Indeed, neither termination nor nontermination is observable.

In this paper, we consider only the style that leads to standard, so-called "imperative" programs, with variables and assignments. Elsewhere, we consider the style of communicating processes. In any case, our purpose is to show the programming process using the predicative formalism.

Specifications

An informal specification of any mechanism is a natural language description that distinguishes satisfactory behavior from unsatisfactory behavior. To make a specification formal, we state the description as a predicate, whose free variables are the quantities of interest. Any values for the variables that satisfy the predicate represent behavior that satisfies the specification; any values that do not satisfy the predicate represent behavior that does not satisfy the specification.

Let the variables of a computation be $x, y, ...$. We use $\overrightarrow{x}, \overrightarrow{y}, ...$ to stand for their initial values, which we provide as input, and $\overleftarrow{x}, \overleftarrow{y}, ...$ to stand for their final values, which the computer provides as output. Altogether, we refer to the variables as v, to their initial values as $\overrightarrow{v}$, and to their final values as $\overleftarrow{v}$. (As a memory aid, we intimate that originally we used a pre-prime $^\backprime v$ for the initial values, and a post-prime $v^\prime$ for the final values.) A specification is a predicate having $\overrightarrow{v}$ and $\overleftarrow{v}$ as its free variables.

Here is an example.

(0) $\qquad \grave{x} \geq 0 \;\Rightarrow\; \acute{y} = 2^{\grave{x}}$

If initially $\grave{x} \geq 0$, then the final value of y is 2 to the initial value of x.

Determination

Let S be a specification. We can classify S for each possible input state $\grave{\nu}$ by the number of corresponding satisfactory output states $\acute{\nu}$.

$\quad\quad S$ is <u>overdetermined</u> for $\grave{\nu}$ if $\quad \neg\exists \acute{\nu}.\ S$
$\quad\quad S$ is <u>deterministic</u> for $\grave{\nu}$ if $\quad \exists 1\, \acute{\nu}.\ S$
$\quad\quad S$ is <u>un(der)determined</u> for $\grave{\nu}$ if $\;\forall \acute{\nu}.\ S$

The word "overdetermined" is synonymous with "unsatisfiable", and means that the number of satisfactory output states is zero.

$\quad\quad S$ is <u>satisfiable</u> for $\grave{\nu}$ if $\quad\quad \exists \acute{\nu}.\ S$

The word "deterministic" means that the number of satisfactory output states is exactly one. (The word "nondeterministic" is sometimes used to mean that more than one output state is satisfactory, allowing a choice of final state.) The words "underdetermined" and "undetermined" are synonymous and mean that all output states are satisfactory; the former word seems appropriate as the opposite of "overdetermined", but the latter seems appropriate as the negation of "determined".

$\quad\quad S$ is <u>determined</u> for $\grave{\nu}$ if $\quad\quad \neg\forall \acute{\nu}.\ S$

We shall find it convenient later to use the symbol ∇ to mean "determined". So we define

$\quad\quad \nabla S \quad =_{df} \quad \neg\forall \acute{\nu}.\ S$

Using example (0),

$$\nabla(\overset{\rightharpoonup}{x} \geq 0 \Rightarrow \overset{\leftharpoonup}{y} = 2^{\overset{\rightharpoonup}{x}}) = (\overset{\rightharpoonup}{x} \geq 0)$$

In general, ∇ tells us what initial values are of interest.

As a comparative, the word "determined" just means the partial ordering of predicates by implication.

$$R \text{ is \underline{as determined as} } S \text{ if } \quad \forall \overset{\rightharpoonup}{v}. \forall \overset{\leftharpoonup}{v}. \ R \Rightarrow S$$

In other words, any behavior satisfying R also satisfies S.

Implementations

It is commonly agreed that any computer behavior producing output $\overset{\leftharpoonup}{v}$ from input $\overset{\rightharpoonup}{v}$ can be represented by a recursive function f such that $\overset{\leftharpoonup}{v} = f(\overset{\rightharpoonup}{v})$. Function f represents an implementation of specification S if f always represents behavior that satisfies S.

$$(1) \qquad \forall \overset{\rightharpoonup}{v}. \forall \overset{\leftharpoonup}{v}. \ \overset{\leftharpoonup}{v} = f(\overset{\rightharpoonup}{v}) \Rightarrow S$$

Some computations never produce output. They are represented by partial functions. According to (1), such unproductive behavior is satisfactory just when S is undetermined. To see this, suppose, for some $\overset{\rightharpoonup}{v}$, that $f(\overset{\rightharpoonup}{v})$ is undefined. Then, for that $\overset{\rightharpoonup}{v}$ and any $\overset{\leftharpoonup}{v}$, $\overset{\leftharpoonup}{v} = f(\overset{\rightharpoonup}{v})$ is undefined — neither true nor false. In order for (1) to be true, the implication must hold for that $\overset{\rightharpoonup}{v}$ and any $\overset{\leftharpoonup}{v}$ by virtue of the consequent being true. So when f is undefined, S must be undetermined. (Note: Our connectives are fully conditional. An implication is true when its consequent is true, even if its antecedent is undefined. Also, an implication is true when its antecedent is false, even if its consequent is undefined.)

In our earlier example, specification (0)

$$\overset{\rightharpoonup}{x} \geq 0 \Rightarrow \overset{\leftharpoonup}{y} = 2^{\overset{\rightharpoonup}{x}}$$

is undetermined for negative $\overset{\rightharpoonup}{x}$. In other words, when the input $\overset{\rightharpoonup}{x}$ is negative, the specification is already satisfied, and an output is not required. But an output is still allowed; in fact, an arbitrary output is satisfactory. As it stands, the specification answers what should happen if nonnegative input is supplied, but leaves the question open when the input is negative. If we care what happens when the input is negative, then we must write a more determined specification.

From (1), we see that an overdetermined specification cannot be implemented. To be implementable, a specification must be universally satisfiable.

$$S \text{ is \underline{implementable} if} \qquad \forall \overset{\rightharpoonup}{v}. \ \exists \overset{\leftharpoonup}{v}. \ S$$

The main concern of this paper is the question: Given a specification, how do we obtain an implementation? But for a moment, let us consider the reverse question. Let f be a (possibly partial) function representing some computer behavior. There may be many specifications implemented by f. The most determined (strongest) specification implemented by f is

$$S = \begin{cases} \overset{\leftharpoonup}{v} = f(\overset{\rightharpoonup}{v}) & \text{if } f(\overset{\rightharpoonup}{v}) \text{ is defined} \\ \textbf{true} & \text{if } f(\overset{\rightharpoonup}{v}) \text{ is undefined} \end{cases}$$

This one specifies f exactly, in the sense that f can be reconstructed from S. But S is also implemented by any function that agrees with f wherever f is defined.

Let g be another function with a similar strongest specification T. The sequential composition of these behaviors (first f then g) is represented by the function $f \circ g$, formed as the functional composition of f and g. Its strongest specification is

$$\begin{cases} \overset{\leftharpoonup}{v} = g(f(\overset{\rightharpoonup}{v})) & \text{if } f(\overset{\rightharpoonup}{v}) \text{ and } g(f(\overset{\rightharpoonup}{v})) \text{ are defined} \\ \textbf{true} & \text{if } f(\overset{\rightharpoonup}{v}) \text{ is defined but } g(f(\overset{\rightharpoonup}{v})) \text{ is not} \\ \textbf{true} & \text{if } f(\overset{\rightharpoonup}{v}) \text{ is undefined} \end{cases}$$

$$= \quad \nabla S \ \Rightarrow \ S \circ T$$

In the same sense as before, this is the exact specification of $f \cdot g$. Similarly, we can obtain the exact specification of any behavior.

Programs

We are interested in the specification of computations, not of programs. If we were to specify programs, perhaps we would be concerned with their length, the relative frequencies of keywords, the choice of identifiers, and the indentation policy; but this is not our concern.

A program is a specification of computer behavior. A computer may not behave as specified by a program for a variety of reasons: a disk head may crash, a compiler may have a bug, or a resource may become exhausted (stack overflow, number overflow), to mention a few. Let us lay to rest all questions that confuse programs with computer behavior. If asked "What does this program do?", we answer "It just sits there on the page (or screen).". If asked "Does this program terminate?", we answer "Yes, all programs terminate.". It is the specified computer behavior that may not terminate.

The language of programs is the implemented subset of the language of specifications. It may be a changing subset, as we find new or better implementation techniques, but it will always be a subset. The language of specifications is not limited. We encourage specifiers to use whatever notations help to make their specifications clear; these may be programming notations, notations from logic, notations from the application area, or notations invented on the spot.

We now present an assortment of programming notations, drawn from various places. Each is defined by an equivalent predicate using standard predicate logic notations. The reader is directed to the paragraphs following these notations, which should be read along with the notations.

ok	$=_{df}$	$\acute{v} = \grave{v}$
$x := e$	$=_{df}$	$\textbf{ok}[\grave{x} : \grave{e}]$
$P \circ Q$	$=_{df}$	$\exists v.\ P[\grave{v} : v] \wedge Q[\acute{v} : v]$
$P ; Q$	$=_{df}$	$\nabla P \Rightarrow P \circ Q$
if b **then** P **else** Q	$=_{df}$	$\grave{b} \wedge P \vee \neg \grave{b} \wedge Q$
if b **then** P	$=_{df}$	**if** b **then** P **else ok**
if $b \to P$ ⬚ $c \to Q$ **fi**	$=_{df}$	$\grave{b} \vee \grave{c} \Rightarrow \grave{b} \wedge P \vee \grave{c} \wedge Q$
P **or** Q	$=_{df}$	$P \vee Q$
var $x:\ T.\ P$	$=_{df}$	$\forall \grave{x}:\ T.\ \exists \acute{x}:\ T.\ P$
loop $P:\ S(P)$	$=_{df}$	$\forall i.\ S^{i}(\textbf{true})$
while b **do** P	$=_{df}$	**loop** $Q:$ **if** b **then** $(P;\ Q)$
repeat P **until** b	$=_{df}$	**loop** $Q:\ (P;\ $ **if** $\neg b$ **then** $Q)$

The first notation, **ok**, is sometimes called "the empty program"; it is the identity relation, in which the final values equal the corresponding initial values (everything is ok the way it is). If there are two variables x and y, then **ok** = $(\acute{x} = \grave{x} \wedge \acute{y} = \grave{y})$.

The second notation is the familiar "assignment". We use **ok**$[\grave{x} : \grave{e}]$ to mean: in the standard predicate notation for **ok**, replace all free occurrences of $\grave{x}$ by $\grave{e}$ (the usual predicate logic substitution rule), where $\grave{e}$ is e but with ` over each variable. For example, in variables x and y,

$$x := x + y \quad = \quad \mathbf{ok}[\grave{x}: \acute{x} + \grave{y}]$$

$$= \quad (\acute{x} = \grave{x} \wedge \acute{y} = \grave{y})[\grave{x}: \acute{x} + \grave{y}]$$

$$= \quad (\acute{x} = \grave{x} + \grave{y} \wedge \acute{y} = \grave{y})$$

A more complete treatment than we have room for here would have to be concerned with whether the expression has a value. In this paper, we shall simply assume it has, and refer the interested reader to [Hehner84a] for a complete definition of "meaning predicates", and to [Hehner84b] for their use in predicative semantics.

The notation $P \circ Q$ is "relational product"; it is formed by binding the final values of P to the initial values of Q. Its implementation is ordinarily sequential execution: first behave according to P, and then according to Q. But when P is undetermined, the implementation is a little trickier: it must be "lazy", or "output driven".

The "composition" notation $P;Q$ is weaker than relational product, so it has more implementations. In particular, composition can always be implemented as sequential execution, even when P is undetermined. To use a programming notation correctly, it is not necessary to know its implementation. (If we were considering the speed of a computation, we would need to know.) It is not necessary that its operands be implementable. This connective, like the previous one, is defined for all specifications, whether implementable or not. It is an ordinary logical connective, like $\wedge$ and $\vee$.

In the **if** notations, b and c are boolean expressions, and P and Q are arbitrary specifications. Again, we are assuming that b and c have values, leaving the problem of undefined expressions to other papers. The **if-then-else** notation is equivalent, by simple boolean algebra, to

$$(\grave{b} \Rightarrow P) \wedge (\neg \grave{b} \Rightarrow Q)$$

Dijkstra's **if** looks particularly nice with one guarded command:

$$\mathbf{if}\ b \rightarrow P\ \mathbf{fi} \quad = \quad (\grave{b} \Rightarrow P)$$

The **or** connective is called "nondeterministic choice"; it is simply logical disjunction. Why should we have two symbols with the same meaning? Indeed, why should we have programming notations at all? We might just have patterns of predicates that we know how to implement, and our task is to express the specification using only these patterns. But pattern matching is hard; a compiler cannot easily decide whether a disjunction is part of the **if** pattern, or part of the **or** pattern. Still, we needn't have provided **or** as a programming notation; we could have insisted that the programmer choose between the disjuncts.

The **var** notation introduces a local variable x of type T into specification P. In standard predicate notation, it is just implementability in x.

The **loop** notation is general recursion (the symbol μ is often used instead of **loop**). It introduces a local (bound) predicate variable P into specification S. If $P = S(P)$ has a least determined solution, then **loop** P: $S(P)$ is that solution. Here is an example.

(2) **loop** P: **if** $x=0$ **then** $y:= 1$ **else** $(x:= x-1;\ P;\ y:= 2{\times}y)$

Let the part of (2) to the right of the colon be $S(P)$. We form a sequence of specifications, starting with the completely undetermined specification, and becoming more determined.

$$S^0(\textbf{true}) \quad = \quad \textbf{true}$$

$$S^1(\textbf{true}) \quad = \quad (\grave{x}{=}0 \Rightarrow \acute{x}{=}0 \land \acute{y}{=}2^{\grave{x}})$$

$$S^i(\textbf{true}) \quad = \quad (0 \le \grave{x} < i \Rightarrow \acute{x}{=}0 \land \acute{y}{=}2^{\grave{x}})$$

Program (2) is the limit, or conjunction, of all these specifications.

$$\forall i.\ S^i(\textbf{true}) \quad = \quad (0 \le \grave{x} \Rightarrow \acute{x}{=}0 \land \acute{y}{=}2^{\grave{x}})$$

Since (2) is more determined than our earlier example specification (0), any implementation of (2) is also an implementation of (0).

The **loop** construct is easily generalized to indirect recursion. It can also be specialized. The **while** and **repeat** notations are familiar specializations.

It is essential that each of our programming notations be monotonic in all predicate variables. This property gives us composability: an implementation of the whole can be constructed from implementations of the parts. Our connectives must also be continuous so that recursion (loops) can be implemented. For further details, we refer the reader to [Hehner84a] or [Hehner84b].

Theorems

Our new connectives have nice properties, and when we become familiar with them, they are as helpful in our reasoning as the old, standard logical connectives. Here is a small sample of theorems about programs that can easily be proven.

$$\textbf{ok};P \;=\; P;\textbf{ok} \;=\; P$$

$$\textbf{true};P$$

$$P;\textbf{true} \;=\; \nabla\neg P$$

$$\textbf{if } b \textbf{ then } P \textbf{ else } P \;=\; P$$

$$\textbf{if } b \textbf{ then } P \textbf{ else } Q \;=\; \textbf{if } \neg b \textbf{ then } Q \textbf{ else } P$$

$$(\textbf{if } b \textbf{ then } P \textbf{ else } Q); R \;=\; \textbf{if } b \textbf{ then } (P; R) \textbf{ else } (Q; R)$$

$$P;(Q \textbf{ or } R) \;=\; (P; Q) \textbf{ or } (P; R)$$

$$P \textbf{ or if } b \textbf{ then } Q \textbf{ else } R$$
$$= \textbf{if } b \textbf{ then } (P \textbf{ or } Q) \textbf{ else } (P \textbf{ or } R)$$

$$\textbf{var } x{:}\,T.\,\textbf{var } y{:}\,U.\,P \;=\; \textbf{var } y{:}\,U.\,\textbf{var } x{:}\,T.\,P$$

$$\textbf{loop } P{:}\,S(P) \;=\; S(\textbf{loop } P{:}\,S(P)) \qquad \text{if } S \text{ is continuous in } P$$

We stress that these are theorems in predicate logic, true of arbitrary specifications P, Q, and R, not just of programs or implementable specifications.

The preceding theorems relate programming notations to each other; in the literature, some are called "optimizations", some "transformations". There are many more such theorems, and many theorems that relate programming notations to other logical connectives. Arbitrary theorem generation is easy. The theorems we want are those that help us to program. Here are some, with a short discussion following.

(3) $P = (\nabla P \Rightarrow P)$

(4) $x := e; P = P[\grave{x}: \grave{e}]$

(5) $P = \textbf{if } b \textbf{ then } (\grave{b} \Rightarrow P) \textbf{ else } (\neg \grave{b} \Rightarrow P)$

(6) $(P;Q) \wedge \acute{R} = P;(Q \wedge \acute{R})$

(7) $\grave{G} \wedge (P; Q) = (\grave{G} \wedge P); Q$

(8) $(\grave{G} \Rightarrow (P; Q)) = ((\grave{G} \Rightarrow P); Q)$

(9) $P; (\grave{I} \wedge Q) \Leftarrow (P \wedge \acute{I}); Q$

(10) $P; Q \Leftarrow (P \wedge \acute{I}); (\grave{I} \Rightarrow Q)$

(11) $(\grave{I} \Rightarrow \textbf{loop } P: S(P)) = (\textbf{loop } P: \grave{I} \Rightarrow S(\grave{I} \wedge P))$

According to (3), we may always assume that a specification is determined. According to (4), an assignment composed with a specification is the same as a substitution in the specification. According to (5), any specification P can be transformed to an equivalent specification that is at least partly in the programming notation; the remaining pieces, $(\grave{b} \Rightarrow P)$ and $(\neg \grave{b} \Rightarrow P)$, are less determined than P, and in that sense they should be easier to implement.

In (6), $\acute{R}$ is any predicate that depends only on the final values of the variables. (R stands for "Result".) Similarly in (7) and (8), $\grave{G}$ is any predicate that depends only on the initial values. (G stands for "Given".) In (9), (10), and (11), $\grave{I}$, like $\grave{G}$, has only accented variables, and $\acute{I}$ is the same as $\grave{I}$ but with all accents flipped. (I stands for "Intermediate").

In (9) and (10), the connective $\Leftarrow$ (pronounced "is implied by", "is solved by", or just "if") is reverse implication. We could equally well have written these theorems the other way round, using the usual implication symbol. Our choice arises from the use of these theorems in programming, where we can always replace a specification by a more determined (but not overdetermined) specification. For example, if a specification is of the form (P; Q), we can replace it by (($P \wedge \acute{I}$); ($\grave{I} \Rightarrow Q$)), because according to (10), any implementation of the latter is also an implementation of the former.

Programming

Given a problem in the form of a specification S, we solve the problem by writing a few theorems that convert S to an equivalent or stronger specification in programming notations. These theorems constitute a constructive proof that S is implementable. As a by-product, we obtain an implementation automatically.

Let us begin again with our example specification (0). From Theorem (5) we know

$$(\grave{x}\geq 0 \;\Rightarrow\; \acute{y}=2^{\grave{x}}) \;\Leftarrow\; \text{if } x{=}0 \text{ then } (\grave{x}{=}0 \;\Rightarrow\; \acute{y}{=}2^{\grave{x}})$$
$$\text{else } (\grave{x}{>}0 \;\Rightarrow\; \acute{y}{=}2^{\grave{x}})$$

We consider the original problem (0) to be solved, but now we have two new problems. The first of these can be solved easily without raising any more problems.

$$(\grave{x}{=}0 \;\Rightarrow\; \acute{y}=2^{\grave{x}}) \;\Leftarrow\; y{:=}1;\; x{:=}3$$

From the left side, we know we need $\acute{y}{=}1$ on the right. The assignment to x

is superfluous; since the problem says nothing about the final value of x, we have perversely assigned x the arbitrary value 3 simply to exercise our freedom. The remaining problem, and those raised subsequently, can be solved as follows.

$$(\grave{x}>0 \;\Rightarrow\; \acute{y}=2^{\grave{x}}) \;\Leftarrow\; (\grave{x}>0 \;\Rightarrow\; \acute{y}=2^{\grave{x}-1}); (\acute{y}=2 \times \grave{y})$$

$$(\grave{x}>0 \;\Rightarrow\; \acute{y}=2^{\grave{x}-1}) \;\Leftarrow\; (\acute{x}=\grave{x}-1); (\grave{x}\geq 0 \;\Rightarrow\; \acute{y}=2^{\grave{x}})$$

$$(\acute{y}=2 \times \grave{y}) \;\Leftarrow\; y:=2 \times y; \; x:=5$$

$$(\acute{x}=\grave{x}-1) \;\Leftarrow\; x:=x-1; \; y:=7$$

Our solution is now complete: every problem raised has been solved.

What we have written are theorems (universally quantified over all variables). A theorem prover (automated, or human, or a combination) should check that they are; if they are not, it should report any error, preferably with a counterexample.

There are many other solutions; the one we have written is neither the simplest nor the most efficient. In the last two lines, we have again made superfluous assignments. Our reason for doing so is didactic; we want to show that our confidence in the correctness of our solution rests on the proofs of these six simple theorems (plus one more that we will see later).

Compilation

Current compilers check programs for syntax errors, but not for logic errors. Future compilers, with built-in theorem provers, will also be able to check for logic errors, pointing out the location of a logic error the same way as they do now with a syntax error.

The other task of a compiler is to translate programs into machine instructions. Translation begins by treating all non-programming notations as identifiers. We illustrate by replacing all the non-programming notations in the previous section with arbitrary single letters. Replacing $(\grave{x}\geq 0 \;\Rightarrow\; \acute{y}=2^{\grave{x}})$ by A, and so on, we obtain

$$A \quad \Leftarrow \quad \textbf{if } x = 0 \textbf{ then } B \textbf{ else } C$$
$$B \quad \Leftarrow \quad y := 1; \ x := 3$$
$$C \quad \Leftarrow \quad D; E$$
$$D \quad \Leftarrow \quad F; A$$
$$E \quad \Leftarrow \quad y := 2 \times y; \ x := 5$$
$$F \quad \Leftarrow \quad x := x - 1; \ y := 7$$

We have six parameterless, scopeless procedure definitions, which call each other. Thanks to the monotonicity of all programming connectives, we can always replace an identifier on the right with something stronger, so we can always replace a procedure call with its body.

$$A \Leftarrow \textbf{if } x = 0 \textbf{ then } (y := 1; \ x := 3)$$
$$\textbf{else } (x := x - 1; \ y := 7; A; \ y := 2 \times y; \ x := 5)$$

A programmer will not usually want to see this stage, or any stage, of the translation to machine instructions; information needed for understanding has been removed.

We hope that our solution now looks sufficiently familiar that the remaining stages of the translation can be taken for granted.

Nondeterminism

Sometimes we may see two or more solutions to a problem. For example,

$$(\overrightarrow{x} > 0 \ \Rightarrow \ \overrightarrow{y} = 2^{\overrightarrow{x}}) \Leftarrow$$
$$\textbf{if } odd(x) \textbf{ then } (x := x - 1; (\overrightarrow{x} \geq 0 \ \Rightarrow \ \overrightarrow{y} = 2^{\overrightarrow{x}}); \ y := 2 \times y)$$
$$\textbf{else } (x := x/2; (\overrightarrow{x} > 0 \ \Rightarrow \ \overrightarrow{y} = 2^{\overrightarrow{x}}); \ y := y \times y)$$

provides a second solution to a problem $(\overrightarrow{x} > 0 \ \Rightarrow \ \overrightarrow{y} = 2^{\overrightarrow{x}})$ solved previously. From a logical point of view, both this and the previous solution are theorems; they coexist peacefully. From an execution point of view, we have two procedure bodies for one procedure name. Any call (occurrence of $(\overrightarrow{x} > 0 \ \Rightarrow \ \overrightarrow{y} = 2^{\overrightarrow{x}})$ on the right) can use either solution. Having two solutions to one problem

$$P \Leftarrow Q$$
$$P \Leftarrow R$$

is the same, both logically and operationally, as having one solution

$$P \Leftarrow Q \textbf{ or } R$$

which uses the nondeterministic choice operator. For the sake of efficiency, if one solution is better than another, it is advisable to delete the worse solution.

Variant

Consider the following "solution" to our example problem.

$$(\grave{x} \geq 0 \Rightarrow \acute{y} = 2^{\grave{x}}) \Leftarrow \textbf{ if } x = 0 \textbf{ then } y := 1 \textbf{ else } (\grave{x} \geq 0 \Rightarrow \acute{y} = 2^{\grave{x}})$$

Although this is a theorem, it is not a proof that $(\grave{x} \geq 0 \Rightarrow \acute{y} = 2^{\grave{x}})$ is implementable, and an implementation cannot be extracted automatically. Two rules of programming must be followed, and the preceding "solution" violates the second. Here are the rules.

> <u>Theorem Rule</u> A problem S is solved by a theorem of the form $S \Leftarrow P$ where P uses only programming notations and solved problems. (Whether they are solved previously, at the same time, or subsequently, is irrelevant; there is no ordering to a collection of theorems.)

> <u>Variant Rule</u> In any collection of theorems, whenever a problem is solved (directly or indirectly) in terms of itself, a variant is required.

We define "variant" in a moment, but first we notice that the variant rule can be followed simply by not solving a problem in terms of itself. This can be accomplished by means of the **loop** notation. If we naïvely attempt to translate our latest "solution" into **loop** notation, we find that

$$(\overleftarrow{x} \geq 0 \Rightarrow \overrightarrow{y} = 2^{\overrightarrow{x}}) \Leftarrow \textbf{loop } P\!: \textbf{if } x{=}0 \textbf{ then } y:= 1 \textbf{ else } P$$

is not a theorem: the right side is equivalent to $(\overleftarrow{x}{=}0 \Rightarrow \overrightarrow{x}{=}0 \wedge \overrightarrow{y}{=}1)$. So the programming error is seen as a violation of the theorem rule. In general, proofs involving the **loop** notation (or its specializations) are difficult, and we prefer not to use it.

When a problem is solved in terms of itself, an execution loop is created. The path (or body) of the loop is readily seen by inspection. In fact, it is an easy job for a compiler, not involving a theorem prover, to point out all loop paths. Let S be a problem solved in terms of itself. Let P be a loop path for S. Let f be an integer expression (not necessarily occurring in the program, nor necessarily using programming notations). Then f is called a variant for P if

$$\nabla S \wedge \overleftarrow{f}{>}0 \wedge P \;\Rightarrow\; 0 \leq \overrightarrow{f} < \overleftarrow{f}$$

is a theorem. This means that for problem S, if f is positive before execution of P, then after execution of P, f will be smaller but not less than zero.

A loop path may go through any programming construct. When it goes through one branch of an **if–then–else** construct, we can replace the other branch with anything we like. To make our proof easiest, we may as well replace the other branch with **false**. Similarly, when a path goes through one side of an **or** construct, we replace the other side with **false**. The reference (call) to the original problem should be replaced with **ok**.

To illustrate, let us look at our example solution.

$$(\overleftarrow{x} \geq 0 \Rightarrow \overrightarrow{y} = 2^{\overrightarrow{x}}) \;\Leftarrow\; \textbf{if } \overleftarrow{x}{=}0 \textbf{ then } (\overleftarrow{x}{=}0 \Rightarrow \overrightarrow{y}{=}2^{\overrightarrow{x}})$$
$$\textbf{else } (\overleftarrow{x}{>}0 \Rightarrow \overrightarrow{y}{=}2^{\overrightarrow{x}})$$

$$(\overleftarrow{x} = 0 \Rightarrow \overrightarrow{y} = 2^{\overrightarrow{x}}) \;\Leftarrow\; y:= 1$$

$$(\overleftarrow{x} > 0 \Rightarrow \overrightarrow{y} = 2^{\overrightarrow{x}}) \;\Leftarrow$$
$$\textbf{if } odd(x) \textbf{ then } (x:= x{-}1; (\overleftarrow{x} \geq 0 \Rightarrow \overrightarrow{y}{=}2^{\overrightarrow{x}}); y:= 2{\times}y)$$
$$\textbf{else } (x:= x/2; (\overleftarrow{x} > 0 \Rightarrow \overrightarrow{y}{=}2^{\overrightarrow{x}}); y:= y{\times}y)$$

These three theorems contain two basic loop paths. A compiler requests a variant f such that

$$\grave{x}{\geq}0 \;\wedge\; \grave{f}{>}0 \;\wedge\; \textbf{if } x{=}0 \textbf{ then false}$$
$$\textbf{else if } odd(x) \textbf{ then } (x{:=} x{-}1;\, \textbf{ok})$$
$$\textbf{else false}$$
$$\Rightarrow\; 0{\leq}\acute{f}{<}\grave{f}$$

$$\grave{x}{>}0 \;\wedge\; \grave{f}{>}0 \;\wedge\; \textbf{if } odd(x) \textbf{ then false}$$
$$\textbf{else } (x{:=} x/2;\, \textbf{ok})$$
$$\Rightarrow\; 0{\leq}\acute{f}{<}\grave{f}$$

are theorems. The programmer supplies one; in this case, the expression x serves the purpose. For further details concerning loop paths, see [Hehner84a].

Invariant

Traditionally, the notion of "invariant" has been associated with loops, and it is most useful in that connection. But it can be defined quite independently of loops. Using the positional notation $I(\grave{v},\, \acute{v})$, here is the general form.

$$\textbf{inv } I.\,P \quad =_{df} \quad \forall v.\; I(v,\, \grave{v}) \wedge \nabla P \;\Rightarrow\; P \wedge I(v,\, \acute{v})$$

Roughly speaking, any state related to the initial state by I must also be related to the final state by I.

To aid our intuition, let us look at some special cases. The two simplest are

$$\textbf{inv true}.\, P \;=\; P$$
$$\textbf{inv false}.\, P \;=\; \textbf{true}$$

Using **true** as invariant leaves a specification unchanged. Using **false** as invariant yields an undetermined specification.

A common special case occurs when the invariant happens to have only $\acute{}$ accents, so that it is really a predicate on a single state. Then

$$\text{inv } \acute{I}.\, P \quad = \quad (\grave{I} \,\wedge\, \nabla P \,\Rightarrow\, P \,\wedge\, \acute{I})$$

This says that if, in addition to the precondition for P, the invariant is also true initially, then P describes the desired behavior with the additional constraint that the invariant must be true finally. For this common case, we adopt the following convention: we allow the invariant to be written without accents. Thus

$$\text{inv } x{>}0.\ \ even(\grave{x}) \Rightarrow \acute{x}{<}\grave{x}$$
$$= \ \grave{x}{>}0 \,\wedge\, even(\grave{x}) \ \Rightarrow\ \acute{x}{<}\grave{x} \,\wedge\, \acute{x}{>}0$$

Another useful special case is the invariant $\acute{e}=\grave{e}$ where e is any expression of any type.

$$\text{inv } \acute{e}{=}\grave{e}.\, P \quad = \quad (\nabla P \,\Rightarrow\, P \,\wedge\, \acute{e}{=}\grave{e})$$

In this case, we refer to e as being constant, and we introduce the notation

$$\text{con } e.\, P \quad =_{\text{df}} \quad \text{inv } \acute{e}{=}\grave{e}.\, P$$

The invariant construct is not always implementable. Here are two such examples.

$$\text{inv } x{=}0.\ \ x{:=}\ 1$$
$$\text{con } x.\ \ x{:=}\ 1$$

The first is equivalent to $\grave{x}{\neq}0$ and the second to $\acute{x}{=}\grave{x}{=}1$; in both cases for $\grave{x}{=}0$ there is no satisfactory $\acute{x}$.

In general, the theorem

$$\text{inv } I.\, P \ \Leftarrow\ P \wedge \text{ok}$$

is not helpful; since P usually requires some variable to change its value, the right side is too strong. One strategy that sometimes helps when P is compound is to distribute the invariant responsibility across the parts of P. Some of the following theorems indicate how this works.

$$\textbf{inv } I. \textbf{ true} \quad = \quad \textbf{true}$$

$$\textbf{inv } I. \textbf{ ok} \quad \Leftarrow \quad \textbf{ok}$$

$$\textbf{inv } I. \ P;Q \quad \Leftarrow \quad (\textbf{inv } I. \ P); (\textbf{inv } I. \ Q)$$

$$\textbf{inv } I. \textbf{ if } b \textbf{ then } P \textbf{ else } Q$$
$$= \textbf{ if } b \textbf{ then inv } I. \ P \textbf{ else inv } I. \ Q$$

$$\textbf{inv } I. \textbf{ if } b \textbf{ then } P \quad \Leftarrow \quad \textbf{if } b \textbf{ then inv } I. \ P$$

$$\textbf{inv } I. \ P \textbf{ or } Q \quad = \quad (\textbf{inv } I. \ P) \textbf{ or } (\textbf{inv } I. \ Q)$$

$$\textbf{inv } I. \textbf{ var } x. \ P \quad = \quad \textbf{var } x. \textbf{ inv } I. \ P$$
if x does not appear in I

$$\textbf{inv } I. \textbf{ while } b \textbf{ do } P \quad \Leftarrow \quad \textbf{while } b \textbf{ do inv } I. \ P$$

$$\textbf{inv } I. \textbf{ repeat } P \textbf{ until } b \quad \Leftarrow \quad \textbf{repeat inv } I. \ P \textbf{ until } b$$

$$\textbf{inv } I. \textbf{ inv } J. \ P \quad = \quad \textbf{inv } I{\wedge}J. \ P$$

Since **con** is a special case of **inv**, these theorems (except the last) also hold for **con**.

Fibonacci

The problem of finding the nth Fibonacci number in $\log n$ time shows **con** to advantage. We define the Fibonacci numbers as

$$f_0 \ = \ 0$$
$$f_1 \ = \ 1$$
$$f_{n+2} \ = \ f_n + f_{n+1}$$

The problem is $(\textbf{con } n. \ \acute{x} = f_{\acute{n}})$; without changing n, set x to f_n. Let n, x, and y be natural variables. The first two steps in the solution are as follows.

$$(\textbf{con } n. \ \acute{x} = f_{\acute{n}}) \quad \Leftarrow \quad (\textbf{con } n. \ \acute{x} = f_{\acute{n}} \ \wedge \ \acute{y} = f_{\acute{n}+1})$$

$$(\textbf{con } n.\ \overleftarrow{x}=f_{\overleftarrow{n}} \wedge \overleftarrow{y}=f_{\overleftarrow{n}+1}) \Leftarrow$$

$$\textbf{if } n=0$$
$$\textbf{then } (x:=0;\ y:=1)$$
$$\textbf{else if } odd(n)$$
$$\textbf{then } (\textbf{con } n.\ \overleftarrow{n}>0 \wedge odd(\overleftarrow{n}) \Rightarrow \overleftarrow{x}=f_{\overleftarrow{n}} \wedge \overleftarrow{y}=f_{\overleftarrow{n}+1})$$
$$\textbf{else } (\textbf{con } n.\ \overleftarrow{n}>0 \wedge even(\overleftarrow{n}) \Rightarrow \overleftarrow{x}=f_{\overleftarrow{n}} \wedge \overleftarrow{y}=f_{\overleftarrow{n}+1})$$

The next step uses the lemmas

$$f_{2k+1} = f_k^2 + f_{k+1}^2$$
$$f_{2k+2} = 2f_k f_{k+1} + f_{k+1}^2$$

In this step, we point out that **con** does not mean that n should not change at all, but only that it must end where it began.

$$(\textbf{con } n.\ \overleftarrow{n}>0 \wedge odd(\overleftarrow{n}) \Rightarrow \overleftarrow{x}=f_{\overleftarrow{n}} \wedge \overleftarrow{y}=f_{\overleftarrow{n}+1}) \Leftarrow$$
$$n:=(n-1)/2;\ (\textbf{con } n.\ \overleftarrow{x}=f_{\overleftarrow{n}} \wedge \overleftarrow{y}=f_{\overleftarrow{n}+1});\ n:=2n+1;$$
$$(\textbf{con } n.\ \overleftarrow{x}=\overleftarrow{x}^2+\overleftarrow{y}^2 \wedge \overleftarrow{y}=2\overleftarrow{x}\overleftarrow{y}+\overleftarrow{y}^2)$$

In the even case, we lower n from $2k+2$ to k, finding f_k and f_{k+1} as x and y. We then calculate the new x as f_{2k+2} and the new y as $f_{2k+1} + f_{2k+2}$.

$$(\textbf{con } n.\ \overleftarrow{n}>0 \wedge even(\overleftarrow{n}) \Rightarrow \overleftarrow{x}=f_{\overleftarrow{n}} \wedge \overleftarrow{y}=f_{\overleftarrow{n}+1}) \Leftarrow$$
$$n:=n/2-1;\ (\textbf{con } n.\ \overleftarrow{x}=f_{\overleftarrow{n}} \wedge \overleftarrow{y}=f_{\overleftarrow{n}+1});\ n:=2(n+1);$$
$$(\textbf{con } n.\ \overleftarrow{x}=2\overleftarrow{x}\overleftarrow{y}+\overleftarrow{y}^2 \wedge \overleftarrow{y}=\overleftarrow{x}^2+\overleftarrow{y}^2+\overleftarrow{x})$$

The remaining two problems are trivial.

$$(\textbf{con } n.\ \overleftarrow{x}=\overleftarrow{x}^2+\overleftarrow{y}^2 \wedge \overleftarrow{y}=2\overleftarrow{x}\overleftarrow{y}+\overleftarrow{y}^2) \Leftarrow$$
$$\textbf{var } oldx:\ natural.\ oldx:=x;\ x:=x^2+y^2;\ y:=2\,oldx\,y+y^2$$

$$(\textbf{con } n.\ \overleftarrow{x}=2\overleftarrow{x}\overleftarrow{y}+\overleftarrow{y}^2 \wedge \overleftarrow{y}=\overleftarrow{x}^2+\overleftarrow{y}^2+\overleftarrow{x}) \Leftarrow$$
$$\textbf{var } oldx:\ natural.\ oldx:=x;\ x:=2xy+y^2;\ y:=oldx^2+y^2+x$$

A variant for each of the loops is n, as the following two theorems show.

$0 < \overset{\grave{}}{n} \;\wedge\;$ **if** $n{=}0$
   then false
   else if $odd(n)$
     then $(n{:=}(n{-}1)/2;\,\textbf{ok})$
     else false $\Rightarrow\;\; 0 \leqslant \overset{\acute{}}{n} < \overset{\grave{}}{n}$

$0 < \overset{\grave{}}{n} \;\wedge\;$ **if** $n{=}0$
   then false
   else if $odd(n)$
     then false
     else $(n{:=}n/2{-}1;\,\textbf{ok})$ $\Rightarrow\;\; 0 \leqslant \overset{\acute{}}{n} < \overset{\grave{}}{n}$

This solution should be judged against any other *log n* solution for its clarity, and it should be noted again that each of the above fragments is a theorem of predicate logic.

Paradigms

Mathematicians do not always prove a theorem from axioms; more often they prove a theorem from other theorems. That way, they build on each other's work. Programming is practical mathematics, and if we want to get very far with it, we must do the same.

An experienced programmer has a mental stock of solutions, or solution patterns. These are sometimes called "program paradigms". Some typical examples are linear search, merge, accumulation, use of a sentinel, and buffering. We shall show that paradigms are just useful theorems, upon which other theorems can be based.

Our first paradigm is even more basic than the examples just cited. Having eschewed the **loop** notation, and finding the loop paths to be still a little complicated, we present a loop paradigm that helps considerably.

Goal

Let f be an integer expression (the variant). Let g be a boolean expression (the goal). Define

$$\text{Goal}(f, g) =_{df} \textbf{inv } f{\geq}0.\ \acute{g}$$

Goal can be used to solve many problems. In turn, it is solved by the following theorem.

$$\text{Goal}(f, g) \ \Leftarrow\ \textbf{while } \neg g \textbf{ do } (\textbf{inv } f{\geq}0.\ \neg\grave{g} \Rightarrow \acute{f}{<}\grave{f})$$

After proving this theorem once, we need never write a loop like it again, nor prove a theorem like it again.

Suppose the problem pot (or job jar) contains the exponentiation problem $(\grave{y} \geq 0 \Rightarrow \acute{z}{=}\grave{x}^{\grave{y}})$. We select this problem and solve it by writing

$$(\grave{y} \geq 0 \Rightarrow \acute{z}{=}\grave{x}^{\grave{y}}) \ \Leftarrow\ z := 1;\ \textbf{con } z{\times}x^{y}.\ \text{Goal}(y,\ y{=}0)$$

We first want $z=1$, then keeping $z{\times}x^{y}$ constant, we want to decrease y until $y=0$. This is not just a strategy, but a theorem that solves the problem. This theorem, which we or a compiler must prove, is a simple one. Expanding the definitions of **con**, Goal, and **inv**, it is

$$(\grave{y} \geq 0 \Rightarrow \acute{z}{=}\grave{x}^{\grave{y}}) \ \Leftarrow$$
$$z := 1;\ (\grave{y}{\geq}0 \Rightarrow \acute{y}{=}0 \wedge \acute{y}{\geq}0 \wedge \acute{z}{\times}\acute{x}^{\acute{y}} = \grave{z}{\times}\grave{x}^{\grave{y}})$$

Using Theorem 4, the right side can be simplified,

$$(\grave{y} \geq 0 \Rightarrow \acute{z}{=}\grave{x}^{\grave{y}}) \ \Leftarrow\ (\grave{y}{\geq}0 \Rightarrow \acute{y}{=}0 \wedge \acute{z}{=}\grave{x}^{\grave{y}})$$

and our problem is solved without any loops. Of course, a compiler will supply a loop, extracted from the Goal theorem.

The compiler also puts a new problem into the pot for us to find and solve at another time. Distributing **con** into the loop body, it is

con $z \times x^y$. **inv** $y \geq 0$. $\grave{y} \neq 0 \Rightarrow \acute{y} < \grave{y}$

It can be solved, for example, by

if $odd(y)$ **then** $(y := y-1;\ z := z \times x)$
else $(y := y/2;\ x := x \times x)$

Another simple example is the factorial problem. Its solution, and the solution to the new problem raised, are as follows:

$(\grave{n} \geq 0 \Rightarrow \acute{x} = \grave{n}!) \Leftarrow x := 1;$ **con** $x \times n!$. Goal$(n, n=0)$

(**con** $x \times n!$. **inv** $n \geq 0$. $\grave{n} \neq 0 \Rightarrow \acute{n} < \grave{n}) \Leftarrow x := x \times n;\ n := n-1$

The problem of reducing a variable modulo 5 gives us a chance to use the invariant construct in its full generality. Here it is, with its solution (all variables are integers).

$(\grave{r} \geq 0 \Rightarrow 0 \leq \acute{r} < 5 \wedge \exists q.\ \acute{r} = \grave{r} - 5 \times q)$
$\Leftarrow$ **inv** $\exists q.\ \acute{r} = \grave{r} - 5 \times q$. Goal$(r, r<5)$

In fact, the reverse implication is also equality. As usual, Goal solves a problem by raising another.

(**inv** $\exists q.\ \acute{r} = \grave{r} - 5 \times q$. **inv** $r \geq 0$. $\grave{r} \geq 5 \Rightarrow \acute{r} < \grave{r}) \Leftarrow r := r-5$

The generality of **inv** is not needed in this example, however, if we allow ourselves the **mod** operator in our predicates. Then we can write

$(\grave{r} \geq 0 \Rightarrow \acute{r} = \grave{r} \bmod 5) \Leftarrow$ **con** $r \bmod 5$. Goal$(r, r<5)$

(**con** $r \bmod 5$. **inv** $r \geq 0$. $\grave{r} \geq 5 \Rightarrow \acute{r} < \grave{r}) \Leftarrow r := r-5$

Linear Search

Let P be a predicate on the natural numbers. Let n be a natural variable. Define

$$\text{LinSrch}(P, n) \quad =_{df} \quad (\forall i: 0 \leq i < \hat{n}. \, \neg P(i)) \wedge P(\hat{n})$$

LinSrch specifies that the final value of n is the first natural number having property P. For LinSrch to be implementable, P must be satisfiable. And when it is,

$$\text{LinSrch}(P, n) \quad = \quad n := 0; \textbf{while } \neg P(n) \textbf{ do } n := n+1$$

Or, if you prefer,

$$\text{LinSrch}(P, n) \quad = \quad n := 0; \text{Goal}(N-n, P(n))$$

where N is the first solution of P.

We can now solve problems using LinSrch. As an obvious example, suppose A is an array indexed from 0 to $N-1$. Then the problem of finding the first occurrence of x in A can be specified and solved as

$$(0 \leq \hat{n} \leq N \wedge (\forall i: 0 \leq i < \hat{n}. \, A[i] \neq x) \wedge (A[\hat{n}] = x \vee \hat{n} = N))$$
$$\Leftarrow \quad \text{LinSrch}(n = N \textbf{ cor } A[n] = x, \, n)$$

where **cor** is semi-conditional **or**. In this example, the problem (as specified in the first line) and solution (as specified in the second) are, in fact, equal. If the second of these two lines is more understandable than the first, then there is no point at all in writing the first line. We should use the second as problem specification, and be done.

Search

Here is a general search paradigm that accommodates linear search, binary search, tree search, and all other searches. Let S be a search space variable. Let P be a predicate over S. Let *present* be a boolean variable. Let x be a variable of the same type as the elements of the search space.

Define

$$\text{Has}(S, P) \;=_{df}\; \exists y \in S.\, P(y)$$

$$\text{Search}(S, P, present, x) \;=_{df}$$
$$(\overrightarrow{present} = \text{Has}(\overleftarrow{S}, P)) \;\wedge\; (\text{Has}(\overleftarrow{S}, P) \;\Rightarrow\; \overrightarrow{x} \in \overleftarrow{S} \wedge P(\overrightarrow{x}))$$

Variable *present* should have final value true if there is an element of the initial search space with property P, and false if there is not. And if there is, x should finally be such an element.

In our solution, Has(S, P) is a constant: if initially true, it remains true, and if initially false, it remains false.

$$\text{Search}(S, P, present, x) \Leftarrow$$
> **if** $S = \{\}$
> **then** $present := $ **false**
> **else** ((**con** $S.\ \overrightarrow{S} \neq \{\} \Rightarrow \overrightarrow{x} \in \overleftarrow{S}$);
>> **if** $P(x)$
>> **then** $present := $ **true**
>> **else** ((**con** Has(S, P). $\overrightarrow{x} \in \overleftarrow{S} \wedge \neg P(\overleftarrow{x}) \Rightarrow \overrightarrow{S} \subset \overleftarrow{S}$);
>>> Search($S, P, present, x$)))

The theorem rule has been followed. The variant rule is satisfied if the initial search space $\overleftarrow{S}$ is finite.

The solution gives us two new problems to be solved: one is to select an element from a non-empty space, and the other is to reduce a non-empty space without losing the last element having property P. Depending on the representation of the search space and the implemented (programming) expressions, we may also have to refine the expression $S = \{\}$.

Any helpful properties of the search space can be used to advantage when selecting an element or reducing its size, if these properties are preserved by the reduction. We could state the property as an invariant, or we can consider such properties to be part of the type of variable S.

To illustrate the use of the general search paradigm, we decided to solve the linear search problem. But to our surprise, the implication went the wrong way.

$$\text{LinSrch}(P, n) \Rightarrow \textbf{var } present: boolean.$$
$$n := 0;$$
$$\text{Search}(\{n, ...\}, P, present, n)$$

The problem is that LinSrch specifies that n should be the first solution of P, but Search does not specify which solution. To solve LinSrch using Search, we need an invariant. Given $\exists n. P(n)$,

$$\text{LinSrch}(P, n) = \textbf{var } present: boolean.$$
$$n := 0;$$
$$\textbf{inv } \forall m < n. \neg P(m).$$
$$\text{Search}(\{n, ...\}, P, present, n)$$

The first of the two new problems raised by Search, after simplification, is $\hat{n} = \overleftarrow{n}$, whose solution is obviously **ok**. The other new problem, after simplification, is

$$\textbf{inv } (\forall m < n. \neg P(m)). \textbf{ con } (\exists y \geq n. P(y)). \neg P(\overleftarrow{n}) \Rightarrow \hat{n} > \overleftarrow{n}$$

whose solution is $n := n+1$.

This example and others, together with proofs of theorems, appear in [Gupta85].

What Remains

In some respects, a paradigm is like a procedure, with procedure parameters. In our formalism, it is a predicate with predicate parameters. We need to decide whether the parameters are syntactic (textual) or semantic (respecting scope), and formalize them properly. As an example, consider a paradigm giving a **for** loop.

$$\text{For}(a, b, P) =_{df} \textbf{;}_{a \leq n \leq b} P(n)$$

$$\text{For}(a, b, P) \Leftarrow \textbf{var } n: integer.$$
$$n := a;$$
$$\textbf{while } n \leq b \textbf{ do } ((\textbf{con } n. P(n)); n := n+1)$$

What is meant when arguments supplied for a, b, and P refer to n?

Eventually we would like a library of helpful paradigms. How should it be organized?

Conclusion

We have defined programming notations in terms of standard logic. This is reasonable if we assume that standard logic is already understood. It may be more reasonable to assume that algorithmic understanding comes before an understanding of logic, or any other mathematics. If so, we should invert our semantics; we should define the logic connectives as programs.

Our programming style bears some similarity to Prolog, particularly in the use of reverse implication. But the resemblance is superficial; the difference is profound. Prolog's theorem-proving is its execution, its "run-time" activity; our theorem-proving is a "compile-time" activity. Our programming is a constructive proof of implementability, much more like Constable's PRL [Constable83].

The search for good programming paradigms is a search for good theorems. They must be general enough to be useful often, and so be worth memorizing. They must not be so general that they hardly help. Finding good paradigms requires experience and good judgement. We have just begun.

Acknowledgement

We thank Tony Hoare, David Gries, Philip Matthews, the members of IFIP Working Group 2.3, and an anonymous referee for helpful comments. This work was supported by The Natural Sciences and Engineering Research Council of Canada.

References

[Constable83] R.L.Constable, J.L.Bates: The Nearly Ultimate PEARL. Cornell TR-83-551, 1983

[Gupta85] L.E.Gupta, Predicative Programs and Paradigms. M.Sc. Thesis, University of Toronto, 1985

[Hehner84a] E.C.R.Hehner: *The Logic of Programming* . Prentice-Hall Int., London, 1984

[Hehner84b] E.C.R.Hehner: Predicative Programming. *C.ACM 27, 2,* pp.134-151, February 1984

Termination Conventions
and
Comparative Semantics

Eric C.R. Hehner
Andrew J. Malton

University of Toronto

Summary

The notion of termination is examined, first for its physical observability, then for its part in six semantic formalisms, with emphasis on predicative semantics.

Observing Termination

Imagine there is a computer in front of you right now. Perhaps it has a screen and keyboard, as is common. You can press the keys, and watch the patterns on the screen. Unfortunately, this computer was built and programmed by Tatooinians, whose language you do not know. The symbols on the keys are meaningless to you; the patterns on the screen are undecipherable. Fortunately, no-one is asking you what is being computed, or what the computation means. You are being asked a simpler question: When has the computation terminated? If you will simply report when the machine is finished, someone else will then interpret the results.

How do you know when termination occurs? If nothing has happened for five minutes, can you report termination? No; perhaps the machine is computing *Ackermann* (6,6), and still has a century to go. It is obvious that nontermination, or infinite looping, is unobservable; without knowing the program, you can only guess that a computation is stuck in a loop. The purpose of this thought-experiment is to convince you that termination is also unobservable.

How do you recognize termination on your own computer, programmed by someone who speaks your language? Probably you look for the word "Done", or something similar, printed as the dying act. Or perhaps you look

NATO ASI Series, Vol. F36
Logic of Programming and Calculi of Discrete Design
Edited by M. Broy
© Springer-Verlag Berlin Heidelberg 1987

for a prompt from the operating system, following termination. It is possible, though not probable, that your computer has broken in mid computation, and is now behaving erratically; it just printed the letters "Done" (or the prompt) by chance as it malfunctions. Or perhaps the program was written by a joker, who thinks it funny to print "Done" (or the prompt) in the middle of the computation, followed in a minute by "Wait, there's more". You cannot be certain when a computation has finished even on your own machine, although the usual indicators are very reliable.

Predicative Semantics

A predicative formalism is a formalism for specifying and describing computations, including the semantics of programs, as predicates. One is invited to decide what observable quantities are of interest, and to express specifications as predicates having these quantities as free variables. A computation satisfies a specification if it instantiates the free variables in a way that satisfies the predicate.

A reasonable choice of "observable quantities of interest" is the communication sequence, or sequences, to and from a computer. In many computer systems and programming languages, there is something that indicates termination of a communication sequence. (In UNIX, it is control-D; in Pascal it is the *eof* function.) But at a basic semantic level, this end-of-file indication is just another communication. It is only by agreement that we give it the special meaning "Don't wait for more". We may decide to enshrine this meaning in a programming language's semantics; there are some advantages in doing so. Similarly, we can design into a language a communication with the meaning "please enter input now", and many other equally useful messages. Or instead, we may decide that the programmers, not the language designers, give meaning to the communications. We leave it to them to decide upon whether and how to prompt, to decide whether and how to say "this message is the last". The benefit is a simpler semantics.

A recent paper [2] presented and used a predicative formalism in which the observable quantities of interest are taken to be the initial values $\grave{x}$, $\grave{y}$, ... and final values $\acute{x}$, $\acute{y}$, ... of some variables. Pointedly, termination and nontermination are not taken to be observable. It is left to the programmers to decide upon their termination convention. We assume knowledge of [2], or of its forerunner [1], and we now discuss the possible termination conventions.

Stability Conventions

A termination convention, or more generally a stability convention, is a predicate $\sigma(v)$ of the program variables (or state) v that is not identically true:

$$\neg \forall v . \sigma$$

We shall see the technical reason for this restriction shortly, but roughly speaking it is just so that we can distinguish "stable" from "unstable". In the notation of [2], we write $\nabla \sigma$, and we say that σ is "determined". Here are two examples.

Convention u (unstable state) Let us call one of the states u. Then, under this convention, we define $\sigma = (v \neq u)$. In words, u is taken to be an unstable state, and all other states are considered stable. (The symbol $\perp$ is sometimes used for this state.)

Convention b (busy bit) Let us call one boolean variable b. Then, under this convention, we define $\sigma = \neg b$. We might implement b as a red light on the console. While it is on (true), the state is unstable and the computation is unfinished. When it goes off (false), the state is stable and the computation has terminated.

From a coding viewpoint, convention u is the most economical; it wastes only one state to indicate instability, leaving all others to indicate results. Convention b makes half the states unstable; still, it wastes only one bit. From a recognition viewpoint, convention b is the most practical; we need to look at only one bit, not all the bits, to determine stability.

Respectfulness

A specification S is said to respect convention σ iff

$$\forall \grave{v} . \ \forall \acute{v} . \ S = (\textbf{inv} \ \sigma . \ S)$$

where (**inv** σ. S) is defined in [2] as $(\eth \wedge \nabla S \Rightarrow S \wedge \acute{\eth})$

Theorem 0: S respects σ iff

$$\forall \grave{v}. \ \nabla S \ = \ \eth \wedge (\forall \acute{v}. \ S \Rightarrow \acute{\eth})$$

For a determined specification, the intent is that the initial state should be stable, and any final state satisfying S should be stable. During the computation, the machine is in an unstable state. Suppose for a moment that we can observe the state during a computation. Under convention u, since there is only one unstable state, we cannot see how the computation is progressing – only that it is. Under convention b, we may be able to watch the sequence of unstable states, and see how the machine works. But our specifications do not speak of intermediate, unstable states; in that sense, they are not "of interest".

Theorem 1: Specification $S(\grave{v}, \acute{v})$ respects convention u iff it is both strict

$$S(u, u)$$

and explosive

$$\forall \grave{v}. \ S(\grave{v}, u) \ \Rightarrow \ \forall \acute{v}. \ S(\grave{v}, \acute{v})$$

This means that from initial state u, final state u is possible; and if, from some initial state, final state u is possible, then, from that initial state, every final state is possible.

Theorem 2: Specification S respects convention b iff it is both strict
$$\forall \grave{v}. \ \exists \acute{v}. \ b \Rightarrow S \wedge b$$
and explosive
$$\forall \grave{v}. \ (\exists \acute{v}. \ S \wedge b) \Rightarrow \forall \acute{v}. \ S$$

Theorem 3: Let S be an arbitrary specification. Then **inv** σ. S respects convention σ.

All our programming connectives that were defined in [2] have the property that if their parts respect some convention, then the whole does.

Theorem 4: If P and Q respect σ, then so do $(P \cdot Q)$, $(P;Q)$, $(P$ **or** $Q)$, and (**if** b **then** P **else** $Q)$. If, assuming P respects σ, $S(P)$ does also, then **loop** P: $S(P)$ respects σ.

It is especially nice that, under any stability convention, the difference between relational product and composition disappears.

Theorem 5: If Q respects some convention σ, then
$$P;Q = P \cdot Q$$

The Need for a Stability Convention

A stability convention is necessary from the practical, human point of view: we must be able to decide when a computation is finished. But it is really of no interest which stability convention we choose. We would like to be able to write a simple specification that refers only to the desired results, not to the arbitrary convention. As a trivial example, we would like to write
$$\acute{x} = \grave{x} + 1$$
to say that x is increased by 1. Unfortunately, this specification does not respect any convention. To obtain a respectful specification, we apply Theorem 3. Under convention b we obtain
$$\neg\grave{b} \Rightarrow \acute{x} = \grave{x} + 1 \wedge \neg\acute{b}$$
and under convention u we obtain
$$\grave{v} \neq u \Rightarrow \acute{x} = \grave{x} + 1$$
assuming that the consequent somehow implies $\acute{v} \neq u$. Even the simple specification **ok** = $(\acute{v} = \grave{v})$ does not respect any convention; we must instead write either $(\neg\grave{b} \Rightarrow \acute{v} = \grave{v})$ or $(\grave{v} \neq u \Rightarrow \acute{v} = \grave{v})$. All specifications become a little more complicated, with extra detail that is of no programming interest.

A stability convention is also necessary for the implementation of semi-colon: to implement $P;Q$ it must be possible to recognize termination of P's execution in order to start Q's execution. The usual convention used for that purpose involves part of the state (the "program counter") that programmers would prefer not to think about. No "higher-level" version of this implementation detail (such as convention u

or convention *b*) is an improvement. Accordingly, semi-colon was defined in [2]

$$P;Q \quad = \quad (\nabla P \Rightarrow P \circ Q)$$

with an antecedent

$$\nabla P \quad = \quad \neg \forall \acute{v}.\ P$$

which says only that there can be a stability convention, but does not specify any particular one. This is the strongest predicate that can be implemented as sequential execution (for proof, see [2]).

Although a stability convention is of no interest to a programmer (in fact, it is an impediment), it allows us to translate among various semantic formalisms, and compare them. That is our purpose in the remainder of this paper. In these translations and comparisons, we shall refer to the predicative semantic formalism as PS.

Dijkstra's wp

According to Dijkstra's "weakest precondition" formalism [0], a program S is defined by a predicate transformer $wp(S, R)$ that maps any postcondition R to the corresponding necessary and sufficient precondition P. Its interpretation is that, starting in a state satisfying P, execution of S will terminate in a state satisfying R.

Suppose we have a PS specification S and a postcondition R, and we want to find precondition $wp(S, R)$. First, extend the state space with at least one unstable state to provide a stability convention σ (defined to be true of exactly the unextended state space). We assume that S respects σ (if not, replace S with (**inv** σ. S) in the following). We also assume $(\forall v.\ R \Rightarrow \sigma)$ (if not, replace R with $R \wedge \sigma$ in the following). Now

$$\acute{w}p(S, R) \quad = \quad (\forall \acute{v}.\ S \Rightarrow \acute{R})$$

(The accent on wp signifies only that the result is a predicate in $\acute{v}$; it may be deleted.) The result of this translation is a precondition P such that $(\forall v.\ P \Rightarrow \sigma)$. The stability convention has now served its purpose; if desired, it can be thrown away by taking σ to be true, thus eliminating the unstable states.

For the reverse translation we are given wp(S, R) for arbitrary R, and we want to express S as a predicate. It is

$$S \quad = \quad \textbf{inv } \sigma. \neg \grave{w}p(S, \acute{v} \neq v)$$

(For the calculation of wp, the $\acute{v}$ are constants; the variables are unaccented. In the resulting precondition, place ` accents on the unaccented variables.) Again, we can throw away σ by letting it be true.

With the stability convention, translations between PS and wp do not lose information; they are reversible. Translation between PS and wp can also be made directly without introducing a stability convention. The translation is

$$\grave{w}p(S, R) \quad = \quad \nabla S \wedge (\forall \acute{v}. \, S \Rightarrow \acute{R})$$

$$S \quad = \quad \neg \grave{w}p(S, \acute{v} \neq v)$$

But in one case (called **havoc** in the catalogue of semantics, later) this is not a reversible translation.

Jones's VDM

In Jones's VDM (Vienna Definition Method) formalism [3], a specification is a pair $(\hat{P}, R)$ in which $\hat{P}$ is a precondition (predicate on the initial state) and R is a relation (predicate on the initial and final states). Its interpretation is that, starting in a state $\grave{v}$ satisfying $\hat{P}$, execution will terminate in a state $\acute{v}$ such that the pair $(\grave{v}, \acute{v})$ satisfies R.

To translate, first extend the state space with at least one unstable state to provide a stability convention σ. Then, given PS specification S respecting σ, we obtain VDM precondition $\hat{P}$ and relation R as follows:

$$\hat{P} = \nabla S \qquad\qquad R = S$$

In VDM, two specifications are considered equivalent if their preconditions are equivalent and their relations agree whenever $\grave{v}$ satisfies the precondition. So we could choose any relation R such that

$$(\nabla S \wedge S) \quad \Rightarrow \quad R \quad \Rightarrow \quad (\nabla S \Rightarrow S)$$

We shall consistently choose R to be as weak as possible.

In the reverse direction, given VDM specification $(\hat{P}, R)$ respecting σ, i.e. such that $(\forall v.\ P \Rightarrow \sigma)$ and $(\forall \hat{v}.\ \forall \acute{v}.\ \hat{P} \wedge R \Rightarrow \acute{\sigma})$, obtain PS specification S as

$$S = (\hat{P} \Rightarrow R)$$

Once again, with the stability convention the translations do not lose information. The translation can be made without any stability convention, but then there is the same single case in which the translation is not reversible.

Translation between VDM and wp is reversible with or without a stability convention. Given wp,

$$\hat{P} = \hat{w}p(S, \textbf{true}) \qquad R = \neg \hat{w}p(S, \acute{v} \neq v)$$

The other way, given $\hat{P}$ and R,

$$\hat{w}p(S, Q) = \hat{P} \wedge (\forall \acute{v}.\ R \Rightarrow \acute{Q})$$

Partial Relation PR

In this formalism, a specification consists of a (possibly partial) relation R, with the following interpretation: if $(\hat{v}, \acute{v})$ satisfies R, then execution starting at $\hat{v}$ must terminate, and $\acute{v}$ is a possible final state. This formalism has been proposed by Robison [5] and independently by von Stengel [6].

An implementable PS specification S can be translated to PR by extending the state space as before, and ensuring that S is respectful. Then

$$R = \nabla S \wedge S$$

The reverse translation is

$$S = ((\exists \acute{v}.\ R) \Rightarrow R)$$

Parnas's LD and RS

In Parnas's LD (Limited Domain) formalism [4], as in Jones's VDM, a specification is a pair $(\hat{C}, R)$. $\hat{C}$ is a predicate on the initial state called the "competence", and R is a relation (predicate on the initial and final states). Its interpretation is a little different than that of VDM: if execution starts in a state $\grave{v}$ satisfying $\acute{C}$, it will terminate in a state $\acute{v}$ such that the pair $(\grave{v}, \acute{v})$ satisfies R ; if it starts in a state $\grave{v}$ not satisfying $\acute{C}$, it will either terminate in a state $\acute{v}$ such that the pair $(\grave{v}, \acute{v})$ satisfies R or it will fail to terminate. Unlike VDM, specifications that differ only when $\grave{v}$ lies outside the competence set are not considered equivalent.

The translation between PS and LD is similar to the translation between PS and VDM for specifications that respect a stability convention. LD differs from VDM in its ability to be disrespectful: an LD specification can say that, for some initial state, nontermination and termination in a limited set of final states are acceptable, but termination in any other final state is unacceptable.

$$\acute{C} = (\forall \acute{v}. S \Rightarrow \acute{\sigma}) \qquad R = S \wedge \acute{\sigma}$$
$$S = (\acute{C} \vee \acute{\sigma} \Rightarrow R)$$

Parnas has also considered a relational semantics called RS. It is similar to LD but the competence is determinable from the relation as

$$\acute{C} = \exists \acute{v}. R$$

and so we can dispense with it. RS can be seen as a variation of PR. In PR, if for $\grave{v}$ there is no $\acute{v}$ such that $(\grave{v}, \acute{v})$ satisfies R , then execution starting at $\grave{v}$ is arbitrary; in RS, nontermination is mandatory.

$$R = \text{if } \forall \grave{v}. (\forall \acute{v}. S \Rightarrow \acute{\sigma}) \vee (\forall \acute{v}. S \Rightarrow \neg\acute{\sigma})$$
$$\text{then } S \wedge \acute{\sigma}$$
$$\text{else inexpressible}$$
$$S = ((\acute{\sigma} \Rightarrow (\exists \acute{v}. R)) \wedge ((\exists \acute{v}. R) \Rightarrow R)$$

Catalogue of Semantics

specification called **abort, chaos** or **disaster**: arbitrary behavior

	with σ	without σ
PS	**true**	**true**
wp(S, R)	**false**	**false**
VDM	**false, true**	**false, true**
PR	**false**	**false**
LD	**false, true**	**false, true**
RS	inexpressible	inexpressible

specification called **havoc** or **chance**: terminating but otherwise arbitrary behavior

	with σ	without σ
PS	$σ̀⇒σ́$	inexpressible
wp(S, R)	$∀v.\ σ⇒R$	$∀v.\ R$
VDM	$σ̀,\ σ̀⇒σ́$	**true, true**
PR	$σ̀∧σ́$	**true**
LD	$σ̀,\ σ̀⇒σ́$	**true, true**
RS	inexpressible	**true**

specification called **skip**, **ok** or **continue**

	with σ	without σ
PS	$σ̀ ⇒ v́=v̀$	$v́=v̀$
wp(S, R)	$σ∧R$	R
VDM	$σ̀,\ σ̀ ⇒ v́=v̀$	**true**, $v́=v̀$
PR	$σ̀ ∧ v́=v̀$	$v́=v̀$
LD	$σ̀,\ σ̀ ⇒ v́=v̀$	**true**, $v́=v̀$
RS	inexpressible	$v́=v̀$

specification called **miracle**

	with σ	without σ
PS	$¬σ̀$	**false**
wp(S, R)	$σ$	**true**
VDM	$σ̀,\ ¬σ̀$	**true, false**
PR	inexpressible	inexpressible
LD	$σ̀,\ ¬σ̀$	**true, false**
RS	inexpressible	inexpressible

assignment $x := e$ in two variables x, y, assuming e is evaluable

	with σ	without σ
PS	$σ̀ ⇒ x́=è ∧ ý=ỳ ∧ σ́$	$x́=è ∧ ý=ỳ$
wp(S, R)	$σ∧R[x:e]$	$R[x:e]$
VDM	$σ̀,\ σ̀ ⇒ x́=è ∧ ý=ỳ ∧ σ́$	**true**, $x́=è ∧ ý=ỳ$
PR	$σ̀ ∧ x́=è ∧ ý=ỳ ∧ σ́$	$x́=è ∧ ý=ỳ$
LD	$σ̀,\ σ̀ ⇒ x́=è ∧ ý=ỳ ∧ σ́$	**true**, $x́=è ∧ ý=ỳ$
RS	inexpressible	$x́=è ∧ ý=ỳ$

sequential composition: satisfy first P then Q

PS	$\nabla P \Rightarrow P{\circ}Q$
wp(S, R)	$\mathrm{wp}(P, \mathrm{wp}(Q, R))$
VDM	$\dot{P}_P \wedge (\forall \acute{v}.\ R_P \Rightarrow \dot{P}_Q),\ R_P{\circ}R_Q$
PR	$(\forall v.\ P(\grave{v}, v) \Rightarrow \exists \acute{v}.\ Q(v, \acute{v})) \wedge P{\circ}Q$
LD	$\check{C}_P \wedge (\forall \acute{v}.\ R_P \Rightarrow \check{C}_Q),\ R_P{\circ}R_Q$
RS	if $\forall \grave{v}.\ (\exists \acute{v}.\ P{\circ}Q) \Rightarrow (\forall v.\ P(\grave{v}, v) \Rightarrow \exists \acute{v}.\ Q(v, \acute{v}))$
	then $P{\circ}Q$
	else inexpressible

deterministic choice: if b is initially true then satisfy P else satisfy Q

PS	$\grave{b} \wedge P \vee \neg \grave{b} \wedge Q$
wp(S, R)	$\grave{b} \wedge \mathrm{wp}(P, R) \vee \neg \grave{b} \wedge \mathrm{wp}(Q, R)$
VDM	$\grave{b} \wedge \dot{P}_P \vee \neg \grave{b} \wedge \dot{P}_Q,\ \grave{b} \wedge R_P \vee \neg \grave{b} \wedge R_Q$
PR	$\grave{b} \wedge P \vee \neg \grave{b} \wedge Q$
LD	$\grave{b} \wedge \check{C}_P \vee \neg \grave{b} \wedge \check{C}_Q,\ \grave{b} \wedge R_P \vee \neg \grave{b} \wedge R_Q$
RS	$\grave{b} \wedge P \vee \neg \grave{b} \wedge Q$

nondeterministic choice: satisfy either P or Q

PS	$P \vee Q$
wp(S, R)	$\mathrm{wp}(P, R) \wedge \mathrm{wp}(Q, R)$
VDM	$\dot{P}_P \wedge \dot{P}_Q,\ \dot{P}_P \wedge \dot{P}_Q \Rightarrow R_P \vee R_Q$
PR	$(\exists \acute{v}.\ P) \wedge (\exists \acute{v}.\ Q) \wedge (P \vee Q)$
LD	$\check{C}_P \wedge \check{C}_Q,\ R_P \vee R_Q$
RS	if $\forall \grave{v}.\ (\exists \acute{v}.\ P) = (\exists \acute{v}.\ Q)$
	then $P \vee Q$
	else inexpressible

joint satisfaction: satisfy both P and Q

PS	$P \wedge Q$
wp(S, R)	wp(P, R) $\vee$ wp(Q, R)
VDM	$\overset{\triangleright}{P}_P \vee \overset{\triangleright}{P}_Q, \; R_P \wedge R_Q$
PR	if $\forall \grave{v}. \; (\exists \acute{v}. \; P \wedge Q) \vee (\neg \exists \acute{v}. \; P) \vee (\neg \exists \acute{v}. \; Q)$
	then $((\exists \acute{v}. \; P \wedge Q) \Rightarrow P \wedge Q)$
	$\wedge ((\neg \exists \acute{v}. \; P) \vee (\neg \exists \acute{v}. \; Q) \Rightarrow P \vee Q)$
	else inexpressible
LD	$\overset{\triangleright}{C}_P \vee \overset{\triangleright}{C}_Q, \; R_P \wedge R_Q$
RS	if $\forall \grave{v}. \; (\exists \acute{v}. \; P \wedge Q) \vee (\neg \exists \acute{v}. \; P) \wedge (\neg \exists \acute{v}. \; Q)$
	then $P \wedge Q$
	else inexpressible

ordering: P satisfied if Q satisfied

PS	$P \Leftarrow Q$
wp(S, R)	$\forall R. \; $wp($P, R$) $\Rightarrow$ wp(Q, R)
VDM	$\overset{\triangleright}{P}_P \Rightarrow \overset{\triangleright}{P}_Q \wedge (R_P \Leftarrow R_Q)$
PR	$(\exists \acute{v}. \; P) \Rightarrow (\exists \acute{v}. \; Q) \wedge (P \Leftarrow Q)$
LD	$\overset{\triangleright}{C}_P \Rightarrow \overset{\triangleright}{C}_Q \wedge (R_P \Leftarrow R_Q)$
RS	$((\exists \acute{v}. \; P) = (\exists \acute{v}. \; Q)) \wedge (P \Leftarrow Q)$

variable declaration: introduce fresh local variable x into P

PS	$\forall \grave{x}. \; \exists \acute{x}. \; P$
wp(S, R)	$\forall x. \; $wp($P, R$)
VDM	$\forall \grave{x}. \; \overset{\triangleright}{P}_P, \; \forall \grave{x}. \; \exists \acute{x}. \; R_P$
PR	$\forall \grave{x}. \; \exists \acute{x}. \; P$
LD	$\forall \grave{x}. \; \overset{\triangleright}{C}_P, \; \forall \grave{x}. \; \exists \acute{x}. \; R_P$
RS	if $\forall \grave{v}. \; \forall \acute{v}. \; (\exists \grave{x}. \; \exists \acute{x}. \; P) \Rightarrow (\forall \grave{x}. \; \exists \acute{x}. \; P)$
	then $\forall \grave{x}. \; \exists \acute{x}. \; P$
	else inexpressible

recursion: to satisfy **loop** P: $S(P)$, satisfy $S($ **loop** P: $S(P)$ $)$

PS	$\forall i.\ S^i(\textbf{true})$
wp(S, R)	$\exists i.\ \text{wp}(S^i(\textbf{abort}), R)$
VDM	$\exists i.\ \grave{P}_{S^i(\textbf{abort})}$, $\forall i.\ R_{S^i(\textbf{abort})}$
PR	not easily expressible
LD	not easily expressible
RS	inexpressible

Comparative Comments

It is questionable whether a semantic formalism that talks only about the initial input state and the final output state, without any interactive input or output during the computation, can be considered adequate. But all the formalisms considered here are of that sort, so it is not a point of comparison.

Five of the formalisms provide a way of saying, for each input state, "specification P requires termination". They are:

wp	wp(P, **true**)
VDM	$\grave{P}_P$
PR	$\exists \acute{v}.\ P$
LD	$\grave{C}_P$
RS	$\exists \acute{v}.\ P$

The negation means, of course, "specification P does not require termination". Only two of the formalisms provide a way of saying "specification P requires nontermination". They are:

LD	$\neg \grave{C}_P \wedge \neg \exists \acute{v}.\ P$
RS	$\neg \exists \acute{v}.\ P$

In PS, ∇P says that P is determined; to observe that a computation satisfies a determined specification, one must observe its final state. But to observe that a computation satisfies an undetermined specification, i.e. when $\forall \acute{v}.\ P$, it is not necessary to observe its final state.

One of the formalisms, wp, is not based on a relation. This makes it awkward to state that the output is to be related to the input. To say that x is to be increased by 1, we may write something like

$$wp(S, x=X+1)$$

accompanied by words that say X is the initial value of x . But formally this allows the unintended solution

$$X := 3; x := 4$$

To be precise, one must write

$$\forall X.\ x=X \Rightarrow wp(S, x=X+1)$$

Clearly, the PS specification

$$\acute{x} = \grave{x}+1$$

is much simpler.

VDM and PS are very close, as seen by the simplicity of the translation. In practice, it often makes sense to think of the precondition separately from the relation, as in VDM. One writes them down with a comma between, as in VDM, or with an implication sign, as in PS. VDM offers us a freedom in stating the relation, and we chose to make it as weak as possible. Consequently,

$$\forall \grave{v}.\ \nabla R \Rightarrow \acute{P}$$

This means that the precondition is entirely superfluous whenever ∇R is true. It gives us further information only for those inputs where ∇R is false. If, for some input, all outputs are acceptable, the precondition tells us whether termination is required. Its only service is to distinguish, for each input state, **chaos** from **havoc**. In judging the value of this service against its cost, keep in mind the fact that termination, by itself, is not observable.

LD differs from VDM in its ability to be disrespectful: an LD specification can say that, for some initial state, nontermination and termination in a limited set of final states are acceptable, but termination in any other final state is unacceptable. Such a specification is very easy to implement: ignore the final states and deliver a nonterminating loop. Hence the ability to be disrespectful is of no practical value in programming. PS, wp, VDM, and PR all hold that (without communications or intermediate results) infinite loops are useless, and there is no point in being particular about possible final states while allowing an infinite loop. One may take the position that LD can describe more mechanisms than PS, wp, VDM, or PR: it can describe those that can nondeterministically either terminate in a particular final state or not terminate. Or, one may instead take the position that mechanisms are deterministic, and that nondeterminism is a property of specifications. In that case, LD is no more descriptive than the other formalisms.

To a specifier, the most important connective is probably joint satisfaction. It is very common to specify by parts, stating properties that must be jointly satisfied. A specifier will therefore appreciate the formalism that makes joint satisfaction simplest.

To a programmer, the most important connective is undoubtedly the ordering, because that is the criterion for correctness of a program. Indeed, the entire programming process is to transform a specification, little by little, to a program, and at each stage to ensure that the new is properly related to the old by the ordering. A programmer will therefore appreciate the formalism that makes the ordering simplest.

Of all these formalisms, PR fits the class of computations best – in fact, perfectly. All implementable specifications are expressible, and all unimplementable specifications are not. That was its design criterion. To achieve this, PR significantly complicates the expression of its connectives, particularly joint satisfaction.

Alone among the formalisms, PS can be criticized for the fact that its semi-colon is not always associative. The counter-example creates, using semi-colon, what would be **havoc** in another formalism. For example, in one integer variable x ,

$$(\acute{x} \neq \grave{x} \ ; \ \acute{x} \neq \grave{x}) \ ; \ \acute{x} = 0 \quad = \quad \textbf{true}$$
$$\acute{x} \neq \grave{x} \ ; \ (\acute{x} \neq \grave{x} \ ; \ \acute{x} = 0) \quad = \quad \acute{x} = 0$$

Our intuition that semi-colon should be associative is simply this: executing first P and then $(Q;R)$ should be the same as executing first $(P;Q)$ and then R . This makes sense when execution of P and $(P;Q)$ terminate. But if P's execution fails to terminate, what does "and then $(Q;R)$ " mean? If $(P;Q)$'s execution fails to terminate, what does "and then R " mean? It is a theorem of PS that semi-colon is associative under all circumstances called for by intuition:

$$\nabla P \ \wedge \ \nabla(P;Q) \quad \Rightarrow \quad (P;(Q;R) = (P;Q);R)$$

In fact, the stronger theorem

$$\nabla(P;Q) \quad \Rightarrow \quad \nabla P \ \wedge \ (P;(Q;R) = (P;Q);R)$$

holds.

More Power

We now present one more semantic formalism, called PF (Powerful Formalism). As in five of the formalisms presented so far, the heart of PF is a relation between input $\grave{v}$ and output $\acute{v}$. Like wp, VDM and LD, it has further information to impart. In PF a specification is a sextuple ($\grave{w}$g, $\grave{w}$lg, $\grave{w}$p, $\grave{w}$lp, R, $\acute{s}$t) in which the first four components are predicates on the initial state, R is the relation, and $\acute{s}$t is a predicate on the final state. These components are to be interpreted as follows.

$\grave{w}$g: true of an initial state from which the computation is required to progress, false of an initial state in which the computation is allowed to get stuck.

$\grave{w}$lg: true of an initial state from which the computation is allowed to progress, false of an initial state in which the computation is required to get stuck.

$\grave{w}$p: true of an initial state for which the computation is required to terminate, false of an initial state for which the computation is allowed to not terminate.

$\grave{w}$lp: true of an initial state for which the computation is allowed to not terminate, false of an initial state for which the computation is required to not terminate.

R: this relation describes the allowed transitions from initial to final state.

$\acute{s}$t: true of a final state iff termination is successful.

Here is a small sample of specifications in PF.

		$\grave{w}$g	$\grave{w}$lg	$\grave{w}$p	$\grave{w}$lp	R	$\acute{s}$t
chaos	=	false,	true,	false,	true,	true,	false
havoc	=	true,	true,	true,	true,	true,	false
random	=	true,	true,	true,	true,	true,	true
break	=	false,	false,	false,	false,	false,	false
miracle	=	true,	true,	true,	true,	false,	true
magic	=	false,	true,	false,	true,	false,	true

$$\text{ok} \quad = \quad \text{true}, \quad \text{true}, \quad \text{true}, \quad \text{true}, \quad \acute{v}{=}\grave{v}, \quad \text{true}$$

$$\text{skip} \quad = \quad \text{false}, \quad \text{true}, \quad \text{true}, \quad \text{true}, \quad \acute{v}{=}\grave{v}, \quad \text{true}$$

$$\text{spin} \quad = \quad \text{true}, \quad \text{true}, \quad \text{false}, \quad \text{false}, \quad \acute{v}{=}\grave{v}, \quad \text{false}$$

In this formalism, we are able to express not only **chaos** and **havoc**, but **random** and **break** as well. We can distinguish **ok** from **skip**, which the other formalisms cannot. One might well ask if **random** and **break** are useful for any purpose; the answer is that they are just as useful as **havoc**. One might be forgiven for wondering how we are to observe "progress" and "success"; the answer is similar to that for "termination". This is indeed an expressive and powerful formalism, and we hope it will receive the attention it deserves.

For many purposes, PF is still not powerful enough. We might well want a seventh component t, this time numeric, to specify the allowed time of execution. For example, we might define

$$P;Q = \grave{w}g_P, \quad \grave{w}lg_P, \quad \grave{w}p_P \wedge (\forall \acute{v}.\, R_P \Rightarrow \grave{w}g_Q),$$

$$\grave{w}lp_P \wedge (\exists \acute{v}.\, R_P \wedge \grave{w}lg_Q), \quad R_P{\circ}R_Q, \quad \acute{s}t_Q, \quad t_P{+}t_Q$$

We have kept PS simple. Those who are uncomfortable without an explicit termination indicator are invited to write their programs and other specifications using their favorite termination convention. Then the initial states for which the computation is required to terminate are those for which $(\forall \acute{v}.\, S \Rightarrow \acute{\sigma})$, *i.e.* for which the specification implies termination. Those interested in execution time are invited to use a time convention. For example, program S

while $x{>}1$ **do**
      if $odd(x)$ **then** $x := 3{*}x{+}1$ **else** $x := x/2$

can be modified to program S_t

$t := 0;$ **while** $x{>}1$ **do**
      $(t := t{+}1;$
          if $odd(x)$ **then** $x := 3{*}x{+}1$ **else** $x := x/2)$

Then the initial states for which the computation terminates in at most n iterations are those for which $(\forall \acute{v}.\, S_t \Rightarrow \acute{t}{\leq}n)$. PS provides the ability to express any convention, but it has none built in.

Conclusion

In all practical circumstances, we can and do observe termination: by means of a termination convention. This is so standard that it may be difficult to realize we are observing a convention, and not termination itself.

We have said that "termination" does not have a physical meaning. We now point out that it does not always have a logical meaning, either. For any semantic formalism and any proof theory, there is a program P such that "P terminates" can neither be proved, nor disproved. There is a model in which it is true, and another in which it is false. For each such program P, the proof theory can be enriched and the model theory constrained to make "P terminates" mean whichever we prefer: true or false. To those who have it firmly fixed in their heads that "termination" means something, this will seem paradoxical.

The simplest of the formalisms, having the properties most convenient for both specifiers and programmers, is PS without a stability convention. Its one "limitation" is its inability to distinguish between **chaos** and **havoc**. But no physical experiment can distinguish between them either. The distinction is a creation of the more complex formalisms.

References

[0] E.W. Dijkstra: *A Discipline of Programming.* Prentice-Hall, Engelwood Cliffs N.J. (1976)

[1] E.C.R. Hehner: Predicative Programming, *Comm.ACM 27*, 2. pp.134-151, February 1984

[2] E.C.R. Hehner, L.E. Gupta, A.J. Malton: Predicative Methodology, *Acta Informatica* (to appear)

[3] C.B. Jones: *Systematic Software Development using VDM.* Prentice-Hall Int., London (1986)

[4] D.L. Parnas: A generalized control structure and its formal definition. *C.ACM 26*, 8 pp.572-581, August .1983

[5]   W.A. Robison: private communication

[6]   B. von Stengel: private communication

PREDICATIVE COMMUNICATIONS

Eric C.R. Hehner
University of Toronto

The essence of the predicative semantic formalism is the following:

(a)   A specification is a predicate whose free variables represent observable quantities of interest. Any values for the variables that satisfy the predicate represent something that satisfies the specification; any values that do not satisfy the predicate represent something that does not satisfy the specification.

(a)   A program is an executable specification of computer behavior.

There are various ways to describe computer behavior. In the paper "Predicative Methodology" we studied a traditional way: in terms of the initial and final state of memory. We now turn our attention to the specification of communicating processes. The quantities of interest here are communication sequences.

Notation

Our sequence notations are summarized below.

λ the empty sequence

3   when used in a context requiring a sequence, this is the sequence consisting of the one item 3 (and similarly for any other one-item sequence)

$\#s$ the length of sequence s

s_i the element of sequence s with index i, $0 \le i < \#s$

$s_{i..}$ the subsequence of s from index i on, $0 \le i \le \#s$

$s \hat{\ } t$ the catenation of sequences s and t

$s \ge t$ sequence s is an extension of sequence t: $\exists u.\ s = t \hat{\ } u$

$s \lesssim t$ sequence s is a tail of sequence t: $\exists r.\ r \hat{\ } s = t$

NATO ASI Series, Vol. F36
Logic of Programming and Calculi of Discrete Design
Edited by M. Broy
© Springer-Verlag Berlin Heidelberg 1987

Specifications

Let a be an input communication channel. We use $\grave{a}$ to stand for the sequence of inputs offered on channel a. These inputs may be available prior to the start of a process (batch), or during the process (interactive); any input that is offered before it is needed is buffered. A process may consume none, some, or all of the input offered to it. We use $\acute{a}$ to stand for the input that remains unconsumed. Clearly, $\acute{a} \preceq \grave{a}$.

Let z be an output communication channel. We use $\grave{z}$ to stand for the sequence of outputs that were produced on channel z prior to the start of a process (computation). For example, if channel z is a terminal screen, then $\grave{z}$ is whatever remains on the screen from a previous computation. We use $\acute{z}$ to stand for the sequence of outputs produced on z before and during a process. Clearly, $\acute{z} \succeq \grave{z}$.

Each channel is designated either as an input channel, or as an output channel, not as both. Usually, our examples will use two channels: input a and output z. But any number of channels is acceptable. Altogether, we refer to the channels as c, and to their associated sequences as $\grave{c}$ and $\acute{c}$. A specification is a predicate having $\grave{c}$ and $\acute{c}$ as its free variables. Here are two examples.

(0) $\qquad \#\grave{a} \geq 10 \implies \acute{z} = \grave{z} \char94 (\sum i: 0 \leq i < 10. \grave{a}_i)$

If at least 10 inputs are offered on channel a, then the sum of the first 10 inputs will be catenated to the output on channel z.

(1) $\qquad \grave{z} = \lambda \implies \forall i: 0 \leq i . \acute{z}_i = i$

Assuming no output has yet been produced on channel z, the output will be the endless stream of natural numbers.

Implementations

An implementation of specification S is any mechanism that is prepared, for arbitrary initial state $\grave{c}$ of the communication sequences, to produce a final state $\acute{c}$ to satisfy S. So, as before, implementability requires

$$\forall \grave{c}.\ \exists \acute{c}.\ S$$

For communicating processes, there are two additional constraints that we place on S in order to consider it implementable. One, roughly speaking, is that it not require a mechanism to change the past. The other is that it not require a mechanism to predict the future.

To state mathematically that a specification does not require a mechanism to change the past, we define a particular specification K. Suppose there are two channels: input channel a and output channel z. Then

$$K \quad =_{df} \quad \acute{a} \succeq \grave{a} \ \wedge \ \acute{z} \succeq \grave{z}$$

In general, K has one conjunct for each channel. It requires nothing of a process except that it be a process, that it proceed by consuming inputs and producing outputs. It says only that consumed input cannot become unconsumed, and produced output cannot become unproduced. Every physical process satisfies this specification. Implementability requires

$$\forall \grave{c}.\ \exists \acute{c}.\ S \wedge K$$

so that S can be satisfied without changing the past. Examples (0) and (1) are implementable, but

$$\acute{z} = 0 \hat{\ } \grave{z}$$

is not.

The following specification is not implementable because it requires a mechanism to predict the future.

$$(\#\acute{a} > 0 \Rightarrow \acute{z} = \grave{z}{}^\frown 1)$$
$$\wedge \, (\#\acute{a} = 0 \Rightarrow \acute{z} = \grave{z}{}^\frown 0)$$

The reason is subtle. If, at some time, an input is available on channel a, then a 1 can be catenated to channel z, and the specification is satisfied. But we do not require that all inputs be available at the start of a computation, nor by any prespecified time. Suppose that no input is available on channel a. If a mechanism ever outputs a 0 on channel z, it risks the possibility that an input may become available later, and it cannot recover from its error. If it never outputs anything, then it certainly does not satisfy the specification. We must change the specification, perhaps to

$$(\#\acute{a} > 0 \Rightarrow \acute{z} = \grave{z}{}^\frown 1)$$
$$\wedge \, (\#\acute{a} = 0 \Rightarrow \acute{z} \geq \grave{z})$$

I do not know how to define implementability for communicating processes to exclude specifications that require a mechanism to predict the future.

Programs

Here is a variety of programming notations taken mainly from Hoare's "Communicating Sequential Processes". Each is defined as a predicate in $\grave{c}$ and $\acute{c}$, where c stands for all channels.

ok	$=_{df}$	$\acute{c} = \grave{c}$
$z!e; P$	$=_{df}$	$P[\grave{z}: \grave{z}\,\hat{}\,e]$
$a?x; P$	$=_{df}$	$\#\grave{a} > 0 \ \wedge\ P[\grave{a}: \grave{a}_{1..}; x: \grave{a}_0]$
		$\vee\ \#\grave{a} = 0 \ \wedge\ K$
$x := e; P$	$=_{df}$	$P[x: e]$
if e **then** P **else** Q	$=_{df}$	$e \wedge P \ \vee\ \neg e \wedge Q$
P **or** Q	$=_{df}$	$P \vee Q$
$a?x; P \ \square\ b?y; Q$	$=_{df}$	$\#\grave{a} > 0 \ \wedge\ P[\grave{a}: \grave{a}_{1..}; x: \grave{a}_0]$
		$\vee\ \#\grave{b} > 0 \ \wedge\ Q[\grave{b}: \grave{b}_{1..}; y: \grave{b}_0]$
		$\vee\ \#\grave{a} = \#\grave{b} = 0 \ \wedge\ K$
loop P: $S(P)$	$=_{df}$	$\forall i.\ S^i(K)$
$P \parallel Q$	$=_{df}$	$P_\alpha \wedge Q_\beta$
chan $a \leftarrow z$: $T.\ P$	$=_{df}$	$\exists \acute{a}.\ \exists \acute{z}.\ P[\grave{a}: \acute{z}; \grave{z}: \lambda]$

If the channels are input a and output z, then

$$\textbf{ok} \ = \ (\acute{a} = \grave{a} \ \wedge\ \acute{z} = \grave{z})$$

This means that no input is consumed, and no output is produced. Here are two input and output examples.

$$z!3;\ \mathbf{ok} \quad = \mathbf{ok}[\acute{z}:\ \grave{z}\,\hat{}\,3]$$
$$= (\acute{a} = \grave{a}\ \wedge\ \acute{z} = \grave{z})\,[\acute{z}:\ \grave{z}\,\hat{}\,3]$$
$$= (\acute{a} = \grave{a}\ \wedge\ \acute{z} = \grave{z}\,\hat{}\,3)$$

$$a?x;\ z!x;\ \mathbf{ok}\ = \quad \#\grave{a} > 0\ \wedge\ (z!x;\ \mathbf{ok})\,[\grave{a}:\ \grave{a}_{1..};\ x:\ \grave{a}_0]$$
$$\vee\ \#\grave{a} = 0\ \wedge\ K$$
$$= \quad \#\grave{a} > 0\ \wedge (\acute{a} = \grave{a}\ \wedge\ \acute{z} = \grave{z}\,\hat{}\,x)\,[\grave{a}:\ \grave{a}_{1..};\ x:\ \grave{a}_0]$$
$$\vee\ \#\grave{a} = 0\ \wedge\ (\acute{a} \preccurlyeq \grave{a}\ \wedge\ \acute{z} \succcurlyeq \grave{z})$$
$$= \quad \#\grave{a} > 0\ \wedge\ \acute{a} = \grave{a}_{1..}\ \wedge\ \acute{z} = \grave{z}\,\hat{}\,\grave{a}_0$$
$$\vee\ \#\grave{a} = 0\ \wedge\ \acute{a} = \lambda\ \wedge\ \acute{z} \succcurlyeq \grave{z}$$

In the first example, a 3 is produced on channel z, and nothing more. In the second example, if there is any input on channel a, the first one is consumed and reproduced on channel z; if not, then of course there is no input to remain unconsumed, and the output on channel z is unspecified. When there is no input in a batch environment, the output on z might be an error message; in an interactive environment, it can never be known that no input will come, so execution must wait.

Input notations, which have the form $(a?x;\ P)$, can be connected by the input choice operator $\square$. The definition shows two alternatives, but it is easily generalized to any number. It says that if input is available on any of the channels, then one such input must be consumed, and execution continues according to the corresponding predicate. If no input is available on any of the channels, then (in an interactive environment) execution must wait.

If the channels c can be partitioned into α and β so that predicate P refers only to α, and predicate Q refers only to β, then $P \parallel Q$ is simply their conjunction. Since P and Q refer to different channels, $P \parallel Q$ can be implemented by concurrent execution.

The **chan** notation introduces two new local channels, one input and one output, with the output channel connected to the input channel. Here is an example.

chan $b \leftarrow w$: *integer.* $(w!3; \textbf{ok}) \parallel (b?x; z!x; \textbf{ok})$

Suppose the global channels are a and z as usual. We must partition the channels a, b, w, and z with w in the first part, and b and z in the second. Let us throw a into the first part. Then our example becomes

$$
\textbf{chan } b \leftarrow w\text{: } integer. \quad (\acute{a} = \grave{a} \;\wedge\; \acute{w} = \grave{w}\,\hat{}\,3)
$$
$$
\wedge \;(\quad \#\acute{b} > 0 \;\wedge\; \acute{b} = \grave{b}_{1..} \;\wedge\; \acute{z} = \grave{z}\,\hat{}\,\grave{b}_0
$$
$$
\vee \; \#\acute{b} = 0 \;\wedge\; \acute{b} \gtrless \grave{b} \;\wedge\; \acute{z} \geq \grave{z} \quad)
$$

$$
= \exists \acute{b}. \,\exists \acute{w}. \quad (\acute{a} = \grave{a} \;\wedge\; \acute{w} = 3)
$$
$$
\wedge \;(\quad \#\acute{w} > 0 \;\wedge\; \acute{b} = \grave{w}_{1..} \;\wedge\; \acute{z} = \grave{z}\,\hat{}\,\grave{w}_0
$$
$$
\vee \; \#\acute{w} = 0 \;\wedge\; \acute{b} \gtrless \grave{w} \;\wedge\; \acute{z} \geq \grave{z} \quad)
$$

$$
= \exists \acute{b}. \,\exists \acute{w}. \; \acute{a} = \grave{a} \;\wedge\; \acute{z} = \grave{z}\,\hat{}\,3 \;\wedge\; \acute{b} = \lambda \;\wedge\; \acute{w} = 3
$$

$$
= \quad \acute{a} = \grave{a} \;\wedge\; \acute{z} = \grave{z}\,\hat{}\,3
$$

Channels can also be connected in other ways.

For the sake of brevity, we sometimes write the notations $a?x$, $z!e$, and $x := e$ without an immediately following semi-colon and predicate. In these cases, the understanding is that the missing predicate is **ok**. Our previous example, by this convention, can be written

chan $b \leftarrow w$: *integer.* $w!3 \parallel (b?x; z!x)$

Theorems

Here are two theorems concerning our new programming notations.

$$
x := e; P \quad = \quad \textbf{chan } b \leftarrow w. \; w!e \parallel (b?x; P)
$$

$$a?x; P \ \square \ b?y; Q \qquad = \qquad \textbf{if } \#\grave{a} > 0 \ \wedge \ \#\grave{b} > 0$$
$$\textbf{then } (a?x; P) \textbf{ or } (b?y; Q)$$
$$\textbf{else if } \#\grave{a} > 0$$
$$\textbf{then } (a?x; P)$$
$$\textbf{else if } \#\grave{b} > 0$$
$$\textbf{then } (b?y; Q)$$
$$\textbf{else } K$$

According to the first of these theorems, the assignment notation can be defined in terms of other programming notations, so we needn't have provided it.

Programming

The programming methods for any predicative formalism are mainly the same. We shall point out what is special about communicating processes shortly. But first, here are some examples.

With sufficient patience and care, we can prove the following two theorems, and so solve the problems given as example specifications (0) and (1).

$$(\#\grave{a} \geq 10 \ \Rightarrow \ \acute{z} = \grave{z} \ \hat{} \ (\textstyle\sum i: \ 0 \leq i < 10. \ \grave{a}_i))$$
$$\Leftarrow \ n := 10; \ s := 0; \ \textbf{loop } P: \textbf{ if } n = 0$$
$$\textbf{then } z!s$$
$$\textbf{else } (a?x; \ n := n-1; \ s := s+x; \ P)$$

$$(\acute{z} = \lambda \ \Rightarrow \ \forall i: 0 \leq i. \ \acute{z}_i = i) \ \Leftarrow \ i := 0; \ \textbf{loop } P: \ z!i; \ i := i+1; \ P$$

Or, to avoid the loop construct and make proofs a lot easier, these problems can be solved by the following theorems.

$$(\#\grave{a} \geq 10 \ \Rightarrow \ \acute{z} = \grave{z} \ \hat{} \ (\textstyle\sum i: \ 0 \leq i < 10. \ \grave{a}_i))$$
$$\Leftarrow \ n := 10; \ s := 0; \ (\#\grave{a} \geq n \ \Rightarrow \ \acute{z} = \grave{z} \ \hat{} \ (\textstyle\sum i: \ 0 \leq i < n. \ \grave{a}_i))$$

$$(\#\acute{a} \geq n \;\Rightarrow\; \acute{z} = \grave{z} \;\hat{}\; (\Sigma i\colon\; 0 \leq i < n.\; \acute{a}_i))$$

$$\Leftarrow \; \textbf{if } n = 0 \textbf{ then } z!s$$
$$\textbf{else } (a?x; \; n := n-1; \; s := s+x;$$
$$(\#\acute{a} \geq n \;\Rightarrow\; \acute{z} = \grave{z} \;\hat{}\; (\Sigma i\colon\; 0 \leq i < n.\; \acute{a}_i)))$$

$$(\acute{z} = \lambda \;\Rightarrow\; \forall i\colon 0 \leq i.\; \acute{z}_i = i) \;\Leftarrow\; i := 0; \; (\acute{z} = \grave{z} \;\hat{}\; i \;\hat{}\; i+1 \ldots)$$

$$(\acute{z} = \grave{z} \;\hat{}\; i \;\hat{}\; i+1 \ldots) \;\Leftarrow\; z!i; \; i := i+1; \; (\acute{z} = \grave{z} \;\hat{}\; i \;\hat{}\; i+1 \ldots)$$

The two rules of programming, "Theorem Rule" and "Variant Rule", apply here just as they did in the paper "Predicative Methodology" using variables instead of communication sequences. The one difference is the definition of "variant"; here it means any communication. When a problem is solved in terms of itself (directly or indirectly), the loop so formed must contain an input or output instruction.

Notes on Logic Programming

J. A. Robinson

Syracuse University

Introduction. The aim of these notes is to give a compact but complete presentation of the basic ideas behind logic programming. The emphasis throughout is on logical principles and on the main ideas of the most useful algorithms. These are concretely realized, although not always in the purest form, in various versions of PROLOG. We shall not be much concerned with how PROLOG is actually implemented, however, since the details vary considerably from system to system and tend to obscure the relatively simple conceptual framework which lies beneath the surface.

Formal symbolic computation. Logic programming is a technique for specifying formal symbolic computations, that is, computations with formal symbolic expressions as data objects. Logicians have long dealt with expressions in this way, and in computer science one must adopt the same approach in dealing formally with programming languages. In most applications these formal expressions have an informal (perhaps even a formal) semantics - the logic programmer means something by them - but in logic programs the expressions are treated purely formally, that is to say, as structured, manipulable syntactic objects of whose meaning no "official" notice is taken at all. Only their (abstract) form is used as a basis for both their analysis and synthesis.   This approach will of course already be especially familiar to those who have used LISP.

Expressions. Atoms = constants + variables. Indeed in dealing formally with expressions we shall use the universal but simple and convenient ontology of LISP. Accordingly we take expressions to be objects generated from two countably infinite, disjoint sets, the set CONST of <u>constants</u> and the set VARS of <u>variables</u>, by a single binary operation, <u>dot</u>.   The set ATOMS is then CONST ∪ VARS. Constants and variables are usually concretely represented by strings over some

NATO ASI Series, Vol. F36
Logic of Programming and Calculi of Discrete Design
Edited by M. Broy
© Springer-Verlag Berlin Heidelberg 1987

suitable alphabet of characters. It does not then much matter what these characters are, but for convenience the various pairs of bracketing characters: < > { } ( ) [ ] should not be among them, nor the space, nor the the comma, nor the character reserved for the dot operation: • . We shall write variables as strings of lower case letters, possibly subscripted, as for example: x, reverse, y_2. All other strings are constants.

Pairs. If A and B are expressions, then so (in the terminology of LISP) is the (dotted) pair P whose **car** is A and whose **cdr** is B, and we write: P = [• A B], aP = A, dP = B. The usual LISP convention is to write the dot infixed, [A • B] rather than [• A B]. In general [• A B] is the same expression as [• B A] only when A and B are the same expression. Nor is the expression [• A[• B C]] ever the same as the expression [•[• A B]C].

Lists. Certain constants are given special roles, most notably the constant NIL, whose role as the <u>empty list</u> is introduced in the following general definition:
- NIL is a list; moreover it is the (only) empty list, and it has length 0 and no elements;
- if L is a list of length n ≥ 0 and A is any expression, then the expression [• A L] is a list of length n+1, and has n+1 elements; its 1st element is A and its (j+1)st element is the jth element of L, for j=1, . . ., n.

So NIL is the only list which is not a pair.

List notation. Although the dotted pair notation is in principle completely adequate for all purposes, we shall mostly be dealing with lists and will therefore use LISP's more intuitive and flexible <u>list notation</u> by following the further convention that allows nested dotted pairs of the form

$$[• A_1[• A_2 \ldots [• A_n \text{ NIL}] \ldots]],$$

namely <u>nonempty</u> lists, to be written without dots or interior parentheses, thus:

$$[A_1 \ A_2 \ldots A_n].$$

The list notation also allows NIL to be written alternatively as: [ ].

Substitutions. We shall have much to do with certain mappings of expressions to expressions, called <u>substitutions.</u> Intuitively, performing a substitution operation on an expression E consists of replacing all of the occurrences of certain variables within E by other expressions (possibly other variables). Each occurrence of the same variable is replaced by an occurrence of the same expression. More precisely, a substitution θ is completely defined, because of the "evaluation" rule given below, by its behavior on the variables.

Formal definition of application of substitutions. For each expression E, the expression Eθ onto which θ maps E is called <u>the value of E under θ</u> The "evaluation" rule then says, intuitively, that the expression Eθ is the result of simultaneously replacing each variable in E by the expression which is the value of that variable under θ. The constants in E are left alone. The "evaluation" rule is very simple and has three parts:

(1) Eθ = E,   when E is a constant ;

(2)   = [• Aθ Bθ],   when E is the expression [• A B]

(3)   = the value of E under θ, when E is a variable.

Bindings. Descriptions of substitutions. In fact, many variables may be mapped onto themselves by θ, and so will be treated by part (3) of the rule exactly as part (1) treats constants. This means that the rule allows us to construct Eθ, for any expression E, if we know the value Xθ under θ of each variable X whose value under θ is different from the variable itself. We say these variables are <u>bound</u> by θ, that the pairs <X Xθ> are the <u>bindings</u> of θ. Finally, in order to have a smooth, flexible notation for describing substitutions, we say that <u>any</u> set of pairs of the form <X Xθ> (where X is a variable) which contains all the bindings of θ, is a

<u>description</u> of θ. Note that any pair in a description of θ which is not a binding of θ must have the form <X X>. It is a common convention, which we have been using above, to use lower case Greek letters to denote substitutions, and to indicate their application to expressions by juxtaposition on the right.

We shall indulge in a benign abuse of notation in which a substitution is identified with a description of it. Thus, we shall write, for example,

θ = { <y [A x] > <x 5> <z [B y] >}

to mean that θ is the substitution <u>described by</u> the right hand side. Then for example we can easily verify that

[A [B x y] [C x y z w]]θ = [A [B 5 [A x]] [C 5 [A x] [B y] w]].

We shall also find it convenient to write Sθ, where S is a <u>set</u> of expressions, to denote the set of all expressions Xθ, where X is in S. Note that the set Sθ may have fewer members than the set S, since it is possible that Xθ = Yθ even though X ≠ Y.

Composition of substitutions. The <u>product</u> θλ of two substitutions θ and λ is simply their composition as mappings, that is, the substitution which maps each expression E onto the expression (Eθ)λ . Thus the product is <u>associative</u>, and has an <u>identity</u>, namely the substitution which maps every expression onto itself. The usual notational convention, which we shall follow, is to denote the identity substitution by the lower case Greek letter ε . Note that { } is a description of ε.

Descriptions of products. Since in actual practice substitutions are represented by their descriptions, we often need to construct a description of θλ, given descriptions of θ and λ. We then use the following easily verified fact:

- if V and W are the sets of variables bound by θ and λ respectively, then the set {< X (Xθ)λ > | X in (V ∪ W)} contains all the bindings of θλ to write a description of $\theta\lambda$, dropping the trivial pairs (if any) of the form: <V V>. So, for example, the product of the substitution

{ <x [A x y] > <v w> }

with the substitution

{<x [C y]> <y [B z x] > < w v>}

is (dropping the trivial pair <v v>) the substitution

{<x [A [C y] [B z x]] > <y B z x]>},

and their product in the reverse order is

{<x [C y]> <y [B z [A x y]] >}.

Unification. The central concept of the theory of substitutions is that of unification. Consider the following unification problem:

- Given any two expressions A and B:

    find (if one exists) a substitution θ such that

    Aθ and Bθ are the same expression, or show

    (if none exists) that this is the case.

A positive solution θ of this problem is said to unify, or to be a unifier of, A and B. More generally, θ is said to unify the set S of expressions if Sθ is a singleton set, that is, if θ maps every expression in S onto the same expression. The set S is then said to be unifiable. It turns out that, if a set of expressions is unifiable at all, it may have many, even infinitely many, different unifiers. However, if in the above problem we ask for a most general unifier of the set {A, B} then the solution is essentially unique if it exists.

Most general unifiers. A substitution σ is a most general unifier of a set S of expressions if it is a unifier of S but also has the property that for any unifier θ of S there exists a substitution λ such that $\theta = \sigma\lambda$. Intuitively: any unifier of S is simply an instance (or special case) of the most general unifier of S. Of all the ideas needed for an understanding of logic programming this idea of most general

<u>unification</u> is undoubtedly the most important.

Example of unification. The expressions

$$A = [[P x y u] [P y z v] [P x v w] [P [K t] t [K t]]]$$

and

$$B = [[P [G r s] r s] [P a [H a b] b] [P x y u] [P u z w]]$$

are unified by the substitution

$$\sigma = \{ <x [G r [K [H r r]]] > \quad <y \; r> \quad <z [H r r] >$$
$$<u [K [H r r]] > \quad <v \; r> \quad <w [K [H r r]] >$$
$$<a \; r> \quad <b \; r> \quad <s [K [H r r]] > \; <t \; [H r r] >\},$$

as may be readily verified by applying σ to A and B and comparing the results. Indeed σ maps both A and B onto the same expression:

$$[\quad [P [G r [K [H r r]]] r [K [H r r]]]$$
$$[P r [H r r] r]$$
$$[P [G r [K [H r r]]] r [K [H r r]]]$$
$$[P [K [H r r]] [H r r] [K [H r r]]] \quad].$$

Now, as it happens, σ is a most general unifier of {A B}: any other unifier θ of {A B} is a product $\sigma\{< r E >\}$ of σ with a some substitution which maps the variable r onto any expression E whatsoever. In particular, if E is a variable, then θ will also be a most general unifier of A and B.

Examples of nonunifiable sets. On the other hand, for example, the set

$$\{[P x y u] [Q a b c]\}$$

is <u>not</u> unifiable. It is easy to see why: any unifier would have to unify the two constants P and Q, which is impossible. Again, the set

$$\{[F x] x\}$$

is not unifiable: any unifier would have to map the variable x into an expression which contained itself as a proper subexpression, which is impossible. These two reasons for nonunifiability are the only two there are.

A simple unification algorithm. We next give a simple <u>unification algorithm</u> which solves all unification problems by finding a most general unifier for a unifiable set of two expressions, and detecting its nonunifiability if it is not unifiable. Unifiers for bigger sets can then be found by iteration, based on the (easily verified) fact:

- $\theta\lambda$ is a most general unifier of a set S containing

  $n \geq 2$ expressions among which are A and B, if θ is

  a most general unifier of {A, B}, and λ is a most

  general unifier of Sθ.

Note that if S has n elements then Sθ will contain at most (n - 1) elements, since Aθ = Bθ, and thus the iteration will stop after at most (n - 1) steps.

Differences between expressions. To help in formulating the unification algorithm in an intelligible (but not yet, as we shall see, fully efficient) way we need the notion of the <u>difference</u> $\Delta(X,Y)$ between any two expressions X and Y. Intuitively, this is the set of all pairs of expressions which occur opposite each other at corresponding positions in X and Y where X and Y are not the same. We have the simple recursive characterization:

$$\Delta(X,Y) = \{\} \qquad\qquad\qquad \text{if } X = Y,$$
$$= \Delta(aX, aY) \ \textbf{U}\ \Delta(dX,dY) \qquad \text{if A and B are both dotted pairs,}$$
$$= \{\{X,Y\}\} \qquad\qquad\qquad \text{otherwise.}$$

Negotiability. Reductions. Such a difference is said to be <u>negotiable</u> if (1) it is nonempty and (2) each pair in it has the property that at least one of its members is a variable and neither member occurs in the other. Thus, because of this condition, for each pair {U, V} in a negotiable difference, at least one of {<U V>} or {<V U>} must be a substitution. These substitutions are called <u>reduction</u>s of the difference.

Examples of differences.   The difference

$$\Delta([P\,x\,y\,z],\ [Q\,a\,b\,c]\,)$$

is the set

$$\{\,\{P, Q\}\ \{x, a\}\ \{y, b\}\ \{z, c\}\,\}.$$

This is <u>not</u> negotiable, because it contains the pair {P,Q} and neither of P, Q is a variable.   Nor is the difference

$$\Delta([F\,x],\,x)\ \ =\ \ \{\,\{[F\,x],\,x\}\,\}$$

negotiable, because x occurs in [F x]. On the other hand, the difference

$$\Delta([P\,x],\,[y\,Q]) = \{\,\{P,y\}\ \{x,Q\}\}$$

<u>is</u>   negotiable, and has the two reductions

$$\mu = \{<y\ P>\}\text{ and }\nu = \{<x\ Q>\}.$$

Unifiers eliminate differences.   The intuitive content of the following proposition is then that the difference between distinct but unifiable expressions is always eliminable:

•   **Negotiability Lemma.** If   A   and   B   are distinct

       expressions, and θ unifies {A, B}, then Δ (A,B) is

       negotiable, and θ unifies each difference in Δ (A, B).

We can now state the

•   **Unification Algorithm**, for two expressions A, B as input:

    1     $\sigma := \epsilon;$

    2   **while** Δ (A σ,B σ) is negotiable **do** $\sigma := \sigma\mu$

       where μ is any reduction of Δ (A σ,B σ);

    3   **return** (**if** Δ (A σ,B σ) is empty **then** σ **else** "FAIL").

We are assured that this algorithm deserves its name by the

Unification Theorem. Let A and B be any two expressions. Then {A B} is unifiable <u>if and only if</u> the above Unification Algorithm terminates, when applied to A and B as input, without returning "FAIL". The σ then returned is, moreover, a most general unifier of {A,B}.

The idea of the proof: termination. At each iteration in step 2 the number of distinct variables in the expressions Aσ, Bσ decreases by 1 (each successive reduction {<U V>} eliminates the variable U, because U does not occur in V). Hence step 2 must terminate after no more iterations than there are distinct variables in the input expressions A and B.

Correctness. If, at step 3, Δ(Aσ, Bσ) is empty, then obviously the σ returned as output is a unifier of A and B, but it must be shown that it is a most general unifier of A and B. This follows from the fact that for every unifier θ of {A,B} the equation

$$\theta = \sigma\theta$$

is an invariant of the computation. It clearly (indeed, trivially) holds after step 1. We can then see that it is preserved throughout step 2 if we note that for any reduction μ of Δ (Aσ,Bσ) the equation $\theta = \mu\theta$ holds, allowing us to calculate:

$$\theta = \sigma\theta = \sigma(\mu\theta) = (\sigma\mu)\theta.$$

Since σ is replaced by $\sigma\mu$ at each iteration the equation $\theta = \sigma\theta$ is an invariant. Thus for any unifier θ we have $\theta = \sigma\lambda$, with $\lambda = \theta$.

Fast unification algorithms. The simple unification algorithm given above has the pedagogical and theoretical advantage of being concise and intuitive. However, it is very inefficient in both time and space. For example, to unify with this algorithm the two expressions

$$[\quad [F\ x_0\ x_0] \quad [F\ x_1\ x_1] \quad [F\ x_2\ x_2] \quad \ldots \quad [F\ x_{n-1}\ x_{n-1}]\ ]$$

$$[\quad x_1 \qquad x_2 \qquad x_3 \qquad \ldots \quad x_n \qquad\qquad]$$

requires time and space proportional to 2^n. It is easy to see that the most general unifier is

$$\{<x_1\ [F\ x_0\ x_0]>$$

$$<x_2\ [F\ [F\ x_0\ x_0]\ [F\ x_0\ x_0]\ ]>$$

$$<x_3\ [F\ [F\ [F\ x_0\ x_0]\ [F\ x_0\ x_0]\ ]\ [F\ [F\ x_0\ x_0]\ [F\ x_0\ x_0]\ ]$$

$$\vdots$$

$$<x_n\ \text{(a term containing "F" } 2n+1 \text{ times and "}x_0\text{" } 2^n \text{ times) > }\}\ .$$

Fortunately it is possible to exploit other aspects of unification in such a way that much more efficient unification algorithms can be devised. The general idea behind all of them is based on the equivalence relations which are induced on sets of expressions by substitutions.

Occurrence graphs. If S is any set of expressions, let us denote by [S] the smallest set of expressions which includes S and contains A and B whenever it contains the pair [• A B]. The <u>occurrence graph of S</u> is then a directed graph whose nodes are the singleton sets {X} where X is an expression in [S], with an arc labelled **a** (respectively **d**) leaving the node {[• A B]} and impinging on the node {A} (respectively {B}). If X is a constant or a variable the the node {X} has no arc leaving it. Clearly, the occurrence graph of S is acyclic.

For each substitution θ we define the equivalence relation $\equiv_\theta$ by:

$$X \equiv_\theta Y \text{ if and only if } X\theta = Y\theta.$$

Now if in the occurrence graph G of $S\theta$ we replace each of its nodes {$X\theta$} by the $\equiv_\theta$-equivalence class in which X lies, we get a graph H which is isomorphic to G. Since G is acyclic, so is H. Let us call H the occurrence graph of $S/\equiv_\theta$. Intuitively,

$H\theta = G$. The equivalence relation $\equiv_\theta$ therefore satisfies the two properties:

[no cycles] the occurrence graph of $S/\equiv_\theta$ is acyclic

[structure]   **for all** distinct X, Y in S:

        if $X \equiv_\theta Y$ **then either** {X, Y} contains a variable

                or X,Y are both dotted pairs

                  and $aX \equiv_\theta aY$ and $dX \equiv_\theta dY$.

The converse also holds: any equivalence relation $\equiv$ on [S] satisfying [no cycles] and [structure] is inducible on S by a substitution. Indeed, a most general substitution σ which induces $\equiv$ on [S] can be immediately constructed from $\equiv$.

Set union algorithm. The idea of the various known fast unification algorithms is to seek to construct, given distinct expressions A and B, an equivalence relation on the set [{A B}] satisfying the above properties. First, one constructs, if possible, an equivalence relation satisfying [structure], for which $A \equiv B$. This is done by imitating the method of the very fast (almost linear in time and linear in space) "set union algorithm" analyzed by R. E. Tarjan [14]. This relation is then checked for the [no cycles] property by the (linear in time and space) "topological sort" method described by Knuth [9].

The remaining details are too many for a complete discussion in these notes. A recent paper by J. S. Vitter and R. A. Simmons [16] contains a full account, and also discusses the potential speed-up of this algorithm if advantage is taken of the opportunities it offers for parallel computations. Gerard Huet described this idea already in his thesis [7], and there are also papers by Paterson and Wegman [11], and by Martelli and Montanari [10], which give strictly linear algorithms.   The following sketch will give a feel for this general approach.

Equivalence classes represented by trees. In the set union algorithm, the classes of an equivalence relation on a set X are represented as trees in a forest defined by a set E of equations between distinct elements of X, no two equations in

E having the same left hand side. If E contains the equation $U = V$ we say that $\underline{E}$ equates $\underline{U}$ to $\underline{V}$, and we think of U and V as being nodes in the same tree, with V the parent of U. The function ROOT is defined for any element A of X and such a set E of equations as arguments, and finds the root of the tree in which A lies:

ROOT A E $=$ **if** E equates A to B **then** ROOT B E **else** A.

The equivalence relation $\equiv_E$ represented by E is then that for which

$$X \equiv_E Y \quad \textbf{iff} \quad ROOT\,X\,E = ROOT\,Y\,E.$$

The [structure] part of the algorithm is then embodied in two cooperating functions EQUIV and EQUATE. In general the function EQUIV, when given as its first and second arguments expressions A, B, and a set E of equations as its third argument, returns either E itself, if $A \equiv_E B$, or a set E' of equations obtained by adding to E the equations required for E' to satisfy [structure] and for $A \equiv_{E'} B$. If no such E' exists, then EQUIV returns the message "FAIL". The function EQUATE has a similar behavior, but assumes that E is not the message "FAIL" and that A and B are roots of E.

We then define UNIFY by

(UNIFY A B) = (EQUIV A B { })

where EQUIV and EQUATE are defined by

EQUIV A B E $=$ **if** E is "FAIL" **then** "FAIL" **else**
      EQUATE (ROOT A E) (ROOT B E) E

EQUATE A B E =	**if**	A = B **then** E	1
else	**if**	{A,B} contains a variable **then** MERGE A B E	2
else	**if**	{A,B} contains a constant **then** "FAIL"	3
else		EQUIV aA aB (EQUIV dA dB (MERGE A B E))	4

Since EQUATE is called only as shown by EQUIV, the input assumption is correct that E is not the message "FAIL" and that A and B are roots of E. The action in line 3 of EQUATE is appropriate to having discovered that [structure] cannot be satisfied, since in view of the tests in lines 1, 2 and 3, one of A, B must be a constant while the other must be either a (distinct) constant or else a dotted pair. The action in lines 2 and 4 is to merge the two trees (i.e. equivalence classes) into a single tree (equivalence class) by equating one root to the other. The action in line 4 is appropriate to having found that both A and B are dotted pairs, so that not only are the two trees (equivalence classes) merged, but the resulting forest (equivalence relation) is modified by such further mergings of equivalence classes as may be necessary to satisfy [structure]. If we use the following simple definition for MERGE

MERGE A B E ≡ **if** A is a variable **then** {A=B} **U** E **else** {B=A} **U** E

then the calls of MERGE from EQUATE preserve the property that

if a tree representing an equivalence class has a variable

as its root, then all expressions in that class are variables.

Balancing and path compression. However, this simple method of merging foregoes the opportunity to imitate fully the set union algorithm, which, when merging, <u>balances</u> the resulting tree by making the root of the <u>taller</u> tree the parent of the root of the <u>shorter</u> tree. The set union algorithm also <u>compresses</u> the trees: each call (ROOT A_0 E) returns a root A_n by accessing a sequence of equations

$$A_i = A_{i+1}, \quad (i = 0, \ldots, n - 1)$$

in E (a "path"). Each of these equations is <u>replaced</u> by the equation $A_i = A_n$, making the root the parent of each node A_i, $(i = 0, \ldots, n - 1)$ (the path is "compressed"). By complicating the fast unification algorithm slightly to reflect these two refinements, an essentially linear cost performance can be achieved.

Logic. After all these preliminaries we can now get to our main topic and set up the <u>clausal predicate calculus</u>. This is is a special machine-oriented version of the predicate calculus, in which one deals principally with only one form of proposition (the clausal sequent) and uses only one inference principle by which to prove the truths among such propositions (the resolution principle).

Clausal sequents.   A clausal sequent is an intuitively meaningful proposition which asserts that a given set of <u>universal disjunctive clauses</u> say, the set P, logically entails a given set of <u>existential conjunctive clauses</u>, say, Q.

Sequent notation. We write the sequent by joining the two sets with a <u>sequent arrow</u>, thus:

$$P \Rightarrow Q$$

and we say that P is the <u>antecedent,</u> and Q the <u>succedent</u>, of the sequent. We read the sequent as "P logically entails Q" or as "Q logically follows from P". If Q happens to be the empty set we can write the sequent simply as

$$P \Rightarrow$$

and read it as "P is logically unsatisfiable". We often write the antecedent and succedent sets by simply listing their clauses in some order (the order being irrelevant) and omitting the external set brackets. Thus, we write

$$A, B, C \ \Rightarrow \ M, N$$

rather than

$$\{A, B, C\} \ \Rightarrow \ \{M, N\}.$$

Meaning of a clausal sequent. Pending the more exact definitions   to be given below, we can say that the sequent $P \Rightarrow Q$ expresses the claim that there is no <u>interpretation</u> of the predicate symbols and function symbols of the clauses in P and Q under which all the clauses in P are true and all those in Q are false.

When Q is a singleton {C} this accords well with our everyday understanding of what it means to say that C logically follows from (the sentences in) P: "C must be true whenever the sentences in P are true".

Universal disjunctive and existential conjunctive clauses. A universal disjunctive (u.d.) clause is a formal sentence of the form:

$$\forall x_1 \ ... \ x_k \ (\sim A_1 \ \vee ... \ \vee \sim A_p \ \vee \ B_1 \ \vee \ ... \ \vee \ B_q \ )$$

which is equivalent to

$$\forall x_1 \ldots x_k \; ((A_1 \wedge \ldots \wedge A_p) \rightarrow (B_1 \vee \ldots \vee B_q))$$

while an existential conjunctive (e.c.) clause is one of the form:

$$\exists x_1 \ldots x_k \; (A_1 \wedge \ldots \wedge A_p \wedge {\sim}B_1 \wedge \ldots \wedge {\sim}B_q)$$

which is equivalent to

$$\exists x_1 \ldots x_k \; ((A_1 \wedge \ldots \wedge A_p) \wedge {\sim}(B_1 \vee \ldots \vee B_q)).$$

In each clause, the expressions $A_1, \ldots, A_p$ and $B_1, \ldots, B_q$ are predications (defined below), and the $x_1, \ldots, x_k$ are all the distinct variables which occur in them. For both kinds of clause we say that

- the set $\{x_1 \ldots x_k\}$ is the <u>prefix</u> of the clause,
- the set $\{A_1 \ldots A_p\}$ is the <u>body</u> of the clause, and
- the set $\{B_1 \ldots B_q\}$ is the <u>head</u> of the clause.

A clause with an empty prefix (i.e. which contains no variables) is called a <u>ground clause</u>.

Empty clauses. When both head and body are empty then (necessarily) also the prefix is empty, and the clause itself is then said to be <u>the empty clause</u> of the one kind or the other. The empty u.d. clause is equivalent to the formal sentence **false,** and the empty e.c. clause is equivalent to the formal sentence **true.** The formal sentence **false** is false in every interpretation (see below), and the formal sentence **true** is true in every interpretation.

The kernel of a clause. A u.d. clause with a given prefix, body and head is transformed into an e.c. clause with the same prefix, body and head under the operation of interchanging $\forall$ with $\exists$, $\wedge$ with $\vee$, and (for each predication P) ${\sim}$P with P. The prefix, body and head are invariants of the transformation. We shall find it useful to define the basic operations and notions of resolution in terms of these invariants alone. We shall call the triple

$$< \{x_1 \ldots x_k\} \; \{A_1 \ldots A_p\} \; \{B_1 \ldots B_q\} >$$

consisting of the prefix, body and head of a clause C the <u>kernel</u> of C, regardless of whether C is a u.d. clause or an e.c. clause. It is convenient to think of the u.d. clause with kernel <X A B> as the tuple <∀ X A B>, and the e.c. clause with kernel <X A B> as the tuple < ∃ X A B>. Notice that when a u.d. clause and an e.c. clause have the same kernel then each is logically equivalent to the <u>negation</u> of the other. It has been the usual practice in clausal predicate calculus to deal only with u.d. clauses, and to call these simply <u>clauses</u> without qualification.   However, this practice leads to unnecessary awkwardness in the later development of the resolution principle. By working with kernels wherever possible we are able to enjoy the conceptual economy of the usual treatment without denying ourselves the richer and more natural means of expression which the availability of both kinds of clause provides.

Predications and terms. Herbrand Universes and Bases. In any particular application, clauses and clausal sequents are all built ultimately out of the variables and the members of a certain set of constants, each constant in which is classified as a <u>predicate symbol</u> or a <u>function symbol</u> and assigned an <u>arity</u>.   (The arity of a symbol may be any natural number. When the arity of a function symbol is 0 the symbol is called an <u>individual symbol</u>). Relative to such a fixed set L of predicate and function symbols (sometimes called a <u>lexicon</u>) we define certain expressions to be the <u>terms over L</u> and the <u>predications over L</u>, and when these expressions contain no variables we say they are <u>ground</u> terms over L and <u>ground</u> predications over L. The definitions are:

- The <u>terms over L</u> are the variables, and also the lists
  $[F\ t_1 \ldots t_n]$ in which F is a function symbol of arity n in
  L, and the t_i are terms over L. The set of all ground
  terms over L is called the <u>Herbrand Universe over L</u>.
- The <u>predications over L</u> are the lists $[P\ t_1 \ldots t_n]$ in
  which P is a predicate symbol of arity n in L, and the
  t_i are terms over L. The set of all ground predications
  over L is called the <u>Herbrand Base over L</u>.

Substitutions extended to tuples. It is useful to extend the substitution notation not only to sets of expressions, but also to _tuples_ whose components are expressions or sets of expressions, in the obvious way: e.g., the triple $< X\ A\ B >\theta$ is the triple $< X\theta\ A\theta\ B\theta >$. We can then readily explain what is meant by a _variant_ of a clause.

Variants. If C is a clause whose kernel is <X A B> and the substitution θ is a bijection on the variables, then $C\theta$ is also a clause, whose kernel is <X A B>θ, and is called a _variant_ of <X A B>. [NOTA BENE: the substitution operates on the variables of the prefix, even though they are from the logical point of view bound variables of the clause. Our substitution operations know nothing about the meanings, if any, that we associate with expressions.] Here we are using kernels for the first but by no means the last time to say two things at once. In particular every clause is a variant of itself (with $\theta = \varepsilon$). Note also that if $C\theta$ is a variant of C then C must be a variant of $C\theta$ since

$$C\theta\theta^{-1} = C\varepsilon = C.$$

Finally, if A is a variant of B and B is a variant of C then A is a variant of C. Thus "being a variant of" is an equivalence relation on clauses.

Separated clauses. Instances. Two clauses are said to be _separated_ if their prefixes are disjoint. A clause D is an _instance_ of a clause C if there is a substitution θ such that $D = C\theta$. (In order for this definition to make sense, the clauses must be construed as tuples). If the prefix of D is empty, it is a _ground instance_ of C.

Herbrand interpretations of L. An Herbrand interpretation J of L is given by specifying, for each predication in the Herbrand Base of L, whether it is _true in J_ or _false in J_. The idea is that such a specification of truth or falsehood can be automatically extended to clauses, since in Herbrand interpretations

- the variables in clauses over L range over the Herbrand Universe of L, which is taken as the domain of individuals of J; so that

- a u.d. (respectively, e.c.) clause is true (respectively, false) in J iff all its ground instances are true (respectively, false) in J; and

- a u.d. (respectively, e.c.) ground clause with body A and head B is false (respectively, true) in J iff each predication in A is true in J and each predication in B is false in J.

Now we can give the following characterization of

Counterexamples of clausal sequents. Let S be a clausal sequent over L. Then an interpretation J of L is a counterexample of S iff every clause in the antecedent of S is true in J, and every clause in the succedent of S is false in J.

Equivalence of clausal sequents. Two sequents over L are equivalent iff every counterexample of one is also a counterexample of the other.

Truth of clausal sequents. A clausal sequent is true iff it has no counterexamples. Being true is in general only a semidecidable property of clausal sequents. There is no general algorithm for detecting the falsehood of every false sequent, but there are, as we shall see, sound and complete systems of proof for clausal sequents, and such a system of proof for clausal sequents is an algorithmic method of recognizing the truth of a clausal sequent if it is in fact true. This is what the resolution principle makes possible, in a reasonably efficient form.

Obvious sequents. Some true clausal sequents are very easy to recognize as such: for example, those which contain **false** in the antecedent or **true** in the succedent. We call these obvious sequents. In general, however, true clausal sequents are not obvious, and we need some other means of establishing their truth. This is the motivation for the resolution principle.

Proving true clausal sequents by means of resolution. The resolution principle is based upon the following construction, involving the unification algorithm, of a _resolvent_ of the kernels of two separated clauses.

Resolvents. Let E, F be two separated clauses whose kernels are <X A B> and <Y C D> respectively. Then a clause R whose kernel is <Z M N> is a _resolvent of E with F on K_ iff K is a unifiable subset of B ∪ C with most general unifier σ, such that both K ∩ B and K ∩ C are nonempty, and such that

- Z = (Xσ ∪ Yσ) ∩ VARS,

- M = Aσ ∪ (Cσ — Kσ),

- N = (Bσ — Kσ) ∪ Dσ.

Note that both the u.d. clause R with kernel <Z M N> and the e.c. clause R with kernel <Z M N> are resolvents of E with F on K.

The resolution principle. The resolution principle is an inference principle for clausal sequents. In the usual treatment [12], resolution is formulated as an inference principle for u.d. clauses, and allows us to infer a u.d. clause as conclusion from two u.d. clauses as premises. By restating the principle for sequents, however, we uncover more of the power and flexibility of the underlying idea, and also allow e.c. clauses to enter into resolution reasoning in a natural way. So we state the resolution principle as follows:

- from a nonobvious clausal sequent S one may infer
  the clausal sequent S + R, and conversely, provided
  that R is a resolvent of two separated variants
  of clauses in S and provided that R is not a variant
  of a clause in S.

By S + R we mean the clausal sequent obtained by adding R to the antecedent of

S, if it is a u.d.clause, or to the succedent of S, if it is an e.c. clause. Any such sequent S + R is then said to be a <u>resolution</u> of the sequent S. The two sequents S and S + R are in fact equivalent.

Comment on the definition. The provision that R should not be a variant of a clause in S eliminates an undesirable source of redundancy and ensures that a given sequent has only finitely many essentially different resolutions. The provision that the sequent S be nonobvious eliminates the possibility of continuing to look for a proof when the proof is in fact complete. This will become clear in the next paragraph.

Resolution series; resolution proofs. A series $S_0, \ldots, S_r$ of sequents in which S_{i+1} is a resolution of S_i, $0 \leq i < r$, is called a <u>resolution series</u>. A resolution series is a <u>resolution proof</u> (of its initial sequent S_0) iff its final sequent S_r is obvious.

Soundness of the resolution principle. The logical justification of the resolution principle rests on the fact (not difficult to establish) that <u>all sequents in a resolution series are equivalent</u>, hence that all sequents in a resolution <u>proof</u> are <u>true</u> - as is clear from the fact that its final sequent, being obvious, is (obviously) true. In particular, the initial sequent of a resolution proof is true, and so the proof really is a proof of its initial sequent. We simply read the proof backwards, starting with an obviously true sequent, and proceeding in truth-preserving steps until we arrive at the initial sequent with the conviction that it too must be true. As a proof system for clausal sequents, in other words, the resolution principle is <u>sound</u>. The significance of the resolution principle for computational logic then rests on two further properties of resolution, <u>local finiteness</u> and <u>completeness</u>, one of which is easy to see, the other of which is not.

Local finiteness. A clausal sequent has only <u>finitely</u> many resolutions, all of which can be effectively constructed. Hence we can effectively find <u>all</u> finite resolution series starting with a given sequent, and therefore all resolution proofs of that sequent, if it has any. This fact allows us to build resolution-proof-finding systems.

Completeness of the resolution principle. Every true sequent has at least one resolution proof. This fact is quite nontrivial. It is what makes resolution-proof-finding systems equivalent to truth-recognition systems for clausal sequents.

Horn sequents. The general resolution-proof-finding procedure as sketched above is attractive, but not yet efficient enough for what we now call logic programming. There are just too many resolutions at each step for it to be feasible to search out all resolution proofs of a given sequent. Nevertheless Green [5] was able to use the general procedure to lay out and motivate the main ideas of logic programming as we know them today. Soon thereafter Colmerauer [4] in his PROLOG system, and Kowalski [8] in a more abstract form, showed that by sacrificing some generality one can achieve a remarkably useful system of logical computation. The key idea is to work with a restricted version of clausal predicate calculus by considering only Horn sequents, rather than clausal sequents in general.

Procedure clauses; goal clauses. A clause is a procedure clause if its head is a singleton, and a goal clause if its head is empty. In both kinds of clauses the predications in the body of the clause are called goals. Both procedure clauses and goal clauses are called Horn clauses. A Horn sequent is a then a clausal sequent whose antecedent contains only procedure clauses and whose succedent contains only goal clauses. A minimal Horn sequent is one which contains only one goal clause.

Logic programs = minimal Horn sequents. A minimal Horn sequent S thus has the form $P \Rightarrow (\exists Y) (G_1 \wedge \ldots \wedge G_n)$, where P is a set of procedure clauses, and $\{G_1, \ldots, G_n\}$ is a nonempty set of goals, while the variables in Y are all those which occur in the goals G_i. The various resolution proofs (if any) of S will include the LUSH resolution proofs which we are about to define, but also many , many more. It turns out that if S is true then not only does it have a resolution proof (which we already know) but it even has a LUSH resolution proof. This is crucial for logic programming purposes. It means that a logic programming engine need only search through the much sparser space of LUSH resolution series starting with a true minimal sequent S, in order to be sure of finding a proof of S.

Selection and removal functions. To help in stating the idea of LUSH resolution we need the idea of a <u>selection</u> function , namely, a function $\uparrow$ defined on every nonempty set M, whose value $(\uparrow M)$ at M is some member of M. For each such selection function we have the corresponding <u>removal</u> function $\downarrow$, which when applied to a nonempty set M returns the set which is the result of removing the expression $(\uparrow M)$ from M.

LUSH resolution series. Let $\uparrow$ be any selection function. Given the resolution series

$$S_0, S_1, \ldots, S_i, \ldots,$$

let us write

$$S_{i+1} = S_i + R_{i+1} \qquad (i \geq 0)$$

to show how at each step the sequent S_{i+1} is obtained by adding the resolvent R_{i+1} to the sequent S_i. Then the series is a <u>LUSH resolution series controlled by</u> $\underline{\uparrow}$ provided that

- each S_i $(i \geq 0)$ is a Horn sequent,

- S_0 is a minimal Horn sequent with goal clause R_0,

- R_{i+1} $(i \geq 0)$ is a resolvent with R_i, on the set $\{H_i \uparrow C_i\}$,

  of (a variant) $\forall X_i (A_i \rightarrow H_i)$ of some procedure clause in S_i, where C_i is the body of R_i.

The clause R_i is called the <u>active clause</u> of the sequent S_i. Thus the active clause of each sequent in the series after the first is the resolvent of some procedure clause in the preceding sequent with the active clause of the preceding sequent. The active clause in the initial sequent is the (only) goal clause in that sequent. Note that in a LUSH resolution series <u>no procedure clauses are generated as resolvents</u>. Note also that each procedure clause can produce <u>at most one</u> resolvent with the active clause, and will do so if, but only if, its head can be unified with the goal selected by ↑ from the body of the active clause. The rapidity with which this can be decided will depend on the complexity of the particular function ↑ being used, on the method of representation of the sets of goals to which it is applied, and on the method of representing the procedure clauses in the initial sequent. PROLOG uses particularly efficient methods, in which an order is imposed on the goals. PROLOG's ↑ respects this ordering in the sense that ↑M is always the first of the most recently added elements of M. The details are too many for further discussion here.

The idea of LUSH resolution is due to Kowalski [8] but the acronymic label is due to Hill [6]. It is intended to suggest: **L**inear resolution with **U**nrestricted **S**election function for **H**orn clauses. The LUSH resolution proofs of a true minimal Horn sequent are far fewer in number than the ordinary resolution proofs of it. Many people, following the example of van Emden and Kowalski [15] and Lloyd [17], prefer to use the acronym SLD (**S**elected **L**inear resolution for **D**efinite clauses) instead of LUSH. However, acronyms are not to be multiplied, or even added, beyond necessity.

LUSH resolution is complete in the following very strong sense: if S is a true minimal Horn sequent, then for <u>all</u> selection functions ↑ there is at least one LUSH resolution proof of S which is controlled by ↑.

Lush resolution series as computations. We can associate with the LUSH resolution series $S_0, S_1, \ldots, S_i, \ldots$, controlled by $\uparrow$, the _computation_ which is the series $C_0, C_1, \ldots, C_i, \ldots$, of _states_ each of which is the body of the active clause R_i of the corresponding sequent S_i. Consider, then, a LUSH resolution series whose initial Horn sequent $P \Rightarrow (\exists Y)C$ corresponds to the state C. The relationship between successive states corresponding to the successive Horn sequents in the series exhibits a repetitive pattern: each successive state C_{i+1} is obtained from its predecessor C_i by the same "computation cycle".

The computation cycle. To obtain the successor of the nonempty state C_i we take some procedure clause in P such that, for some suitable variant

$$<X_i \, A_i \, \{H_j\}>\theta_i ,$$

of its kernel $<X_i \, A_i \, \{H_j\}>$, the set $\{\uparrow C_i, H_i\theta_i\}$ is unifiable with most general unifier σ_i. If no such procedure clause exists, then the state C_i is a "failure". and has no successors. Otherwise, the new state C_{i+1} is formed by the construction

$$C_{i+1} = A_i\theta_i \sigma_i \cup (\downarrow C_i) \sigma_i .$$

In general there may be more than one procedure clause for which this construction can be made. In other words, a state may have more than one successor.

Stacklike behavior of successive states. This computation cycle does indeed abstractly resemble the basic cycle of a simple stack-oriented computer if we think of $\uparrow$ as returning, and $\downarrow$ as removing, the "top" element of the "stack". The states C_i are then the successive contents of the "stack". The cycle thus consists, partly, of "popping" the "top" goal from the stack and "pushing" the goals of the procedure body onto the stack. This is what PROLOG actually does. Unfortunately this simple analogy does not yet account for the application, to each goal in the stack, of the most general unifier σ_i. However, by means of an idea due originally to Boyer and Moore in their Edinburgh resolution theorem prover [1], we can find a natural computational role in this analogy for the substitutions θ_i and σ_i of this basic cycle: that of the <u>environment of bindings</u> for the variables.

Implicit representation of expressions. The idea of Boyer and Moore is to represent an expression $E\theta$ "implicitly" by the pair $<E \ \theta>$ instead of actually carrying out the work of applying θ to E. This pair can be viewed as a "closure" or a "delayed evaluation". The pair $<E \ \theta>$ can be treated in all respects as though it were the explicit expression $E\theta$ that it implicitly represents: for example the result $E\theta\lambda$ of applying λ to the expression represented by the pair $<E \ \theta>$ is itself represented by the pair $<<E \ \theta> \ \lambda >$, and so on. When pairs are nested to the left like this we follow an "association to the left" convention and drop the inner brackets. In general, the expression implicitly represented by $<E \ \theta_1 \ldots \theta_n>$ can be found simply by carrying out the "delayed" work of applying the successive substitutions, to yield the explicit expression: $((E\theta_1) \ldots \theta_n)$. It is straightforward to adapt the procedures UNIFY, EQUIV, EQUATE, ROOT, MERGE, etc., to this method of implicit representation of expressions. We just supply, as separate parameters, the substitution components of the implicit representations of the argument expressions. We can then use the Boyer-Moore idea to represent the successive states of a LUSH computation. Instead of actually constructing C_{i+1} by applying the most general unifier σ_i to the set $(A_i\theta_i \cup \uparrow C_i)$ we can simply represent C_{i+1} by pairing this set with σ_i:

$$C_{i+1} = < (A_i\theta_i \cup \uparrow C_i) \ \sigma_i >.$$

The set $A_i\theta_i$ can also be represented in the same way, so that the equation can be written

$$C_{i+1} = <(<A_i \ \theta_i> \cup \uparrow C_i) \ \sigma_i>.$$

Computations on the machine will of course use this implicit representation wherever possible. In particular the successive unification substitutions will be separate components of each state. The successive states of the computation corresponding to a LUSH resolution proof of the minimal Horn sequent

$$P \Rightarrow (\exists Y)C$$

are then the following (in Boyer-Moore form):

$$C_0 = < C \ \varepsilon >$$

$$C_1 = < (<A_1 \ \theta_1> \cup \uparrow C_0) \qquad \sigma_1 >$$

$$C_2 = < (<A_2 \ \theta_2> \cup \uparrow C_1) \qquad \sigma_1 \ \sigma_2 >$$

$$\vdots$$

$$C_{j+1} = < (<A_{j+1} \ \theta_{j+1}> \cup \uparrow C_j) \qquad \sigma_1 \ \sigma_2 \ \dots \ \sigma_{j+1}>$$

$$\vdots$$

$$C_t = < \{\} \qquad\qquad\qquad \sigma_1 \ \sigma_2 \ \dots \ \sigma_j \ \dots \sigma_t >$$

with the successive kernels $<X_1 \ A_1 \ \{H_1\}>, \dots, <X_t \ A_t \ \{H_t\}>$ of (not necessarily different) procedure clauses in P supplying the sets A_j of new goals at each step, and with each substitution σ_j satisfying the equation:

$$\sigma_j = (\text{UNIFY } H_j \ \theta_j \ (\uparrow C_j) \ <\sigma_1 \dots \sigma_{j-1}>), \qquad (j \geq 1).$$

Throughout this LUSH computation no expression need actually be constructed explicitly. At termination, the substitution $(\sigma_1 \ \sigma_2 \ \dots \ \sigma_t)$ is available to construct the output of the computation.

The computation tree. The procedure clause chosen at each step of the computation is one of the only finitely many occurring in the antecedent P of the sequent. This gives rise to a <u>computation space</u> which is a finitary (but not necessarily finite) tree. The various branches of the tree correspond to the various LUSH resolution series starting with the given initial sequent. The root of the tree is the body of the goal clause (= the active clause) of the initial sequent, and in general each node of the tree is <u>either</u>

* empty, and a leaf of the tree, (a "success") <u>or</u>

* nonempty but with no successors, and a leaf of the tree, (a "failure") <u>or</u>

* nonempty and with one or more successors.

The "success" branches (if any) of the computation tree are the completed computations corresponding to the various LUSH resolution proofs of the initial minimal sequent $P \Rightarrow (\exists Y)C$ the body C of whose active clause $(\exists Y)C$ is the root of the tree.

Each completed computation yields an output. It is then natural to view the equation

$$Y = (Y\sigma_1\sigma_2 \ldots \sigma_t)$$

as the <u>output</u> of the completed computation, where the state $< \{ \} \ \sigma_1 \ \sigma_2 \ \ldots \ \sigma_t >$ is its terminal node. The term(s) $Y\sigma_1\sigma_2 \ldots \sigma_t$ are expressions constructed stepwise by the successive unifiers $\sigma_1, \sigma_2, \ldots, \sigma_t$.

Nondeterminacy. For every true initial sequent S there is at least one such computation since the sequent has at least one LUSH resolution proof. S may, however, have many, even infinitely many, such proofs; and for the computation corresponding to each proof there will be a possibly different output. It is the purpose of the various logic programming engines, such as a PROLOG machine, to obtain <u>all</u> such outputs when given a true minimal Horn sequent. This it does by making a complete exploration of the search space. If the search space is infinite then it may contain infinitely many success branches (and it may also contain infinitely many failure branches). A properly designed engine should presumably generate the search tree "fairly", i.e., in such a way (and there are many options) as to reach any given node in the tree after only finitely much time. Unfortunately, most PROLOG engines are designed unfairly (for the sake of speed) as "depth-first backtracking" devices.

Example 1. The minimal Horn sequent sequent

- $\forall x: [\text{NUMBER } x] \rightarrow [\text{NUMBER } [1+ x]]$
- $[\text{NUMBER } 0]$

$\Rightarrow \quad \exists y: [\text{NUMBER } y]$

is true, and has infinitely many LUSH resolution proofs.

The outputs of the corresponding computations are the equations:

$$y = 0$$
$$y = [1+ 0]$$
$$y = [1+ [1+ 0]]$$

and so on.

At the jth step $(j > 0)$ the active clause is (understanding y_0 as just y itself):

$$\exists y_j: [\text{NUMBER } [1+ \ldots [1+ y_j] \ldots]] \quad (\text{with } j \ 1+\text{'s})$$

and the next resolution can be obtained by choosing either the second procedure clause

(*)   [NUMBER 0]

or the [j+1]st variant

(**) $\forall y_{j+1}$: [NUMBER y_{j+1}] → [NUMBER [1+ y_{j+1}]]

of the first procedure clause.   The   choice of (*) will yield an obvious sequent ,
and the output will be

y = [1+ ... [1+ 0] ...]   (with j 1+'s)

The choice of (**) will produce the new active clause

$\exists y_{j+1}$: [NUMBER [1+ ... [1+ y_{j+1}] ...]]   (with j+1   1+'s).

A depth-first backtracking device which chose (**) before (*) at each level would
therefore delay permanently the choice of (*) at the first level, and never reach even
the first success node in the search tree. Merely reversing the order of the choice
would produce a complete (although nonterminating) traversal of the search tree.

Example 2. The two procedure clauses

P1: $\forall x$: [CAT [ ] x x]
P2: $\forall x,a,b,c$:   [[CAT a b c] → [CAT [• x a] b [• x c]]]

intuitively define [CAT x y z] to mean that the list z is the result of conCATenating
the lists x and y in that order. The goal clause

Q: $\exists p,q: [CAT\ p\ q\ [\bullet\ 1\ [\bullet\ 2\ [\bullet\ 3\ NIL]]]\ ]$

intuitively says that the list [1 2 3] is the result of concatenating two lists, p and q, in that order. The minimal Horn sequent {P1 P2} $\Rightarrow$ Q is true, and has four different LUSH resolution proofs, the simplest of which is obtained by adding of just one resolution invoking the procedure clause P1. The corresponding computation has the output

[p q] = [NIL [1 2 3]]

describing the construction [1 2 3] = [ ]++[1 2 3]. The other three proofs consist respectively of one, two and three successive invocations of the procedure clause P2 followed by an invocation of the procedure clause P1. The outputs of the corresponding computations describe respectively the constructions

[1 2 3] = [1]++[2 3], [1 2 3] = [1 2]++[3], [1 2 3] = [1 2 3]++[ ].

Another view of LUSH resolution proofs. Clark [3] has pointed out an interesting alternative way to view a computation with output $Y = Y\theta$ corresponding to a LUSH resolution proof of a true minimal Horn sequent

$$P \Rightarrow (\exists Y)(G_1 \wedge \ldots \wedge G_n).$$

Namely, it can be interpreted as the construction of n separate hyper-resolution proofs by which n unconditional procedure clauses

$$(\forall X_1)H_1, \ldots, (\forall X_n)H_n$$

are simultaneously deduced from the procedure clauses in P, and which are such that the expressions

$$[H_1, \ldots, H_n] \quad \text{and} \quad [G_1 \ldots G_n]$$

are unifiable with most general unifier θ.

Hyper-resolution. Hyper-resolution is an inference pattern for u.d. clauses which requires a <u>conditional</u> procedure clause

(1) $(\forall X)(A_1 \wedge \ldots \wedge A_k \rightarrow B)$

with $k \geq 1$ goals $A_1, \ldots, A_k$, as <u>major premise,</u> and k <u>unconditional</u> procedure clauses

(2) $(\forall X_1)B_1, \ldots, (\forall X_k)B_k$,

separated from it and from each other, as <u>minor premises</u>, such that the expressions

$$[A_1 \ldots A_k] \quad \text{and} \quad [B_1 \ldots B_k]$$

are unifiable with most general unifier σ. The <u>conclusion</u> of the hyper-resolution inference is then the unconditional procedure clause

(3) $(\forall Z)C$

where $C = B\sigma$, and $Z = (X \cup X_1 \cup \ldots \cup X_k)\sigma \cap \text{VARS}$. It is quite straightforward to verify that the clause (3) is indeed a logical consequence of the clauses (2) together with the clause (1).

One may use this inference pattern to obtain, from a set P of procedure clauses, a series $P_0, P_1, \ldots$, of sets of procedure clauses all of which are logical consequences of P, as follows. The set P_0 is the set of unconditional procedure clauses in P. The set P_{j+1} is the result of adding to the set P_j all the unconditional procedure clauses which can be inferred by a single application of hyper-resolution with major premise in the set P and minor premises in the set P_{j+1}. Clearly the union

$$P^k = P_0 \cup P_1 \cup \ldots \cup P_k$$

of the first k of these sets contains all the unconditional procedure clauses deducible from P by no more than k steps of hyper-resolution. It is natural to organize a deduction from P of such an unconditional procedure clause as a tree with that clause as its root and with members of P_0 as leaves. Each nonleaf node in the tree is the immediate consequence, by hyper-resolution, of its immediate descendents in the tree (as minor premises) and some conditional clause in P as major premise.

LUSH resolution and hyper-resolution. Now consider again a LUSH resolution proof whose initial sequent is $P \Rightarrow (\exists Y)(G_1 \wedge \ldots \wedge G_n)$ and whose output is $Y = Y\theta$. Let

$$C_0, \ldots, C_t$$

be the successive states of the corresponding computation and let

$$D_0, \ldots, D_t$$

be the successive procedure clauses D_i such that D_i is used with C_i to get C_{i+1}. Note that

$$C_0 = \{G_1, \ldots, G_n\}.$$

Clark observes that the ith step of the computation can be interpreted as attaching the goals in the body of D_i as immediate successors to the goal $\uparrow C_i$. These goals then become, together with those in the set $\downarrow C_i$, the goals in the set C_{i+1}. In this manner n trees are grown, each nonleaf node in which follows, by a single application of hyper-resolution, from its immediate successors (as minor premises) and some procedure clause in P (as major premise). Clark's interpretation is most illuminating, for it shows where the extraordinary freedom of the LUSH resolution scheme (to use any selection function whatsoever) comes from. It comes from the fact that it does not matter at all in what order the nodes of the n hyper-resolution trees are treated as these trees are grown.

Negation as failure. The preceding notes have dealt only with the pure Horn clause case of logic programming. In practice, one can work (as first explained in Clark [2]) with pseudo-Horn clauses by generalising the definition of Horn clauses in the following way. Instead of restricting the bodies to be sets of predications (= unnegated atomic sentences) we can allow them to be literals , that is, either predications or negated predications. However, both the definition of procedure clauses as having a head containing exactly one predication, and the definition of goal clauses as having an empty head, are retained. The basic computation cycle is then extended to deal with the case that the goal $\uparrow C_i$ can now be a negated predication, say, $\sim G$ (hence not unifiable with the head of any procedure clause).

If G is a ground expression an attempt is then made to prove the sequent $P \Rightarrow G$. This attempt can have three outcomes:

1. it can terminate with a proof, in which case $\sim G$ is "disproved" and C_i has no successors

2. it can terminate without finding a proof ("finite failure"), in which case ("negation by failure") $\sim G$ is "proved" and C_i has the successor $\downarrow C_i$

3. it can fail to terminate, in which case the attempt must be eventually aborted without any decision as to the provability of G from P.

Evidently, **1** assumes the simple consistency of P, while **2** assumes something like the completeness of P ("if G were true it would be provable from P") for ground literals. We cannot discuss further here this important and interesting topic, which is the subject of much current research. We refer the reader to Clark [2] and Lloyd [17] for further details.

References.

[1] Boyer, R.S. and Moore, J S.

The sharing of structure in theorem proving programs.

Machine Intelligence 7, Edinburgh University Press, 1972, 101 - 116.

[2] Clark, K.L.

Negation as failure.

In Logic and Databases, edited by Gallaire and Minker,

Plenum Press, 1978, 293 - 322.

[3] Clark, K.L.

Predicate logic as a computational formalism.

Ph.D. Thesis, Imperial College, London, 1979.

[4] Colmerauer, A., et al.

Un systeme de communication homme-machine en francais.

Groupe d'Intelligence Artificielle, U.E.R. de Luminy, Universite

d'Aix-Marseille, Luminy, 1972.

[5] Green, C.C.

Application of theorem proving to problem solving.

Proceedings of First InternationalJointConference on

Artificial Intelligence, Washington D.C., 1969, 219 - 239.

[6] Hill, R.

LUSH resolution and its completeness.

DCL Memo 78, University of Edinburgh Department

of Artificial Intelligence, August 1974.

[7] Huet, G.

Resolution d'equations dans les langages d'ordre 1, 2, . . . , ω.

These d'Etat, Universite Paris VII (1976).

[8] Kowalski, R.A.

Predicate logic as programming language.

Proceedings of IFIP Congress 1974, North Holland, 1974, 569 - 574.

[9] Knuth, D. E.

The Art of Computer Programming, Volume 1, Addison-Wesley 1969,
258 - 268.

[10] Martelli, A. and Montanari, U.

Unification in linear time and space.

Technical Report B76-16, University of Pisa, Italy, 1976.

[11] Paterson, M. S., and Wegman, M. N.

Linear unification. Journal of Computer and Systems Sciences
16, 1978, 158 - 167.

[12] Robinson, J. A.

A machine-oriented logic based on the resolution principle.

Journal of the Association for Comp[uting Machinery 12, 1965, 23 - 41.

[13] Robinson, J. A.

Automatic deduction with hyper-resolution.

International Journal of Computer Mathematics 1, 1965, 227 - 234.

[14] Tarjan, R. E.

Efficiency of a good but not linear set union algorithm.

Journal of the Association for Computing Machinery 22, 1975, 215 - 225.

[15] van Emden, M.H., and Kowalski, R.A.

      The semantics of predicate logic as a programming language.

      J.ournal of the Association for Computing Machinery 23, 1976, 733 - 742.

[16] Vitter, J. S., and Simmons, R. A.

      New classes for parallel complexity: a study of unification

      and other complete problems for *P.*

      I.E.E.E.Transactions on Computers, Vol C-35, May 1986, 403 - 417.

[17] Lloyd, J. W.

      Foundations of logic programming.

      Springer-Verlag, 1984.

C.A.R. Hoare

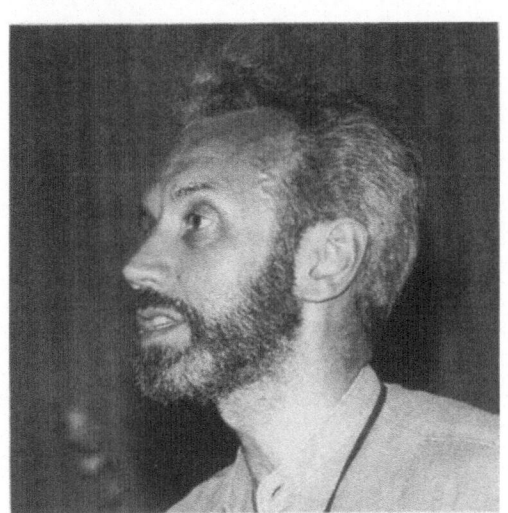

C.B. Jones

M. Broy

Part II

Specification and Verification Calculi

The specification, not only of programs, but also of problems and computation structures, is the basis of proper program design. The transition from an informal problem description to a formal one is a decisive step. It determines which aspects of the considered problem are to be represented and which may be neglected. A formal specification has to be validated to ensure that it fits the informally posed problem. Then a program has to be verified with respect to the formal specification to ensure its correctness. Both for the validation of specifications and for the verification of programs, rules are needed that form calculi for the specification and verification.

Program Specification and Verification in VDM

C.B. Jones
Department of Computer Science
Manchester University
M13 9PL, United Kingdom

Abstract

Formal methods employ mathematical notation in writing specifications and use mathematical reasoning in justifying designs with respect to such specifications. One avenue of formal methods research is known as the Vienna Development Method. *VDM* has been used on programming language and non-language applications. In this paper, programming languages and their compilers are ignored; the focus is on the specification and verification of programs.

VDM emphasizes the model-oriented approach to the specification of data. The reification of abstract objects to representations gives rise to proof obligations; one such set which has wide applicability assumes an increase in implementation bias during the design process. The incompleteness of this approach and an alternative set of rules are discussed.

The decision to show the input/output relation by post-conditions of two states is also a feature of *VDM*. In early publications, the proof obligations which support decomposition were poorly worked out; those presented below are as convenient to use as the original "Hoare-logic". Recent work on a logic (which is tailored to partial functions) is also described.

1 Introduction

The term "Formal Methods" applies to the use of mathematical notation in the specification, and the use of such specifications as a basis for the verified design, of computer systems. There are several more-or-less distinct approaches in use. The approach which matches normal software development practice most closely is to specify a task in a specification language; to record design decisions in languages which are close to the final implementation language; and to then generate and discharge consequent proof obligations.

A second approach (see, for example, [10]) is to make the starting point of the development a very clear description which can—possibly with very poor performance—be executed. Design steps then consist of transforming such a description into a "program" of acceptable efficiency.

The third general approach (see [11]) also begins with a specification but then provides a constructive proof of the existence of a result; from this proof a program can be extracted.

The so-called *Vienna Development Method* (*VDM*) subscribes to the first of these approaches. In [33] it is shown how specifications can be written using pre-/post-conditions which are truth-valued functions over state-like objects. Such states are models defined in terms of basic objects like sets. Design proceeds by *data reification* and *operation decomposition*.

Steps of data reification make the transition from abstract objects to objects which are representable in the chosen implementation language. Operation decomposition is the process of realizing implicit specifications by statements written in the programming language. For significant systems, several steps of both sorts of design step might be required.

NATO ASI Series, Vol. F36
Logic of Programming and Calculi of Discrete Design
Edited by M. Broy
© Springer-Verlag Berlin Heidelberg 1987

Either sort of design step gives rise to *proof obligations*. These are sequents which must be true for the design step to satisfy its specification. The required proofs can be conducted at an appropriate level of formality.

In the extreme, these proof obligations could be compared to the output of *verification condition generators* (VCG) (cf. [7]). The VCG approach has received considerable criticism because of the difficulty of relating the created logical expressions to the original programming task. This author's own experience both with hand proofs and with Jim King's *EFFIGY* system (cf. [18]) has confirmed the validity of this criticism. The attempt to prove a complete program correct using VCG's is like trying to solve equations in large numbers of variables— unfortunately, failure to find a proof corresponds to the lack of a solution and the ensuing hunt for alternative assertions is very tedious. How does *VDM* avoid this problem? The approach is to use the steps of development themselves as a way of decomposing the correctness argument. Well-chosen steps provide an informal proof outline of the type used by mathematicians. This reduces the need for formal proof. If it is decided to construct a formal proof, such a proof is likely to be relatively simple. Perhaps most importantly, any errors are relatively easy to locate. An essential property is "compositionality" in the development method. This point is discussed further below. It has been argued elsewhere (e.g. [32]) that this approach can increase the productivity of the development process by locating—soon after insertion—any errors which are made in the early stages of design.

This paper reviews some recent and on-going research relevant to formal methods like *VDM*. Sections 2 and 3 review, respectively, work on data reification and operation decomposition. The need to establish a logic which recognises the rôle of partial functions is reviewed in Section 4. A separate paper ([35]) discusses the form of support system which might help in the use of formal methods. The general direction of this work can be seen in [12,13]. (The *VDM* approach to language specification is not discussed in this paper. Interested readers are referred to [5].)

2 Data Reification

In order to achieve full advantage from the application of formal methods, it is necessary to apply them to the early stages of development. Clearly, this implies the construction of formal specifications. After that, one must ask: what activities are most common in the early (high-level) design stages? Typically the choice of data representations is made before detailed algorithm design. Thus *VDM* tends to put more emphasis on proof of data reification than on operation decomposition[1]. This section reviews the most straightforward rules for the justification of design steps of data reification, the shortcomings of these rules, and a new set of rules which are—in some sense—complete.

A specification in *VDM* normally consists of a set of states and a set of operations which rely on, and transform, these states. Operation specifications are discussed below; initially, attention is focussed on the objects which comprise the states.

Many computing applications need some form of access to data via a *Key*. A convenient *map* object is used in *VDM* which makes it possible to define:

Keyed = map *Key* to *Data*

with an initial object corresponding to the empty map[2]:

$m_0 = \{\,\}$

---

[1]It is an accident of history—reiterated, as Kuhn predicts, in many text books—that operation decomposition proofs were studied first: see, for example, [43].

[2]The identification of a set of initial states in [33] differs from [30] where initialising operations were used.

Such an abstraction is very convenient in the specification precisely because it hides all of the implementation problem. Clearly, the design process must choose—and justify—a representation.

One possible way of storing large volumes of keyed data is in a binary tree. Such a set of trees can be described by[3]:

$Bintree = [Binnode]$

$$Binnode :: \quad lt \ : \ Bintree$$
$$k \ : \ Key$$
$$d \ : \ Data$$
$$rt \ : \ Bintree$$

where:

$inv\text{-}Binnode(mk\text{-}Binnode(lt, k, d, rt)) \quad \triangle$
$\quad (\forall lk \in collkeys(lt) \cdot lk < k) \wedge (\forall rk \in collkeys(rt) \cdot k < rk)$

$collkeys : Bintree \rightarrow$ set of Key

$collkeys(t) \quad \triangle \quad$ cases t of
$$nil \rightarrow \{\,\}$$
$$mk\text{-}Binnode(lt, k, d, rt) \rightarrow collkeys(lt) \cup \{k\} \cup collkeys(rt)$$
end

The set of objects is considered to be restricted by the invariant[4]—thus:

$Binnode =$
$\quad \{ mk\text{-}Binnode(lt, k, d, rt) \mid$
$\quad\quad lt, rt \in Bintree \wedge k \in Key \wedge d \in Data \wedge inv\text{-}Binnode(mk\text{-}Binnode(lt, k, d, rt)) \}$

The initial object corresponds to the empty tree:

$t_0 = nil$

The representation, *Bintree*, must be related to the abstraction *Keyed*. In early work in Vienna this was normally done by a relation or (cf. [39]) by building up a combined state with an invariant to control the relationship to the *ghost variables*. During the late 60's, it was realized that a special case arose very often in design. It was noticed (cf. [26]) that a one-to-many relation often existed between elements of the abstraction and those of the representation. This was no accident. It is desirable to make states of specifications as abstract as possible; the structure of the implementation language (or machine) forces the introduction of extra information and redundancy; it is, therefore, very common that a one-to-many relationship arises[5]. Precisely this situation holds here. There are many possible tree representations of any (non-trivial) map

---

[3]The optional brackets define:

$\quad Bintree = Binnode \cup \{nil\}$

The "::" notation defines *Binnode* in terms of a constructor or projection function:

$\quad mk\text{-}Binnode: Bintree \times Key \times Data \times Bintree \rightarrow Binnode$

[4]This, more central, rôle for invariants is also a change from [30].

[5]In fact, this discussion gives rise to the notion of *bias* discussed in [29] where the avoidance of redundancy is taken as a test for the acceptability of a set of states to be used as the basis of a specification.

object. Both [24] and [26] relate the set of abstractions to their representations by a function from the latter to the former. Here they are called (following [28]) *retrieve functions* because they get back the abstract values from the representation details. For the example in hand:

$$retrm : Bintree \rightarrow Keyed$$

$retrm(t)$ $\triangleq$
    cases t of
$$nil \rightarrow \{\,\}$$
$$mk\text{-}Binnode(lt, k, d, rt) \rightarrow retrm(lt) \cup \{k \mapsto d\} \cup retrm(rt)$$
    end

In the set of rules used most commonly in *VDM*, such retrieve functions must be total. That this property is satisfied by *retrm* follows from the invariant which ensures that the domains of the maps to be united are disjoint. Another property required of the representation (strictly— with respect to the retrieve function) is *adequacy*: there must be at least one representation for each abstract element. For the case in hand:

$$\forall m \in Keyed \cdot \exists t \in Bintree \cdot retrm(t) = m$$

It is straightforward to prove this by induction on the domain of m. It is, in fact, worth providing a function which inserts *Key/Data* pairs into a tree (cf. *insb* below) and use this. In practice, it would be worth defining a number of functions and developing the *theory* of the data type. For example:

$$\forall t \in Bintree \cdot \mathsf{dom}\ retrm(t) = collkeys(t)$$

can be proved by structural induction on *Bintree*. One of the advantages of this set of proof rules is that they do isolate useful proof obligations about the state alone and, in practice, these proofs are a very useful check on a representation before proceeding to look at the individual operations. It is, however, also necessary to consider the operations. The initial states are trivially related:

$$retrm(t_0) = m_0$$

On *Keyed*, the insert operation is specified trivially:

$INSERT$ $(k\!:Key, d\!:Data)$
ext wr m : $Keyed$
pre $k \notin$ dom m
post $m = \overleftarrow{m} \cup \{k \mapsto d\}$

Such a specification[6] defines a partial and possibly non-deterministic state transformation. The pre-condition defines the set of states over which the implementor must make the operation terminate and yield a result which, together with the input state (variables decorated with backwards pointing hooks) must satisfy the post-condition[7].

---

[6] The rôle of the side effect on the external variables is emphasized in *VDM* by the presentation of operation specifications. The meaning is:

$INSERT\!:Key \times Data \times Keyed \rightarrow Keyed$
$\forall k \in Key, d \in Data, \overleftarrow{m} \in Keyed \cdot k \notin \mathsf{dom}\ \overleftarrow{m} \land INSERT(k, d, \overleftarrow{m}) = m \;\Rightarrow\; m = \overleftarrow{m} \cup \{k \mapsto d\}$

[7] During the Summer School, Bernard von Stengel pointed out that more expressive power could be achieved by adding the requirement that, if termination did occur even for states not satisfying the pre-condition, the results should still be constrained by the post-condition.

Such a specification should satisfy the *implementability* proof obligation, in this case:

$$\forall \overleftarrow{m} \in Keyed, k \in Key, d \in Data \cdot$$
$$pre\text{-}INSERT(k, d, \overleftarrow{m}) \;\Rightarrow\; \exists m \in Keyed \cdot post\text{-}INSERT(k, d, \overleftarrow{m}, m)$$

The corresponding operation on *Bintree* is defined:

$INSERT_B$ $(k: Key, d: Data)$

ext wr t : $Bintree$

pre $k \notin collkeys(t)$

post $t = insb(k, d, \overleftarrow{t})$

The auxiliary function is defined:

$insb$ $(k: Key, d: Data, t: Bintree)$ $r: Bintree$

pre $k \notin collkeys(t)$

$insb(k, d, t)$ $\triangle$

    cases t of

$$\text{nil} \rightarrow mk\text{-}Binnode(\text{nil}, k, d, \text{nil})$$

      $mk\text{-}Binnode(lt, mk, md, rt) \rightarrow$

          If $k < mk$

          then $mk\text{-}Binnode(insb(k, d, lt), mk, md, rt)$

          else $mk\text{-}Binnode(lt, mk, md, insb(k, d, rt))$

    end

The relevant proof obligations are:

$$\forall t \in Bintree \cdot pre\text{-}INSERT(k, d, retrm(t)) \;\Rightarrow\; pre\text{-}INSERT_B(k, d, t)$$

$$\forall \overleftarrow{t}, t \in Bintree \cdot pre\text{-}INSERT(k, d, retrm(\overleftarrow{t})) \wedge post\text{-}INSERT_B(k, d, \overleftarrow{t}, t) \;\Rightarrow$$
$$post\text{-}INSERT(k, d, retrm(\overleftarrow{t}), retrm(t))$$

The first of these requires that the domain of the operation on the representation is large enough; the second requires that the transition on the representation—when viewed under the retrieve function—nowhere contradicts the specification on the abstract states. Proofs of these results are straightforward—the first appeals to the lemma mentioned above.

These proof rules are more general than required for this situation but it should be remembered that the post-condition of $INSERT_B$ could have been:

$$retrm(t) = retrm(\overleftarrow{t}) \cup \{k \mapsto d\}$$

which is non-deterministic[8]. Furthermore, at the next stage of development, the operations on *Bintree* would play the part of the specification so the rules need to cater with partial, non-deterministic operations in both the specification and the representation[9].

The interest here, however, focuses on the *incompleteness* of the above rules. It was known at the time the rules were published in [30] that there were valid steps of development which

---

[8] This is illustrative of the way in which non-determinacy is most useful in the design process: with a deterministic specification, and the intention to design a deterministic program, non-determinism can be used to structure the design decisions (e.g. the more general *post-INSERT$_B$* could be used to reflect the fact that the precise tree balancing algorithm has not been chosen at this design step).

[9] A second step of development of the abstract *Bintree* objects onto Pascal records and pointers is given in [33].

they would not support. In particular, it was obvious that any step of development which reversed the normal one-to-many relationship between abstraction and representation (e.g. to have *Bintree* in the specification and *Keyed* in the design) could not be justified since a retrieve function could not be found. This restriction was viewed as a virtue in so far as it tended to minimize the danger of biased specifications. Lockwood Morris also pointed out a technical problem in the need to tighten invariants so as to fulfil the requirements on retrieve functions.

What has become apparent more recently is that there are perfectly good specifications for which valid implementations cannot be justified by the above set of rules. The essence of the problem is explained below—an example is presented first.

In her work (cf. [42]) on the specification of GKS, Lynn Marshall uncovered a situation where more information was needed in the specification state than in that of valid implementations: there is a need to place, in the state, information required only to express non-determinacy; an implementation which is constrained to a deterministic answer needs less information. A simple example (due to Ib Sørensen) of this situation results from the specification:

$$s_0 = \{\,\}$$

ARB () $r:\mathbf{N}$

ext wr s : set of $\mathbf{N}$

pre true

post $r \notin \overleftarrow{s} \land s = \overleftarrow{s} \cup \{r\}$

This requires that each invocation of the operation ARB returns a result which it has never returned before. The state is initialized to the empty set and ARB adds each element which it returns. This specification is (unboundedly!) non-deterministic. An implementation which simply returns the "next" natural number on each invocation violates none of the specified requirements—thus:

$$n_0 = 0$$

ARB_n () $r:\mathbf{N}$

ext wr n : $\mathbf{N}$

pre true

post $r = \overleftarrow{n} \land n = \overleftarrow{n} + 1$

Intuitively ARB_n is correct with respect to the specification ARB: it has the same domain and yields answers which do not contradict the specification. This notion of *satisfaction* can be formalised. An operation is defined by a pair:

$$(S, R)$$

where S is the set of states over which termination is guaranteed and R is the relation expressing the input/output relation[10]. There is a requirement that:

$$S \subseteq \text{dom } R$$

---

[10]There is not a requirement for bounded non-determinacy.

For a specification, the corresponding semantic object is[11]:

$$(\{\sigma \mid pre\text{-}OP(\sigma)\}, \{(\overleftarrow{\sigma}, \sigma) \mid post\text{-}OP(\overleftarrow{\sigma}, \sigma)\})$$

The formal notion of satisfaction is defined[12]:

$$(S_1, R_1) \text{ sat } (S_2, R_2) \triangleq S_2 \subseteq S_1 \wedge S_2 \lhd R_1 \subseteq R_2$$

That is (S_1, R_1) satisfies (S_2, R_2) iff the termination domain S_1 is at least as large as S_2 and the meaning relation R_1—restricted to the required termination set—nowhere contradicts R_2. Notice that sat is a partial order. Thus, with appropriate use of the retrieve function, it can be seen that ARB_n satisfies ARB but it cannot be proved by the rules used above for the development of *Bintree*. Were this the only sort of counter-example, it would be possible to introduce special steps of development for the situation where a reduction in non-determinacy reduces the complexity of states. There is, unfortunately, another class of counter-examples. The root of the further weakness discovered in the proof obligations used above for *Bintree* is that they were formulated around the aim of showing that each individual operation on the representation satisfied the corresponding abstract operation. This property is not necessary since it is the external behaviour of the collection of operations which needs to be preserved. Once this point is recognised it is a simple matter to generate further counter-examples.

The problems discussed above have been overcome by a rule which is based on a relation between the abstract and representation state spaces:

$$\_ \sqsubseteq \_ : Rep \times Abs \to \mathbf{B}$$

There are no proof obligations such as adequacy on $\sqsubseteq$; those for the operations are:

$$\forall a \in Abs, r \in Rep \cdot r \sqsubseteq a \wedge pre_A(a) \Rightarrow pre_R(r)$$

$$\forall \overleftarrow{a} \in Abs, \overleftarrow{r}, r \in Rep \cdot \overleftarrow{r} \sqsubseteq \overleftarrow{a} \wedge post_R(\overleftarrow{r}, r) \Rightarrow \exists a \in Abs \cdot post_A(\overleftarrow{a}, a) \wedge r \sqsubseteq a$$

It is possible to avoid the need for special rules on the initial states if an initialization operation is included which behaves like a (possibly non-deterministic) constant. The other omission from these rules is an assumption in the result rule of $pre_A(\overleftarrow{a})$. To see that this is not required, it is necessary to realize that the simulation relation ($\sqsubseteq$) need only involve those elements of *Abs* which are reachable by the operations[13].

Basically similar forms of this rule were found independently by Tobias Nipkow and researchers at the Programming Research Group in Oxford. This work led to joint discussions and is reported in [44], [45], [20] and [21].

The rule given here is certainly more powerful than that used above on the *Bintree* example. It is natural to question whether it is complete. Loosely what this amounts to is the question whether any correct data reification can be verified by the rule. But what is the independent notion of "correct"? If the behaviour of sequences of the operations is to be used in defining this notion, one approach is to define a language for combining operations. Issues such as the presence or absence of (angelic or otherwise) non-deterministic statements must be resolved. This linguistic approach is taken in [45] and the rule proven to be complete under suitable assumptions.

This then leaves the pedagogic question of which rule to teach (first). It is argued in [17] that their version of the above rule is easier to use; [33] takes a different view. It can be claimed

---

[11]The requirement corresponding to $S \subseteq \text{dom } R$ is referred to in [33] as the *implementability* proof obligation.

[12]$S \lhd R \triangleq \{(x, x') \in R \mid x \in S\}$

[13]The insertion of $pre_A(\overleftarrow{a})$ does however make the link to the **sat** relation above more obvious. This link can be seen simply by substituting the identity relation for $\sqsubseteq$; in the form present here, the identity must be suitably restricted.

that the avoidance of bias (cf. Section 9.1 of [33]) is an important objective in specifications and that this, combined with the use of proof obligations which avoid the need for existential quantifiers, justifies the use of the older ([30]) rule whenever it is applicable. Even the need to tighten invariants can be seen as an advantage in that it makes both the task of changing a specification safer and the range of potential representations clearer. A final argument in favour of the more restrictive rule is that the isolation of the adequacy proof obligation makes it possible to conduct a significant part of the verification work once (on the state) rather than delaying it to the (many) operation proofs.

3 Decomposition Rules with Input/Output Relations

The need to have post-conditions which relate final to initial states[14] is illustrated above by the choice of examples. It is such a natural way of thinking about the specification of a system that it comes as a surprise to notice that much of the work on program proofs uses post-conditions of the final state alone (cf. [23], [14], [16], [3] but not [25]). Since most computer programs are clearly written to transform a state, some way of describing the input/output relation must be found. One way of achieving this (cf. [16]) is to store the initial values of variables in the state. This would not always be acceptable in the final program but such variables can be marked as "ghost variables" and dropped once they have played their part in the proof. Strictly, this approach still needs a way of expressing the fact that these special variables cannot be changed during execution (cf. **glocon, glovar**, etc. in [14]). A second approach to the gap left by post-conditions having no direct way of referring to the initial state is to use free variables[15]. Unfortunately, the fact that such variables span more than one formula makes their treatment difficult.

A third approach to the gap is to govern the relationship by a free predicate symbol—thus, using the weakest precondition of [14]:

$$wp(GCD, p(x)) = p(gcd(x, y))$$

None of these methods is entirely satisfactory and this section presents proof obligations which directly handle post-conditions of two states[16].

Another issue which divides some specification methods from *VDM* is its separation of the pre-condition. It should be clear that (a form of) the pre-condition could be conjoined to the post-condition so as to yield a single predicate which comprises the whole specification of an operation. In *Z*, for example, there is one predicate to define an operation (cf. [19]). The decision to separate the pre- and post-conditions in *VDM*'s operation specification was initially motivated by purely pragmatic considerations. It does appear to be good discipline to make a distinction between the assumptions (that an implementor is invited to make) and the requirement that the (output of the created) program must satisfy. In many industrial specifications with which this author has had contact, the requirement was far better thought out than the assumption. Thus, it seems wise to put some focus on the pre-condition. It so happens that the separation of the pre-condition has a number of formal advantages including the rôle that pre-conditions play in the various data reification proof obligations.

What form are the proof rules for operation decomposition to have when post-conditions do relate final to initial states? Unfortunately, the proof obligations given in [30] are rather heavy. They do succeed in splitting the task of checking a decomposition step into small, separate,

---

[14]It must be conceded that the term "post-condition" is not well-chosen; its wide use, however, makes it preferable to the introduction of a new term like "input/output relation".

[15]These free variables can be made more apparent by selecting some special fount.

[16]The method used here should be compared with [49].

proof steps. But the rules are certainly not memorable. The suggestions made by Peter Aczel (cf. [2]), however, have led to rules which bear comparison with those in [23].

The process of operation decomposition also gives rise to proof obligations. There follows an explanation of the proof obligations and a style in which programs can be annotated with their correctness arguments. Ways in which the proof ideas can be used in the development of programs are discussed at the end of this section.

This section presents proof rules[17] only for some simple programming language constructs. The general form of these rules is similar to those of logic. Here, the conditions under which a rule can be applied require that certain properties hold for sub-operations and the conclusions are that (other) properties hold for combinations of the sub-operations. The proof rules facilitate proofs that pieces of program satisfy specifications. Thus it can be shown that:

If $i < 0$ then $i,j := -i, -j$ else skip

satisfies the specification:

$MAKEPOS$
ext wr $i: \mathbf{Z}$, wr $j: \mathbf{Z}$
pre true
post $0 \le i \wedge i * j = \overleftarrow{i} * \overleftarrow{j}$

For small examples, it is convenient to record the specification and its implementation together, thus:

$MAKEPOS$
ext wr $i: \mathbf{Z}$, wr $j: \mathbf{Z}$
pre true
If $i < 0$ then $i,j := -i, -j$ else skip
post $0 \le i \wedge i * j = \overleftarrow{i} * \overleftarrow{j}$

Such an annotated program is written when the code has been shown to satisfy the specification. The name of the operation and the externals line are sometimes omitted when they are clear from context.

A natural extension of this style is to write specifications for sub-operations—rather than their code; see Figure 1. This can be read as saying that the composition of two sub-operations $MAKEPOS$ and $POSMULT$ would satisfy the specification of $MULT$. The sub-operations are not (yet) coded—rather, their specifications are given[18]. The proof rule for sequential execution is discussed below.

When programs are presented in this way, the effect is intentionally similar to natural deduction proofs (cf. Section 4). There are, however, some important differences which are discussed below. The proof rules are somewhat similar to the deduction rules for logic. Broadly,

---

[17]It is, in part, the form of the proof rules used here which prompted the decision to mark initial values with a hook (rather than priming the final values) in post-conditions.

[18]A design can be presented as a combination of (specified) sub-problems. A *compositional* development method permits the verification of a design in terms of the specification of its (syntactic) sub-programs. Thus, one step of development is independent of subsequent steps in the sense that any implementation of a sub-program can be used to form the implementation of the specification which gave rise to the sub-specification. In a non-compositional development method, the correctness of one step of development might depend on the subsequent development of the sub-programs.

MULT
ext wr $i, j, m: \mathbf{Z}$
pre true
   MAKEPOS
   ext wr $i, j: \mathbf{Z}$
   pre true
   post $i \geq 0 \wedge i * j = \overleftarrow{i} * \overleftarrow{j}$

   ;
   POSMULT
   pre $i \geq 0$
   post $m = \overleftarrow{i} * \overleftarrow{j}$
post $m = \overleftarrow{i} * \overleftarrow{j}$

Figure 1: Example of Specifications in Place of Code

there is one proof rule for each language construct. In order to present the proof rules[19] in a compact way, the pre- and post-conditions are written in braces before and after the piece of code to which they relate—thus:

$$\{pre\} S \{post\}$$

It is sometimes necessary to use information from a pre-condition in the post-condition. Decorating P with a hook to denote a logical expression which is the same as P except that all free variables are decorated with a hook, the relevant proof rule is:

$$\frac{\{P\} S \{R\}}{\{P\} S \{\overleftarrow{P} \wedge R\}}$$

Thus, for example, from:

$$\{fn = 1\} FACTB \{fn = \overleftarrow{fn} * \overleftarrow{n}!\}$$

it follows that:

$$\{fn = 1\} FACTB \{fn = \overleftarrow{fn} * \overleftarrow{n}! \wedge \overleftarrow{fn} = 1\}$$

and thus:

$$\{fn = 1\} FACTB \{fn = \overleftarrow{n}!\}$$

Notice that the hooking of P (and thus its free variables) is crucial—it is not true that, in the final state:

$$fn = 1$$

---

[19]Readers who are familiar with the original form of Hoare-logic should be reassured that the assertions written here are for total correctness: termination is required for all states satisfying *pre*.

The most basic way of combining two operations is to execute them in sequence. It would be reasonable to expect that the first operation must leave the state so that the pre-condition of the second operation is satisfied. In order to write this, a distinction must be made between the relational and single-state properties guaranteed by the first statement. The names of the truth-valued functions have been chosen as a reminder of the distinction between:

$$P: \Sigma \to \mathbf{B}$$
$$R: \Sigma \times \Sigma \to \mathbf{B}$$

Writing:

$$R_1 \mid R_2$$

for[20]:

$$\exists \sigma_i \cdot R_1(\overleftarrow{\sigma}, \sigma_i) \wedge R_2(\sigma_i, \sigma)$$

the sequence rule is:

$$\frac{\{P_1\}S_1\{P_2 \wedge R_1\}, \; \{P_2\}S_2\{R_2\}}{\{P_1\}S_1; S_2\{R_1 \mid R_2\}}$$

The predicate P_2 can be seen as the designer's choice of interface between S_1 and S_2 whereas R_1 and R_2 fix the functionality of the two components.

Referring to Figure 1, the first conjunct of *post-MAKEPOS* is also seen in *pre-POSMULT*: this defines the interface between the two (as yet to be coded) components. The condition given as *post-POSMULT* is the same as *post-MULT* but the position of the former shows that its hooked variables refer to values which will arise between the execution of *MAKEPOS* and *POSMULT*. The second conjunct of *post-MAKEPOS* is the simplest expression (for R_1 in the rule) which ensures that *post-MULT* is satisfied—in detail, *post-MAKEPOS* can be written as:

$$post\text{-}MAKEPOS(\overleftarrow{i}, \overleftarrow{j}, \overleftarrow{m}, i, j, m) \;\; \triangleq \;\; i * j = \overleftarrow{i} * \overleftarrow{j} \wedge m = \overleftarrow{m}$$

(The non-appearance of m in the external clause of *MAKEPOS* justifies the second conjunct.) Also:

$$post\text{-}POSMULT(\overleftarrow{i}, \overleftarrow{j}, \overleftarrow{m}, i, j, m) \;\; \triangleq \;\; m = \overleftarrow{i} * \overleftarrow{j}$$

Thus:

$$post\text{-}MAKEPOS \mid post\text{-}POSMULT$$

becomes:

$$\exists i_i, j_i, m_i \cdot i_i * j_i = \overleftarrow{i} * \overleftarrow{j} \wedge m_i = \overleftarrow{m} \wedge m = i_i * j_i$$

from which:

$$m = \overleftarrow{i} * \overleftarrow{j}$$

---

[20]This is, of course, familiar relational composition. The reason that this does not imply "angelic non-determinism" is the assumption (implementability) given above on pre/post pairs.

follows.

In practice, it is not normally necessary to proceed formally with such proofs. It becomes rather easy to check an annotated text like that for *MULT*. The only care required is the association of the hooked variables with the values at the beginning of the appropriate operation. A good visual check is given by the nesting. (The generalization to a sequence of more than two statements is straightforward.)

The proof rule for conditional statements is:

$$\frac{\{P \wedge B\} TH \{R\}, \ \{P \wedge \neg B\} EL \{R\}}{\{P\} \text{ if } B \text{ then } TH \text{ else } EL \{R\}}$$

Looking at this proof rule, it would appear that the designer has little freedom of choice other than the selection of cases. Consideration of even a simple case—again taken from the multiplication example—shows how the designer's freedom actually arises:

$MAKEPOS$
ext wr $i, j : \mathbf{Z}$
pre true
    if $i < 0$
    then   pre $i < 0$
                post $0 \leq i \wedge i = - \overleftarrow{i} \wedge j = - \overleftarrow{j}$
    else   pre $0 \leq i$
                post $0 \leq i \wedge i = \overleftarrow{i} \wedge j = \overleftarrow{j}$
post $0 \leq i \wedge i * j = \overleftarrow{i} * \overleftarrow{j}$

Formally, this argument is also using a rule which permits the use of (stronger pre-conditions or) weaker post-conditions:

$$\frac{PP \Rightarrow P, \ \{P\} S \{RR\}, \ RR \Rightarrow R}{\{PP\} S \{R\}}$$

The post-conditions of the two statements imbedded within the conditional have been chosen to express the intentions of the designer rather than just being copies of *post-MAKEPOS*. In this way—on a problem of greater size—the designer decouples the design of sub-components from their context.

The proof obligation for iteration—as would be expected—is the most interesting. The general form is:

$$\frac{\{P \wedge B\} S \{P \wedge R\}}{\{P\} \text{ while } B \text{ do } S \{P \wedge \neg B \wedge R^*\}}$$

R is required to be well-founded and transitive. The logical expression R is irreflexive, for example:

$$x < \overleftarrow{x}$$

Since the body of the loop might not be executed at all, the state might not be changed by the while loop. Thus the overall post-condition can (only) assume R^* which is the reflexive closure of R—for example:

$$x \leq \overleftarrow{x}$$

There is a significant advantage in requiring that R be well-founded (and thus irreflexive) since the above proof obligation then establishes termination. The rest of this rule is easy to understand. The expression P is an invariant which is true after any number (including zero) of iterations of the loop body. This is, in fact, just a special use of a data type invariant. (Notice that such an invariant could fail to be satisfied within the body of the loop.) The falseness of B after the loop follows immediately from the meaning of the loop construct[21]. Returning again to the multiplication example, $POSMULT$ might be implemented as in Figure 2. The reader should check carefully how the terms in these logical expressions relate to the proof rule. Notice that rel is well-founded, since i is always positive and cannot be decreased indefinitely (cf. Inv).

$POSMULT$
ext wr $i, m : \mathbf{Z},$ rd $j : \mathbf{Z}$
pre $0 \leq i$
$\quad m := 0$
$\quad ;$
$\quad$ pre $0 \leq i$
$\quad\quad$ while $i \neq 0$ do
$\quad\quad$ Inv $0 \leq i$
$\quad\quad\quad i := i - 1;$
$\quad\quad\quad m := m + j;$

$\quad\quad$ rel $m = \overleftarrow{m} + (\overleftarrow{i} - i) * \overleftarrow{j} \wedge i < \overleftarrow{i}$
$\quad$ post $m = \overleftarrow{m} + \overleftarrow{i} * \overleftarrow{j}$
post $m = \overleftarrow{i} * \overleftarrow{j}$

Figure 2: Development for Multiplication Example

The implementation in Figure 2 is slow in that it is linear in the value of i. Using the ability of a binary computer to detect the difference between even and odd numbers (by checking the least significant bit) and to multiply or divide by two (by shifting), an algorithm which takes time proportional to the logarithm (base 2) of i is shown in Figure 3. The outer loop of these two algorithms is the same. Notice, however, that the externals clause of $POSMULT$ has been modified to permit the necessary assignments to j; the rel clause of the loop has also been changed to cater for the more general case[22]. In both cases the relation is transitive.

The comparison is made above between annotated program texts and natural deduction proofs. Although this similarity can be useful, it is important to notice the differences. In the program texts, the same expression denotes different things in different places. The effect of assignment statements is to destroy so-called "referential transparency". It is therefore *not* possible to simply refer to any earlier line in a text in the same way as is done in natural deduction proofs.

It would be reasonable, at this point, to ask how the Inv/rel expressions are discovered. The discovery of proofs from code is not the main objective, and this discussion is avoided. It is, however, possible to observe that the proof step is, in some sense, the inverse of the program design activity. As such it serves as a check in the same way that differentiation of an expression derived by integration is a standard check in the infinitesimal calculus.

---

[21] The proof rule here and its use of R can be compared with the "decreasing function" in [14]—there it is used only in the termination proof. (This function is called a "variant" in [22].)

[22] A comparison of these two predicates is actually quite interesting. The earlier one shows directly the remaining work to be done; the latter predicate shows an expression whose value is to be kept constant.

POSMULT
ext wr $i, j, m: \mathbf{Z}$
pre $0 \leq i$
   $m := 0$
   ;
   pre $0 \leq i$
      while $i \neq 0$ do
      inv $0 \leq i$
         ext wr $i, j: \mathbf{Z}$
         pre $i \neq 0$
            while *is-even*(i) do
            inv $1 \leq i$
               $i := i/2$
               $j := j * 2$

            rel $i * j = \overleftarrow{i} * \overleftarrow{j} \wedge i < \overleftarrow{i}$
         post $i * j = \overleftarrow{i} * \overleftarrow{j} \wedge i \leq \overleftarrow{i}$
         ;
         $m := m + j$;
         $i := i - 1$

      rel $m + i * j = \overleftarrow{m} + \overleftarrow{i} * \overleftarrow{j} \wedge i < \overleftarrow{i}$
    post $m = \overleftarrow{m} + \overleftarrow{i} * \overleftarrow{j}$
post $m = \overleftarrow{i} * \overleftarrow{j}$

Figure 3: Alternative Development for Multiplication Example

It is now shown how the proof obligations for programming constructs can be used to stimulate program design steps. It is, however, important that one does not expect too much from this idea. Design requires intuition and cannot, in general, be automated. What is offered is a framework into which the designer's commitments can be placed. If done with care, the verification then represents almost no extra burden. Even so, false steps of design cannot be avoided in the sense that even a verified decision can lead to a blind alley (e.g. a decomposition which has unacceptable performance implications). If this happens, there is no choice but to reconsider the design decision which led to the problem. A mould is being given into which a design explanation can be fitted; it aims only to show that the need for verification can also help the design process.

An obvious example of the way in which a proof rule can help a designer's thoughts about decomposition is given by the rule for sequential composition—the assertion P_2 fixes an interface between the two sub-operations. There are advantages in not making such interfaces unnecessarily restrictive. The choice of a general pre-condition for the second operation can result in the specification—and eventual implementation—of a piece of software which is applicable outside the context of the first operation. Such meaningful decompositions are to be sought in all designs.

The design problems presented by iterative constructs are more interesting. Here, judicious use of the rel/inv clauses can lead to the specification of the loop body. In fact, two different approaches to the problem of design can be illustrated on the simple example of computing (general) addition by successor. The first of these programs in its annotated form is[23]:

pre $j \geq 0$
   $t := 0; r := i$
   ;
   pre $t \leq j \wedge r = i + t$
      while $t \neq j$ do
      inv $t \leq j \wedge r = i + t$
         $t := t + 1;$
         $r := r + 1$
     rel $\overleftarrow{t} < t \wedge i = \overleftarrow{i} \wedge j = \overleftarrow{j}$
   post $r = \overleftarrow{i} + \overleftarrow{j}$
post $r = \overleftarrow{i} + \overleftarrow{j}$

The overall post-condition here is

$$r = \overleftarrow{i} + \overleftarrow{j}$$

The design decisions to not change i and j and to introduce a temporary variable (t) suggests an invariant (inv):

$$r = i + t$$

to express the progress of the calculation. This easy to establish by initialization. This only leaves, for the relation (rel), the establishment of termination (the relation must be well-founded) and the preservation of the initial values. It is obvious that this relation is transitive. (Strictly in a subsequent step of development) the assignment statements in the body of the loop can be seen to preserve the invariant and to satisfy the relation.

A different program which satisfies the same overall specification is:

---

[23]These should really be presented in a step-by-step design but their size is such that this is a waste of space.

```
pre j ≥ 0
   r := i
   ;
   pre 0 ≤ j
      while j ≠ 0 do
      Inv 0 ≤ j
         j := j − 1;
         r := r + 1
      rel r = ⃖r + ⃖j − j ∧ j < ⃖j
   post r = ⃖r + ⃖j
post r = ⃖i + ⃖j
```

In this program, the decision to avoid a temporary variable gives rise to a different pattern. The initialization does not obviously establish an invariant which relates the variables. The plan to reduce j suggests something like:

$$r = i + (\overleftarrow{j} - j)$$

but this is not an expression in a single state. However, rel does not have to be: it reflects the work which remains to be done. This time the invariant is simpler because it only serves as a data type invariant (which plays a part in checking that rel is well-founded).

The following table attempts to capture the main differences between loops which work "up" using temporary variables and those which work "down" avoiding temporaries[24].

	"up"	"down"
	compute the required function of temporary variables	eliminate work "remaining" at each iteration
temporaries	yes	no
initialization	temporaries and results set to "zero"	reflect whole task as "remaining"
initial state	undisturbed	changed
Inv	locals = f (temporaries)	data type invariant (only)
rel	current = initial temporaries decreased	f(current) = f(initial) distances to intial decreased
loop test	temporary = some initial	test for "zero"

The two approaches to the task of computing factorial yields a similar analysis of the assertions. The overall post-condition is:

$$fn = \overleftarrow{n}\,!$$

Taking this as an invariant of the temporary variable leaves only the preservation of n and well-foundedness for rel—see Figure 4. The body of the loop can be completed with the assignments shown.

With the version of the program which does not have a temporary variable, the factorial is computed backwards $(n * (n - 1) * \ldots)$. This is done by overwriting the value in n, and rel captures this with an expression equivalent to:

$$fn * n! = \overleftarrow{fn} * \overleftarrow{n}\,!$$

pre $0 \leq n$

  $fn := 1; t := 0$

  ;

  pre $t \leq n \wedge fn = t!$

    while $t \neq n$ do

    inv $t \leq n \wedge fn = t!$

      $t := t + 1; fn := fn * t$

    rel $n = \overleftarrow{n} \wedge \overleftarrow{t} < t$

  post $fn = t! \wedge t = n = \overleftarrow{n}$

post $fn = \overleftarrow{n}\,!$

Figure 4: Development of Factorial

pre $0 \leq n$

  $fn := 1$

  ;

  pre $0 \leq n$

    while $n \neq 0$ do

    inv $0 \leq n$

      $fn, n := fn * n, n - 1$

    rel $fn = \overleftarrow{fn} * \overleftarrow{n}\,!/n! \wedge n < \overleftarrow{n}$

  post $fn = \overleftarrow{fn} * \overleftarrow{n}\,!$

post $fn = \overleftarrow{n}\,!$

Figure 5: Alternative Development of Factorial

pre $j \neq 0$

  $q := 0$

  ;

  pre true

    while $i \geq j$ do

    inv true

      $i, q := i - j, q + 1$

    rel $j = \overleftarrow{j} \wedge i < \overleftarrow{i} \wedge j * q + i = \overleftarrow{j} * \overleftarrow{q} + \overleftarrow{i}$

  post $\overleftarrow{j} * (q - \overleftarrow{q}) + i = \overleftarrow{i} \wedge i < \overleftarrow{j}$

post $\overleftarrow{j} * q + i = \overleftarrow{i} \wedge i < \overleftarrow{j}$

Figure 6: Development of Integer Division Algorithm

This gives rise to the development shown in Figure 5.

A straightforward development of an integer division algorithm which does overwrite its initial values is shown in Figure 6. As an illustration of a more interesting problem, consider describing how a mechanical calculator performs the same task. In a first stage (SL), j is shifted left until it is larger than i—the number of shifts is recorded in n. The second stage (SR) shifts j back and at each step keeps the expression $j * q + i$ constant. There are two places this must be done: shifting at SRS and re-establishing $i < j$ by stepping down i at SRC. The presentation in Figure 7 is made simpler by assuming that all variables are natural numbers.

pre $j \neq 0$

    pre $j \neq 0$ $\{SL\}$

        ext rd i, wr j, q, n

        $n := 0$;

        while $j \leq i$ do

        Inv true

            $j, n := j * 10, n + 1$

        rel $j * 10^{\overleftarrow{n}} = \overleftarrow{j} * 10^n \wedge j > \overleftarrow{j}$

    post $j = \overleftarrow{j} * 10^n \wedge i < j$

    ; $q := 0$;

    pre 10^n divides $j \wedge i < j$ $\{SR\}$

        while $n \neq 0$ do

        Inv 10^n divides $j \wedge i < j$

            $n, j, q := n - 1, j/10, q * 10$; $\{SRS\}$

            while $j \leq i$ $\{SRC\}$ext wr i, q, rd j

            Inv $(0 \leq i)$

                $i, q := i - j, q + 1$

            rel $\overleftarrow{j} * \overleftarrow{q} + \overleftarrow{i} = j * q + i \wedge i < \overleftarrow{i}$

        rel $j/10^n = \overleftarrow{j}/10^{\overleftarrow{n}} \wedge j * q + i = \overleftarrow{j} * \overleftarrow{q} + \overleftarrow{i} \wedge n < \overleftarrow{n}$

    post $j = \overleftarrow{j}/10^{\overleftarrow{n}} \wedge j * q + i = \overleftarrow{j} * \overleftarrow{q} + \overleftarrow{i} \wedge i < j$

post $\overleftarrow{j} * q + i = \overleftarrow{i} \wedge i < \overleftarrow{j}$

Figure 7: Development of Alternative Integer Division Algorithm

---

[24]It would be interesting to try to present these strategies in the "d-Calculus" proposed by Michel Sintzoff elsewhere in these proceedings.

Programs for searching and sorting (cf. [36]) provide many interesting examples for proof construction. In the case of searching, the basic vector involved is not changed and proofs using input/output relations differ little from those which use post-conditions of the final state alone. The utility of the more general post-conditions becomes apparent on sorting examples where the basic vector is changed[25]. Consider the following specification:

$SORT$ ()

ext wr l : seq of $\mathbf{N}$

post $is\text{-}ord(l) \wedge is\text{-}perm(l, \overleftarrow{l})$

The truth-valued function for ordering:

$is\text{-}ord$: seq of $\mathbf{N} \to \mathbf{B}$

and that for permutations:

$is\text{-}perm$: seq of $\mathbf{N} \times$ seq of $\mathbf{N} \to \mathbf{B}$

are obvious (although it might be interesting to define the latter via its properties rather than directly).

A very simple sorting strategy is to absorb, at each iteration of the loop, the "next" element into its correct position. This design decision can be shown by:

$SORT$
var i: $\mathbf{N}$
$i := 1$;
while $i \neq n$ do
inv $is\text{-}ord(l(1, \ldots, i))$
$\quad i := i + 1$
$\quad ;$
$\quad BODY(i)$
pre $i \in$ dom l
post $l(i+1, \ldots) = \overleftarrow{l}(i+1, \ldots) \wedge$
$\quad\quad \exists j \in \{1, \ldots, i\} \cdot$
$\quad\quad\quad l(j) = \overleftarrow{l}(i) \wedge \overleftarrow{l}(1, \ldots, i-1) = del(l(1, \ldots, i), j)$
rel $is\text{-}perm(l, \overleftarrow{l})$
post $is\text{-}ord(l) \wedge is\text{-}perm(l, \overleftarrow{l})$

An equally simple (and similarly inefficient) sorting algorithm is one which picks the lowest of the remaining elements and moves it to the next position on each iteration. The additional property is clearly shown in the following invariant:

---

[25]During the Summer School, Jon Garnsworthy pointed out that the same problem arises in the so-called "Dutch National Flag" problem—cf. [14].

SORT

var $i : \mathbf{N}$

$i := 0;$

whlle $i \neq n - 1$ do

Inv $is\text{-}ord(l(1, \ldots, i)) \wedge$
$$\forall m \in \{1, \ldots, i\}, n \in \{i + 1, \ldots\} \cdot l(m) \leq l(n)$$

$i := i + 1$

;

$BODY(i)$

pre $i \in \text{dom } l$

post $l(1, \ldots, i - 1) = \overleftarrow{l}(1, \ldots, i - 1) \wedge$
$$\exists j \in \{i, \ldots\} \cdot$$
$$l(i) = \overleftarrow{l}(j) \wedge l(i + 1, \ldots) = del(\overleftarrow{l}(i, \ldots), j)$$

rel $is\text{-}perm(l, \overleftarrow{l})$

post $is\text{-}ord(l) \wedge is\text{-}perm(l, \overleftarrow{l})$

A comparison of *post-BODY* in the two cases shows the essence of the work to be performed. The development of more efficient algorithms is left as an exercise to the interested reader.

This section should have established that post-conditions of two states (input-output relations) can be profitably used in program design. The proof rules shown above[26] are only slightly more complicated than those in [23] and the examples here have shown that the separation of, for example, invariants and relations can actually aid the design process. (Although the rules in [30] are heavy, it is interesting to see how they can be used as a useful check list in design.)

Several recent papers have attempted to show how programming and specification notation can be merged by translating the former into predicates (see, for example, [25,22,1]). In [25] a motivation is provided for the idea of "weakest pre-specification". The ordering corresponding to sat above is relational containment and does not cope with termination as here. The paper by Eric Hehner in these proceedings manages to use an implication ordering on predicates in a way which gives very attractive properties. The single predicate is formed, essentially, by an expression of the form:

pre $\Rightarrow$ post

As such, the definition is very similar to that used in this paper. Apart from the pragmatic arguments for separating the pre-condition, the system used here does allow additional distinctions to be made between specifications. In both [25] and [22], the basic definitions are used to derive convenient algebraic laws for programming constructs. The presence of these laws blurs the distinction made in the introduction to this paper between the transformational and specify/design/verify approaches to program development.

4 Logic for Partial Functions

One area of *VDM* research which has recently made some progress is the choice of a logic which handles partial expressions in a convenient way. Such partial expressions arise naturally in the specification and design of programs but earlier treatments have not been fully successful. As well as reviewing the sources of partial expressions, this section offers some requirements for an appropriate logic and compares the proposal in [4], [8] with the requirements.

---

[26]The proof rules presented above can be justified with respect to a denotational semantics of the programming language in question. For the whlle construct, this is done in Appendix A along with other consequences of the definitions.

Many of the operators on the basic *VDM* data types are partial (e.g. hd, map application). They arise in expressions like:

$$t = [\,] \vee t = append(\text{hd } t, \text{tl } t)$$

if ρ is a member of map *Id* to *Den*:

$$id \in \text{dom } \rho \wedge \rho(id) \in Proctype$$

The fact that the operators are partial gives rise to terms which may fail to denote a value. Another obvious source of partial terms is recursion—for example:

$$subp : \mathbf{N} \times \mathbf{N} \to \mathbf{N}$$

$$subp(i,j) \quad \triangleq \quad \text{if } i = j \text{ then } 0 \text{ else } subp(i, j+1) + 1$$

Providing that $i \geq j$, this function yields a defined result. This prompts the writing of expressions like:

$$\forall i, j \in \mathbf{N} \cdot i \geq j \;\Rightarrow\; subp(i,j) = i - j$$

It can clearly be seen how the problem of undefined terms propagates up to the meaning of the logical operators: what does this last expression mean when the antecedent of the implication is false?

There have been a number of historical approaches to this problem. John McCarthy showed how logical expressions could be defined by conditionals ([41])—for example:

$$p \wedge q$$

is defined as:

If p then q else false

Operators defined in this way are obviously not commutative. Thus VDL's (cf. [40]) adoption of such a set of operators led to a logic in which familiar properties do not hold. This was unfortunate because many of the operands were completely defined and proofs were hamstrung unnecessarily.

In [27] and [14][27], a distinction is made between the conditional (cand, cor) and the classical (and, or) operators. Unfortunately, neither reference offers an axiomatization of the logic and there are some slightly messy properties. For example, while it is obvious that:

$$\neg(E_1 \underline{or} (E_2 \underline{cand} E_3)), \neg E_1 \underline{and} (\neg E_2 \underline{cor} \neg E_3)$$

are equivalent, it is perhaps less obvious that:

$$E_1 \underline{and} (\neg E_1 \underline{cor} E_2), E_1 \underline{cand} E_2$$

are equivalent.

In [30] an attempt was made to limit variables by bounded quantifiers as a way of avoiding undefined terms—for example:

$$is\text{-}ordered : \text{seq of } \mathbf{N} \to \mathbf{B}$$

$$is\text{-}ordered(t) \quad \triangleq \quad \forall i \in \{1, \ldots, \text{len } t - 1\} \cdot t(i) \leq t(i+1)$$

Figure 8: Ordering for Truth Values

This does not always work and in other places explicit conditional expressions were written. None of these approaches is satisfactory when judged against the following criteria:

- Both a model and a proof theory should be given and the latter should be proved consistent and complete with respect to the former.

- There should be clear links to classical logic—for example:

  - The proof rules should be consistent with classical logic;
  - conjunction and disjunction should be commutative;
  - most standard laws of logic should hold;
  - and there should be a clear way of building a link to those which do not hold;
  - familiar operators should be monotone with respect to the ordering in Figure 8;
  - implication should fit the standard abbreviation($p \Rightarrow q$ as $\neg p \vee q$).

- If there is a need for non-classical, non-monotonic operators, their use should be localized and not inflicted on the developer of standard programs;

- It should be possible to prove results about functions (e.g. *subp*) without a separate proof of definedness of terms[28].

The model theory of [4] is summarized in the following truth tables in which $*$ is used to denote a missing value. The extended truth table for disjunction is:

$\vee$	true	$*$	false
true	true	true	true
$*$	true	$*$	$*$
false	true	$*$	false

Notice that the truth table is symmetrical, as also is that for conjunction:

$\wedge$	true	$*$	false
true	true	$*$	false
$*$	$*$	$*$	false
false	false	false	false

The table for negation is:

---

[27]The notation of the latter is used here since it is more widely known.

[28]This requirement was added after several proposals (e.g. Manfred Broy's proposals elsewhere in these proceedings which do require such a separation) were made at the Summer School.

¬	
true	false
*	*
false	true

The truth tables for implication and equivalence are derived by viewing them as the normal abbreviations:

⇒	true	*	false
true	true	*	false
*	true	*	*
false	true	true	true

⇔	true	*	false
true	true	*	false
*	*	*	*
false	false	*	true

The proof rules for this logic (derived from [37]) are presented in a way which is intended to be used in (linear-style) natural deduction proofs. The proof rules support the deduction of sequents of the form:

$$\Gamma \vdash E$$

where Γ is a list of expressions. The intended interpretation of such sequents is that E should be true in all worlds where all of the expressions in Γ are true. Notice that the sequent:

$$E_1 \vdash E_2$$

is valid if E_1 is false or undefined, whatever the value of E_2.

For the basic propositional operators ($\neg$, $\vee$) there are the obvious introduction and elimination rules. In addition, it is necessary to have rules for negated disjunctions (i.e. $\neg\vee$-I). The need for these rules arises from the fact that the "law of the excluded middle" does not hold in this logic. (All of the rules are given in Appendix B.) Conjunction and implication are introduced by definitions and their introduction and elimination rules are proved as derived results. An example of a natural deduction proof using these rules to show:

$$(E_1 \vee E_2) \wedge (E_1 \vee E_3) \vdash E_1 \vee E_2 \wedge E_3$$

is given in [34][29]. This proof would be valid in classical logic whereas the normal proof written in classical logic (cf. [16]) is not valid here because it uses the "law of the excluded middle".

The axiomatization of the predicate calculus follows a similar pattern with the existential quantifier being treated as basic and the universal quantifier being introduced as an abbreviation for which inference rules have to be derived (cf. Appendix B). The main point with this treatment is to constrain the bound variable of a quantified expression to range only over "proper elements"[30].

The basic characterization of sets like the natural numbers is given by constructor functions:

$$0 : \mathbf{N}$$
$$succ : \mathbf{N} \to \mathbf{N}$$

---

[29] The functional style of the justifications permits compositions of steps to be used—the whole style is very much in the spirit of the "d-Calculus" proposed by Michel Sintzoff elsewhere in these proceedings.

[30] Considerable effort has been put into the development of derived rules for this version of logic. Many of the proofs are contained in [34].

and an induction axiom:

$$\text{N-ind} \qquad \frac{p(0); \ n \in \mathbf{N}, p(n) \vdash p(n+1)}{n \in \mathbf{N} \vdash p(n)}$$

Notice that the induction rule is presented via a turnstile rather than using implication. This simplifies subsequent proofs because it avoids the need to use the $\Rightarrow$-I rule. The induction rule is also presented without quantifiers which can be inserted using the $\forall$-I rule.

For recursively defined types such as *Binnode* an induction rule is generated for each type, thus for:

$$\begin{aligned}
Binnode \ :: \ & lt \ : \ [Binnode] \\
& k \ : \ Key \\
& d \ : \ Data \\
& rt \ : \ [Binnode]
\end{aligned}$$

the induction rule is:

$$Binnode\text{-ind} \qquad \frac{\begin{array}{c} p(\text{nil}); \\ k \in \mathbf{N}, d \in Data, lt, rt \in Binnode, p(lt), p(rt) \vdash \\ p(mk\text{-}Binnode(lt, k, d, rt)) \end{array}}{bn \in Binnode \vdash p(bn)}$$

The requirement to minimize the use of non-monotonic operators has proved the most elusive and several attempts have been made in order to minimize the occurrence of undefined values or non-monotonic operators in normal proofs. The approach in [4] was to handle definitions like that for *subp* by generating inference rules of the form:

$$d_b \qquad \frac{}{subp(n, n) = 0}$$

$$d_i \qquad \frac{n_1 \neq n_2; \ subp(n_1, n_2 + 1) = n_3}{subp(n_1, n_2) = n_3 + 1}$$

The reason that this works revolves around the distinction between strong ($==$) and weak ($=$) equality and, in particular, the use of the latter in the hypothesis of d_i (rule d_i relies on the fact that the second hypothesis is undefined in exactly the cases needed to avoid relying on the conclusion of the rule). The differences between the strict weak equality and the non-monotonic strong equality can be seen from the following tables (here, the undefined values are shown as "bottom" elements ($\perp$)).

$=$	0	1	2	$\ldots$	$\perp_\mathbf{N}$
0	true	false	false		$\perp_\mathbf{B}$
1	false	true	false		$\perp_\mathbf{B}$
2	false	false	true		$\perp_\mathbf{B}$
$\ldots$					
$\perp_\mathbf{N}$	$\perp_\mathbf{B}$	$\perp_\mathbf{B}$	$\perp_\mathbf{B}$		$\perp_\mathbf{B}$

$==$	0	1	2	$\ldots$	$\perp_\mathbf{N}$
0	true	false	false		false
1	false	true	false		false
2	false	false	true		false
$\ldots$					
$\perp_\mathbf{N}$	false	false	false		true

The justification of such rules (with respect to the definition of *subp*) does require the use of—and reasoning about—strong equality; but the proof of the appropriate property in the referenced paper only uses the rules d_b and d_i.

In [33] a slightly different approach is used which obviates the need to create the inference rules. The idea is to use definition rules in direct substitutions (cf. $=$-*subs*, $\triangle$-*subs*, if-*subs*). This permits proofs to avoid mentioning undefined values. The only non-obvious step in devising the proof shown in Figure 9 was deciding to conduct the main induction on $subp(i, i - n)$.

	from $i, j \in \mathbf{N}$	
1	$i - 0 = i \in \mathbf{N}$	h,N
2	$subp(i, i - 0) = 0$	ifth-subs/$subp$(h,1)
3	$0 \leq i \ \Rightarrow \ subp(i, i - 0) = 0$	vac $\Rightarrow$ -I(2)
4	from $n \in \mathbf{N};\ n \leq i \ \Rightarrow \ subp(i, i - n) = n$	
4.1	from $n + 1 \leq i$	
4.1.1	$n \leq i$	h4.1, N
4.1.2	$subp(i, i - n) = n$	vac $\Rightarrow$ -E(h4,4.1.1)
4.1.3	$i \neq i - (n + 1)$	N, h4
4.1.4	$n + 1 = n + 1$	=-term(h4, N)
4.1.5	$subp(i, i - n) + 1 = n + 1$	=t-subs(4.1.2, 4.1.4)
	Infer $subp(i, i - (n + 1)) = n + 1$	ifel-subs/$subp$(h,4.1.3,4.1.5)
4.2	$(n + 1 \leq i) \in \mathbf{B}$	h4, N
	Infer $n + 1 \leq i \ \Rightarrow \ subp(i, i - (n + 1)) = n + 1$	$\Rightarrow$-I(4.1,4.2)
5	$\forall n \in \mathbf{N} \cdot n \leq i \ \Rightarrow \ subp(i, i - n) = n$	$\forall$-I(N-ind(3,4))
6	from $i \geq j$	
6.1	$i - j \in \mathbf{N}$	N,h6
6.2	$0 \leq j \ \Rightarrow \ subp(i, j) = i - j$	$\forall$-E(5,6.1),N
	Infer $subp(i, j) = i - j$	vac $\Rightarrow$ -E(6.2,h)
7	$(i \geq j) \in \mathbf{B}$	h,N
	Infer $i \geq j \ \Rightarrow \ subp(i, j) = i - j$	$\Rightarrow$-I(6,7)

Figure 9: Proof about *subp*

The principal differences between *LPF* ("Logic for Partial Functions") and classical logic should be noted. It is an obvious consequence of the truth-tables that the law of the excluded middle does not hold. Nor does the deduction theorem hold without an additional hypothesis (cf. $\Rightarrow$ -I). For weak equality it is not necessarily true that $t = t$ for an arbitrary term t.

On the other hand, $\wedge$ and $\vee$ are commutative and monotone. Properties like:

$$x \in \mathbf{R} \vdash x = 0 \vee x/x = 1$$

are easily proved. The implication operator fits its normal abbreviation and also has an interpretation which fits the needs of the result on *subp*. Many of the results from classical logic do hold (cf. Appendix B—even most of the properties of $\leftrightarrow$ presented by Edsger Dijkstra in his Royal Society Lecture of 1985) although simple tautologies have to be re-expressed as sequents. Where properties would otherwise fail to hold, hypotheses can be added as to the definedness of expressions which bring the results back to those of classical logic.

In [8] (which should also be consulted for a full list of references) a number of completeness results are given:

- The operators tt, ff, uu, $\neg$, $\wedge$, $\vee$ form a set which are expressively complete for monotonic operators (result due to Koletsos).

- The set $\neg$, $\vee$, uu, $\triangle$ are expressively complete for all operators (Cheng 3.1(1)).

- The basic axiomatization is consistent and complete (propositional calculus—Cheng 3.3; predicate calculus—Cheng 4.3/4.4).

- The "cut elimination" theorem holds (Cheng 5).

- The I/E rules for linear-style natural deduction proofs are consistent and complete (Cheng 7.4).

The thesis also contains a discussion of the influence of equality on the logic. There are, of course, still unresolved questions:

- Before this logic can be compared with others such as those in [46], [47], [6], [1], it will be necessary to conduct a number of experiments with typical application proofs.

- The use of undefined predicates needs further study.

- The problems caused by implementing such a monotonic logic in a programming language must be assessed.

Other approaches are the use of LCF in [15], the constructive approach in [11] and the work of Dana Scott (see, for example, [48]). A forthcoming paper will make a fuller comparison with the usability of various systems ([9])[31].

Acknowledgements

The author is grateful to the directors of the Summer School for the invitation to present this material. The ideas presented owe much to other researchers: Section 2 to Tobi Nipkow, Section 3 to Peter Aczel, and Section 4 to Jen Cheng. Jeff Sanders read the preprint in detail and suggested a number of corrections. Julie Hibbs typed and revised the LaTeX script. The author also acknowledges the financial support of SERC and the stimulus of the meetings of IFIP's WG 2.3.

References

[1] "Programming as a Mathematical Exercise", J.R. Abrial, in "Mathematical Logic and Programming Languages", (eds.) C.A.R. Hoare and J.C. Shepherdson, Prentice-Hall International, pp113–139, 1985.

[2] "A Note on Program Verification", P. Aczel, private communication, 1982.

[3] "Program Construction and Verification", R.C. Backhouse, Prentice-Hall International, 1986.

---

[31]This will include a comparison with the work of Jean-Raymond Abrial and the Oxford group which was brought into discussion by Mike Spivey and the proposal by Oliver Schoett to use "existential equality".

[4] "A Logic Covering Undefinedness in Program Proofs", H. Barringer, J.H. Cheng and C.B. Jones, Acta Informatica, Vol 21, No. 3, pp251–269, 1984.

[5] "Formal Specification and Software Development", D. Bjørner and C.B. Jones, Prentice-Hall International, 1982.

[6] "Partial Valued Logic", S.R. Blamey, Ph.D. Thesis, Oxford University, 1980.

[7] "A Verification Condition Generator for FORTRAN", R.S. Boyer and J. Strother Moore, pp9–101 in "The Correctness Problem in Computer Science", (eds.) R.S. Boyer and J. Strother Moore, Academic Press, 1981.

[8] "A Logic for Partial Functions", J.H. Cheng, Ph.D Thesis, University of Manchester, 1986.

[9] "On the Usability of Logics which Handle Partial Functions", J.H. Cheng and C.B. Jones, forthcoming.

[10] "The Munich Project CIP —Volume 1: The Wide Spectrum Language CIP-L", CIP Language Group, Springer-Verlag, Lecture Notes in Computer Science, Vol.183, 1985.

[11] "Implementing Mathematics with the Nuprl Proof Development System", R.L. Constable, et al., Prentice-Hall, 1986.

[12] "Project Support Environments for Formal Methods", I.D. Cottam, C.B. Jones, T. Nipkow, A.C. Wills, M.I. Wolczko, A. Yaghi in "Integrated Project Support Environments", (ed.) J. McDermid, Peter Peregrinus Ltd., 1985.

[13] "Mule—An Environment for Rigorous Software Development", I.D. Cottam, C.B. Jones, T.N. Nipkow, A.C. Wills, M. Wolczko and A. Yahgi, final Report to the SERC, June 1986.

[14] "A Discipline of Programming", E.W. Dijkstra, Series in Automatic Computation, Prentice-Hall, 1976.

[15] "Edinburgh LCF", M. Gordon, R. Milner and C. Wadsworth, Springer-Verlag, Lecture Notes in Computer Science, Vol.78, 1979.

[16] "The Science of Computer Programming", D. Gries, Springer-Verlag, 1981.

[17] "Data Refinement Refined", $H^3.M.S^4$, Oxford, Programming Research Group, draft typescript dated May 1985.

[18] "An Introduction to Proving the Correctness of Programs", S.L. Hantler and J.C. King, ACM Computing Surveys, Vol. 8, No. 3, pp331–353, September 1976.

[19] "Specification Case Studies", I. Hayes, to be published by Prentice-Hall International, 1987.

[20] "Data Refinement Refined: Resume", J. He, C.A.R. Hoare and J.W. Sanders, ESOP '86, (eds.) B. Robinet and R. Wilhelm, Springer-Verlag, Lecture Notes in Computer Science, Vol. 213, 1986.

[21] "Prespecification in Data Refinement", J. He., C.A.R. Hoare and J.W. Sanders, submitted to Information Processing Letters, 1986.

[22] "The Logic of Programming", E.C.R. Hehner, Prentice-Hall International, 1984.

[23] "An Axiomatic Basis for Computer Programming", C.A.R. Hoare, CACM Vol.12, No.10, pp576–580, October 1969.

[24] "Proof of Correctness of Data Representations", C.A.R. Hoare, Acta Informatica, Vol.1, pp271–281, 1972.

[25] "Laws of Programming: A Tutorial Paper", C.A.R. Hoare, He Jifeng, I.J. Hayes, C.C. Morgan, J.W. Sanders, I.H. Sørensen, J.M. Spivey, B.A. Sufrin and A.W. Roscoe, Oxford University Technical Monograph, PRG-45, May 1985.

[26] "A Technique for Showing that Two Functions Preserve a Relation between their Domains", C.B. Jones, IBM Laboratory, Vienna, LR 25.3.067, April, 1970.

[27] "Formal Development of Correct Algorithms: An Example Based on Earley's Recogniser", C.B. Jones, Proceedings of the 1972 Las Cruces Conference, SIGPLAN Notes, Vol. 7, No.1, 1972. (Full version published as IBM Technical Report TR 12.095, IBM U.K. Laboratories, Hursley, December 1971.)

[28] "Formal Definition in Compiler Development", C.B. Jones, IBM Laboratory Vienna, TR 25.145, February 1976.

[29] "Implementation Bias in Constructive Specifications of Abstract Objects", C.B. Jones, 1977.

[30] "Software Development: A Rigorous Approach", C.B. Jones, Prentice-Hall International, 1980.

[31] "Development Methods for Computer Programs including a Notion of Interference", C.B. Jones, Oxford University, PRG-25, June 1981.

[32] "Systematic Program Development", C.B. Jones, in "Mathematics and Computer Science", (eds.) J.W. de Bakker, M. Hazewinkel and J.K. Lenstra, CWI Monographs, North Holland Publishers, pp19–50, 1986.

[33] "Systematic Software Development using VDM", C.B. Jones, Prentice-Hall International, 1986.

[34] "Teaching Notes for Systematic Software Development using VDM", C.B. Jones, Department of Computer Science Technical Report, UMCS-86-4-2, Manchester University, 1986.

[35] "Some Requirements for Formal Reasoning Support", C.B. Jones and C.P. Wadsworth, forthcoming.

[36] "Sorting and Searching", D.E. Knuth, in 'The Art of Computer Programming', Vol. III, Addison-Wesley Publishing Company, 1975.

[37] "Sequent Calculus and Partial Logic", G. Koletsos, M.Sc. Thesis, Manchester University, 1976.

[38] "Abstraction and Specification in Program Development", B. Liskov and J. Guttag, MIT Press, 1986.

[39] "Two Constructive Realizations of the Block Concept and their Equivalence", P. Lucas, IBM Laboratory Vienna, Technical Report TR 25.085, June, 1968.

[40] "On The Formal Description of PL/I", P. Lucas and K. Walk, Annual Review in Automatic Programming, Vol. 6, Part 3, Pergamon Press, 1969.

[41] "A Basis for a Mathematical Theory for Computation", J. McCarthy, in "Computer Programming and Formal Systems", (eds.) P. Braffort and D. Hirschberg, North-Holland Publishing Company, pp33–70, 1967.

[42] "A Formal Specification of Straight Lines on Graphic Devices", Lynn S. Marshall, (in) "Formal Methods and Software Development", Proceedings of the Int. Joint Conference on Theory and Practice of Software Development (TAPSOFT), Berlin, Vol 2: Colloquium on Software Engineering, Springer Verlag, Lecture Notes in Computer Science, Vol. 186, pp129–147, March, 1985.

[43] "An Early Program Proof by Alan Turing", F.L. Morris and C.B. Jones, "Annals of the History of Computing", Vol.6 No.2, pp139–143, April, 1984.

[44] "Non-Deterministic Data Types: Models and Implementations", T. Nipkow, Internal Report, University of Manchester, June 1985.

[45] "Non-Deterministic Data Types: Models and Implementations", T. Nipkow, Springer-Verlag, Acta Informatica Vol. 22, pp629–661, 1986.

[46] "An Approach to Program Reasoning Based on a First Order Logic for Partial Functions", O. Owe, privately circulated, June 1984 .

[47] "Partial Function Logic", G. D. Plotkin, Lectures at Edinburgh University, 1985.

[48] "Existence and Description in Formal Logic", in "Bertrand Russell, Philosopher of the Century", (ed.), Schoemann, Allen and Unwin, 1967.

[49] "A Language of Specified Programs", A. Tarlecki.

A Proofs about Operation Decomposition

The semantic model used here is a pair consisting of a termination set and a meaning relation. This model can be used to link the semantics of specifications and programs. For the latter:

$$M: Stmt \rightarrow P(\Sigma \times \Sigma)$$

$$T: Stmt \rightarrow P(\Sigma)$$

Thus, for the simple composition of two statements:

$$M[\![S_1; S_2]\!] \triangleq M[\![S_1]\!]; M[\![S_2]\!]$$
$$T[\![S_1; S_2]\!] \triangleq T[\![S_1]\!] - \mathsf{dom}\,(M[\![S_1]\!] \rhd T[\![S_2]\!])$$

The value of $\mathsf{dom}\,M[\![S]\!]$ defines the set over which S could terminate; the set over which it is guaranteed to terminate is given by $T[\![S]\!]$ which is always a subset of $\mathsf{dom}\,M[\![S]\!]$. This might be more obvious if the following equation is studied:

$$T[\![S_1; S_2]\!] = \{\overleftarrow{\sigma} \in T[\![S_1]\!] \mid \forall \sigma \cdot (\overleftarrow{\sigma}, \sigma) \in M[\![S_1]\!] \Rightarrow \sigma \in T[\![S_2]\!]\}$$

Here, attention is focussed on the while construct because its semantics alone presents technical challenge (other parts of the language are studied in [31]). The termination set is defined[32].

$$W: \text{while } B \text{ do } S$$
$$W': \text{while } B \text{ do } S'$$

---

[32]The meta-brackets ($[\![\ ]\!]$) are used to delimit (abstract) program text; $\overline{p}$ is the set satisfying the truth-valued function p; fix is the fixpoint operator.

$$\mathcal{M}[\![W]\!] \triangleq fix(\lambda r \cdot (\overline{\neg B} \lhd I) \cup \overline{B} \lhd \mathcal{M}[\![S]\!]; r)$$
$$\mathcal{T}[\![W]\!] \triangleq fix(\lambda ss \in P(\Sigma) \cdot \overline{\neg B} \cup ((\overline{B} \cap \mathcal{T}[\![S]\!]) - dom\,(\mathcal{M}[\![S]\!] \rhd ss)))$$

The notion of *satisfaction* is defined above. In the notation used here:

$$[\![S']\!] \text{ sat } [\![S]\!] \triangleq \mathcal{T}[\![S]\!] \subseteq \mathcal{T}[\![S']\!] \wedge \mathcal{T}[\![S]\!] \lhd \mathcal{M}[\![S']\!] \subseteq \mathcal{M}[\![S]\!]$$

It is necessary to establish that the property of the $\mathcal{T}[\![s]\!]$ set being contained in dom $\mathcal{M}[\![s]\!]$ holds for all constructs—thus:

Lemma (W1)

$$\mathcal{T}[\![S]\!] \subseteq dom\,\mathcal{M}[\![S]\!] \vdash \mathcal{T}[\![W]\!] \subseteq dom\,\mathcal{M}[\![W]\!]$$

There is a technical problem since $\mathcal{T}$ is not ω-continuous. Define:

$$\mathcal{F}(ss) \triangleq \overline{\neg B} \cup \{\overrightarrow{\sigma} \in \overline{B} \mid \exists \sigma \in \Sigma \cdot (\overrightarrow{\sigma}, \sigma) \in \mathcal{M}[\![S]\!] \wedge \sigma \in ss\}$$

This is continuous and:

$$\mathcal{F}(ss) = \overline{\neg B} \cup dom\,(\overline{B} \lhd \mathcal{M}[\![S]\!] \rhd ss)$$

Furthermore with:

$$\mathcal{G}(r) \triangleq (\overline{\neg B} \lhd I) \cup \overline{B} \lhd \mathcal{M}[\![S]\!]; r$$

it follows that:

$$\forall n \geq 0 \cdot \mathcal{F}^n(\{\,\}) \subseteq dom\,\mathcal{G}^n(\{\,\})$$

can be proved by induction and the lemma follows[33].

The main result here (Theorem Th4) establishes that the constructor while is monotone in the sat ordering. This result justifies a compositional development style in which objects which satisfy a specification can safely be inserted in place of those specifications. Two preliminary lemmas are given:

Lemma(W2)

$$[\![S']\!] \text{ sat } [\![S]\!] \vdash \mathcal{T}[\![W]\!] \subseteq \mathcal{T}[\![W']\!]$$

Lemma (W3)

$$\mathcal{T}[\![S]\!] \lhd \mathcal{M}[\![S']\!] \subseteq \mathcal{M}[\![S]\!] \vdash \mathcal{T}[\![W]\!] \lhd \mathcal{M}[\![W']\!] \subseteq \mathcal{M}[\![W]\!]$$

Theorem (W4)

$$[\![S']\!] \text{ sat } [\![S]\!] \vdash [\![W']\!] \text{ sat } [\![W]\!]$$

The link between the proof obligation for while and the $\mathcal{T}/\mathcal{M}$ semantics given above can be established. Program texts can be decorated with assertions in a Hoare-like style:

$$\{P\}S\{R\}$$

where:

$$P\colon \Sigma \to \mathbf{B}$$
$$R\colon \Sigma \times \Sigma \to \mathbf{B}$$

The definition is:

$$\{P\}S\{R\} \triangleq \overline{P} \subseteq \mathcal{T}[\![S]\!] \wedge \overline{P} \lhd \mathcal{M}[\![S]\!] \subseteq \overline{R}$$

In the proof obligation for while, a transitive, well-founded, relation R is used. This gives rise to a (complete) induction rule:

---

[33]The full proofs will be contained in a Manchester Technical Report version of this paper.

$$R\text{-ind} \quad \frac{\forall \sigma \in \Sigma \cdot \sigma \in \mathsf{dom}\, R \;\Rightarrow\; pr(\sigma)}{\forall \sigma' \in \Sigma \cdot R(\sigma,\sigma') \;\Rightarrow\; pr(\sigma')}}{\sigma \in \Sigma \vdash pr(\sigma)}$$

The proof obligation for while is justified with respect to the above semantics (two preliminary lemmas are used).

B Inference rules for LPF

Conventions

1. $E, E_1, \ldots$ denote logical expressions.

2. $x, y, \ldots$ denote variables over proper elements in a universe.

3. $c, c_1, \ldots$ denote constants over proper elements in a universe.

4. $s, s_1, \ldots$ denote terms which may contain partial functions.

5. $E(x)$ denotes a formula in which x occurs free.

6. $E(s/x)$ denotes a formula obtained by substituting all free occurrences of x by s in E. If a clash between free and bound variables would occur, suitable renaming is performed before the substitution.

7. $E[s_2/s_1]$ denotes a formula obtained by substituting some occurrences of s_1 by s_2. If a clash between free and bound variables would occur, then suitable renaming is performed before the substitution.

8. X is a non-empty set.

9. An "arbitrary" variable is one about which no results have been established.

General Properties

$$\text{inf} \quad \frac{E_1 \vdash E_2;\; E_1}{E_2}$$

$$\text{var-I} \quad \overline{x^{34} \in X}$$

commutativity ($\vee / \wedge / \Leftrightarrow$-comm)

$$\frac{E_1 \vee E_2}{E_2 \vee E_1} \qquad\qquad \frac{E_1 \wedge E_2}{E_2 \wedge E_1} \qquad\qquad \frac{E_1 \Leftrightarrow E_2}{E_2 \Leftrightarrow E_1}$$

associativity ($\vee / \wedge / \Leftrightarrow$-ass)

---

[34] x is arbitrary

$$\frac{(E_1 \vee E_2) \vee E_3}{E_1 \vee (E_2 \vee E_3)} \quad \frac{(E_1 \wedge E_2) \wedge E_3}{E_1 \wedge (E_2 \wedge E_3)} \quad \frac{(E_1 \Leftrightarrow E_2) \Leftrightarrow E_3}{E_1 \Leftrightarrow (E_2 \Leftrightarrow E_3)}$$

transitivity ($\Rightarrow$ /$\Leftrightarrow$-trans)

$$\frac{E_1 \Rightarrow E_2; \; E_2 \Rightarrow E_3}{E_1 \Rightarrow E_3} \quad \frac{E_1 \Leftrightarrow E_2; \; E_2 \Leftrightarrow E_3}{E_1 \Leftrightarrow E_3}$$

substitution

=t-subs
$$\frac{s_1 = s_2; \; E}{E[s_2/s_1]}$$

=v-subs
$$\frac{s \in X; \; x \in X \vdash E(x)}{E(s/x)}$$

=-comm
$$\frac{s_1 = s_2}{s_2 = s_1}$$

=-trans
$$\frac{s_1 = s_2; \; s_2 = s_3}{s_1 = s_3}$$

$f : D \to R$

$f(d) \overset{\triangle}{=} e$

$e_0 = e(d_0/d)$

$\triangle$-subs
$$\frac{d_0 \in D; \; E(e_0)}{E[f(d_0)/e_0]}$$

$\triangle$-inst
$$\frac{d_0 \in D; \; E(f(d_0))}{E[e_0/f(d_0)]}$$

$f(d) \overset{\triangle}{=}$ if e then et else ef

if-subs
$$\frac{d_0 \in D; \; e_0; \; E(et_0)}{E[f(d_0)/et_0]} \quad \frac{d_0 \in D; \; \neg e_0; \; E(ef_0)}{E[f(d_0)/ef_0]}$$

Definitions of Connectives

f-defn
$$\frac{\neg true}{false}$$

$\wedge$-defn
$$\frac{\neg(\neg E_1 \vee \neg E_2)}{E_1 \wedge E_2}$$

⇒-defn $$\frac{\neg E_1 \lor E_2}{E_1 \Rightarrow E_2}$$

⇔-defn $$\frac{(E_1 \Rightarrow E_2) \land (E_2 \Rightarrow E_1)}{E_1 \Leftrightarrow E_2}$$

∀-defn $$\frac{\neg \exists x \in X \cdot \neg E(x)}{\forall x \in X \cdot E(x)}$$

Relationships between Operators

deM $$\frac{\neg (E_1 \lor E_2)}{\neg E_1 \land \neg E_2} \qquad \frac{\neg (E_1 \land E_2)}{\neg E_1 \lor \neg E_2}$$

$$\frac{\neg \exists x \in X \cdot E(x)}{\forall x \in X \cdot \neg E(x)} \qquad \frac{\neg \forall x \in X \cdot E(x)}{\exists x \in X \cdot \neg E(x)}$$

dist $$\frac{E_1 \lor E_2 \land E_3}{(E_1 \lor E_2) \land (E_1 \lor E_3)} \qquad \frac{E_1 \land (E_2 \lor E_3)}{E_1 \land E_2 \lor E_1 \land E3}$$

∃∨-dist $$\frac{\exists x \in X \cdot E_1(x) \lor E_2(x)}{(\exists x \in X \cdot E_1(x)) \lor (\exists x \in X \cdot E_2(x))}$$

∃∧-dist $$\frac{\exists x \in X \cdot E_1(x) \land E_2(x)}{(\exists x \in X \cdot E_1(x)) \land (\exists x \in X \cdot E_2(x))}$$

∀∨-dist $$\frac{(\forall x \in X \cdot E_1(x)) \lor (\forall x \in X \cdot E_2(x))}{\forall x \in X \cdot E_1(x) \lor E_2(x)}$$

∀∧-dist $$\frac{(\forall x \in X \cdot E_1(x)) \land (\forall x \in X \cdot E_2(x))}{\forall x \in X \cdot E_1(x) \land E_2(x)}$$

Substitution

∧-subs $$\frac{E_1 \land \ldots \land E_i \land \ldots \land E_n; \ E_i \vdash E}{E_1 \land \ldots \land E \land \ldots \land E_n}$$

∨-subs $$\frac{E_1 \lor \ldots \lor E_i \lor \ldots \lor E_n; \ E_i \vdash E}{E_1 \lor \ldots \lor E \lor \ldots \lor E_n}$$

∃-subs $$\frac{\exists x \in X \cdot E_1(x); \ E_1(x) \vdash E(x)}{\exists x \in X \cdot E(x)}$$

contr $$\frac{E_1; \ \neg E_1}{E_2}$$

⇒-contrp $$\frac{E_1 \Rightarrow E_2}{\neg E_2 \Rightarrow \neg E_1}$$

$$INTRODUCTION(op\text{-}I) \qquad ELIMINATION(op\text{-}E)$$

$\neg\neg$

$$\frac{E}{\neg\neg E} \qquad\qquad \frac{\neg\neg E}{E}$$

$\vee$

$$\frac{E_i}{E_1 \vee E_2 \vee \ldots \vee E_n} \qquad \frac{E_1 \vee \ldots \vee E_n;\quad E_1 \vdash E;\ \ldots;E_n \vdash E}{E}$$

$\wedge$

$$\frac{E_1;\ E_2;\ \ldots;\ E_n}{E_1 \wedge E_2 \wedge \ldots \wedge E_n} \qquad \frac{E_1 \wedge E_2 \wedge \ldots \wedge E_n}{E_i}$$

$\neg\vee$

$$\frac{\neg E_1;\ \neg E_2;\ \ldots;\ \neg E_n}{\neg(E_1 \vee E_2 \vee \ldots \vee E_n)} \qquad \frac{\neg(E_1 \vee E_2 \vee \ldots \vee E_n)}{\neg E_i}$$

$\neg\wedge$

$$\frac{\neg E_i}{\neg(E_1 \wedge \ldots \wedge E_n)} \qquad \frac{\neg(E_1 \wedge \ldots \wedge E_n);\quad \neg E_1 \vdash E;\ \ldots;\ \neg E_n \vdash E}{E}$$

$\Rightarrow$

$$\frac{E_1 \vdash E_2;\ E_1 \in \mathbf{B}}{E_1 \Rightarrow E_2}$$

vac $\Rightarrow$

$$\frac{E_2}{E_1 \Rightarrow E_2} \qquad \frac{E_1 \Rightarrow E_2;\ \neg E_2}{\neg E_1}$$

$$\frac{\neg E1}{E_1 \Rightarrow E_2} \qquad \frac{E_1 \Rightarrow E_2;\ E_1}{E_2}$$

$\Leftrightarrow$

$$\frac{E_1 \wedge E_2}{E_1 \Leftrightarrow E_2} \qquad \frac{E_1 \Leftrightarrow E_2}{E_1 \wedge E_2 \vee \neg E_1 \wedge \neg E_2}$$

$$\frac{\neg E_1 \wedge \neg E_2}{E_1 \Leftrightarrow E_2}$$

$\neg\Leftrightarrow$

$$\frac{E_1 \wedge \neg E_2}{\neg(E_1 \Leftrightarrow E_2)} \qquad \frac{\neg(E_1 \Leftrightarrow E_2)}{E_1 \wedge \neg E_2 \vee \neg E_1 \wedge E_2}$$

$$\frac{\neg E_1 \wedge E_2}{\neg(E_1 \Leftrightarrow E_2)}$$

$$\exists \qquad \frac{s \in X;\ E(s/x)}{\exists x \in X \cdot E(x)} \qquad\qquad \frac{\begin{array}{c}\exists x \in X \cdot E(x);\\ y^{35} \in X, E(y/x) \vdash E_1\end{array}}{E_1}$$

$$\forall \qquad \frac{x^{36} \in X \vdash E(x)}{\forall x \in X \cdot E(x)} \qquad\qquad \frac{\forall x \in X \cdot E(x);\ s \in X}{E(s/x)}$$

$$\neg\exists \qquad \frac{x \in X \vdash \neg E(x)}{\neg\exists x \in X \cdot E(x)} \qquad\qquad \frac{\neg\exists x \in X \cdot E(x);\ s \in X}{\neg E(s/x)}$$

$$\neg\forall \qquad \frac{s \in X;\ \neg E(s/x)}{\neg\forall x \in X \cdot E(x)} \qquad\qquad \frac{\begin{array}{c}\neg\forall x \in X \cdot E(x);\\ y^{37} \in X, \neg E(y/x) \vdash E\end{array}}{E}$$

Miscellaneous

$\exists$split
$$\frac{\exists x \in X \cdot E(x,x)}{\exists x, y \in X \cdot E(x,y)}$$

$\forall$fix
$$\frac{\forall x, y \in X \cdot E(x,y)}{\forall x \in X \cdot E(x,x)}$$

$\forall \rightarrow \exists$
$$\frac{\forall x \in X^{38} \cdot E(x)}{\exists x \in X \cdot E(x)}$$

$$\frac{\exists x \in X \cdot \forall y \in Y \cdot E(x,y)}{\forall y \in Y \cdot \exists x \in X \cdot E(x,y)}$$

$$\frac{\forall x \in X \cdot E_1(x) \Leftrightarrow E_2(x)}{(\forall x \in X \cdot E_1(x)) \Leftrightarrow (\forall x \in X \cdot E_2(x))}$$

=-contr
$$\frac{\neg(s = s)}{E}$$

=-term
$$\frac{s \in X}{s = s}$$

---

[35] y is arbitrary and not free in E_1
[36] x is arbitrary
[37] y is arbitrary and not free in E
[38] X is non-empty

=-comp
$$\frac{s_1, s_2 \in X}{(s_1 = s_2) \vee \neg(s_1 = s_2)}$$

Δ-I
$$\frac{E}{\Delta E} \qquad\qquad \frac{\neg E}{\Delta E}$$

Δ-E
$$\frac{\Delta E;\ E \vdash E_1;\ \neg E \vdash E_1}{E_1}$$

$\neg\Delta$-I
$$\frac{\Delta E \vdash E_1;\ \Delta E \vdash \neg E_1}{\neg \Delta E}$$

$\neg\Delta$-E
$$\frac{\neg\Delta E \vdash E_1;\ \neg\Delta E \vdash \neg E_1}{\Delta E}$$

==-refl
$$\frac{}{s == s}$$

==-subs
$$\frac{s_1 == s_2;\ E}{E[s_2/s_1]}$$

==-comm
$$\frac{s_1 == s_2}{s_2 == s_1}$$

==-trans
$$\frac{s_1 == s_2;\ s_2 == s_3}{s_1 == s_3}$$

==$\rightarrow$=
$$\frac{s_1 == s_2;\ s_i \in X}{s_1 = s_2}$$

=$\rightarrow$==
$$\frac{s_1 = s_2}{s_1 == s_2}$$

Equational Specification of
Partial Higher Order Algebras

Manfred Broy
Fakultät für Mathematik und Informatik
Universität Passau
Postfach 2540
D-8390 Passau

Abstract

The theory of algebraic abstract types specified by positive conditional formulas formed of equations and a definedness predicate is outlined and extended to hierarchical types with "nonstrict" operations, partial and even infinite objects. Its model theory is based on the concept of partial interpretations. Deduction rules are given, too. Models of types are studied where all explicit equations have solutions. The inclusion of higher order types, i.e. types comprising higher order functions are treated, leads to an algebraic ("equational") specification of algebras including sorts with "infinite" objects and higher order functions ("functionals"). Finally concepts of implementations of algebraic types are studied.

1. Introduction

Axiomatic property-oriented ("equation-oriented") descriptions of data structures provide a powerful concept for the specification, the design, and the development of algebras, consisting of families of object sets and of families of operations on them. In the meantime the usefulness of algebraic specifications of abstract data types is widely accepted.

However, for making algebraic specifications into a powerful practical tool for software engineering purposes their theory and their methodology has to be further developed. Central questions here are the structuring of specifications, the treatment of functions the effect of the application of which is not defined for certain arguments, the model-theoretic framework (the semantics) and the deductive theory of algebraic specifications.

Clearly, for the practical use of algebraic specifications not only theoretical but more pragmatic questions may be decisive: what is needed is a well worked-out methodology and a flexible formalism ("specification-language") as well as the availability of support tools. But one should be aware of the fact that languages, methodologies, and tools have to be based on an appropriate foundational framework.

However, still the theory of algebraic types is incomplete. There are some shortcomings and open questions for instance concerning the treatment of higher order functions and the treatment of "diverging" expressions especially in conjunction with partial "nonstrict" operations, which are well-understood in the meanwhile in domain theory of denotational semantics. A theory capable to deal with nonstrict operations is needed even if only an equational treatment of the if-construct is required.

Algebraic specifications (using conditional equations) including higher order functions can be written in a straightforward way. We consider identifiers for functions in higher order axioms very similar to identifiers for objects not ranging over the space of all functions with the resp. functionality (the whole function space), but only over the set of those functions that can be represented by functional terms i.e. by composing given functions (term-generated functions).

NATO ASI Series, Vol. F36
Logic of Programming and Calculi of Discrete Design
Edited by M. Broy
© Springer-Verlag Berlin Heidelberg 1987

In the following a theoretical framework for an equational approach to nonstrict operations and infinite objects in abstract types with higher order functions is given. Basically we understand our approach as a further extension of the algebraic approach developed by the Munich CIP group.

The paper is organized as follows: At first we give some basic definitions including the notion of term and context. Then we define the notion of partial interpretation. We treat the notions of algebraic extension and of hierarchical data types and of higher order signatures and higher order algebras. Finally we discuss shortly concepts of implementations of algebraic types.

2. Basic Notions

In this section we introduce the basic notions needed in the following chapters. We start with a number of "syntactical" concepts.

2.1. Signatures, Terms, Contexts, Polynomials

A signature provides sets of names for sets and functions. Basically a signature can be understood as defining an (abstract) syntax.

A (first-order) signature Σ consists of a pair (S, F) where

- S is a set of sorts and

- F is a set of function symbols,

where we assume that for every $f \in F$ an arity arity$(f) \in S^* \times S$ is predefined.

A function symbol $f \in F$ with arity$(f) = <s>$ for some sort s is called nullary.

Signatures can be represented by directed graphs (signature graphs) where all sorts are represented by nodes and all function symbols are represented by arcs (with multiple sources).

We often shall write in type specifications

$$\textbf{fct} \; (\, s_1, ... , s_n \,) \, s_{n+1} \quad f$$

for specifying

$$\text{arity}(f) = <s_1 ... s_{n+1}>$$

A subsignature $\Sigma' = (S', F')$ of a signature $\Sigma = (S, F)$ is a signature (i.e. arity$(f) \in S'^* \times S'$ for all $f \in F'$) with $S' \subseteq S$, $F' \subseteq F$.

Example: The signature $\Sigma_{NAT} = (S_{NAT}, F_{NAT})$ of the numbers is given by

$$S_{NAT} = \{ \; \textbf{nat, bool} \; \}$$
$$F_{NAT} = \{ \quad \text{true, false, not, and, or, ...}$$
$$\text{zero, succ, pred, iszero, ... } \}$$

$$\text{arity(true)} = < \textbf{bool} >$$

arity(false) = < **bool** >

arity(not)   = < **bool bool** >
arity(and)   = < **bool bool bool** >

.

.

.

arity(zero)   = < **nat** >
arity(succ)   = < **nat nat** >
arity(pred)   = < **nat nat** >
arity(iszero) = < **nat bool** >

The signature Σ_{BOOL} specified by

$$\Sigma_{BOOL} = (\{ \text{ \textbf{bool} } \}, \{\text{true, false, not, and, or }\})$$

forms a subsignature of the signature Σ_{NAT}.

end of example

Often we have two classes of sorts and function symbols in a signature. The sorts and function symbols in the first class are well-understood. Therefore they will be called primitive. The sorts and function symbols in the second class are not well-understood and can be explained in terms of the primitive ones. Therefore they will be called nonprimitive. According to this concept of structuring and observability we consider often hierarchical signatures:

A signature Σ is called hierarchical iff a subsignature PRIM(Σ) is designated as being primitive. Note that PRIM(Σ) can itself be hierarchical again.

For instance in the example above the subsignature Σ_{BOOL} could be designated as primitive for Σ_{NAT}. Then Σ_{NAT} forms a hierarchical signature.

Often the actual names for the sorts and functions are not important. Rather the structure of the signature is relevant. Therefore sometimes one may be interested in renaming sorts or function symbols. This can be done by a signature morphism.

A signature morphism σ from Σ to Σ' for signatures $\Sigma = (S, F)$, $\Sigma' = (S', F')$ is a pair ($\sigma 1, \sigma 2$) of mappings

$\sigma 1: S \rightarrow S'$, $\sigma 2 : F \rightarrow F'$

with

$\text{arity}(\sigma 2(f)) = < \sigma 1(s_1) \dots \sigma 1(s_{n+1}) >$

for every $f \in F$ with $\text{arity}(f) = < s_1 \dots s_{n+1} >$. For reasons of simplicity we often denote $\sigma 1$ as well as $\sigma 2$ simply by σ. In particular a signature morphism represents a graph morphism between the resp. signature diagrams.

Given a signature Σ we can form terms. The family of sets $W_\Sigma(s)$ of terms of sort s (formed over the signature Σ) is defined as follows:

- for $f \in F$ with $\text{arity}(f) = < s >$ we have $f \in W_\Sigma(s)$

- for $f \in F$ with arity(f) = $< s_1 ... s_n \, s >$ and terms $t_1 \in W_\Sigma(s_1), ..., t_n \in W_\Sigma(s_n)$ we have

$f(t_1, ..., t_n) \in W_\Sigma(s)$

We take the smallest (in the inclusion ordering) sets of terms for $W_\Sigma(s)$ that fulfil the definition. If the signature Σ does not contain nullary function symbols, then all sets $W_\Sigma(s)$ are empty.

The set $W_\Sigma(s)$ of terms of sort s over a signature Σ is a member of the family $(W_\Sigma(s))_{s \in S}$ of sets (also called the carrier sets of the <u>word-algebra</u> W_Σ, term algebra, Herbrand universe). The elements of $W_\Sigma(s)$ are often called <u>ground terms</u>.

Given an S-sorted family $X = (X_s)_{s \in S}$ of (disjoint) infinite sets X_s of identifiers, then $W_\Sigma(X)$ defines the algebra of terms with free identifiers from X, i.e. the term algebra over the extended signature $(S, \{ x \in X_s : s \in S \} \cup F)$ with arity(x) = $< s >$ for $x \in X_s$. By $W_\Sigma(s, X)$ the set of terms from $W_\Sigma(X)$ of sort s are denoted. The terms from $W_\Sigma(s, X)$ are also called Σ-<u>polynomials</u> of sort s over X.

Example: For the signature Σ_{NAT} we obtain as ground terms of sort **nat**:

zero, succ(zero), pred(zero), ...

and the ground terms of sort **bool**,

true, false, not(true), not(false), and(true, false), ...

and also

iszero(zero), izero(succ(zero)), ...

Assuming $X_{nat} = \{n, n1, n2, ... \}$, $X_{bool} = \{b, b1, b2, ... \}$ we obtain polynomials of sort **bool** and **nat** resp. such as

b, n, iszero(n), not(b), ...

end of example

An important operation on terms is the substitution function (for any s, s$'$ $\in$ S)

[. /.]: $W_\Sigma(s', X) \times W_\Sigma(s, X) \times X_s$ -> $W_\Sigma(s', X)$

that allows to replace all occurrences of an identifier in a term by some other term. It is defined by (for t $\in$ $W_\Sigma(s, X)$, y, x $\in$ X_s)

y[t/x] = y   if x and y are distinct identifiers
x[t/x] = t
$f(t_1, ..., t_n)[t/x] = f(t_1[t/x], ..., t_n[t/x])$

As usual we also use the simultaneous substitution denoted by

$t'[t_1/x_1, ..., t_n/x_n]$

which is just a straightforward extension of the concept simple substitution.

Similar to the universe of terms the universe of contexts may be defined over Σ. Contexts are closely related to polynomials and to the functions one may define over a given family of functions. They play an important role in all term-oriented calculi such as algebraic specifications (cf. observability by primitive contexts) or in term rewriting. Other interesting examples where contexts are considered are positional logic or the treatment of attributes in compiler construction. In the sequel we are going to give a very "functional" definition of a context.

Similar to the universe of terms the universe of contexts is defined over a given signature Σ. A Σ-context c of sort s_{n+1} for (terms or polynomials of) the sorts $s_1, \ldots, s_n$ is a particular function on terms:

$$c : W_{\Sigma}(s_1, X) \times \ldots \times W_{\Sigma}(s_n, X) \rightarrow W_{\Sigma}(s_{n+1}, X)$$

such that there exists a polynomial $t \in W_{\Sigma}(s_{n+1}, X)$ and identifiers $x_1, \ldots, x_n$ where

$$c[t_1, \ldots, t_n] = t[\, t_1/x_1, \ldots, t_n/x_n]$$

If in t each of the identifiers $x_1, \ldots, x_n$ occurs in t exactly once, then c is called simple context.

If t is x_i then we write also $\bullet_i$ for c. The set of those contexts will be denoted by $C_{\Sigma}(s_1,\ldots,s_n)$ and the set of all contexts is denoted by C_{Σ}.

Contexts are very similar to polynomials. However, in contrast to contexts in polynomials the free identifiers have a relevant identity and are not linearly ordered.

The terms built over signatures and their structures are especially interesting for algebraic specifications. All what we can really write down are terms that carry the intended information. Therefore we study the term structure in detail.

A term t1 is called a subterm of a term t2 and we write t1 $\leq_{sub}$ t2 if

$$\exists\, c \in C_{\Sigma} : c[t1] = t2$$

One easily proves that $\leq_{sub}$ is a partial order.

For contexts we may define two partial orderings in a straightforward way: For a multiple context c1 a context c2 is called a subcontext, if

$$\exists\, c \in C_{\Sigma} : c[c2] = c1$$

and we write c1 $\leq_{sub}$ c2.

For a context c2 a context c1 is called a more general context and we write c1 $\leq_{gen}$ c2, if

$$\exists\, c_1, \ldots, c_n \in C_{\Sigma} : c1[\, c_1, \ldots, c_n\,] = c2$$

Trivially the identity function is the most general context. Again $\leq_{gen}$ defines a partial ordering modulo the ordering for the arguments.

Proposition:

(1) The ordering $\leq_{sub}$ on contexts coincides with the pointwise ordering $\leq_{sub}*$ induced by $\leq_{sub}$ on contexts as functions.

(2) The ordering $\leq_{gen}$ is consistently complete, i.e. whenever two contexts have an upper bound there exists a least upper bound.

Proof: (1) We have by definition

$$c1 \leq_{sub}* c2 \text{ iff } \forall t_1,...,t_n : c1(t_1,...,t_n) \leq_{sub} c2(t_1,...,t_n)$$

this is equivalent to

$$\forall t_1, ... , t_n : \exists c \in C_\Sigma : c[c1(t_1,...,t_n)] = c2(t_1,...,t_n)$$

(2) Induction on the structure of the contexts:

Assume contexts c1, c2, c with

$$c1 \leq_{gen} c \wedge c2 \leq_{gen} c$$

then if $c1 = \bullet_i$ take c2 as least upper bound for c1 and c2; if $c2 = \bullet_j$ take c1 as least upper bound. If both $c1 \neq \bullet_i$ and $c2 \neq \bullet_j$ then we must have

$$c1 = f(c^1_1, ..., c^1_k) \wedge c2 = f(c^2_1, ..., c^2_k) \wedge c = f(c_1, ..., c_k)$$

and $c^1_i \leq_{gen} c_i$, $c^2_i \leq_{gen} c_i$. By induction hypothesis there exists c^0_i that are least upper bounds for c^1_i and c^2_i. $f(c^0_1, ..., c^0_k)$ is a least upper bound for c1 and c2.

end of proof

Given two contexts c1 and c2, then a context c is also called a <u>unifier</u> of c1 and c2, if

$$c1 \leq_{gen} c \text{ and } c2 \leq_{gen} c$$

Note since $\leq_{gen}$ is a partial ordering we immediately may also talk about a least (most general) unifier. If there exists a unifier for c1 and c2, then according to the lemma above there exists always a <u>most general unifier</u>, i.e. a least upper bound for c1 and c2.

2.2. Σ-Formulas and abstract types

For having the possibility to write axioms for specifying abstract types we define the set of Σ-formulas: A <u>Σ-formula</u> over the family of identifiers X is defined inductively by

- for t1, t2 $\in W_\Sigma(X)$ of identical sort the equation t1 = t2 and the expression DEF(t1) are (atomic) Σ-formulas,

- for Σ-formulas e1, e2: $\neg$e1, e1 $\wedge$ e2, e1 $\vee$ e2, el => e2, $\forall$ s x: e1, $\exists$ s x : e2 are

Σ-formulas (provided $x \in X_s$ and $s \in S$).

A Σ-formula of the form $\forall s_1 x_1: ... \forall s_m x_m: e_1 \wedge ... \wedge e_n => e_{n+1}$ where the e_i either are equations or of the form DEF(t) or $\neg$DEF(t) is called a <u>Horn-formula</u>. If none of the e_i is of the form $\neg$DEF(t), then we speak of a <u>definedness positive Horn-formula</u>; if none of the e_i is of the form DEF(t), then we speak of a <u>definedness negative Horn-formula</u>.

A partial abstract type T = (Σ, E) consists of a signature Σ and a set E of Σ-formulas. Generally we always provide a name for an abstract type. A first example for an abstract type is the type BOOL:

type BOOL =

   sort bool,

   fct bool true, false,
   fct (bool) bool not,
   fct (bool, bool) bool or, and,

   DEF(true),
   DEF(false),

   $\neg$(true = false),

   not(false) = true,
   not(not(x)) = x,

   or(true, x) = true,
   or(x, true) = true,
   or(false, x) = x,
   or(x, false) = x,

   and(false, x) = false,
   and(x, false) = false,
   and(true, x) = x,
   and(x, true) = x

                                                  end of type

The axioms are all assumed to be universally quantified. The axiom

       $\neg$(true = false)

will be the only negated equation that we use throughout this paper. The formula

       DEF(true)

expresses that the result of the nullary function true is defined.

A <u>hierarchical type</u> T = (Σ, E, PRIM(T)) consists of a signature Σ a set of axioms E and a primitive type PRIM(T) which may be simple or hierarchical.

A first example of a hierchical type is the type NAT:

type NAT =

based_on BOOL,

sort nat,

fct nat zero,
fct (nat) nat succ,
fct (nat x : not (iszero(x))) **nat** pred,
fct (nat) bool iszero,

pred(succ(x)) = x,
iszero(zero) = true,
iszero(succ(x)) = false,

fct (nat, nat) nat add, mult, sub,

add(zero, y) = y,
add(succ(x), y) = succ(add(x, y)),

sub(x, zero) = x,
sub(x, succ(y)) = pred(sub(x, y)),

mult(x, zero) = zero
mult(x, succ(y)) = add(mult(x, y), x)

end of type

The indication

based_on BOOL

specifies that the type BOOL is the primitive subtype of type NAT and that all the sorts and function symbols as well as the axioms of BOOL are also contained in the type NAT.

The restriction

fct(nat x: not(iszero(x))) **nat** pred

is a shorthand for the axiom

DEF(pred(x)) => not(iszero(x)) = true

In the presence of partial functions we immediately discover question like "does the following equation hold?"

or(iszero(pred(zero)), true) = true

Certainly pred(zero) is not defined and therefore for "strict" functions iszero

iszero(pred(zero))

should be not defined, too. However, due to the equation

or(x, true) = true

we might conclude also

(*)   or(iszero(pred(x)), true) = true.

However assuming or and iszero to be strict we may conclude that

or(iszero(pred(x)), true)

is not defined. In the sequel we are going to develop a semantic framework for algebraic types where iszero is strict and and nevertheless the equation (*) holds. An even more significant example are conditionals.

We easily can add an operation

fct (bool, nat, nat) nat if

to the type NAT with the axioms

if(true, x, y) = x,
if(false, x, y) = y,
DEF(if(b, x, y)) => DEF(b)

We want to have for instance

if(true, zero, pred(zero)) = zero

although pred(zero) is not defined. Then if is "nonstrict": from

¬DEF(y)

we cannot conclude

¬DEF(if(b, x, y))

It is rather clear that we would like to have an algebraic framework for treating strict and nonstrict functions side by side.

A further example is given by the algebraic type SEQ:

type SEQ =

based_on DATA, BOOL,

sort seq,

fct seq eseq,
fct (data) seq m,
fct (seq, seq) seq conc,
fct (seq) bool iseseq,
fct (seq s : not(iseseq(s))) **seq** lr, rr,
fct (seq s : not(iseseq(s))) **data** first, last,

conc(conc(s1, s2), s3) = conc(s1, conc(s2, s3)),
conc(s, eseq) = s = conc(eseq, s),

iseseq(eseq) = true,
iseseq(m(x)) = false,
iseseq(conc(s, r)) = and(iseseq(s), iseseq(r)),

lr(conc(s, m(x))) = s,
rr(conc(m(x), s)) = s,
first(conc(m(x), s)) = x,
last(conc(s, m(x))) = x

end of type

Here in connection with nonstrict functions we might even ask a more complex question. If we want to solve equations like

x = conc(m(zero), x)

then if conc is strict, then "x not defined" is a trivial solution of the equation. However if conc is nonstrict then "x not defined" is not a solution and we may look for nontrivial solutions. This way we may include "infinite" objects.

From the equation and the axioms of SEQ we may derive for x:

first(rr^i(x)) = zero

for all i. This can be shown by induction on i. For i = 0 we obtain:

first(rr^0(x)) = first(x) = first(conc(m(zero), x)) = zero

By induction on i: rr^i(x) = x

rr^{i+1}(x) =
rr(rr^i(x)) =
rr(x) =
rr(conc(m(zero), x)) = x

In the following we are going to provide a purely equational framework in which questions as outlined above can be tackled.

3. Model Theory for Partial Types

In this section we introduce the notion of partial interpretations. Partial interpretation will be associated as a model-theoretic meaning to abstract types.

3.1. Partial Heterogeneous Algebras

Signatures provide names for sets and functions. If families of sets and families of functions are given for the names, then we speak of an algebra.

Let the signature Σ = (S, F) be given. A <u>partial, heterogeneous Σ-algebra</u> A is a pair $((s^A)_{s \in S}, (f^A)_{f \in F})$ consisting of a family of <u>carrier sets</u> s^A and a family of <u>partial mappings</u>

$$f^A : s_1{}^A \times ... \times s_n{}^A \dashrightarrow s_{n+1}{}^A$$

for every f $\in$ F with arity(f) = < s_1 ... s_{n+1} >. Thus the arity of a function symbol indicates the range and domain of the resp. function in an algebra.

A Σ-algebra A is called <u>total</u>, if all functions in A are total.

Example: With the signature Σ_{NAT} of the example above we obtain a Σ_{NAT}- algebra A by defining.

$$\text{nat}^A \ =_{\text{def}} \mathbb{N}$$

$$\text{bool}^A \ =_{\text{def}} \mathbb{B}$$

where $\mathbb{B}$ denotes the set of logical values, i.e. $\mathbb{B} = \{$ tt, ff $\}$ and $\mathbb{N}$ denotes the natural numbers. With the function symbols we denote the usual functions; for instance

$$
\begin{array}{ll}
\text{zero}^A & = 0 \\
\text{succ}^A(x) & = x+1 \\
\text{pred}^A(x) & = x\text{-}1 \quad \text{if } x > 0 \\
\text{pred}^A(0) & \quad \text{is not defined}
\end{array}
$$

and so on.

end of example

For an arbitrary signature the families of ground terms $W_\Sigma(s)$ form a total Σ-algebra if we associate the resp. term-building operations with the function symbols.

Also the contexts form an algebra. More precisely for the signature $\Sigma = (S, F)$ the contexts build a (S^*, C_Σ)-algebra. Interestingly in the context-algebra every object in a carrierset also occurs as a function associated with a function symbol.

Let now $\Sigma' = (S', F')$ be a subsignature of Σ. A Σ'-algebra A is called $\underline{\Sigma'\text{-subalgebra}}$ of the Σ-algebra B iff

(1) $\forall \ s \in S' : s^A \subseteq s^B$,

(2) $\forall \ f \in F' : f^A = f^B|_A$.

Here $f^B|_A$ denotes the restriction of the mapping f^B to the elements of the carrier sets of A. In a Σ'-subalgebra certain sorts and objects may be missing with respect to a given Σ-algebra and for the remaining sorts some objects may be missing, too.

A Σ'-subalgebra A is called $\underline{\Sigma'\text{-reduct}}$ of a Σ-algebra B if Σ' is a subsignature of Σ and

(1) $\forall \ s \in S' : s^A = s^B$,

(2) $\forall \ f \in F' : f^A = f^B$.

Thus a Σ'-reduct is a special case of a Σ'-subalgebra. If we replace the equality "=" in the condition (2) of these definitions by the less-defined ordering "$\leq_\perp$" we speak of weak $\underline{\Sigma'\text{-subalgebras}}$ and $\underline{\text{weak } \Sigma'\text{-reducts}}$ resp. For partial functions the ordering "$\leq_\perp$" is defined as usual by

$$f \leq_\perp g \qquad \text{iff} \qquad \forall \ x : f(x) \text{ is not defined or } f(x) = g(x).$$

Example: For our example signature Σ_{NAT} we can define a second Σ_{NAT}-algebra D by

$$\mathbf{nat}^D = \mathbb{Z}$$

$$\mathbf{bool}^D = \mathbb{B}$$

$$\mathbf{zero}^D = 0$$

$$\mathbf{succ}^D(x) = x+1$$

$$\mathbf{pred}^D(x) = x-1 \dots$$

Then the Σ_{NAT}-algebra A defined in the example above forms a weak Σ-subalgebra of D.

end of example

A Σ-algebra A is called <u>strictly term-generated</u> (finitely generated), if A does not contain a proper Σ-subalgebra. Both the Σ_{NAT}-algebras A and D are strictly term-generated. However, if we replace in D $\mathbf{pred}^D$ by the function $\mathbf{pred}^A$ the application of which is not defined for the argument 0 then the resulting algebra is no longer term-generated, since it contains A as proper Σ_{NAT}-subalgebra. Note that every Σ-algebra contains exactly one strictly term-generated Σ-subalgebra.

Trivially a hierarchy on a signature Σ induces a hierarchy on every Σ-algebra A. Then A is called a <u>hierarchical Σ-algebra</u>. Then A contains a PRIM(Σ)-reduct which is sometimes also called the primitive PRIM(Σ)-subalgebra of A.

Signature morphisms can be used to rename Σ-algebras. Given the two signatures $\Sigma 1 = (S1, F1)$ and $\Sigma 2 = (S2, F2)$ and a signature morphism

$$\sigma : \Sigma 1 \rightarrow \Sigma 2$$

then every $\Sigma 2$-algebra A2 can be seen containing a subalgebra that can be renamed into a $\Sigma 1$-algebra A1 by taking

- for the carrierset s^{A1} associated with the sort $s \in S1$ the set $\sigma(s)^{A2}$

- for the function f^{A1} in A1 the function $\sigma(f)^{A2}$ where $s \in S$, $f \in F$.

We denote the $\Sigma 1$-algebra A1 that is induced by the signature morphism σ on A2 by $\sigma^{-1}(A2)$.

Often we are interested to study the relationship between algebras with the same signatures. This can be done by particular families of functions.

For Σ-algebras A and B a family $\varphi = (\varphi_s)_{s \in S}$ of partial mappings

$$\varphi_s : s^A \dashrightarrow s^B$$

is called a (partial) <u>Σ-homomorphism</u>, iff for every $f \in F$ with $\text{arity}(f) = < s_1 \dots s_{n+1} >$ the following two conditions are fulfilled (for simplicity of notation we drop the index s in φ_s):

$\forall \, a_1 \in s_1{}^A, ..., a_n \in s_n{}^A:$

if both $\varphi(f^A(a_1, ..., a_n))$ and $f^B(\varphi(a_1), ..., \varphi(a_n))$ are defined, then:

(*) $\varphi(f^A(a_1, ..., a_n)) = f^B(\varphi(a_1), ..., \varphi(a_n))$

$\forall \, a_1, a_1' \in s_1{}^A, ..., a_n, a_n' \in s_n{}^A$

(**) $\varphi(a_1) = \varphi(a_1') \wedge ... \wedge \varphi(a_n) = \varphi(a_n') => \varphi(f^A(a_1, ..., a_n)) = \varphi(f^A(a_1', ..., a_n'))$

The condition (**) assures that φ induces a congruence relation on A and condition (*) says that ihe function f^B behaves like the function induced by φ on B for f^A. The equality "=" used here is assumed to be <u>strong</u>, i.e. $\varphi(a_1) = \varphi(a_2)$ holds iff both sides are defined and are identical or if both $\varphi(a_1)$ and $\varphi(a_2)$ are not defined. Note that $\varphi(f^A(a))$ (and similarly $f^B(\varphi(a))$) is not defined whenever $f^A(a)$ is not defined or $f^A(a) = a'$ is defined, but $\varphi(a')$ is not defined. Note that the composition of homomorphisms may not be a homomorphism again.

Trivially if f^A, f^B and φ are total functions, then the equation (*) must always hold, the condition (**) is trivially fulfilled and we obtain the classical notion of a homomorphism. This in particular means that if $f^A(a_1, ..., a_n)$ and $f^B(\varphi(a_1), ..., \varphi(a_n))$ are defined, so is $\varphi(f^A(a_1, ..., a_n))$ and (*) holds.

From now on for notational convenience we always drop the sort index s from φ_s and write for homomorphisms $\varphi : A \dashrightarrow B$.

Our notion of partial homomorphism is more liberal than the one in [Broy, Wirsing 82]. The more restricted notion of a homomorphism used there is introduced later by restricting the notion of partial homomorphism as defined above.

Homomorphisms are mainly used to compare Σ-algebras A and B. Partial homomorphisms compare fragments of Σ-algebras. In the classical case of total algebras with total homomorphisms, a homomorphism between term-generated algebras A and B basically induces a congruence relation on A such that the resp. quotient structure is isomorphic to B. So B can be seen as arising from A by identifying certain elements.

For partial algebras and partial homomorphisms we always may ask whether the homomorphic images of two elements from A are equal and whether the homomorphic image of an element from A is defined. In connection with operations f^A in A and f^B in B we can ask similar questions for their images.

A partial Σ-homomorphism

$\varphi: A \longrightarrow B$

always defines a weak Σ-subalgebra A´ of A, consisting of the subsets of the carriersets the objects of which have defined images. i.e.for all $s \in S$ we define

$s^{A'} = \{ \, a \in s^A : \varphi(a) \text{ is defined } \}$

and the resp. weakening of the functions to the carrier sets of A´, i.e. for $f \in F$ with $arity(f) = < s_1, ... , s_{n+1} >$ the resp. functions $f^{A´}$ in A´ are defined by

$$f^{A´}(a_1, ..., a_n) = f^A(a_1, ... , a_n)$$

if $\varphi(a_i)$ are defined for all i, $1 \le i \le n$ and $\varphi(f^A(a_1, ... , a_n))$ is defined and $f^{A´}(a_1, ..., a_n)$ is not defined otherwise. Then by

$$\varphi´ : A \rightarrow A´$$

we denote the partial identity with

$$\varphi´(a) = a$$

if $\varphi(a)$ is defined. By

$$\varphi{\sim}: A´ \rightarrow B$$

we denote the total Σ-homomorphism from A´ to B which is the restriction of φ to A´. So every partial Σ-homomorphism from the Σ-algebra A to the Σ-algebra B defines a weak Σ-subalgebra A´ of A and a total Σ-homomorphism from A´ to B.

For a (total) Σ-homomorphism

$$\varphi{\sim}: A´ \rightarrow B$$

we always can isolate a weak Σ-subalgebra B´ of B consisting just of the elements that are images of elements in A, i.e. we define the carrier sets of B´ by

$$s^{B´} = \{ b \in s^B : \exists a \in s^A : \varphi{\sim}(a) = b \}$$

and for $f \in F$ with $arity(f) = < s_1, ... , s_{n+1} >$ the resp. functions $f^{B´}$ in B´ are defined by

$$f^{B´}(b_1, ..., b_n) = \varphi{\sim}(f^A(a_1, ... , a_n)) \text{ where } \qquad b_i = \varphi{\sim}(a_i) \text{ and } DEF(f^B(b_1,...,b_n))$$

Due to the definition of B´ such a_i do exist and due to the definition of homomorphism the definition is independent of the choice of the a_i and thus consistent. By this we get a total surjective homomorphism

$$\varphi´´: A´ \rightarrow B´$$

such that

$$\forall a_1 \in s_1^A, ..., a_n \in s_n^A: \quad \varphi´´(f^{A´}(a_1, ..., a_n)) = f^{B´}(\varphi´´(a_1), ..., \varphi´´(a_n))$$

By construction B´ is a weak Σ-subalgebra of B. Therefore there exists a total Σ-homomorphism

$\phi''': B' \to B$

which is the identity on the elements of the carrier sets of B'.

We obtain a decomposition (factorization) of homomorphisms ϕ

$$A \xrightarrow{\phi'} A' \xrightarrow{\phi''} B' \xrightarrow{\phi'''} B \quad \text{with} \quad \phi = \phi' \circ \phi'' \circ \phi'''$$

where ϕ' is the partial identity (a weakening of the identity) and ϕ''' is the identity (the embedding of B' into B), and ϕ'' is a total Σ-homomorphism. This decomposition shows very explicitly the structure of a partial homomorphism.

For certain parts of A (those not in A') and certain parts of B (those not in B') a homomorphism ϕ does not establish any correpondence. For some sort $s \in S$ and some element $a \in s^A$ we may have:

$f^A(a)$ may be defined whereas

$f^B(\phi(a))$ is undefined and vice versa

The notion of a homomorphism can be restricted to enforce a closer relationship between A and B. We now study a number of those restrictions that will be used later for classifying interpretations of algebraic specifications.

A partial homomorphism ϕ is called <u>strict</u>, iff for every $f \in F$ with arity$(f) = \langle s_1 \ldots s_{n+1} \rangle$ we have:

$$\forall a_1 \in s_1{}^A, \ldots, a_n \in s_n{}^A: \phi(f^A(a_1, \ldots, a_n)) = f^B(\phi(a_1), \ldots, \phi(a_n))$$

In particular this implies the $\phi(f^A(a_1, \ldots, a_n))$ is not defined whenever $\phi(a_i)$ is not defined for some i, $1 \leq i \leq n$. Strictness ensures that the image of ϕ defines a Σ-subalgebra for B (and not just a weak Σ-subalgebra). In particular in the decomposition of ϕ above ϕ'' is strict. If ϕ is strict, then B' is just the Σ-subalgebra of B.

A Σ-homomorphism ϕ is called <u>strengthening</u>, if $f^B(\phi(a_1), \ldots, \phi(a_n))$ is defined, whenever $\phi(f^A(a_1, \ldots, a_n))$ is defined. For unary functions f this condition is equivalent to the condition

$$f^A \circ \phi \leq_\perp \phi \circ f^B$$

In particular in the decomposition of ϕ above ϕ''' is strengthening. In terms the decomposition of homomorphisms for a strengthening homomorphism we obtain in addition: ϕ''' is strengthening. Total strengthening Σ-homomorphisms coincide again with the classical notion.

A Σ-homomorphism is called <u>weakening</u> if $\phi(f^A(a_1, \ldots, a_n))$ is defined whenever $f^B(\phi(a_1), \ldots, \phi(a_n))$ is defined. For unary functions f this is equivalent to the condition

$$\varphi \circ f^B \leq_\perp f^A \circ \varphi$$

In particular in the decomposition of φ above φ' is weakening. In terms the decomposition of homomorphisms for a strengthening homomorphism we obtain in addition: φ' is weakening. Total strengthening Σ-homomorphisms coincide again with the classical notion.

The notion of a partial Σ-homomorphism that we use here is rather liberal. The existence of general partial homomorphisms between Σ-algebras A and B does not tell very much about the structural relationship between the Σ-algebras A and B since the everywhere undefined function trivially always represents a partial Σ-homomorphism.

Homomorphisms can be used to designate particular elements in classes of algebras.

Given a class C of Σ-algebras an algebra $A \in C$ is called (weakening, strengthening, strictly or totally resp.) initial in C iff for all $B \in C$ there exists a unique (strict or total resp.) Σ-homomorphism φ: A --> B.

An algebra $A \in C$ is called (weakening, strengthening, strictly or totally) terminal (or final) iff for all $B \in C$ there exists at least one (strict or total) Σ-homomorphism φ: B --> A.

The notions of initiality and terminality are very important since they characterize certain models up to isomorphism.

Proposition: If algebras A and B are (strictly, weakening, strengthening, totally) initial in a class of algebras, then A and B are isomorphic.

Proof: Assume (strict, weakening, total) Σ-homomorphisms

$$\varphi : A \to B$$
$$\tau : B \to A$$

Then $\varphi \circ \tau$ is a (strict, total) Σ-homomorphism.

$$\varphi \circ \tau : A \to A$$

Since the identity is a (strict, total) Σ-homomorphism and the Σ-homomorphism is unique for A $\varphi \circ \tau$ must be the identity function, and also $\varphi \circ \tau$. So τ must be the inverse to φ.

end of proof

In the case of of general partial Σ-homomorphisms initiality is not a very interesting notion, since only the Σ-algebra A with empty carrier sets is initial (if A is initial there exists only one Σ-homomorphism A —> A; the totally undefined function as well as the identity are such partial Σ-homomorphisms. So if A is initial, both coincide; so all carriers must be empty).

For a Σ-algebra A every context $c \in C_\Sigma(s_1 \dots s_{n+1})$ can be interpreted by a partial function

$$c^A : s_1{}^A \times ... \times s_n{}^A \rightarrow s_{n+1}{}^A$$

which can be inductively defined by on the term structure.

Every Σ-homomorphism trivially is also a homomorphism w.r.t. all context functions c^A and c^B with $c \in C_\Sigma$.

So far we did not require any particular properties of a general partial homomorphism for cases where one of the sides of a homomorphic equation is not defined. The strictness condition and the weakening and strengthening conditions, however, are rather strong - too strong for some interesting cases. Therefore we now consider a weaker requirement for the cases where the value of a homomorphism is not defined.

A partial homomorphism

$$\varphi : A \dashrightarrow B$$

is called <u>regular</u> iff for all $a \in s^A$ with $\varphi(a)$ not defined we have for all unary contexts c and all objects $a0$

$$(***) \quad \varphi(c^A(a)) \text{ defined } \Rightarrow \varphi(c^A(a0)) \text{ defined}$$

This condition is equivalent to the condition

$$\varphi(a) \text{ not defined } \wedge \varphi(c^A(a0)) \text{ not defined} \Rightarrow \varphi(c^A(a)) \text{ not defined}$$

or to the equivalent condition

$$\varphi(c^A(a)) \text{ defined } \Rightarrow \quad \varphi(a) \text{ defined or } \varphi(c^A(a0)) \text{ is defined for all } a0$$

The condition (***) includes a "weak" monotonicity condition for φ as it will be demonstrated in the following sections. Trivially every strict homomorphism is regular.

The regularity condition imposes special restrictions for the φ-images of objects in A that are results of $f^A(a_1, ..., a_n)$ where $\varphi(a_i)$ is not defined. Regularity is of special interest when we consider interpretations which are homomorphisms from the term-algebra into partial algebras.

3.2. Partial Interpretations

For a given signature Σ and a given Σ-algebra A every weakening partial homomorphism

$$I^A : W_\Sigma \dashrightarrow A$$

is called a <u>(partial) interpretation</u> of Σ-terms in A. Note that the term-algebra W_Σ is a total algebra. If I^A is strict, we speak of a <u>strict interpretation</u>. For every Σ-algebra A there exists a uniquely determined strict interpretation I^A of terms in A called the <u>natural interpretation</u>. For terms $t \in W_\Sigma$ we denote the natural interpretation $I^A[t]$ also by t^A.

Of course we are not only interested in the interpretation of terms but also in the interpretation of polynomials. For studying interpretations of polynomials we introduce environments.

Given a signature Σ and an S-sorted family X of identifiers and a Σ-algebra A, then a <u>partial (X, A)-environment</u> is a family $\{ \eta_s \}_{s \in S}$ of partial mappings where

$$\eta_s : X_s \dashrightarrow s^A$$

for every $s \in S$. Again for simplicity we drop the indexes s and write η both for $\{ \eta_s \}_{s \in S}$ and η_s. The set of all partial (X, A)-environments will be denoted by ENV(X, A). By Ω we denote the everywhere undefined environment.

In the case of strict interpretations every interpretation of terms can be extended uniquely to polynomials. For nonstrict interpretations this is not true, if we consider identifiers with undefined interpretations and there do not exist terms the interpretation of which is not defined. If we consider for instance the classical boolean algebra B with the sort **bool** and the operations true, false, not, and, or, then for the environment Ω for the polynomial

and(x, false)

the interpretation is not fixed by B. Therefore interpretations of polynomials will be considered in the sequel.

A function

$$I^A : \text{ENV}(X, A) \to W_\Sigma(X) \dashrightarrow A$$

is called a partial <u>(regular) interpretation</u> of a Σ-polynomial in a given Σ-algebra A (we write also $I^A_\eta(t)$ for $I^A(\eta)(t)$) if for a given (X, A)-environment η

$$I^A_\eta[x] = \eta(x), \qquad \text{for x from the family of identfiers X}$$

and I^A_η is a partial (regular) interpretation of terms where for all polynomials we require $I^A_\eta[t]$ = $I^A_{\eta'}[t]$ whenever $\eta(x) = \eta'(x)$ for all x occurring in t.

If we add a simple further assumption to the class of algebras that for every sort there should be at least a term with not defined interpretation, then for those algebras there exists for a given regular interpretation of terms exactly one regular interpretation of Σ-polynomials, i.e. the regular interpretation of Σ-polynomials is uniquely defined by a given regular interpretation of terms. For this reason we assume a special nullary function symbol "omega" for every sort the interpretation of which is always undefined. We shall even use omega without mentioning it in the signatures explicitly. This assumption is equivalent to the consideration of partial interpretations of polynomials.

Note the difference to domain theory where the element "$\bot$" is introduced into the semantic models and not into the function symbols.

According to the "denotation principle" we often consider just Σ-algebras where all elements are denotable by terms. This corresponds to the principle of finite term-generability:

For a given interpretation an algebra is called <u>term-generated</u>, if for every object a of A there exists a term t such that $I^A[t] = a$ or a polynomial such that $I^A_\Omega[t] = a$. Note the difference between term-generability and strict term-generability. Only for strict interpretations both notions coincide.

The importance of the notion of strictly term-generated algebras can be seen by the following proposition:

Proposition: A Σ-algebra A is strictly term-generated, iff the strict interpretation

$$\varphi: W_\Sigma \dashrightarrow A$$

is a surjective Σ-homomorphism, i.e. iff A is a strict partial homomorphic image of W_Σ.

Proof: φ defines a Σ-subalgebra A´ for A by the set of objects that are in the range of φ. On A´ φ is surjective. So A = A´ iff φ is surjective on A.

$\qquad\qquad\qquad\qquad\qquad\qquad\qquad\qquad\qquad\qquad\qquad\qquad\qquad$ **end of proof**

Given two partial Σ-interpretations of Σ-polynominals I^A and I^B:

$$I^A: ENV(X, A) \to W_\Sigma(X) \dashrightarrow A$$

$$I^B: ENV(X, B) \to W_\Sigma(X) \dashrightarrow B$$

and a partial Σ-homomorphism $\varphi: A \dashrightarrow B$ then φ is called partial Σ-homomorphism from the interpretation I^A to I^B if for all terms $t \in W_\Sigma(X)$ and all partial (X, A)-environments η

$$\varphi(I^A{}_\eta[t]) = I^B{}_{\eta \circ \varphi}[t] \quad \text{whenever} \quad \varphi(I^A{}_\eta[t]) \text{ and } I^B{}_{\eta \circ \varphi}[t] \text{ defined}$$

The notions of strict, strengthening, weakening generalize straightforward.

With this definition we may also speak about initial or terminal interpretations. In the case of strict interpretations the existence of the homomorphism between the algebras A and B is sufficient for the existence of a homomorphism between the interpretations.

3.3. On the Principle of Extensionality

The concept of hierarchical algebras leads to an abstraction concept, the concept of extensionality. This concept supports an abstract view on the nonprimitive terms for a given partial interpretation in a hierarchical algebra.

Let $\Sigma = (S, F)$ be a hierarchical signature with primitive subsignature $PRIM(\Sigma) = (PRIM(S), PRIM(F))$.

Given a partial interpretation I^A in a hierachical Σ-algebra A then two nonprimitive terms t and t', i.e. two terms t, t' $\in W_\Sigma(s)$ of the nonprimitive sort s $\in$ S\PRIM(S), are called extensionally equivalent, if for all primitive sorts p we have:

$$\forall c \in C_\Sigma(s\ p): I^A[c[t]] = I^A[c[t']]$$

We then also write t $\sim_{I}A$ t'. Two nonprimitive terms are extensionally equivalent, if they lead to the same primitive effects.

The priniciple of extensionality is well-known for functions: two functions are equivalent, if their results coincide for all possible arguments.

A partial interpretation I^A in a hierachical Σ-algebra A is called <u>fully abstract</u>, if for all nonprimitive sorts s we have:

$$\forall\ t, t' \in W_{\Sigma}(s):\ I^A[t] = I^A[t']\ <=>\ t \sim_I A\ t'$$

Based on the principle of extensionality we can also study the relationship between hierarchical algebras with identical primitive subalgebras.

Given a partial interpretation I^A in a hierachical Σ-algebra A and a partial interpretation I^B in a hierachical Σ-algebra B where A and B are assumed to have identical primitive subalgebras, then the interpretations I^A and I^B are called <u>extensionally equivalent</u>, if for all primitive sorts p we have:

$$\forall\ t \in W_{\Sigma}(p):\ I^A[t] = I^B[t]$$

Now we can prove a very basic lemma on the existence of fully abstract interpretations.

Lemma: For every partial interpretation I^A in a term-generated algebra A there exists an extensionally equivalent partial interpretation that is fully abstract.

Proof: We can construct the <u>behavioural term algebra</u> B for A where all nonprimitive terms are interpreted by the family of functions mapping primitive contexts to primitive terms.

We define B as follows. For $s \in PRIM(S)$ we define

$$s^B = s^A$$

For $s \in S\backslash PRIM(S)$ we define

$$s^B = \{ h_t{}^s : t \in W_{\Sigma}(s) \}$$

where the $h_t{}^s = \{ h_t{}^{s,p} \}_{p \in PRIM(S)}$ are families of functions

$$h_t{}^{s,p} : C_{\Sigma}(s\ p) \rightarrow p^A$$

defined by

$$h_t{}^{s,p}(c) = I^A[c[t]]$$

Now we define the functions f^B associated with the function symbols $f \in F$ by

$$f^B(\ map(\ h_{t1}{}^{s1}\ ),\ ...,\ map(\ h_{tn}{}^{sn}\ )\ ) =\ map(\ h_{f(t1,\ ...,\ tn)}{}^{sn+1}\ )$$

where map is defined by

$$
map(\ h_t{}^s\ ) = \begin{cases} h_t{}^s & \text{if the sort s is not primitive} \\ I^A[t] & \text{otherwise} \end{cases}
$$

The consistency of these definitions and the full abstractness of B as well as the extensional equivalence of A and B are easily proved.

end of proof

This is a very interesting lemma since it shows that every programming language with a fixed extensional behavior has a fully abstract denotational ("compositional") semantic model.

We even may compare hierarchical algebras with distinct primitive subalgebras via homomorphisms between the primitive algebras or homomorphisms between the interpretations of terms of primitive sort.

3.4. Totalization of Partial Algebras

We now study shortly the possibility of dealing with total algebras instead of partial ones in connection with partial interpretation. It can be demonstrated that all the concepts introduced so far could also be introduced in the framework of total algebras, if a special element $\perp$ is assumed for every carrier set.

Given a partial Σ-homomorphism

$$\varphi: A \longrightarrow B$$

we can totalize the homomorphism φ to a total function $\varphi^{\perp}$ and the algebra $B^{\perp}$ to the total algebra $B^{\perp}$ where

$$\varphi^{\perp}: A \longrightarrow B^{\perp}$$

and for $s \in S$:

$$s^{B^{\perp}} = s^{B} \cup \{\perp\}$$

and for $a \in s^{A}$:

$$\varphi^{\perp}(a) = \begin{cases} \varphi(a) & \text{if } \varphi(a) \text{ defined} \\ \perp & \text{otherwise} \end{cases}$$

and for $f \in F$ with $\text{arity}(f) = \langle s_1 \ldots s_{n+1} \rangle$ we define

$$f^{B^{\perp}}(b_1, \ldots, b_n) = f^{B}(b_1, \ldots, b_n)$$

if $f^{B}(b_1, \ldots, b_n)$ is defined (and $b_i \neq \perp$); and

$$f^{B^{\perp}}(b_1, \ldots, b_n) = \varphi^{\perp}(f^{A}(a_1, \ldots, a_n))$$

if there exist $a_1, \ldots, a_n$ with $\varphi^{\perp}(a_i) = b_i$ for all i, $1 \leq i \leq n$ and $\varphi(f^{A}(a_1, \ldots, a_n))$ defined and

$$f^{B\perp}(\,b_1, \,...,\, b_n\,) = \perp$$

otherwise. Due to the homomorphism condition this definition is consistent.

So the interpretation can also be represented by total algebras with a distinguished element $\perp$. However, we prefer to work with partial algebras to emphasis the special role of terms with not defined interpretations.

3.5. Analysis of Terms with Not Defined Interpretations

In domain theory the phenomenon of diverging computations is dealt with by the introduction of a special "element" called "$\perp$" or "ω". Additionally a complete partial order is introduced motivated by the concept of approximation. All functions considered are required to be monotonic or even continuous which allows to prove the existence of least fixed points. Also nonstrict functions are included. "Infinite" objects can be represented by the least solution of fixed point equations or by the set of their finite approximations w.r.t. the used ordering. For all these purposes in domains partial orderings are essential.

Domains are rather order-theoretic than equation-oriented. Of course, we can use axiomatic techniques for defining the partial ordering in domains (cf. [Möller 85]), but a purely algebraic approach based on equational axioms has the significant advantage that equational axioms are more simple and can be used much more flexibly. Moreover, as it will be shown, there are examples of equationally specified algebras for which order-theoretic specifications do not exist.

In the classical theory of partial functions the introduction of an artificial object $\perp$ representing "undefined" is completely avoided. Partial functions naturally correspond to strict functions (functions that produce $\perp$ if some argument is $\perp$), if they are totalized (naturally extended) by the introduction of the artificial object $\perp$.

Terms the interpretation of which is not defined have to be treated somewhat different to terms with defined interpretation from a point of view of computation. This is done by introducing the requirement of regularity. Regularity is a weak form of monotonicity.

The intuitive meaning of undefinedness in connection with partial functions and partial interpretations is less obvious than one might expect. There are at least three reasons for considering a term as being not defined (being without defined interpretation), or more precisely considering the result of the application of a function to certain arguments as not defined:

- there is no meaningful result for a function application (for example when asking for the first element of an empty sequence);

- the assumption of total functions might lead to a contradiction (in cases of overspecification like in fixed point equations over numbers such as $f(x) = f(x)+1$);

- it is not possible to treat (axiomatize) all the cases in a (uniquely) defined way (in cases of underspecification such as for functions with nonrecursive domains; an example is the specification of an interpreter).

Often all three ways of using partiality occur side by side within one formal framework. However, the different reasons require different techniques. In fixed point theory monotonicity (and often even continuity) of functions is assumed for guaranteeing the existence of uniquely defined least (w.r.t. definedness) fixed points.

In an equational axiomatisation of partial algebras and partial interpretations we need not prove the existence of fixed points but simply can postulate the existence of (least) fixed points for all functions and all explicit equations as part of the axioms of algebraic specifications. In particular an order-theoretic treatment is not needed. However, one has to be careful about the treatment of terms containing subterms with not defined interpretations.

To illustrate the relationship between partial homomorphisms and interpretations and domain theory we now introduce for a given partial interpretation a relation $\leq_\perp$ on the term algebra and the algebra A that carries the interpretation. This way we can introduce classical notions from domain theory:

An operation $f \in F$ with $\text{arity}(f) = \langle s_1 \ldots s_{n+1} \rangle$ is called <u>strict</u>, if for all terms $t_1, \ldots, t_n$ of the resp. sorts $I^A[f(t_1, \ldots, t_n)]$ is not defined if for one of the terms t_i the interpretation $I^A[t_i]$ is not defined.

Given a regular Σ-interpretation I^A in a term-generated Σ-algebra A we may analyse the set of terms the interpretations of which are not defined. Let t, t´ be ground terms. If t contains subterms $t_1, \ldots, t_n$ with undefined interpretations, i.e. if there is a context c such that

$$c[t_1, \ldots, t_n] = t$$

and there are terms $t_1´, \ldots, t_n´$ where $t´ = c[t_1´, \ldots, t_n´]$, then we write $t \leq_\perp t´$.

Lemma: The relation $\leq_\perp$ is a preordering on W_Σ.

Proof: Reflexivity is trivial (choose n = 0). Transitivity is shown as follows: Assume

$$t \leq_\perp t´ \leq_\perp t''$$

then there exist terms and contexts such that

$$t = c[t_1, \ldots, t_n], \quad t´ = c[t´_1, \ldots, t´_n], \quad t´ = c'[r_1, \ldots, r_m], \quad t'' = c'[r´_1, \ldots, r´_m]$$

The contexts c and c' can be chosen $\leq_{gen}$-minimal. Hence $c \leq_{gen} c'$ must hold due to the regularity assumption. Thus $t \leq_\perp t''$.

end of proof

Note that $\leq_\perp$ is not a partial ordering, but only a preordering.

Theorem: All contexts are monotonic w.r.t. $\leq_\perp$, i.e. for all contexts c and all terms t and t':

$$t \leq_\perp t' \Rightarrow c[t] \leq_\perp c[t']$$

Proof: If $t \leq_\perp t'$, then due to the definition there exists terms $t_1, \ldots, t_n$ and $t_1´, \ldots, t_n´$ with the interpretations of $t_1, ..., t_n$ not defined and a context $c0$ such that

$t = c0[t_1, ..., t_n]$ and $t' = c0[t_1', ..., t_n']$.

Now

$c[t] = c[c0[t_1, ..., t_n]] = c(c0)[t_1, ..., t_n],$

$c[t'] = c[c0[t_1', ..., t_n']] = c(c0)[t_1', ..., t_n']$

i.e. $c[t] \leq_\perp c[t']$.

end of proof

Now we are going to study the properties of the relation induced by the relation $\leq_\perp$ and the partial interpretation I^A on the carrier sets s^A of the term-generated algebra A. Trivially $\leq_\perp$ is reflexive on term-generated algebras. But it is not antisymmetric, in general. And it is not even transitive in general.

Therefore we define for every sort $s \in S$ with carrier s^A the relation $\leq_\perp$ on s^A to be the transitive closure of the relation induced by by the relation $\leq_\perp$ on terms via the interpretation I^A, i.e. $\leq_\perp$ is the least transitive relation on s^A for $s \in S$ such that for all terms t, t':

$$t \leq_\perp t' \implies I^A[t] \leq_\perp I^A[t']$$

We immediately obtain the corollary

Corollary: For all objects a1, a2 and contexts c:

$a1 \leq_\perp a2 \implies c^A[a1] \leq_\perp c^A[a2]$

end of corollary

In particular, since functions are contexts all functions f^A are $\leq_\perp$-monotonic.

The term t is called <u>partial</u> and its interpretation $I^A[t]$ is called a <u>partial object,</u> if there exists a term t' with $t \leq_\perp t'$, but not $t' \leq_\perp t$ and $a = I^A[t]$, $a' = I^A[t']$ and a is distinct from a'.

A regular interpretation I^A in a Σ-algebra A is called <u>flat,</u> if at most the terms with undefined interpretation are partial, i.e. if there do not exist any partial objects.

3.6. Validity of Σ-Formulas

A Σ-equation $t1 = t2$ with polynomials t1 and t2 of identical sort is called <u>valid</u> under a partial interpretation I^A (in a Σ-algebra A) for the partial environment η if

$I^A_\eta[t1] = I^A_\eta[t2]$ and we write then $I^A_\eta \models t1 = t2$

The formula DEF(t) is valid under a partial interpretation I^A for the environment η if $I^A_\eta[\, t\,]$ is defined. We then write also $I^A_\eta \models DEF(t)$. If t1 and t2 are of the same sort, then we have

$$(I^A_\eta \models \neg DEF[t1] \wedge \neg DEF[t2]\,) \Rightarrow (I^A_\eta \models t1 = t2\,)$$

Note that for every context c regularity can be expressed by a definedness negative Horn-formula:

$$\neg DEF(x) \wedge \neg DEF(c(y)) \Rightarrow \neg DEF(c(x))$$

For the logical operators we assume the classical interpretations. Since the interpretations of an equation or of a formula DEF(t) are always either true or false, we can use classical "total" (two-valued) logic and we do not have to extend the logical operators to arguments that are not defined. For universally quantified formulas of the form $\forall\, s\, x : e$ we define two forms of validity as follows: For formulas without quantifiers strict and regular validity coincide.

$\forall\, s\, x : e$ is called <u>strictly valid</u> for the total environment α and the strict interpretation I^A if for all total environments η with $\alpha(y) = \eta\,(y)$ for all identifiers y with $x \neq y$ we have: e is strictly valid in A for η.

$\forall\, s\, x : e$ is called <u>regularly valid</u> for the partial environment α and the regular interpretation I^A if for all partial environments η with $\alpha(y) = \eta(y)$ for all identifiers y with $x \neq y$ we have: e is regularly valid under I^A for η.

The validity for existential quantification is defined analogously. In connection with quantification we observe a similar effect as well-known from the semantics of function application in first order applicative languages: there is a call-by-value treatment and a call-by-name treatment for the actual parameters possible. The same distinct concepts for the identifiers used in quantifications are possible.

A Σ-formula e is called <u>strictly valid for a Σ-algebra A</u> (with strict interpretation I^A) and we write

$$A \models_{strict} e \qquad\qquad (\text{or } I^A \models_{strict} e)$$

if for all total environments α the formula e is strictly valid.

e is called <u>regularly valid for (the regular interpretation)</u> I^A (in a Σ-algebra A) and we write

$$I^A \models_{reg} e$$

if for all partial environments η the formula e is regularly valid.

Strict and regular validity do not coincide for a given partial interpretation and one does not imply the other, in general. However, as long as we consider only Horn-formulas, then regular validity implies strict validity.

Examples: Consider the signature Σ_{NAT} with the classical interpretation. Then

$pred(succ(x)) = x$

is regularly valid and strictly valid. The formula

$iszero(succ(x)) = false$

is strictly valid, but not regularly valid. The formula

$DEF(x)$

is always strictly valid but never regularly valid. The formula

$\exists\ s\ x: \neg DEF(x)$

is always regularly valid, but not strictly valid.

end of example

The two different forms of validity lead to different interpretations of algebraic specifications.

3.7. Equationally Complete Σ-algebras and Algebraic Extensions

So far we have studied equational formulas mainly as a tool for writing axiomatic specifications of algebras. Now we study special forms of equations (socalled systems of explicit or recursive equations) that can be used for specifying ("describing") objects or families of objects as solutions of equations (fixed points).

We assume that we are given a Σ-algebra A, a S-sorted family X of identifiers, and a regular interpretation I^A of Σ-polynomials in A. A set EE of equations between polynomials is called a finite or infinite family of <u>explicit equations</u>, if there is a finite or infinte (countable) set IND of indexes, such that

$EE = \{ x_i = t_i : i \in IND \}$

where the x_i are pairwise distinct identifiers and the t_i are polynomials.

The environment η or more precisely the vector of values $\eta(x_1), ..., \eta(x_i), ...$ are then called a <u>fixed point</u> of EE, if for all $i \in IND$, we have $I^A_\eta \models_{reg} x_i = t_i$. A fixed point is called <u>minimal</u> (or also minimally defined), if for every environment η' which is also fixed point of EE we have

$\eta' \leq_\perp \eta \Rightarrow \eta \leq_\perp \eta'.$

The interpretation I^A is called <u>Σ-equationally complete</u>, if every finite or infinite set of explicit equations between finite terms has a solution.

Then in particular for all contexts $c_0, ..., c_n \in C_\Sigma$:

$I^A \models_{reg} \exists\ x_0, ..., x_n : x_0 = c_0[x_0, ..., x_n] \wedge ... \wedge x_n = c_n[x_0, ..., x_n]$

A Σ-algebra A is called <u>Σ-algebraic</u>, if for every object a in A there is a set of explicit equations EE and an environment η such that $a = \eta(x_0)$ and η is a minimally defined fixed point of EE.

This means that for every sort s every object $a \in s^A$ can be obtained either by interpreting a finite term or as a minimal solution of (a set of) explicit equations between finite terms.

Theorem: In an equational complete Σ-algebra every finite system of explicit equations has a minimal fixed point.

end of theorem

An algebra A is called $\underline{\Sigma\text{-generated}}$ by the Σ-interpretation I^A, if there does not exist a regular Σ-interpretation $I^{A'}$ in a proper Σ-subalgebra A' of A that is equationally complete and where

$$I^A = I^{A'}$$

Theorem: If the Σ-interpretation I^A in the Σ-algebra A is Σ-generated, then A is Σ-algebraic.

end of theorem

Here we use a purely algebraic, equational technique very much in the spirit of algebraic extensions in classical algebra.

The classical approaches used for dealing with fixed point equations are rather order-theoretic. Here we do not require that there exist least fixed points. If uniquely defined least fixed points exist for every system of explicit equations, then it is clear that in Σ-algebraic interpretations every system of explicit equations has exactly one minimal fixed point and every object is least fixed point of a set of equations.

Theorem: Every interpretation I^A in a term-generated model A can be extended to an equationally complete interpretation I^A such that A is a Σ-subalgebra of A'.

Proof: Add for systems of explicit equations without fixed points the equations as formal elements to the carrierset.

end of proof

As well-known given a signature Σ we can also define the set of infinite terms (the infinite term-algebra $W^\infty{}_\Sigma$) by taking the ideal completion $C^\infty{}_\Sigma$ of $(C_\Sigma, \leq_{gen})$ and defining

$$W^\infty{}_\Sigma = \{ c[omega, ..., omega] : c \in C^\infty{}_\Sigma[s_1,..., s_n] \},$$

$$W^{omega}{}_\Sigma = \{ c[omega, ..., omega]: c \in C_\Sigma[s_1, ..., s_n] \}$$

A Σ-algebra A is called $\underline{\text{continuously term generated}}$ if for all sorts s the preorder $\leq_\perp$ is a partial order on the carrier sets s^A and we have

$$\forall M \subseteq W^{omega}{}_\Sigma: M \leq_\perp \text{-directed} => \exists a \in s^A: a = \text{lub} \{ I^A[t]: t \in M \}$$

$$\forall a \in s^A: \exists M \subseteq W^{omega}{}_\Sigma: M \leq_\perp \text{-directed and } a = \text{lub} \{ I^A[t]: t \in M \}$$

and all f^A for $f \in F$ are $\leq_\perp$ continuous. We do not require that A is complete. There might be directed sets in the carrier sets of A that do not have least upper bounds. Only those directed sets that are interpretations of directed sets of terms should have least upper bounds. This is sufficient for proving the existence of least fixed points of term equations. Trivially we obtain:

Theorem: Every total interpretation in a continuously term-generated Σ-algebra is equationally complete.

end of theorem

Note that the reverse does not hold, in general.

The consideration of equationally complete interpretations again can be considered as additional semantical requirement for the interpretations of algebraic specifications. As long as we consider strict interpretations (with regular validity) this requirement is trivial: Ω always is a fixed point then. For general regular interpretations families of explict equations may occur where Ω is not a fixed point and therefore nontrivial fixed points must be associated.

4. A Deductive Theory for Partial Types

Given a set of Σ-formulas E then we can define rules of inference that allow to deduce new formulas from E. Similar to the different forms of validity we get different forms of deductive theories depending on the decision whether we want to deal with regular or strict interpretations. We write

$$E \vdash_{strict} e \qquad \text{and} \qquad E \vdash_{reg} e$$

resp. if e follows from E by the classical rules of equational logic using the strict rule or the regular rule resp. for the instantiation of identifiers. A particular set of deduction rules will be given in the sequel.

Basically we obtain a first-order equational theory and can use the classical calculus of first order predicate logic. However, due to the fact that we have partial functions, sorted expressions and identifiers, and we assume a regular interpretation and a definedness predicate we obtain special rules of inference that will be studied in the following.

4.1. Deduction Rules for Equations

In the rules most of the time we drop the conditions of sort correctness. Sort correctness of terms is a simple syntactic property. Of course rules of inference should only be applied to sort correct formulas and only if the resulting formulas are sort correct, too.

Of course we assume for the equality symbol "=" all the classical laws of congruence relations.

<u>Reflexivity</u>

$t = t$

<u>Symmetry</u>

$t1 = t2$
___
$t2 = t1$

<u>Transitivity</u>

$t1 = t2, t2 = t3$
___
$t1 = t3$

<u>Congruence</u>: let $f \in F$

$t_1 = t_1{'}, ..., t_n = t_n{'}$
___

$$f(t_1, ..., t_n) = f(t_1{'}, ..., t_n{'})$$

Note that there are no restrictions on these laws, although we deal with partial interpretations. So we can use classical first-order equational calculus.

4.2. Rules for Quantifiers

For replacing free identifiers in terms by an arbitrary term (of the resp. sort) we use the rule of instantiation.

Rule of instantiation for regular validity

Let $t \in W_\Sigma(s)$, x identifier of sort s

$$\frac{e}{e[t/x]}$$

where e[t/x] denotes the replacement of x in e by t. Note that this rule does not hold for strict validity. For strict validity first the definedness of the term t has to be shown.

Rule of instantiation for strict validity

Let $t \in W_\Sigma(s)$, x identifier of sort s

$$\frac{e, \; DEF(t)}{e[t/x]}$$

According to the occurrence of instantiations of partial functions the rule of universal quantification reads for regular interpretations:

$$\frac{\forall \, s \, x : e}{e}$$

For strict interpretation this rule is only correct, if the carrier set associated with sort s is not empty. For regular interpretations the quantification never is done over an empty set since the everywhere undefined environment Ω can always be taken. Since we assume sorted identifiers, the sort information in the quantification is redundant.

4.3. Deduction Rules for the Definedness Predicate

Now due to the regularity conditions for partial interpretations we get special rules for talking about the definedness of terms.

Rules for strong equality

$$\frac{\neg DEF(t1), \; \neg DEF(t2)}{t1 = t2}$$

$$\frac{\neg(t1 = t2)}{}$$

$$DEF(t1) \lor DEF(t2)$$

The regularity condition gives special rules for deriving the definedness as well as the undefinedness of terms.

<u>Rules for regularity</u>

$$\frac{\neg DEF(t1[t/x]), \ \neg DEF(t2)}{\neg DEF(t1[t2/x])}$$

The reverse rule reads:

$$\frac{DEF(t[t1/x])}{DEF(t[t2/x]) \lor DEF(t1)}$$

This rule can be reformulated:

$$\frac{DEF(C[t1]), \quad \neg DEF(C[t2])}{DEF(t1)}$$

Later we will in addition study rules connected with induction. For strict interpretation we can use stronger rules

<u>Rule of stricness</u>

Let $0 \leq i \leq n$; then for every n-ary function symbol $f \in F$

$$\frac{\neg DEF(t_i)}{\neg DEF(f(t_1, \dots, t_n))}$$

The reverse rule reads:

$$\frac{DEF(f(t_1, \dots, t_n))}{DEF(t_i)}$$

We do not give any of the classical rules of inference for predicate logic for the logical connectives and quantification; they are assumed to be valid.

4.4. Deduction Rules for Equationally Complete Types

In an equationally complete type every explicit equation has a solution. Thus we have the rule (let $x_1 \in X_{s1}, \dots, x_n \in X_{sn}, t_1 \in W_\Sigma(s_1, X)), \dots, t_n \in W_\Sigma(s_n, X))$:

$$\exists\, s_1\, x_1: \ldots \exists\, s_n\, x_n: \quad x_1 = t_1 \wedge \ldots \wedge x_n = t_n$$

For existential quantifiers we assume the classical rules of quantification. The Skolem functions that we can associate with the existential quantifiers above correspond to a fixed point operator and will betreated later in connection with higher order types.

Another deduction principle that will be treated later is induction. Of course it has different forms in term-generated algebras and in Σ-generated algebras.

5. Abstract Types: Algebraically Specified Classes of Algebras

Abstract types are specifications of signatures (and therefore a term algebra) and a family of partial interpretations for the polynomials.

5.1. Interpretations for Abstract Types

An abstract type T is a pair (Σ, E) where Σ is a signature and E is a set of Σ-formulas. A Σ-algebra A is called a strict model of a type $T = (\Sigma, E)$ iff

(1) $\forall\, e \in E: A \models_{strict} e$

(2) A is strictly term-generated

A regular interpretation I^A (in a Σ-algebra A) is called regular model of a type $T = (\Sigma, E)$ iff

(1) $\forall\, e \in E: I^A \models_{reg} e$

(2) A is term-generated by I^A

If we replace (2) by

(2′) A is Σ-generated by I^A

then we speak of an equationally complete regular model.

It seems a little bit more complicated and less elegant that not just algebras but algebras together with interpretations are considered as models. But this is necessary since there may be several possible partial interpretations for a given algebra. There is always the natural interpretation in a given partial algebra.

A very basic example for algebraically specified types is the type BOOL of boolean values given in section 2.

For the type BOOL every regular model (i.e. every regular interpretation) is carried by an algebra that is strictly term-generated. Hence every model is flat. Trivially every ground term can be reduced to (i.e. can be shown to be equal to) true or false by the axioms.

Generally, every regular model of a data type T includes a strict interpretation which, however, not necessarily is a strict model of T.

A type is called (strictly or regularly) monomorphic, if it has up to isomorphism exactly one (strict or regular resp.) model. If it has (up to isomorphism) more than one model, then it is called polymorphic.

For any type T = (Σ, E) that includes the type BOOL we can prove a lemma that allows to show the definedness of certain terms.

Lemma: Let f be a function symbol with arity (f) = <s **bool**> and let t, t′ be terms such that

E |- f(t) = true,

E |- f(t′) = false

then the interpretations of both t and t′ must be defined in every regular model of T.

Proof: Due to the definition of homomorphisms and regular interpretations $I^A[t] = I^A[t′]$ does not hold in any model since ¬(true = false). Thus at least t or t′ must have a defined interpretation. Assume $I^A[t]$ is not defined and $I^A[t′]$ is defined. We have with context c where c[x] = or(omega, f(x)):

$$c[t] = or(omega, f(t)) = or(omega, true) = true$$
and
$$c[t′] = or(omega, f(t′)) = or(omega, false) = omega$$

thus t must be defined, too, since otherwise we obtain a contradiction to the regularity property. The definedness of t′ is proved analoguously.

end of proof

A (regular or strict) model (interpretation) I^A of an abstract type is called <u>minimally defined</u> for the type T if for every every interpretation I'^A which is a model of T we have

$$I'^A \leq_\perp I^A => I^A \leq_\perp I'^A$$

Note that we have chosen a very liberal concept of models where the only restriction is term generability. From a specification point of view there is no good reason to restrict oneself to initial algebras or terminal algebras. However, sometimes it might be interesting to consider minimally defined models only.

5.2. Properties of Abstract Data Types

Abstract types provide a very powerful tool for the specification of algebraic structures. However, not all abstract types should be considered as proper specifications. An abstract type should fulfil at least some simple consistency properties.

For simplicity we assume from now on that every data type includes the type BOOL as a subtype.

A type T = (Σ, E) then is called <u>consistent</u>, if for every Σ-formula e at most e or ¬e can be proved, i.e. if in particular true = false cannot be proved.

By assuming the type BOOL to be a subtype for every type that we consider from now on, we can also introduce classical constructs like the conditional, which have proved being difficult to be defined in full generality in an appropriate way in total (without artificial element ⊥) or strict algebras.

In our framework of regular interpretations we easily can add an operation

funct (**bool, s, s**) **s** if

to every type and for every sort s with the axioms

if(true, x, y) = x,
if(false, x, y) = y,
DEF(if(b, x, y)) => DEF(b)

An abstract data type T = (Σ, E) is called <u>BOOL-complete</u>, if for every Σ-term t of sort **bool** one of the formulas DEF(t) => t = true or DEF(t) => t = false can be proved.

The type T = (Σ, E) is called <u>definedness-complete</u> (for a sort s) if for every term t (of sort s) either DEF(t) or $\neg$DEF(t) can be proved. An abstract data type T = (Σ, E) is called <u>complete</u>, if for every Σ-formula e the validity of e or $\neg$e can be proved.

Theorem: If an abstract type T is complete and consistent, then it is <u>monomorphic</u>, i.e. it has (up to the isomorphism) exactly one term-generated regular model.

Proof: Immediately a term model can be constructed according to the assumed consistency and completeness. Assume there are two models, i.e. two regular interpretations I^A and I^B in the term-generated algebras A and B. Now we define

$$\varphi_A: A \to B , \qquad \varphi_B: B \to A$$

by (for t $\in$ W_Σ)

$$\varphi_A(I^A[t]) = I^B[t] \qquad \varphi_B(I^B[t]) = I^A[t]$$

Due to the principle of term generation and completeness this way φ_A and φ_B are uniquely and consistently defined. Trivially $\varphi_A \circ \varphi_B$ and $\varphi_B \circ \varphi_A$ denote the identity.

end of proof

In algebraically specified types there are two important properties that characterize a term-generated model up to isomorphism:

-    which of the terms have identical interpretations and

-    the interpretation of which terms is not defined.

According to the different concepts of Σ-homomorphisms (partial, total, weakening, srengthening, strict) we get different concepts of initiality.

Proposition: Let C be a class of partial regular term-generated Σ-interpretations. If the regular interpretation I^A is

- (totally, partially, weakening, strictly) initial in C then for all interpretations I^B and for all Σ-terms t1, t2 with $I^A \models_{reg} DEF(t1) \wedge DEF(t2)$ and $I^B \models_{reg} DEF(t1) \wedge DEF(t2)$ we have:

$$I^A \models_{reg} t1 = t2 \quad => \quad I^B \models_{reg} t1 = t2$$

end of proposition

Similarly according to the different concepts of Σ-homomorphisms (partial, total, weakening, strict) we get different concepts of terminality.

Proposition: Let C be a class of partial regular term-generated Σ-interpretations. If the regular interpretation I^A is

- (totally, partially, weakening, strictly) terminal in C, then all interpretations I^B and for all Σ-terms t1, t2 with $I^A \models_{reg} DEF(t1) \land DEF(t2)$ and $I^B \models_{reg} DEF(t1) \land DEF(t2)$ we have:

$$I^B \models_{reg} t1 = t2 \implies I^A \models_{reg} t1 = t2$$

end of proposition

If the treatness of definedness in abstract types is complete, then a classical lemma on the existence of initial models holds.

Lemma: If a type T has only Horn-formulas as axioms and T is definedness-complete and consistent, then T has an initial model.

end of lemma

In connection with axiomatic specifications we simply can indicate in the axioms whether the interpretation of certain terms should be defined or definitely not defined.

However, often a specification is not definedness complete. For all terms where nothing is said about definedness we can either be liberal and accept all kinds of models. Those where the terms where nothing can be concluded about their definedness are defined and those where those terms are not defined. Another possibility is to take only maximally defined models (all terms are defined the undefinedness of which cannot explicitly deduced) or minimally defined models (all terms are undefined the definedness of which cannot be explicitly deduced).

These different options of taking minimally or maximally defined models can especially be expressed by the different forms of homomorphisms and by taking initial or terminal models resp. as it is indicated by the lemmas above.

Structured algebraic specifications are of particular interest in computing science. Therefore we consider now hierarchical algebras.

5.3. Hierarchical Abstract Types

A <u>hierarchical abstract type</u> T is a triple $(\Sigma, E, PRIM(T))$ where Σ is a hierarchical signature with primitive subsignature $PRIM(\Sigma)$ and E is a set of Σ-formulas where a subset $PRIM(E)$ $\subseteq$ E of $PRIM(E)$-formulas is designated as <u>primitive</u> such that $PRIM(T) = (PRIM(\Sigma), PRIM(E))$ forms a type called the <u>primitive subtype</u> of T.

A classical example that is often used is the type FINSET over a given type DATA with some specified equality function eq, i.e. DATA is assumed to be any given type with at least a function eq of functionality < **data data bool** >. The fact that DATA (together with the always included type BOOL) forms the primitive subtype of FINSET is expressed by the declaration **based_on** DATA.

type FINSET =

   based_on DATA

   sort fset,

   fct fset eset,
   fct (fset, data) fset add,
   fct (fset) bool iseset,

fct (fset, data) fset delete,
fct (fset, data) bool isel,

iseset(eset) = true,
iseset(add(s, x)) = false,

delete (eset, x) = eset
eq(x, y) = true => delete (add(s, y), x) = delete (s, x),
eq(x, y) = false => delete (add(s, y), x) = add(delete(s, x), y),

isel(eset, x) = false,
eq(x, y) = true => isel(add(s, y), x) = true,
eq(x, y) = false => isel(add(s, y),x) = isel(s, x),

add(add(s, x), y) = add(add(s, y), x),
isel(s, x) = true => add(s, x) = s

end of type

The type FINSET specifies finite sets of objects of sort **data**. Note that in a strict interpretation the elimination of the last two axioms would not change the terminal model but the initial one!

In a regular interpretation even adding undefined terms does not lead to undefined sets. For instance we obtain the equation

iselem(add(s, omega), x) = add(s, x)

The notion of hierarchical types seems very fundamental. It reflects precisely a situation found in programming very often: Some of the sorts stand for carrier sets the objects of which are well-known and for which the programmer has a very concrete understanding. Examples are booleans, natural numbers, characters, etc. For these objects generally external representations exist. They are used as input and output of programs. Such sorts and their basic operations correspond to the primitives of an abstract type. For other "nonprimitive" objects that can be constructed using the primitive ones external representations often do not exist. Such non-primitive objects are called TOI-objects by Guttag (for type-of-interest). For instance for a data base, which of course can be seen as an abstract object, generally nobody would expect to have an external standard representation.

A hierarchical type can always be seen as an enrichment of a given well-understood type (that forms the primitive subtype then) by certain sorts and operations. The hierarchy is also useful for introducing the concept of observability (also called input/output behaviour or extensional equivalence) in a straightforward way. The observable identity of an abstract object, i.e. of some term t of abstract sort, is completely defined in some interpretation for the primitive subtype by the values of terms c[t] of primitive sorts, where c is some context of primitive sort.

If the nonprimitive axioms do not introduce unnecessary inequalities then the observable (extensional) equality of nonprimitive terms corresponds to the equality in the terminal models.

Clearly one wishes that the hierarchy defined on the signature and on the axioms of some type is properly reflected in every model. In particular every model of the primitive type should be extendable to a complete model of the whole type: the nonprimitive axioms should not impose any new equalities or inequalities for primitive terms. Vice versa all primitive objects should be nameable by primitive terms: the non-primitive operations should not generate additional objects for the primitive sorts.

A Σ-algebra A is called strict (hierarchical) model of a hierarchical type T = (Σ, E) iff

(1) $\forall\, e \in E: A \models_{strict} e$

(2) A is strictly term-generated

(3) The (primitive) PRIM(Σ)-reduct of A is strictly term-generated

A regular interpretation I^A (in a Σ-algebra) A is called <u>regular (hierachical) model</u> of a hierarchical type $T = (\Sigma, E)$ iff

(1) $\forall\, e \in E: I^A \models_{reg} e$

(2) A is term-generated (or Σ-generated)

(3) The (primitive) PRIM(Σ)-reduct of $I^A(W_\Sigma)$ is PRIM(Σ)-algebraic

Since the axioms of the overall type include those of the primitive one, all first order Horn formula properties of the primitive type remain valid in the overall type - independent whether they concern defined terms or not.

A hierarchical type $T = (\Sigma, E)$ is called <u>weakly sufficiently complete</u> if for every term $t \in W_\Sigma(s)$ of primitive sort $s \in$ PRIM(S) such that $E \vdash$ DEF(t) there exists a primitive term $p \in W_{PRIM(\Sigma)}(s)$ with

$$E \vdash t = p.$$

A hierarchical type $T = (\Sigma, E)$ is called <u>sufficiently complete</u> if for every term $t \in W_\Sigma(s)$ of primitive sort $s \in$ PRIM(S) either $E \vdash \neg$DEF(t) or there exists a primitive term $p \in W_{PRIM(\Sigma)}(s)$ with

$$E \vdash t = p.$$

Sufficient completeness is a sufficient condition that no additional primitive elements are added by the nonprimitive functions i.e. no junk is generated.

However, there are examples of types that are not sufficiently complete, but in all models no junk is generated. As an example consider the type EX-FINSET:

type EX-FINSET =

    extends FINSET,

    fct (**fset** s : not(iseset(s)) **data** any,

    iseset(s) = false => isel(s, any(s)) = true   **end of type**

Every strict (strictly term-generated) model of this type for which we asume that the carrier set associated with **bool** has exactly two elements is a strict hierarchical model, too, although the type is not sufficiently complete.

The hierarchical type T is called <u>hierarchy-consistent</u>, if for all ground PRIM(Σ)-formulas e :

$$E \vdash e <=> PRIM(E) \vdash e.$$

A well-known example of a hierarchical type is the type SEQ that specifies sequences of objects of sort **data** (see section 2).

In the type SEQ we definitely have partial operations. This is expressed by restriction of the resp. function by terms of boolean sort. So

fct (**seq** s : not(iseseq(s))) **data** first

stands for the axiom

DEF(first(s)) => iseseq(s) = false

In a strict interpretation we obtain the classical algebra of sequences. However in a regular nonstrict interpretation we obtain "partial" sequences, i.e. sequences that contain data terms the interpretation of which is not defined. The interpretation of m(omega) has to be defined, since iseseq(m(x)) is defined and distinct from iseseq(eseq).

We obtain more strict variations of the type of sequences by inserting DEF(x) as premises for some of the axioms. Examples are algebras with a strict function m and left-strict or right-strict versions of the function conc leading to streams. We also may now consider equational complete interpretations of the type sequence. Then explicit equations such as

$$x = conc(m(d), x)$$

with arbitrary objects d of sort **data** do have only nontrivial solutions in equationally complete models.

5.4 Strict versus Regular Interpretations of Abstract Types

Strict validity can also be expressed by particular axioms with regular interpretations, if we assume that all carrier sets of the algebras that we consider are not empty. Given a regular interpretation I^A in a Σ-algebra A and a Horn-formula e of the form:

$$t_1 = r_1 \wedge ... \wedge t_n = r_n \wedge DEF(q_1) \wedge ... \wedge DEF(q_m) => t_{n+1} = r_{n+1}$$

such that

$$I^A \models_{strict} e$$

where $x_1, ..., x_n$ are the only identifiers occurring in e then

$$I^A \models_{reg} DEF(x_1) \wedge ... \wedge DEF(x_n) \wedge e$$

The strictness of a function symbol f with arity(f) = $<s_1... s_{n+1}>$ can be specified by the axioms (let $1 \le i \le n$)

DEF(f($x_1, ..., x_n$)) => DEF(x_i)

Therefore every algebraic type T for which a strict interpretation is assumed can be transformed into algebraic type T′ with a class of regular interpretations which has exactly the class of models that is the class of strict models of T. Therefore strict algebraic types can be understood as a special case of regular types.

This can be demonstrated by an example. Consider the algebraic type NAT with a strict interpretation:

type NAT =

  based_on BOOL

sort nat,

fct nat zero,
fct (nat) nat succ,
fct (nat x : not (iszero(x))) pred,
fct (nat) bool iszero,

pred(succ(x)) = x,
iszero(zero) = true,
iszero(succ(x)) = false

end of type

It can be transformed by the techniques described above into a type NAT'with regular interpretation:

type NAT' =

based_on BOOL

sort nat,

fct nat zero,
fct (nat) nat succ,
fct (nat x : not (iszero(x))) pred,
fct (nat) bool iszero,

DEF(succ(x)) => DEF(x),
DEF(pred(x)) => DEF(x),
DEF(iszero(x)) => DEF(x),

DEF(x) $\land$ pred(succ(x)) = x,
iszero(zero) = true,
DEF(x) $\land$ iszero(succ(x)) = false

end of type

Thus abstract types with strict interpretations can always be transformed into abstract types with regular interpretations that have the same models. Strictly interpreted abstract types can be seen as a specification scheme for regular interpretations with strict functions only.

5.5 Equational Specifications versus Order-theoretic Specifications

Now we give an example for a regular algebraic type for which an equivalent order-theoretic algebraic specification does not exist. At first we give a simple analysis of the type NAT given above, specifying natural numbers, however with a regular interpretation including "partial" numbers.

Assuming a strict interpretation the type NAT has just the classical set of natural numbers as model. In a nonstrict (regular) interpretation in every minimally defined model we have also "partial" elements such as the interpretation of succ(pred(zero)). In every model pred(zero) does not have a defined interpretation. However, succ(pred(zero)) must have a defined interpretation since iszero(succ(pred(zero))) is defined (and false) and iszero(zero) = true, so due to the regularity conditions both zero and succ(pred(zero)) must be defined (and distinct).

Moreover, all interpretations of terms

$succ^n(pred(zero))$

must be defined for $n > 0$, since $iszero(pred^m(succ^n(pred(zero))))$ is defined for $n > m$ and undefined otherwise. In equationally complete models the equation

$$x = succ(x)$$

does have a solution. A solution x is distinct to the interpretation of ground terms, since $iszero(pred^m(x)) = false$ holds for all m.

Now consider the following type very similar to the type FINSET:

type FSET =

   based_on NAT,

   sort fset,

   fct fset emptyset,
   fct (nat, fset) fset put,
   fct (nat, fset) bool iselem,

   put(x, put(y, s)) = put(y, put(x, s)),
   put(x, put(x, s)) = put(x, s)
   iselem(x, put(y, s)) = or(eq(x, y), iselem(x, s))

                                                              end of type

Let us consider the two terms (let omega stand for pred(zero))

   t1: put(omega, put(succ(omega), put(succ(succ(omega)), emptyset)))

   t2: put(omega, put(succ(succ(omega)), emptyset)).

Both terms are interpreted differently in certain minimally defined models: there is no way to conclude the equality of these two terms from the axioms.

However, whenever we assume $\leq_\perp$ to be a partial ordering on our models, then we obtain (since the interpretation of omega is not defined) $I^A[\,t1] \leq_\perp I^A[\,t2\,]$ and $I^A[\,t2\,] \leq_\perp I^A[\,t1\,]$, i.e. $I^A[\,t1\,] = I^A[\,t2\,]$. So assuming $\leq_\perp$ to be a partial ordering leads to unwanted identifications. Or more precisely: there are equationally specified structures that cannot be specified by $\leq_\perp$-ordered continuous algebras.

5.6. Structural Induction

There is a simple but nevertheless powerful technique for proving properties for all term-generated models of an algebraic type, namely the technique of structural induction. Trivially $\leq_{sub}$ forms a Noetherian ordering on W_Σ. So we can apply the classical techniques of structural induction. More refined versions of induction can be obtained by the definition of term-normal forms or even unique term normal forms which allow to reduce the proof overhead considerably.

Based on the relation $\leq_{sub}$ structural induction for term-generated interpretations on the term structure reads

$$\forall\, t \in W_\Sigma: (\forall\, t' \in W_\Sigma: t' \leq_{sub} t \wedge t' \neq t => P(t')) \;=>\; P(t)$$

$$P(t)$$

Note once more that proofs by structural induction on the term structure can only be applied to term-generated interpretations.

Even for Σ-algebraic algebras methods of structural induction work. Then the induction must be carried out over all polynomials (contexts) that may occur as right-handsides of explicit equations. Another possibility which will be studied in the next chapter in connection with higher order algebras is to work with term generated algebras that include an explicit fixed point operator.

6. Higher Order Data Types

In some applications it seems convenient to include second and even higher order functions into algebraic specifications. However, this leads to the question how to interpret second order or even higher order equational formulas. More precisely, the key question is how to handle universal quantification for function identifiers. Following the concept of term-generability for objects and contexts we may introduce the concept of "term-generated sets of functions".

6.1. Higher Order Signatures and Higher Order Algebras

Let S be a set of basic sorts. The set of higher order functionalities $S^{->}$ is defined as follows

- for all $s \in S$ we have $s \in S^{->}$

- if $u_1, ..., u_{n+1} \in S^{->}$ then $< u_1 ... u_{n+1} > \in S^{->}$

$S^{->}$ is assumed to be the least set fulfilling these conditions. This construction is very similar to the constructions of the types in typed λ-calculus. A higher order signature $\Sigma = (S, F)$ consists of a set of basic sorts S, a set of (higher order) function symbols F, and a functionality function **fct**: $F \to S^{->}$.

Given a higher ordersignature $\Sigma = (S, F)$ and a $S^{->}$-sorted family $X = \{ X_s \}_{s \in S^{->}}$ of (pairwise disjoint) sets of identifiers, then we can define for higher order sorts $u \in S^{->}$ the set $W_\Sigma(u)$ of terms of sort u and the set $W_\Sigma(u, X)$ of polynomials of sort u. The <u>higher order term algebra</u> W_Σ over the higher order signature Σ consists of the family of sets $W_\Sigma(u)$ for $u \in S^{->}$.

$W_\Sigma(u)$ and $W_\Sigma(u, X)$ are defined by inductively by the following rules:

(0) for $f \in F$ with **fct**(f) = u we have

$$f \in W_\Sigma(u) \text{ and } f \in W_\Sigma(u, X)$$

for $x \in X_u$ we have:

$$x \in W_{\Sigma}(u, X)$$

(1) for $f \in F$ with $\mathbf{fct}(f) = < u_1 \dots u_{n+1} >$ we have for $t_1 \in W_{\Sigma}(u_1), \dots, t_n \in W_{\Sigma}(u_n)$

$$f(t_1, \dots, t_n) \in W_{\Sigma}(u_{n+1})$$

and for $t_1 \in W_{\Sigma}(u_1, X), \dots, t_n \in W_{\Sigma}(u_n, X)$ we have

$$f(t_1, \dots, t_n) \in W_{\Sigma}(u_{n+1}, X)$$

(2) **λ-abstraction**

If $t \in W_{\Sigma}(u, X)$ and the pairwise distinct identifiers $x_1, \dots, x_n$ are of sorts $u_1, \dots, u_n$ then

$$(\lambda x_1, \dots, x_n : t) \in W_{\Sigma}(< u_1 \dots u_n u >, X)$$

If $x_1, \dots, x_n$ are the only free identifiers in t then

$$(\lambda x_1, \dots, x_n : t) \in W_{\Sigma}(< u_1 \dots u_n u >)$$

(3) **Fixed point operator**

Let $f \in W_{\Sigma}(<u\ u>)$ then **fix** f is a term of sort u   i.e.

$$\mathbf{fix}\ f \in W_{\Sigma}(u).$$

Let $f \in W_{\Sigma}(<u\ u>, X)$ then **fix** f is a polynomial of sort u   i.e.

$$\mathbf{fix}\ f \in W_{\Sigma}(u, X).$$

Higher order equations are formulas between higher order polynomials. Higher order equations can be interpreted the same way like classical first order equations. Note here that the validity of higher order equations strongly depends on the range of the carrier sets and that we do <u>not</u> associate with the higher order sort $< u_1 \dots u_{n+1} >$ the set of all (partial) functions

$$u_1{}^A \times \dots \times u_n{}^A \to u_{n+1}{}^A$$

but only those functions that are contained in the resp. sort. In term-generated algebras this means that they can be represented by some term.

A <u>higher order Σ-algebra</u> A consists of a family of carrier sets s^A for every $s \in S^{->}$ and a family of partial functions f^A for every $f \in F$ with range and domain according to the functionality of f. If $s = < u_1 \dots u_{n+1} >$ then we assume $s^A \subseteq (u_1{}^A \times \dots \times u_n{}^A \to u_{n+1}{}^A)$.

We do not give a model theory in terms of partial interpretations here for higher order types.

6.2. Deduction Rules for Higher Order Signatures

For higher order signatures we use besides other laws the classical rules of deduction namely the law of <u>extensionality</u>. We again assume sort correctness for the terms involved (let $\mathbf{fct}(g) = \mathbf{fct}(f) = <u_1 ... u_{n+1}>$)

$$\frac{\forall\ x_1, ..., x_n\colon f(x_1, ..., x_n) = g(x_1, ..., x_n)}{f = g}$$

The other classical law for (higher order) functions is the <u>law of instantiation</u> (let $t_i \in W_\Sigma(u_i, X)$ for $1 \le i \le n$):

$$\frac{g = f}{g(t_1, ..., t_n) = f(t_1, ..., t_n)}$$

In addition of course we assume the laws given for the compositional forms for functions. For λ-terms we assume the laws of α-conversion:

$$(\lambda\, x_1, ..., x_n : t) = (\lambda\, y_1, ..., y_n : t[y_1/x_1, ... , y_n/x_n])$$

and the laws of β-conversion:

$$(\lambda\, x_1, ..., x_n : t)(t_1, ..., t_n) = t[t_1/x_1, ..., t_n/x_n]$$

In connection with higher order algebras we have to distinguish carefully between a term of sort s and a nullary function f with $\mathbf{fct}(f) = <s>$. Then $f()$ is a term of sort s.

For **fix** f we assume the equation:

$$f(\mathbf{fix}\ f) = \mathbf{fix}\ f$$

and the equation (let x not occur in C and f):

$$(\exists\, \mathbf{s}\, x : x = f(x) \land \neg\mathrm{DEF}(C(x))) => \neg\mathrm{DEF}(C(\mathbf{fix}\ f))$$

which is equivalent (since x does not occur in the conclusion):

$$x = f(x) \land \neg\mathrm{DEF}(C(x)) => \neg\mathrm{DEF}(C(\mathbf{fix}\ f))$$

The law of extensionality is not a Horn clause and therefore higher-order types are significantly distinct to first-order types with Horn clause specifications.

6.3 Examples of Higher Order Types

We now give some examples for higher order specifications of data types. In the type BOOL we may introduce a function

$$\mathbf{fct}\ (\ \mathbf{bool}\ )\ \mathbf{fct}(s, s)s\quad cd$$

defined by

$$cd(true) = \lambda\, x, y : x$$

$$cd(false) = \lambda\, x, y : y$$

Trivially we obtain

$$if(b, t1, t2) = cd(b)(t1, t2)$$

This demonstrates how we can work with currying and other techniques from functional programming in higher order types.

If we assume a given element d_0 of sort **data** we can specify the type MAP based on anarbitrary type DATA without introducing a new sort:

high type MAP =

    based on BOOL, DATA,

    fct fct(data)data init,

    fct (fct(data)data, data, data) fct(data)data update,

    init = $\lambda\, x: d_0$,

    update(f, d1, d2) (d1) = d2,

    eq(d1, d) = false => update(f, d1, d2)(d) = f(d)

                                                end of high type

For the type sequence we may introduce a star operation:

high-type STAR =

    based_on SEQ,

    fct(fct(data)data) fct(seq)seq star,

    star(f)(empty) = empty

    star(f)(conc(m(d), s)) = conc(m(f(d)), star(f)(s))

                                                end of high type

If we assume a type STATE with an update function in analogy to the type MAP, then we can define a type PL denoting a simple programming language straightforward:

high-type PL = **based_on** STATE, IDENTIFIER, MAP,

    fct (sta) sta nop,

    fct (id, fct(sta)int) sta assign,

    fct (fct(sta)bool, fct(sta)sta, fct(sta)sta) fct(sta)sta if,

    fct (fct(sta)sta, fct(sta)sta) fct(sta)sta semi,

fct (fct(sta)bool, fct(sta)sta) fct(sta)sta while,

nop = λ x : x,

semi(c1, c2)(x) = c2(c1(x)),

b(s) = true => if(b, c1, c2) (s) = c1(s),

b(s) = false => if(b, c1, c2) (s) = c2(s),

DEF(v(s)) => assign(x, v)(s) => update(s, v, x),

while(b, c) = if(b, semi(c, while(b, c)), nop)

end of high type

The axiom for while could also be replaced by a definition using the fixed point operator.

while(b, c) = **fix** λ x : if(b, semi(c, x), nop)

Here a tuned notation could help to improve the readability of the signatures where we are allowed to abbreviate function sorts by simple sort identifiers.

Higher order types as well as "types with nonstrict operations" can be modelled in classical strict first order algebraic specifications if we model the term-structure there as objects. Then we just have to add the operation apply for representing function application. But there the law of extensionality causes problems, too, if it is to be axiomatized.

Higher order algebraic types can just be seen as a notational extension (a mechanism for schematic extensions) of abstract types leading into the rich styles of functional programming or typed λ-calculus. With higher order abstract types all phases of program development can be treated within the algebraic framework.

6.5 Deduction Rules based on Least Fixed Point Properties and Continuity Assumptions

If we assume that **fix** chooses the least defined function that fulfils an equation we may use the deduction rule

x = t $\wedge$ $\neg$DEF(C[x]) $\Rightarrow$ $\neg$DEF(C(**fix** λ x: t))

Due to the regularity conditions this way no inconsistencies are introduced in types with definedness positive axioms where no axioms for the fixed point operator are included besides the basic definition that it fulfils the fixed point equation.

The principle of computational induction can be formulated as follows:

$\forall$ i $\in$ N: $\neg$DEF(t_i[x]), where t_0 = t, t_{i+1} = C[t_i]

$\neg$DEF(λx: C[x])

With this rule of computational induction we can only prove undefinedness of terms. The equality of fixed point definitions is closely connected with the extensional equality. For proving the extensional equality of fixed points one may combine techniques using fixed point properties and computational induction.

For certain types the assumption of the validity of computational induction may lead to inconsistencies.

6.6. Hierarchical Higher Order Types

Often one is interested in hierarchical types T with primitive subtypes with a complete deductive theory (for regular term-generated models). This means that we can prove for all primitive terms t and t'

$$DEF(t) \quad\quad \text{or} \quad\quad \neg DEF(t)$$

and

$$t = t' \quad\quad \text{or} \quad\quad \neg(t = t').$$

All nonprimitive axioms are assumed to be definedness positive Horn clauses, where only equations occur in the conclusions. Let us furthermore assume that the type is weakly sufficiently complete and hierarchy-consistent and all primitive sorts are flat. Under these assumption we can prove the following theorem.

Theorem:
Under the condition given above we have:

(1) There exists a fully abstract model of T

(2) If the equality between primitive terms is decidable and the definedness of primitive terms is positive semidecidable, then the equality between nonprimitive terms is negative semidecidable and their definedness is positive semidecidable.

Proof:
(1) Define for (nonprimitive) terms t, t'

$$t \sim t' \quad \text{if for all contexts C of primitive sort} \quad C[t] = C[t']$$

~ is a congruence relation and so defines a fully abstract model on the term algebra. Define for nonprimitive t

$$DEF(t) \text{ is valid}$$

if there exists a context C of primitive sort such that

$$\neg(C[t] = C[t']) \text{ and } DEF(C[t])$$

can be deduced for some term t', otherwise assume $\neg DEF(t)$.

(2) All contexts of primitive sort are recursively enumerable. Also all terms are enumerable. Therefore we can search for a given term t, for a term t' and a primitive (boolean) context such that $\neg(C[t] = C[t'])$. Note that the equality between primitive terms is assumed to be decidable. Then DEF(t) is valid.

end of proof

Sometimes we study only minimally defined models where every term of primitive sort is assumed to be undefined if it cannot be reduced to a primitive term.

7. Algebraic Abstract Types in Program Design

In the program development process abstract types are useful in at least three respects.

- They can be used to specify the basic computation structures that are to be used in programs.

- The axioms of a type can be used immediately as transformation and verification rules in program development.

- They provide a clear notion of implementation that allows one to replace one type by another (more machine-oriented) one in program development. This proceeding can be repeated until the programs just use types implementations of which are provided by the target programming language or the target hardware.

In the following we give some brief introduction to the realisation and implementation of abstract types.

Abstract types provide just specifications. But of course it is the purpose of a specification to serve as the starting point for the construction of a mechanism that satisfies the specification.

In the following sections we briefly study three aspects of the realisation of an algebraic specification:

- implementation of abstract types by other abstract types: We speak of algebraic ("abstract") implementations;

- inference mechanism based realisation of abstract types by techniques from logic programming implementing the deductive theory;

- realisation of abstract types by data structure definitions in programming languages.

All three methods are related, are useful in the design of software, and can be based on special techniques forming a methodological framework.

7.1 Algebraic Implementations of Abstract Types

Throughout this section for simplicity we consider just strict types. In the following we want to write implementations of abstract types in terms of other, more basic abstract types. Then the concept of an implementation can be formalized as a specific relation between types.

Given the hierarchical types $T = (\Sigma, E)$ and $T^+ = (\Sigma^+, E^+)$ with identical primitive subtypes $PRIM(T) = PRIM(T^+)$ and a signature morphism

$$\sigma : \Sigma \rightarrow \Sigma^+$$

which is the identity for the primitive subsignature $PRIM(\Sigma)$, then (T^+, σ) is called algebraic implementation of T if for every model A^+ of T^+ there exists a total Σ-homomorphism from the term-generated Σ-subalgebra of $\sigma^{-1}(A^+)$ onto a model of T. According to this definition every model of an algebraic implementation of a type T can be renamed such that it contains a Σ-subalgebra that is extensional equivalent to some model of T.

An implementation of an abstract type T_A in terms of a given type T_I can be constructed as follows: We assume that both T_A and T_I are hierarchical types with identical primitive subtype $PRIM(T_A) = PRIM(T_I)$ all nonprimitive sorts and function symbols are distinct and that both types T_A and T_I are sufficiently complete. Now we assume the following three steps for the construction of an implementation of T_A in terms of T_I.

(1) <u>Enrich</u>:
T_I is extended ("enriched") by a number of operations leading to the type T^+ with primitive subtype T_I. Again T^+ is assumed to be sufficiently complete and hierarchy-consistent w.r.t. $PRIM(T^+) = T_I$.

(2) <u>Relate (and forget sorts, functionsymbols, and elements)</u>
We define a signature morphism σ that maps the signature Σ_A of type T_A to the signature Σ^+ of type T^+. σ should be the identity on the primitive subsignature $PRIM(\Sigma_A)$.

(3) <u>Identify</u>
We construct a type T_C. T_C is only needed for verification purposes and contains the following operations: For every nonprimitive sort $s1 \in S_A$ with $\sigma(s1) = s2$ the type T_C contains a function

fct (s2) s1 abs$_s$

and the following equations: For every nonprimitive function symbol $f \in F_A \backslash PRIM(F_A)$ with arity(f) = $<s_1 ... s_{n+1}>$ and with $\sigma(f) = f'$ the type T_C contains the equation

$$abs_{s_{n+1}}(f(x_1, ..., x_n)) = f'(abs_{s1}(x_1), ..., abs_{sn}(x_n))$$

For primitive sorts s we replace $abs_s(x_i)$ by x_i. Now we have the following theorems:

Theorem: Let the definitions of $PRIM(T_A)$, T_I, T_A, T^+, σ, T_C be like above: Then the type T_C is sufficiently complete w.r.t. $PRIM(T_A)$, T_I and T_A.

Proof: Trivially every ground term containing applications of the functions abs$_s$ can be translated by the axioms for abs$_s$ in a term without applications of the function abs$_s$. The sufficient completeness of T_I and T_A immediately implies the sufficient completeness of T_C w.r.t. $PRIM(T_A)$.

end of proof

Now we give the basic theorem of this section. It demonstrates that the proof of correctness of an implementation basically can be understood as a proof of hierarchy consistency.

Theorem: The type T^+ provides an implementation for type T_A if T_C is hierarchy-consistent w.r.t. both T_A and T_I.

Proof: Assume T_C is hierarchy consistent. Then the functions abs$_s$ define a homomorphism for every model of T^+ from a Σ_A-subalgebra to a model of T_A.

end of proof

Note that hierarchy-consistency is a sufficient but not a necessary condition. Due to our condition of abstract implementation T^+ might impose additional constraints on T_A which is simply due to the fact that an implementation may choose to implement one particular model of T_A. We can reduce our requirement to the following condition: T_C must be hierarchy-consistent w.r.t. $PRIM(T_A)$, provided all nonprimitive axioms in T_A are positive Horn-clauses.

Note that the hierarchy-consistency of T_C w.r.t. T^+ is trivial, since T_C does not add any equations for T^+ terms.

Proving hierarchy-consistency is a very abstract requirement. Therefore in the remaining parts of this section we show in a more concrete style how to prove that some type represents an implementation for another type as well as how to construct an implementation.

Such a more concrete method for constructing an implementation and proving its correctness is obtained by the construction of a concrete model (and proving it correct) of the type T_A in terms of an arbitrary model of the type T_I by introducing explicitly the congruence relation induced by the homomorphism.

For proving the correctness of an implementation we specify two predicates for every sort s in S_A:

- a predicate REP_s specifying which terms of sort $\sigma(s)$ are used for representing the objects of the abstract type T_A,

- a predicate EQU_s specifying whether two objects of sort $\sigma(s)$ for which REP_s holds represent the same abstract objects of sort s.

For every model I of T^+ there has to exist a model A of T such that there exist two families of functions:

the abstraction functions $\{ ABS_s \}_{s \in S}$ where

$$ABS_s : \sigma(s)^I \to s^A$$

the implementation functions $\{ IMP_s \}_{s \in S}$ where

$$IMP_s : s^A \to P(\sigma(s)^I).$$

For simplicity we drop the sort indices whenever this can be done without leading to confusions..

The functions ABS_s have to be partial, surjective, and Σ-homomorphic.

The functions IMP_s are total and set-valued (one-to-many) where the set must not be empty.

Their interrelationship is specified by the following formulas (let $s \in S$) which represent the verification conditions.:

(0) EQU_s is a congruence relation

(1) $\forall x \in s^A$: $ABS_s(IMP_s(x)) = \{x\}$,

(2) $\forall \, y \in \sigma(s)^I : REP_s(y) => y \in IMP_s(ABS_s(y))$,

(3) $\forall \, y1, y2 \in \sigma(s)^I : REP_s(y1) \wedge REP_s(y2) \wedge ABS_s(y1) = ABS_s(y2) \; => \; EQU_s(y1, y2)$,

(4) $\forall \, y \in \sigma(s)^I : DEF(ABS_s(y)) => REP_s(y)$,

If the above formulas are proved and in addition every law e of the type T can be verified for T^+ if we replace the equality "=" by EQU and restrict the quantification to elements x for which REP(x) holds, then the type T^+ defines a correct implementation.

Note that the functions ABS, EQU and IMP are completely determined by the choice of σ and REP.

In principle an implementation can be constructed using the laws of the given type. To give a simple example we construct an implementation of the type FINSET in terms of the type SEQ.

At first we have to choose the representations for the sorts:

$\sigma(\textbf{fset}) = \textbf{seq}$

Trivially we may choose

$\sigma(eset) = eseq$, $\sigma(iseset) = iseseq$,

To find representations for the other functions in FINSET we have to enrich the type SEQ by the functions

fct (seq, data) seq add´,
fct (seq, data) seq delete´,
fct (seq, data) bool iselem´,

such that we can choose

$\sigma(eset) = eseq$,
$\sigma(iseset) = isseq$,
$\sigma(add) = add´$,
$\sigma(delete) = delete´$,
$\sigma(iselem) = iselem´$

Now there are several alternatives for choosing the representation of the constructor function add´.

First alternative: It is rather suggestive to use the equation:

$add´(s, x) = conc(s, m(x))$

This axiom immediately induces the axioms for the other functions by simply taking the resp. axioms of type FINSET:

delete´(eseq, x) = eseq,
eq(x, y) = true => delete´(conc(s, m(x)),y) = delete´(s,y),
eq(x, y) = false => delete´(conc(s, m(x)),y) = conc(delete´(s, y), m(x)),
isel´(eseq, x) = false,
isel´(conc(s, m(x)), y) = or(eq(x, y), isel´(s, y)).

Furthermore we obtain

REP(s) = true   for all objects s of sort **seq**

and

EQU(sl, s2) = ∀ **data** x : iselem´(sl, x) = isel´(s2, x)

Using the laws of SEQ also a recursive version can be obtained for delete´ using the substitution in the axioms

iseseq(s) = false => s = conc(lr(s), m(last(s)))

By that one obtains:

deletes(s, x) =
if iseseq(s)   **then** eseq
                else   **if** eq(x, last(s))   **then** delete´(lr(s), x)
                                      else   conc(delete´(lr(s), x), m(last(s)))
                                fi
fi

Note that this is a recursive version of delete´ based on sequences and may be further developed into a procedural program by the techniques of section 3.

Second alternative: Now we choose a more refined axiom for add´:

add´(s, x) = **if** isel´(s, x) **then** s **else** conc(s, m(x))) **fi**

The axioms for delete´ and isel remain the same as before. But for REP we now may use a stronger predicate:

REP(conc(s, m(x))) = and(**not**(isel´(s, x)), REP(s)),

REP(eseq) = true.

Accordingly we use only sequences for representing sets where each element occurs at most once. With this invariant assertion the recursive version of delete´ may be simplified to

delete´(s, x) =
if iseseq(s)   **then** eseq
            else if eq(x, last(s))   **then** lr(s)
                            else conc(delete´(lr(s), x), m(last(s))) **fi fi**

The two alternative implementations of type FINSET by the type SEQ show significantly different properties of efficiency.

The construction of an implementation of an abstract type in terms of another type generally is a difficult and complex task and also very error-prone. Therefore here verification and a design based on formal rules is an indispensible requisit for being sure about the correctness of the constructed implementation.

7.2 Implementation of Types based on the Deductive Theory

With an algebraic type $T = (\Sigma, E)$ a deductive theory is associated. It consists of a number of rules of inference which of course have to be consistent with the model theory. In its simplest view the deductive theory allows to prove a number of equations between terms and/or the definedness of certain terms.

The deductive theory forms a purely logical proof calculus. However, as we know from logic programming a proof theory can also be used as the basis of a method of evaluation. If certain terms (terms in "normal form") are specified to denote ("represent") objects, then we can use a deductive theory for reducing terms to normal forms as follows. If for a given term t we are able to prove from the axioms E of a type $T = (\Sigma, E)$ some equation

$$t = t'$$

or more precisely $E \mid- t = t'$ where t' is in normal form, then we can say that we have evaluated t to t'. This corresponds to solving the explicit equation

$$x = t \qquad \qquad \text{where x is required to be in normal form}$$

i.e. to find a term t' for x with t' in normal form such that the equation above is fulfilled.

Explicit equations like the one given above are only a special case of arbitrary equations or even systems of equations between polynomials for which we would like to find solutions. It is rather clear that in a brute force search we can recursively enumerate all terms for the free identifiers in the system. For each tuple of terms (for instance for the left-hand side of the system of equations) we can recursively enumerate all equivalent terms. This way we find all solutions of a system of equations. However, this is a rather inefficient way of doing it. A more sophisticated way of finding such solutions is <u>conditional narrowing</u> which uses techniques from term rewriting and logic programming. In the following we give a short explanation of such a technique following [Hussmann 85].

For explaining the conditional narrowing process we generalize the problem of solving a system of equations. We start by introducing term environments. For a given signature Σ and a set of identifiers X a <u>term environment</u> is a mapping

$$\eta: X \to W_\Sigma(X)$$

which is assumed to be sort consistent.

An environment η is called <u>simple</u> if for all identifiers $x \in X_s$ (for arbitrary sorts $s \in S$) we have: if $\eta(x) = t$ then for all identifiers occurring in t we have $\eta(y) = y$. If η and α are simple environments so is the environment $\eta \circ I_\alpha$ provided that

(*) for all $x, z \in X_s$ (with arbitrary $s \in S$) we have if $\eta(x) \neq x$ then $\alpha(x) = x$ and x does not

occur in some $\alpha(z)$ for $z \neq x$.

Here I_α denotes the interpretation of terms in the algebra of polynomials $W_\Sigma(X)$ under the environment α.

Given the type $T = (\Sigma, E)$ and a finite set of equations

$$D = \{ t_i = t_i' : 1 \le i \le k \}$$

then a simple term environment η is called <u>solution</u> of D if

$$E \vdash I_\eta[t_i] = I_\eta[t_i']$$

for all i, $1 \le i \le n$. Since we can understand D as specifying the task of finding a solution, D is also called a <u>task</u>.

Now for a finite system of equations D and an environment α where for all x occurring in D we assume $\alpha(x) = x$ by

D **where** α

we denote a <u>generalized task</u> (also called a <u>goal</u>). If a simple environment η is a solution of D, then $\eta \circ I_\alpha$ is called a <u>solution</u> of the generalized task (we assume condition (*)).

With the identity function ι (i.e. $\iota(x) = x$ for all $x \in X$, which is a simple term environment, too, a simple environment η is a solution of the generalized task

D **where** ι

iff $\eta \cdot I_\iota = \eta$ is a solution of D, i.e. iff η is a solution of D. This way every task can be trivially generalized to a generalized task. For the generalized task

D **where** α

where there exists a most general unifier η, i.e. $I_\eta[t_i] = I_\eta[t_i']$ for all i, $1 \le i \le k$, the simple term environment $\eta \cdot I_\alpha$ is a solution of the task D. Then the task is also called <u>solved</u>. Every task with an empty set of equations is solved.

Now given an abstract type $T = (\Sigma, E)$ and a system D of equations between Σ-polynomials, we can try to find a solution for D by looking at the associated generalized task and trying to transform this task using the axioms from E until the task is solved.

For a given generalized task

(*) $\{ t_i = t_i' : 1 \le i \le k \}$ **where** α

we can obtain a new generalized task by applying an axiom from E (if possible) as follows. Let (w.l.o.g. we assume that all identifiers in the axioms are distinct to the identifiers occurring in the t_i and t_i')

$$a_1 = b_1 \wedge ... \wedge a_j = b_j => a_{j+1} = b_{j+1}$$

be an axiom from E.

We obtain a new generalized task if there exists a subterm u (which is not just an identifier, i.e.

we require $\neg(u \in X))$ in some of the terms t_i or $t_i{}'$ such that for u and a_{j+1} there exists a unifier (let w.l.o.g. be i = k).

Let η be the most general term environment (representing the most general unifier) such that

$$I_\eta[u] = I_\eta[a_{j+1}]$$

and $\alpha \circ I_\eta$ is simple (this can always be achieved by renaming η). Then we consider the new task

$$\{ I_\eta[t_i] = I_\eta[t_i{}'] : 1 \leq i \leq k\text{-}1 \} \qquad \cup$$
$$\{ I_\eta[t_k[b_{j+1}/u]] = I_\eta[t_k{}'] \} \qquad \cup$$
$$\{ I_\eta[a_i] = I_\eta[b_i] : 1 \leq i \leq j \} \qquad\qquad \textbf{where} \ \ \alpha \circ I_\eta$$

Trivially every solution of this task is a solution of the generalized task (*).

Based on the algorithm which provides a deduction tree for generalized tasks a system has been implemented at the University of Passau for the evaluation of tasks over algebraic types. For results about the completeness of the method cf. [Hussmann 85].

7.3 Implementations of Types by Programs

Generally the required result of a program development process is not an algebraic specification but a program written in some programming language. This corresponds rather to a system of sort (mode) declarations based on direct union (variant) and product (record), recursion and maybe also some more machine-oriented concepts like program variables and pointers. In another application area one might be interested in versions of algebraic types that can be used interactively or even concurrently by communicating processes running in parallel.

Using the concept of abstraction functions also in the case of programs representing computation structures the correctness of an implementation may be made explicit.

The most rigorous approach here would be to give an algebraic description of the programming language and to show the algebraic laws of the type that is to be implemented for the implementing constructions by the algebraic laws for the used language constructs.

We could also use a enriched signature and an enriched term algebra that provides for each tuple of sort resp. constructors and destructors for forming tuples and similar constructs for union (variant sorts) etc. (cf. [CIP 85]). We give an example only considering tupling.

Often we are interested to represent abstract objects by tuples of concrete objects. Then the type that should carry the implementation has to be extended by further sorts representing tuples of other sorts and by the respective tupling and projection functions. This can be done in a very schematic way.

Let S be a set of sorts. The set of tuple sorts $S^{<>}$ is defined as follows

- if $s \in S$ then $s \in S^{<>}$

- if $s_1, ..., s_n \in S$ then $<s_1 ... s_n> \in S^{<>}$

$S^{<>}$ is assumed to be the least set fulfilling these conditions. The tuple signature $\Sigma^{<>} = (S^{<>}, F^{<>})$ for a given signature $\Sigma = (S, F)$ consists of a set of sorts $S^{<>}$, and $F^{<>}$ the set of function symbols F is defined as follows

(0) <u>projection functions</u>:

for every i, $n \in \mathbb{N}$ with $1 \le i \le n$ and $s \in S^{<>}$ with $s = <u_1 ... u_n u_i>$ by Π_i^s we denote a function symbol from $F^{<>}$ of functionality s for which we assume the equation

$$\Pi_i^s(t_1 ... t_n) = t_i$$

we drop s in Π_i^s and write Π_i^n or just Π_i whenever the sort information s or the arity information can be omitted without the danger of confusions.

(1) <u>tupeling</u>:

Let $s = <u_1 ... u_n> \in S^{<>}$. $[]_s$ is a functional term of functionality $<u_1 ... u_n>$. Its application is defined by the equation:

$$[]_s(x_1, ... , x_n) = (x_1, ..., x_n)$$

(2) <u>function symbols</u>: Let $f \in F$ with $arity(f) = <s_1 ... s_{n+1}>$; then $f \in F^{<>}$ with $arity(f) = <s_1 ... s_{n+1}>$.

We can introduce additional function symbols or we can use functional terms as defined in higher order types.

Now we can define signature morphisms also between a given abstract signature $\Sigma_A = (S_A, F_A)$ and $(\Sigma_I)^{<>} = (S_I^{<>}, F_I^{<>})$, where $\Sigma_I = (S_I, F_I)$ is a given concrete signature. By using this concept a lot of explicit definitional overhead can be avoided.

8. Conclusions

Algebraic specifications of partial higher order algebras provide a powerful and flexible framework for the requirement specification as well as design specification. By including appropriate definitions the transition to particular programming styles is possible such that a coherent programming framework can be built.

However, still a lot of work remains to be done for forming a powerful tractable methodology based on appropriate support tools.

References

[ADJ 75]
J.A. Goguen, J.W. Thatcher, E.G. Wagner, J.B. Wright: Initial algebra semantics and continuous algebras. IBM Research Report RC-5701, November 1975, JACM 24 (1977) 68-95

[Bauer et al. 81]
F.L. Bauer et al.: Programming in a wide spectrum language: A collection of examples. SCP 1, (1981) 73 - 114

[Birkhoff, Lipson 70]
G. Birkhoff, J.D. Lipson: Heterogeneous algebras. J. of Combinatorial Theory 8 (1970) 115-133

[Broy 84]
M. Broy: Algebraic Methods for program construction: The project CIP. In: P. Pepper (ed.): Program Transformation and Programming Environments. Springer 1984, 199 - 222

[Broy 85]
M. Broy: On modularity in programming. In: H. Zemanek (ed.): 25 years of IFIP. North Holland Publ. Company 1986, 347-362

[Broy, Wirsing 81]
M. Broy, M. Wirsing: On the algebraic extensions of abstract data types. J. Diaz, I. Ramos (eds): International Colloquium on Formalization of Programming Concepts, Peniscola, April 1981, Lecture Notes in Computer Science 107, Berlin-Heidelberg-New York: Springer 1981, 244-251

[Broy, Wirsing 82]
M. Broy, M. Wirsing: Partial abstract data types. Acta Informatica 18:1, November 1982, 47-64

[Broy, Wirsing 84]
M. Broy, M. Wirsing: Generalized heterogeneous algebras and partial interpretations. In: Proc. CAAP 84. Lecture Notes in Computer Science 159, Berlin-Heidelberg-New York: Springer 1984, 1-34

[Broy et al. 84]
M. Broy, J.C. Pair, M. Wirsing: A systematic study of models of abstract data types. TCS 33 (1984), 139-174

[Broy et al. 86]
M. Broy, B. Möller, P. Pepper, M. Wirsing: Algebraic implementations preserve program correctness. To appear in Science of Computer Programming

[Burstall, Goguen 77]
R.M. Burstall, J.A. Goguen: Putting theories together to make specifications. IJCAI 77, 1045-1058

[CIP 85]
CIP-L. Lecture Notes in Computer Science 183, Springer 1985

[Ehrich 82]
H.-D. Ehrich: On the theory of specification, implementation and parameterization of abstract data types. JACM 29:1, 1982

[Ehrich, Lipeck 80]
H.D. Ehrich, U. Lipeck: Proving implementations correct - two alternative approaches. In: Lavington, D. (ed.): IFIP - Congress 80. Amsterdam: North - Holland, pp. 83 - 88 (1980)

[Ehrig, Mahr 85]
H. Ehrig, B. Mahr: Fundamentals of algebraic specification 1. Springer 1985

[Ehrig et al. 82]
H. Ehrig, H.-J. Kreowski, B. Mahr, P. Padawitz: Algebraic implementation of abstract data types. TCS 20 (1982) 209-263

[Goguen et al. 78]
J.A. Goguen, J. W. Thatcher, E.G. Wagner An initial algebra approach to the specification,

correctness and implementation of abstract data types. In: Current Trends in Programming Methodology IV: Data 1978

[Grätzer 68]
G. Grätzer: Universal algebra. Princeton: Van Nostrand, 1968

[Guttag, Horning 78]
J.V. Guttag, J.J. Horning: The algebraic specification of abstract data types. Acta Informatica 10 (1978) 27-52

[Guttag et al. 78]
J.V. Guttag, E. Horowitz, D.R. Musser: Abstract data types and software validation. CACM 21:12 (1978) 1048-1064

[Hoare 72]
C.A.R. Hoare: Proof of correctness of data representation. Acta Informatica 1:4 (1972) 271-281

[Huet, Oppen 80]
G. Huet, D.C. Oppen: Equations and rewrite rules: a survey. In: R. V. Book: Formal Language Theory: Perspectives and Open Problems, Academic Press 1980

[Hussmann 85]
H. Hussmann: Unification in conditional-equational theories. Universität Passau, Fakultät für Mathematik und Informatik, Report MIP-8502, 1985

[Kleene 52]
S.C. Kleene: Introduction to metamathematics. New York: Van Nostrand 1952

[Laut 80]
A. Laut: Safe procedural implementations of algebraic types. IPL 11:4,5 (1980) 147-151

[Liskov, Zilles 75]
B. Liskov, S. Zilles: Specification techniques for data abstraction. IEEE Transactions on Software Engineering 1:1, 7 - 18 (1975)

[Manna 74]
Z. Manna: Mathematical theory of computation. New York: McGraw Hill 1974

[Möller 82]
B. Möller: Unendliche Objekte und Geflechte. Technische Universität München, Institut für Informatik, TUM-I8213, Ph. D. Thesis 1982

[Möller 86]
B. Möller: Algebraic specifications with higher order operators. In: L. Meertens (ed.): Proc. IFIP TC2 Working Conference on Program Specification and Transformation, Bad Tölz, April 1986. Amsterdam: North-Holland (to appear)

[Parnas 72]
D. Parnas: On the criteria being used to decompose modules into systems. CACM 15 (1972) 1053-1058

[Poigne 84]
A. Poigne: Higher order data structures - cartesian closure versus λ-calculus. Proc. STACS 1984, Lecture Notes in Computer Science 166, Berlin-Heidelberg-New York: Springer 1984, 174-185

[Scott 70]
D. Scott: Outline of a mathematical theory of computation. Proc. 4th Annual Princeton

Conference on Information Sciences and Systems 1970, 169-176

[Wirsing, Broy 80]
M. Wirsing, M. Broy: Abstract data types as lattices of finitely generated models. In: Dembinski, P. (ed.): Mathematical Foundations of Computer Science - 9th Symposium, Rydzyna, Poland, Sept. 1-5, 1980. Lecture Notes in Computer Science 88. Berlin-Heidelberg-New York: Springer 1980, 673-685

[Wirsing et al. 80]
M. Wirsing, P. Pepper, H. Partsch, W. Dosch, M. Broy: On hierarchies of abstract data types. Acta Informatica 20, 1983, 1-33

Extreme solutions of equations

Prof. Dr. Edsger W. Dijkstra
Department of Computer Sciences
The University of Texas at Austin
Austin, TX 78712 - 1188
USA

In the previous chapter we have encountered a number of statements S, for which the predicate transformers wlp(S,?) and wp(S,?) were given in closed form. In the next chapter we shall encounter a statement for which the predicates wlp(S,X) and wp(S,X) are given as solutions of equations of the form

$$(0) \qquad Y : [b.(X,Y)].$$

Here, b is a function from predicate pairs to predicates, i.e. b.(X,Y) is a boolean structure, [b.(X,Y)] is a boolean expression in X and Y , which for given X and Y is either true or false.

In (0) we have followed our convention of notationally distinguishing between boolean expressions and equations: by prefixing the boolean expression [b.(X,Y)] by "Y:" we indicate that the boolean expression should be viewed as equation in the unknown Y.

<u>Remark</u> We found the convention of explicitly identifying the unknown(s) preferable to the convention of using reserved letters for the unknowns. It enables us to distinguish between the quadratic equation

$$x:(x^2+a \cdot x+b = 0)$$

and the linear equation

$$b:(x^2+a \cdot x+b = 0).$$

(End of Remark.)

Which predicates Y are solutions of (0) -if any- depends in general on which predicate we have chosen for X. A thing we would like to show -and we shall do so- is that the b's we shall encounter when defining semantics are such that (0) is solvable for any predicate X.

A minor problem is that -for a single X- (0) has often many solutions. Fortunately, we can strengthen (0) into equations that have at most one solution, viz.

NATO ASI Series, Vol. F36
Logic of Programming and Calculi of Discrete Design
Edited by M. Broy
© Springer-Verlag Berlin Heidelberg 1987

(1)   Y: ([b.(X,Y)] ∧ (AZ:[b.(X,Z)] : [Y ⇒ Z]))

(2)   Y: ([b.(X,Y)] ∧ (AZ:[b.(X,Z)] : [Z ⇒ Y])).

The solution of (1) is called "the strongest solution of (0)" since it implies all solutions of (0); the solution of (2) is called "the weakest solution of (0)" since it follows from all solutions of (0). Together they are referred to as "the extreme solutions of (0)". In due time we shall show that the b's we shall encounter in the definition of semantics are such that for any predicate   X equations   (1)   and (2)   are solvable, i.e. that the extreme solutions of   (0) exist for any predicate X.

Before proceeding to do so, however, we shall demonstrate that extreme solutions are unique, i.e. that   (1)   and   (2)   each have at most one solution.

<u>Proof</u>

We prove the uniqueness of the solution of   (1); for   (2),   the proof is very similar.

To this end we observe - for fixed   X-

    (P and Q solve (1))
=   {def.of (1) and rearrangement of terms}
    [b.(X,P)] ∧ (AZ : [b.(X,Z)] : [Q ⇒ Z]) ∧
    [b.(X,Q)] ∧ (AZ : [b.(X,Z)] : [P ⇒ Z])
⇒   {instantiate Z:=P and Z:=Q respectively}
    [Q ⇒ P] ∧ [P ⇒ Q]
=   {predicate calculus}
    [P ≡ Q]   (End of Proof.)

Thus we have established that the extreme solutions are each unique, provided that they exist. Instead of showing the existence of strongest solutions separately from the existence of weakest solutions, we shall first establish a duality theorem by means of which we can halve the length of the existence proof.

Two introductory remarks first. Let b be such that   (1)   has a solution for any X, or - equivalently- that   (0) has a strongest solution for any X. Since that strongest solution depends in general on the predicate X, which occurs as parameter in the equation, it is a function of X; accordingly we denote it by g.X, thus indicating explicitly its dependence on X. Furthermore we shall formulate and prove the duality theorem only for a special form of the function b, viz. the form that allows the most elegant formulation of the duality (and, not surprisingly, is the only form in which we shall need it). After these preliminaries we can present

Theorem 5.0 (Duality Theorem.)

(g.X is the strongest solution of Y:[p.(X,Y) $\Rightarrow$ q.(X,Y)]) $\equiv$
(g*.X is the weakest solution of Y:[p*.(X,Y) $\Leftarrow$ q*.(X,Y)]).

Proof 5.0

(g.X is the strongest solution of   Y:[p.(X,Y) $\Rightarrow$ q.(X,Y)])
= {definition of strongest solution, see (1)}
(AX:: [p.(X,g.X) $\Rightarrow$ q.(X,g.X)]$\wedge$(AZ:[p.(X,Z) $\Rightarrow$q.(X,Z)]:[g.X $\Rightarrow$ Z]))
= {transforming the dummies: X:= $\neg$X , Z := $\neg$Z}
(AX:: [p.($\neg$X, g.($\neg$X)) $\Rightarrow$ q.($\neg$X,g.($\neg$X))] $\wedge$

(AZ: [p.($\neg$X, $\neg$Z) $\Rightarrow$ q.($\neg$X, $\neg$Z)] : [g.($\neg$X) $\Rightarrow$ $\neg$Z]))
= {definition of conjugate, property of $\Rightarrow$ and$\Leftarrow$}
(AX:: [p*.(X,g*.X) $\Leftarrow$ q*.(X, g*.X)] $\wedge$

(AZ: [p*.(X,Z) $\Leftarrow$ q*.(X,Z)] : [g*.X $\Leftarrow$ Z]))
= {definition of weakest solution, see (2)}
(g*.X is the weakest solution of   Y:[p*.(X,Y) $\Leftarrow$ q*.(X,Y]).

(End of Proof 5.0)

The previous theorem is about extreme solutions provided that they exist. We now turn to existence of extreme solutions; in view of Theorem 5.0, we only need to define and prove them for strongest solutions; sometimes we shall formulate the dual theorem as well. Since in this context nothing is gained by dragging the parameter X around -all the time we would be quantifying universally over it- we leave it out.

The first (general) step of coming to grips with the existence of a strongest solution is the consideration that the only candidate for a strongest solution is the conjunction of all solutions. Indeed we have

Theorem 5.1   Consider equation

(3)   Y:[b.Y]   ;   then
(equation (3) has a strongest solution) $\equiv$
((AZ : [b.Z]: Z) solves (3)).

Proof 5.1

(equation (3) has a strongest solution)
= {see (1)}
(EY:: [b.Y] $\wedge$ (A.Z : [b.Z] : [Y $\Rightarrow$ Z]))
= {in order to get Y outside the universal quantification we
first interchange quantifications}

$(EY:: [b.Y] \wedge [(AZ : [b.Z] : Y \Rightarrow Z)])$

=   {and use that the antecedent distributes over universal quantification}

$(EY:: [b.Y] \wedge [Y \Rightarrow (AZ : [b.Z] : Z)])$

=   {now we have $(AZ: [b.Z]: Z)$ as subexpression; but note that the inverse implication follows from $[b.Y]$}

$(EY:: [b.Y] \wedge [Y \Leftarrow (AZ : [b.Z] : Z)]$

$\wedge [Y \Rightarrow (AZ : [b.Z] : Z)])$

=   {predicate calculus}

$(EY :: [b.Y] \wedge [Y \equiv (AZ : [b.Z] : Z)])$

=   { one-point rule}

$[b. (AZ : [b.Z] : Z)]$

=   {(3)}

($(AZ : [b.Z] : Z)$ solves (3)).   (End of Proof 5.1)

Note that in the above proof, until the application of the one-point rule, we have only massaged the existentially quantified term, which is nothing else but the body of the equation for the strongest solution of (3). Consequently, if $(AZ: [b.Z]: Z)$ solves (3), it is also (3)'s strongest solution.

Remark The dual of Theorem 5.1 is

(equation (3) has a weakest solution) $\equiv ((EZ:[b.Z]: Z)$ solves (3)).

(End of Remark.)

Our next theorem states the existence of the strongest solution for a special b, viz. such that we can show that the equation is solved by the conjunction of its solutions.

Theorem 5.2 Let equation (4) be given by

(4) $Y: [p.Y \Rightarrow q.Y]$,

let p be monotonic, and let q be conjunctive over the set of solutions of (4). Then equation (4) has a strongest solution. (The dual theorem states that for monotonic q, and for p disjunctive over the set of solutions of (4), equation (4) has a weakest solution.)

Proof 5.2 Thanks to Theorem 5.1, it suffices to show that the conjunction of (4)'s solutions solves (4). The calculation is straightforward

$p.(AZ : [p.Z \Rightarrow q.Z]: Z)$

$\Rightarrow$ {p is monotonic}

  (AZ: [p.Z $\Rightarrow$ q.Z]: p.Z)

$\Rightarrow$ {predicate calculus}

  (AZ: [p.Z $\Rightarrow$ q.Z]: q.Z)

= {q is conjunctive over the solution set of (4)}

  q. (AZ: [p.Z $\Rightarrow$ q.Z]: Z)

(End of Proof 5.2)

And now we are ready for the famous

Theorem 5.3 (In the oral tradition known as the "Theorem of Knaster-Tarski".) For monotonic f

(5) Y: [f.Y $\equiv$ Y]

has the same strongest solution as

(6) Y: [f.Y $\Rightarrow$ Y]

and has the same weakest solution as

(7) Y: [f.Y $\Leftarrow$ Y]

Proof 5.3   We can confine ourselves to demonstrating the existence and equality of the strongest solutions of (5) and (6), as existence and equality of the weakest solutions of (5) and (7) is merely the dual.

Choosing in Theorem 5.2 f for p , and for q the identity function (which is universally conjunctive), we conclude that (6) has a strongest solution, i.e. calling it Q , we have

(8)   [f.Q $\Rightarrow$ Q]

(9)   (AZ:[f.Z $\Rightarrow$ Z] : [Q $\Rightarrow$ Z]) .

  In order to show that Q solves (5) we observe

  [f.Q $\equiv$ Q]

= {predicate calculus; rewriting the equivalence as mutual
    implication is suggested by (8)}

  [f.Q $\Rightarrow$ Q] $\wedge$ [Q $\Rightarrow$ f.Q]

= {(8)}

  [Q $\Rightarrow$ f.Q]

$\Leftarrow$ {(9) tells us what Q implies, hence instantiate (9) with
      Z := f.Q}

$[f.(f.Q) \Rightarrow f.Q]$

$\Leftarrow$ {now we can use f's monotonicity}

$[f.Q \Rightarrow Q]$

$=$ {(8) again}

true

In order to show that Q implies all solutions of (5) we observe

$(\underline{A}Z: [f.Z \equiv Z] : [Q \Rightarrow Z])$

$\Leftarrow$ {fortunately $[f.Z \equiv Z] \Rightarrow [f.Z \Rightarrow Z]$, i.e. (5) is the least tolerant equation}

$(\underline{A}Z: [f.Z \Rightarrow Z] : [Q \Rightarrow Z])$

$=$ {(9)}

true. (End of Proof 5.3)

The Theorem of Knaster-Tarski is of profound methodological significance. It allows us to characterize the common strongest solution of (5) and (6) for monotonic f as the unique solution of

(10) $Y: ([f.Y \equiv Y] \wedge (\underline{A}Z: [f.Z \Rightarrow Z] : [Y \Rightarrow Z]))$

or as the unique solution of

(11) $Y: ([f.Y \Rightarrow Y] \wedge (\underline{A}Z: [f.Z \equiv Z]: [Y \Rightarrow Z]))$.

Note that both conjuncts in the body of (11) are weaker than the corresponding conjuncts in the body of (10). Yet, for monotonic f, these two equations have the same unique solution!

Hence, in a proof in which a predicate has been given to be such a strongest solution, we tend to <u>use</u> that it solves (10); in an argument in which we have to show that a predicate is such a strongest solution, it suffices to show that it solves (11).

The usefulness of the above device is enhanced by the fact that f only needs to be monotonic, i.e. only need to enjoy the weakest junctivity property.

We have seen that if $Y:[f.Y \Rightarrow Y]$ has a strongest solution, $(\underline{A}Z: [f.Z \Rightarrow Z]: Z)$ gives that solution in closed form. This closed form, however, is not one with which we can do very much. It is therefore good to know that for <u>or</u>-continuous f there exists a closed expression for the strongest solution which is more easily manipulated. The next two theorems deal with that; the first one is a stepping-stone.

<u>Theorem 5.4</u> For monotonic f and any Y

$[f.Y \Rightarrow Y] \Rightarrow [(\underline{E} i : i \geq 0 : f^i. \text{ false}) \Rightarrow Y)]$.

Proof 5.4   The dummy i ranging over the natural numbers and functional iteration being defined recursively, a proof by mathematical induction over the natural numbers seems indicated. Hence we try to massage the consequent so as to make it amenable to an inductive proof:

$\quad$ [(Ei : i $\geq$ 0 : f^i. false) $\Rightarrow$ Y]
= $\quad$ {quasi-distribution of the consequent}
$\quad$ [(Ai: i $\geq$0: f^i.false $\Rightarrow$ Y)]
= $\quad$ {interchange of quantifications}
$\quad$ (Ai: i>0: [f^i.false $\Rightarrow$ Y]).

This we shall demonstrate by mathematical induction over i under the assumptions that f is monotonic and [f.Y $\Rightarrow$ Y]. The base is easy; neither assumption is needed.

Base $\quad$ [f^0. false $\Rightarrow$ Y]
= $\quad$ {definition of functional iteration}
$\quad$ [false $\Rightarrow$ Y]
= $\quad$ {predicate calculus}
$\quad$ true

Step $\quad$ [f^{i+1}. false $\Rightarrow$ Y]
= $\quad$ {definition of functional iteration}
$\quad$ [f.(f^i.false) $\Rightarrow$ Y]
$\Leftarrow$ $\quad$ {let us use [f.Y $\Rightarrow$ Y] to get f in the consequent}
$\quad$ [f.(f^i.false) $\Rightarrow$ f.Y]
$\Leftarrow$ $\quad$ {f is monotonic}
$\quad$ [f^i. false $\Rightarrow$ Y]

$\hfill$ (End of Proof 5.4)

Theorem 5.4 states that, for monotonic f, (Ei : i $\geq$ 0: f^i.false) implies any solution of Y:[f.Y $\Rightarrow$ Y], just as its strongest solution does. And this raises the question whether (Ei:i$\geq$0:f^i.false) could itself be that strongest solution. This question is answered in

<u>Theorem 5.5</u>   For <u>or</u>-continuous f

  (<u>E</u>i: i ≥ 0: f^i.false)

is the strongest solution of

(6)   Y: [f.Y ⟹ Y]

(The dual is that, for <u>and</u>-continuous f, the weakest solution of
Y: [f.Y ⟸ Y] is (<u>A</u>i: i ≥ 0: f^i.true).)

<u>Proof 5.5.</u> Since an <u>or</u>-continuous f is monotonic, (6) has a
strongest solution. In view of Theorem 5.4 it suffices to show that
(<u>E</u>i: i ≥ 0: f^i.false) solves (6). To this end we shall first show
that its terms form a weaking sequence, i.e.

  (<u>A</u>i : i ≥ 0: [f^i. false ⟹ f^{i+1}.false]).

This is done by mathematical induction:

<u>Base</u> [f^0.false ⟹ f^1.false]
=   {definition of functional iteration}
    [false ⟹ f.false]
=   {predicate calculus}
    true.

<u>Step</u> [f^{i+1}.false ⟹ f^{i+2}.false]
=   {definition of functional iteration}
    [f.(f^i.false) ⟹ f.(f^{i+1}.false)]
⟸   {f is montonic}
    [f^i.false ⟹ f^{i+1}.false].

Finally we observe

    f.(<u>E</u>i : i ≥ 0: f^i.false)
=   {f is <u>or</u>-continuous, sequence is weaking}
    (<u>E</u>i : i ≥ 0 : f^{i+1}.false)
=   {renaming the dummy i:=j−1; [f^0.false ≡ false]}
    (<u>E</u>j : j ≥ 1: f^j.false) ∨ f^0.false
=   {predicate calculus}
    (<u>E</u>i : i ≥ 0: f^i.false)

                                (End of Proof 5.5)

  Continuity derives a lot of its significance from the above
theorem; it enables us to prove properties of an extreme solution
by means of mathematical induction over the natural numbers. It is,

however, possible that the importance of this possibility has been overrated

*   *   *

We now reintroduce our parameter X in the equation and turn our attention to equation

(12) Y: [f.(X,Y) ≡ Y]

for monotonic f. Such an f being also monotonic in the individual components of its argument, in particular in the second component, Theorem 5.3 (Knaster-Tarski) asserts that its extreme solutions exist.

In what follows, g.X denotes the strongest solution of (12) and h.X denotes the weakest solution of (12). In analogy with (10), we capture our knowledge about g and h in the formally strongest way: we have for all X and Z

(13) [f.(X,g.X) ≡ g.X]

(14) [f.(X,Z) ⇒ Z] ⇒ [g.X ⇒ Z]

(15) [f.(X,h.X) ≡ h.X]

(16) [f.(X,Z) ⇐ Z] ⇒ [h.X ⇐ Z].

The ultimate goal of this section is to prove junctivity properties of g and h , given the junctivity properties of f. As we go along, we shall see that the proofs can be smoothly derived with a minimum of invention or trial and error by each time realizing which of the formulae (13) through (16) is the appropriate one to appeal to.

Let in the demonstrandum an application of g occur in the consequent. For that g , an appeal to (14) is of no interest: (14) allows us to conclude that an application of g implies something and not what it is implied by. Therefore, for such an application, only (13) can be of interest (and in all probability has to be used).

Conversely, if the demonstrandum has an application of g as its antecedent, an appeal to (14) is almost certainly required as (13), all by itself, fails to express how strong g really is.

For the choice between (15) and (16), similar considerations apply.

A major decision is often whether to start massaging the antecedent so as to show that it implies the consequent, or to start massaging the consequent so as to show that it follows from the antecedent. It may surprise the reader that we call this decision "major", since the two proofs are each other's reverse and, hence, logically identical. The point is that steps that in the one direction are almost dictated by what has been written down, may in the other direction require clairvoyance for their justification. The general advice is to start at the most complicated side (if there is one): usually the more complicated expression shows more explicitly which transformation is appropriate.

We have also minor decisions to take, such as the order in which to apply different transformations. We call them minor because as a rule they do not influence our ability to prove the theorem; they may influence the length of our proofs and are therefore preferably taken wisely.

Just to show how well these heuristics work, let us prove

Theorem 5.6   Let p and q be monotonic functions from predicate pairs to predicates;
let (P,Q) be the strongest solution of

$$(X,Y): [(p.(X,Y), q.(X,Y)) \equiv (X,Y)];$$

let g.X be the strongest solution of

$$Y: [q.(X,Y) \equiv Y] \qquad .$$

Then we have [g.P ≡ Q].

Proof 5.6   For the sake of completeness we observe that both strongest solutions exist - (p.(X,Y), q.(X,Y)) being a monotonic function of (X,Y) for monotonic p and q -.

Our formal knowledge about P and Q is - expressed in the separate components - (analogously to (13) or the first conjunct of (10)):

(17) [p.(P,Q) ≡ P]

(18) [q.(P,Q) ≡ Q]

and analogously to (14) or the second conjunct of (10):

(19) [p.(X,Y) ⇒ X] ∧ [q.(X,Y) ⇒ Y] ⇒ [(P,Q) ⇒ (X,Y)]

Our formal knowledge about g is similarly captured by

(20) [q.(X,g.X) ≡ g.X]

(21) [q.(X,Y) ⇒ Y] ⇒ [g.X ⇒ Y].

So much for what has been given. Not surprisingly in this context, we shall prove the equivalence by mutual implication. Let us tackle [Q ⇒ g.P] first. (That is one of those "minor decisions".)

[Q ⇒ g.P]
=   {we can tackle g.P via (20) or try to tackle Q via (19);
      let us take the minor decision to do the latter; in view of
      (19) we rewrite}
[(P,Q) ⇒ (P, g.P)]
⇐   {(19) with X,Y := P, g.P}
[p.(P,g.P) ⇒ P] ∧ [q.(P, g.P) ⇒ g.P]
=   {for the consequent g.P of the second conjunct, only (20)
      can be of interest, so (20) with
      X := P}
[p.(P, g.P) ⇒ P] ∧ [q.(P, g.P) ⇒ q.(P, g.P)]
=   {predicate calculus}
[p.(P, g.P) ⇒ P]
=   {for the consequent P, only (17) can be of interest}
[p.(P, g.P) ⇒ p.(P, Q)]
⇐   {fortunately, p is monotonic}
[g.P ⇒ Q]
⇐   {we can tackle the consequent Q via (18) or the
      antecedent g.P via (21); let us take the minor decision to
      do the latter; (21) with X,Y := P,Q}
[q.(P,Q) ⇒ Q]
=   {now we tackle consequent Q with (18)}
[q.(P,Q) ⇒ q.(P,Q)]
=   {predicate calculus}
true

Notice that in the mean time we have proved the other implication as well and that, hence, our proof obligation has been met. Notice also that we have appealed to each of the given formulae (17) through (21) precisely once, and since we need all of them, our proof is in that sense the shortest possible one.

<u>Remark</u> Trusting that the reader has read the above proof very carefully and has absorbed the heuristics, we shall in future abbreviate the heuristics. We shall also combine steps, such as omitting the two intermediate results preceding "{predicate calculus}". (End of Remark.)

(End of Proof 5.6)

After this interlude we return to the junctivity properties of g and h, given the junctivity properties of f. As a starter we establish Theorem 5.7. (It will be subsumed in later theorems, for whose proofs it will be used.)

<u>Theorem 5.7</u>   For monotonic f, g and h are monotonic.

<u>Proof 5.7</u>   To prove the monotonicity of g, we have to show for arbitrary predicates P and Q

$$[P \Rightarrow Q] \Rightarrow [g.P \Rightarrow g.Q],$$

using that g is given by

(13) $[f.(X, g.X) \equiv g.X]$ and

(14) $[f.(X,Z) \Rightarrow Z] \Rightarrow [g.X \Rightarrow Z].$

   To this end we observe
   $[g.P \Rightarrow g.Q]$
$\Leftarrow$ {tackle g.P via (14) with X,Z := P, g.Q}
   $[f.(P, g.Q) \Rightarrow g.Q]$
$=$ {tackle g.Q via (13) with X:=Q}
   $[f.(P, g.Q) \Rightarrow f.(Q, g.Q)]$
$\Leftarrow$ {f is monotonic, hence monotonic in 1st comp.}
   $[P \Rightarrow Q].$
   The monotonicty of h is merely the dual of the above.
                                          (End of Proof 5.7)

   And now we are ready to demonstrate the beautiful

<u>Theorem 5.8</u>   Any type of conjunctivity enjoyed by f is enjoyed by h as well.

   (Its dual is: Any type of disjunctivity enjoyed by f is enjoyed by g as well.)

<u>Proof 5.8</u>   With f enjoying some type of conjunctivity, f is monotonic; hence - Theorem 5.7 - h is monotonic.

   In order to show that h is conjunctive over some V, i.e.

$$[h.(\underline{A}X: X \in V : X) \equiv (\underline{A}X: X \in V: h.X)]$$

we show that either side implies the other.

(i) Because h is monotonic we have

$$[h.(\underline{A}X: X \in V : X) \Rightarrow (\underline{A}X: X \in V: h.X)].$$

(Here we see what good use we can make of Theorem 5.7 when showing a junctivity property of extreme solutions; the latter being monotonic, we get the implication in the one direction for free.)

(ii) To show the implication in the other direction we begin by observing

$$[h.(\underline{A}X: X \in V : X) \Leftarrow (\underline{A}X: X \in V: h.X)]$$

$\Leftarrow$ {the h. in the consequent is to be tackled via (16) with

$$X, Z := (\underline{A}X: X \in V : X), (\underline{A}X: X \in V: h.X)\}$$

$$[f.((\underline{A}X: X \in V:X), (\underline{A}X: X \in V: h.X)) \Leftarrow (\underline{A}X: X \in V: h.X)]$$

= {simplification of f's argument: quantification distributes over pair forming}

$$[f.(\underline{A}X : X \in V: (X, h.X)) \Leftarrow (\underline{A}X: X \in V : h.X)]$$

= {the h. in the antecedent is to be tackled via (15)}

$$[f.(\underline{A}X: X \in V: (X, h.X)) \Leftarrow (\underline{A}X: X \in V: f.(X, h.X))]$$

Now the -minor- complication is that whereas h's conjunctivity is related to a bag of predicates, f's conjunctivity is related to a bag of predicate pairs. To be formally precise, we construct a bag W of predicate pairs by

$$(22) \quad (X,Y) \in W \equiv X \in V \wedge [Y \equiv h.X]$$

and observe that, thanks to the monotonicity of h, V and W are of the same junctivity type. Hence it suffices to show the above implication under the assumption that f is conjunctive over W. The formal demonstration proceeds as follows

$$f.(\underline{A}X: X \in V: (X, h.X))$$

= {one-point rule to introduce Y}

$$f.(\underline{A}X: X \in V: (\underline{A}Y: [Y \equiv h.X] : (X,Y)))$$

= {unnesting and (22) to introduce W}

$$f.(\underline{A}X,Y : (X,Y) \in W: (X,Y))$$

= {f conjunctive over W}

$$(\underline{A}X,Y : (X,Y) \in W: f.(X,Y))$$

= {elimination of W with (22) and nesting}

$$(\underline{A}X: X \in V: (\underline{A}Y: [Y \equiv h.X]: f.(X,Y)))$$

= {one-point rule to eliminate Y}

$$(\underline{A}X: X \in V: f.(X,h.X)).$$

Remark   The last 5 steps of the above proof are not very exciting. Note that a number of them were needed to introduce Y and to get rid of it again, obligations caused by the way in which we defined W. Had we used the "bagifier" $\underline{B}$, we could have defined W by

$$W = (\underline{B}X: X \in V: (X,h.X))$$

and with rules how to manipulate expressions for such bags, there would have been no need to refer explicitly to the one-point rule. (End of Remark.)

(End of Proof 5.8)

Whereas Theorem 5.8 dealt with the conjunctivity properties of the weakest solution of

(12) Y:[f.(X,Y) ≡ Y],

Theorem 5.10 will do so for its strongest solution. But first we state and prove Theorem 5.9 -g.X and h.X denoting, as before, the strongest and the weakest solution of (12)-.

Theorem 5.9   For finitely conjunctive f and predicates X and Y satisfying

  [f.(X,Y) ≡ Y]

we have

  [g.X ≡ g.true ∧ Y].

(The dual states that for finitely disjunctive f and such X and Y we have

  [h.X ≡ h.false ∨ Y].)

In other words: the strongest solution of (12) is for finitely conjunctive f the conjunction of an arbitrary solution of (12) and the constant predicate -i.e. independent of X - g.true.

Proof 5.9   Given are

(23) [f.(X,Y) ≡ Y]
(13) [f.(X',g.X') ≡ g.X']
(14) [f.(X',Z) ⇒ Z] ⇒ [g.X' ⇒ Z].

We shall prove the equivalence by proving that either side implies the other.

(i)   [g.X ⇒ g.true ∧ Y]
=   {predicate calculus}
  [g.X ⇒ g.true] ∧ [g.X ⇒ Y]
⇐ {g is monotonic; (14) with Z:=Y}
  [X ⇒ true] ∧ [f.(X,Y) ⇒ Y]
=   {predicate calculus; (23)}
  true

(ii) [g.true ∧ Y ⇒ g.X]
= {predicate calculus, so as to tackle g.true via (14)}
   [g.true ⇒ g.X ∨ ¬Y]
⇐ {(14) with X', Z := true, g.X ∨ ¬Y}
   [f.(true, g.X ∨ ¬Y) ⇒ g.X ∨ ¬Y]
= {predicate calculus, preparing for f's conjunctivity}
   [f.(true, g.X ∨ ¬Y) ∧ Y ⇒ g.X]
= {(23), the only thing given about Y!}
   [f.(true, g.X ∨ ¬Y) ∧ f.(X,Y) ⇒ g.X]
= {f is finitely conjunctive; predicate calculus}
   [f.(X, g.X ∧ Y) ⇒ g.X]
= {(23) and (14) with X',Z := X,Y}
   [f.(X, g.X) ⇒ g.X]
= {(13) with X' := X}
   true

(End of Proof 5.9)

Theorem 5.9 is most interesting for the weakest possible choice for Y, viz. h.X. And so we get as first corollary

<u>Theorem 5.9.0</u>   For finitely conjunctive f

[g.X ≡ g.true ∧ h.X].

The second corollary is

<u>Theorem 5.9.1</u> For finitely conjunctive f

[g.(X ∧ Y) ≡ g.X ∧ h.Y].

<u>Proof 5.9.1</u>

   g.(X ∧ Y)
= {Theorem 5.9.0 with X := X ∧ Y}
   g.true ∧ h.(X ∧ Y)
= {f conjunctive, hence h conjunctive, Theorem 5.8}
   g.true ∧ h.X ∧ h.Y
= {Theorem 5.9.0}
   g.X ∧ h.Y

(End of Proof 5.9.1)

<u>Remark</u> The last two corollaries capture the important outcome of Theorem 5.9. We could have proved Theorem 5.9.1 directly - Theorem 5.9.0 then follows- instead of Theorem 5.9. We have not done so, firstly because Theorem 5.9.1 is more specific (in its mentioning

of h) and, secondly, because the formulae of the proof would have been quite a bit longer. (End of Remark.)

Having expressed - Theorem 5.9.0 - g.X in terms of (a constant predicate and) h.X, and having established - Theorem 5.8 - that h inherits the conjunctivity of f, we are ready for

Theorem 5.10   With the exception of universal conjunctivity and and-continuity, the conjunctivity of f is enjoyed by g as well.

(Its dual states that with the exception of universal disjunctivity and or-continuity, the disjunctivity of f is enjoyed by h as well.)

Proof 5.10   For monotonic f, the monotonicity of g is asserted in Theorem 5.7. For the remaining types of conjunctivity (i.e. unbounded, denumerable or finite), f is finitely conjunctive and hence - Theorem 5.9.0 - we have

[g.X ≡ g.true ∧ h.X].

Theorem 5.8 states that h enjoys the conjunctivity of f, and g inherits the conjunctivity of h, universal conjunctivity excepted.
(End of Proof 5.10)

*   *   *

Theorems 5.9 and 5.10 are less beautiful than Theorem 5.8, which states that h inherits without constraint or exception the conjunctivity enjoyed by f. To show that these constraints and exceptions are not void - i.e. have not entered the picture merely as a result of our weakness as theorem provers - we shall construct counter-examples.

Theorem 5.9 is restricted to finitely conjunctive f. All other forms of conjunctivity imply monotonicity, and, for a really convincing counter-example, it therefore suffices to come up with a monotonic - but not finitely conjunctive!- f such that the conclusion of 5.9 or 5.9.0 or 5.9.1 does not hold.

Let us look for the simplest example we can come up with that is monotonic but not finitely conjunctive; [f.(X,Y) ≡ X],

[f.(X,Y) ≡Y], and [f.(X,Y) ≡ X ∧ Y] won't do, because they are finitely conjunctive, but

[f.(X,Y) ≡ X ∨ Y]

is monotonic and passes the test of non-conjunctivity. (In general we have ¬[(X ∧ X') ∨ (Y ∧ Y') ≡ (X ∨ Y) ∧ (X' ∨ Y')].) With this choice for f, equation

(12) $Y:[f.(X,Y) \equiv Y]$

becomes

$\qquad Y: [X \Rightarrow Y]$

with the obvious extreme solutions $[g.X \equiv X]$ and $[h.X \equiv true]$. Substituting these in the conclusion of Theorem 5.9.0, viz. $[g.X \equiv g.true \wedge h.X]$ would yield $[X]$ which is not true for any X. We have been fortunate: the simplest proposal for f that we could think of provided the counter-example. So much for the constraint of Theorem 5.9 to conjunctive f.

In order to show that Theorem 5.10's exception of universal conjunctivity is justified, we should look for a universally conjunctive f such that $\neg[g.true]$. Here the simple choice $[f.(X,Y) \equiv Y]$ does the job. With this choice, (12) becomes

$\qquad Y: [Y \equiv Y]$

with the obvious extreme solutions $[g.X \equiv false]$ and $[h.X \equiv true]$; g is not universally conjunctive.

In order to show, finally, that also Theorem 5.10's exception of and-continuity is justified, we look for an f that is and-continuous, but is not finitely conjunctive. In our first counter-example we found the simple f, given by $[f.(X,Y) \equiv X \vee Y]$, that was not finitely conjunctive, but we cannot use that because the corresponding strongest solution is the identity function, which is and-continuous. But we can use that f by using it as a source of inspiration, and by complicating it a little: replacing Y by p.Y for a carefully chosen p.

We look for a p that is and-continuous, so that f is and-continuous. We look for a p that is also or-continuous so that -Theorem 5.5 - we have a closed form for g.X. And we would like p so simple that there is hope of tackling that closed form analytically. In a state space that has z as one of its integer coordinates, we suggest wp("z:= z+1, Y) for p.Y, i.e. we consider f given by

$\qquad [f.(X,Y) \equiv X \vee Y^z_{z+1}].$

According to Theorem 5.5 and the fact that f is or-continuous in its second argument, g.X is given by

$\qquad [g.X \equiv (\underline{E}.i : i \geq 0 : k^i.false)]$

where k is given by $[k.U \equiv X \vee U^z_{z+1}]$, which - via induction over i - leads to

$[g.X \equiv (\underline{E}i : i \geq 0 : X^z_{z+i})]$.

Consider now the strengthening sequence of predicates $C.j$ given by $[C.j \equiv z \geq j]$ for $j \geq 0$. Then

$\neg[g.(\underline{A}j : j \geq 0 : C.j) \equiv (\underline{A}j : j \geq 0 : g.(C.j))]$.

for:

```
      g.(Aj: j ≥ 0: C.j)
=       {def. of C}
      g.(Aj: j ≥ 0: z ≥ j)
=       {predicate and integer calculus}
      g.false
=       {last expression for g.X}
      false                                    and
```

```
      (Aj : j ≥ 0 : g.(C.j))
=       {def. of C}
      (Aj: j ≥ 0 : g.(z ≥ j))
=       {last expression for g.X}
      (Aj: j ≥ 0: (Ei : i ≥ 0: z+i ≥ j))
=       {predicate and integer calculus}
      (Aj: j ≥ 0: true)
=       {predicate calculus}
      true.
```

And this concludes the construction of the third and last counter-example. We would like to add that the sequence $C.j$ used above is a standard ingredient for showing non-<u>and</u>-monotonicity. (Similarly, the weakening sequence $z \leq j$ is used to show that <u>or</u>-continuity has been lost.) This knowledge makes the choice of our last f less surprising.

Logic Based on Programming

Eric C.R. Hehner
University of Toronto

Platonism and Formalism

A map of the world would be the same if the shorelines had been discovered in a different order. The world exists independent of our knowledge of it. That, at least, is the opinion of most people. Similarly, it is the opinion of most mathematicians that mathematical objects exist (in some abstract sense), and that mathematical truths about them are discovered. This opinion is called "platonism". According to a platonist, the order of discovery may be partly a historical accident, and our way of expressing truths may be a product of human design, but the truths themselves are independent of us, timeless and universal.

The opposing opinion is called "formalism". According to a formalist, mathematics is not discovered but created. The expressions and the rules for manipulating expressions constitute the subject. The word "truth" should not be used, but if it must be, it simply means "theorem", which is an expression obtained according to a definite procedure, or program. The various programs for obtaining theorems are called "theories". It is entirely possible for an expression to be "true" (i.e. a theorem) according to one theory, and not according to another. Theories are human creations, and each is influenced by its predecessors.

Platonists and formalists speak slightly different languages, and this has caused some awkward misunderstandings for computer scientists. Just as we can write the word "table" on a piece of paper and use it to refer to a physical object, so we can write number-expressions (numerals), set-expressions, predicate-expressions, function-expressions, and so on, and if we are platonic we use them to refer to numbers, sets, functions, predicates, and other mathematical objects. "Syntax" tells us how to write and read the expressions, and "semantics" tells us what objects they refer to. But how can we give the semantics? Most mathematicians are not concerned with this question, but computer scientists who design, implement, and use programming languages are pre-occupied with it. So-called "axiomatic semantics" of programming languages does not qualify as a real semantics to a platonist, because it provides only a purely syntactic proof theory. Denotational semantics is a translation from programs to (usually) function-expressions, but that just reduces the

NATO ASI Series, Vol. F36
Logic of Programming and Calculi of Discrete Design
Edited by M. Broy
© Springer-Verlag Berlin Heidelberg 1987

problem to the problem of giving semantics to function-expressions. Predicative semantics, viewed as a translation to predicate-expressions, suffers the same criticism. To give people the meaning of the word "table" without pushing the problem onto another language, we take them to a table, and let them see it, feel it, and experience it in any way they can. We cannot do the same for number-expressions, set-expressions, predicate-expressions, or function-expressions. But we *can* do it for programs: we can take them to a computer and let them watch it run the program, let them interact with it. We have physical experience upon which to base our understanding of programs. The direction of platonist semantics, from program to mathematical expression to abstract object, is reversed by the formalist: from mathematical expression to program to activity. Indeed, our earliest understanding of mathematics is formalist. For the past few decades, computer scientists have looked to logicians for a firm foundation; perhaps we should trade places.

Formalists, whose world is not populated with abstract objects, find it cumbersome to have to call their subject matter "number-expression", "set-expression", "predicate-expression", and "function-expression"; they prefer to say simply "number", "set", "predicate", and "function". It is common in programming circles to talk about the syntax of a function. The platonist complains that well-established, standard mathematical terminology is being abused.

The criticisms made by platonists against formalism concern not only the language, but also the purpose and scope of mathematics. If the purpose of mathematics is not to discover truths, then what is it? Platonists object that formalists make mathematics meaningless — an arbitrary exercise in symbol manipulation. They believe that Gödel showed us that there are truths that are not theorems, no matter how big the formalism. And finally, platonists say that a large part of mathematics cannot be formalized (reduced to procedure). In particular, they believe that Cantor demonstrated that sets of uncountable cardinality cannot even be listed, much less explained, by a program. If formalism does not have room for the real numbers, and does not seek the truth, then a platonist cannot be satisfied with it. Platonists do not reject formalism, but they consider it to be a small part of mathematics.

I am a formalist. I shall rebut the criticisms referring to Cantor and Gödel in their own separate sections. Let me briefly give the formalist position concerning the purpose of mathematics. Often, mathematical structures are created as models of physical processes. The physical language used in mathematics, that of objects and existence, helps to make the analogies clear. The success of mathematics in providing useful models, ones that aid us in thinking about the world, makes it worthwhile to learn it as early in life as possible. We begin counting and adding before we can appreciate abstract analogies. We are misled by the physical language of mathematics to believe that numbers "exist", with a body of facts, a notion of "truth". "Five" is a noun in mathematics, not an adjective as in English. A platonist requires the world of mathematical objects to be a model of a theory; to a formalist, a theory is a model of the world.

Not all mathematics is created as a model, like a drawing. Some mathematical structures are created just for their elegance and beauty, like music. This may be called "arbitrary symbol manipulation" by anyone who would call music "arbitrary sound manipulation". Most of us would not. Although I cannot define "beauty", and I grant that it leaves room for variety and difference, it nonetheless serves as a criterion for much of mathematics. And some of that mathematics finds application later.

Another criticism of the formalist position is that formal arguments are lengthy, tedious, and error-prone; insistence on formal proof, quoting axiom and proof-rule, prevents us from getting very far. As evidence, critics cite Russell and Whitehead's *Principia Mathematica*. This criticism likens formal proofs to machine-language programs. The axioms and proof-rules are indeed the machine-language of Logic. But the criticism is misdirected: formalists do not insist that proofs must be at that level. Just as a programmer structures a program in a high-level language, using packaged procedures and utilities, a mathematician should structure a formal proof, using previous theorems and derived proof-rules.

A formalist does not insist that all arguments must be formal, but only that they must be formalizable. When a proof is presented to a machine, then it must be formal, but to a human, a convincing informal argument, perhaps containing a "you know what I mean" in the form of three dots, is usually welcome. But we must be able to remove the three dots, to fill in the detail and produce a machine-checkable proof if asked. One obtains a licence to be informal by demonstrating the ability to be formal. Informality does not entail platonism, if one is careful.

Many mathematicians feel too constrained, or limited, by the requirement that all proofs be formalizable. It is indeed a severe limitation: it limits proofs to those that mathematicians can agree on. If there were a dispute, then at least in principle a machine could be arbitrator. The much-vaunted universality of mathematics, the ability of mathematicians to agree, is just the mechanical nature of formal proof. Although we can agree, given a theory, what the theorems (truths) are, we certainly have our differing preferences for theories. The design of a good one is shaped by trade-offs and criticisms. It requires good taste and judgment, like any other human activity. To a formalist, mathematics is an attitude, a method of thinking, not a collection of facts or truths.

Classical and Constructive Logic

"Constructive Logic" is claimed by its adherents to be the logic of computation, and so it may be confused with formalism. But the two are independent: there are constructive platonists and classical formalists, as well as constructive formalists and classical platonists. Constructivism arose from intuitionism, which was invented to make mathematical "existence" model physical existence better. We cannot sit in our rooms and reason about the existence of a physical object with some property; we must observe it, at least indirectly, to say it exists. By analogy, in intuitionistic or constructive logic, a proof of $\exists x.\ p(x)$ requires a term t such that $p(t)$ is a theorem. And so a proof of $\forall \hat{v}.\ \exists \acute{v}.\ S(\hat{v}, \acute{v})$ is a program for constructing from input $\hat{v}$ a satisfactory output $\acute{v}$. This is the same formula used to define implementability of a specification in the Predicative formalism, but with an essential, classical difference: for some specifications S we must consider $\forall \hat{v}.\ \exists \acute{v}.\ S(\hat{v}, \acute{v})$ proved without producing a term t for $\acute{v}$. Otherwise we require every program execution to halt, and our logic is inconsistent.

The constructive view of "$\exists$" is applied by its advocates also to "$\lor$". A proof of $a \lor b$ requires either a proof of a or a proof of b. Most people, however, are willing to agree that "either God exists or God does not exist" without a proof of either disjunct. (A constructive proof of the first disjunct would be interesting.) Similarly, it is possible to accept
$$1/0 = 5 \ \lor \ 1/0 \neq 5$$
without assenting to or denying either disjunct.

> *Aside.* It is also reasonable to extend (enrich) Peano's Logic with a point at infinity such that $1/0 = \infty$ and $5 \neq \infty$. Then $1/0 \neq 5$ becomes true and $1/0 = 5$ becomes false. The logic is

more complete, provides answers to more questions, and for that reason is perhaps more attractive. But we are not compelled to make this extension. *End of Aside*.

Computation requires (is!) formalism, not constructivism. And classical logic is simpler, with a richer set of laws, than constructive logic. To demonstrate the relation between programming and proving in any chosen proof system, here is "the universal program". It is extremely inefficient, but it is a completely general implementation of any implementable specification.

Let P be a proof system. Then P is defined by a program for generating proofs. Let us call specification $S(\grave{v}, \acute{v})$ P-implementable if $\forall \grave{v}.\ \exists \acute{v}.\ S$ is a theorem of P. Here is a program for S.

```
x := input v̀;
loop U: generate next proof in P;
        if this proof has S(x, y) as its last line
        then output v́ := y
        else U
```

Cantor and the Uncountable

Cantor's "diagonal argument" is supposed to show that there are more real numbers than integers. It is usually presented informally, platonically. Without loss of generality, we shall consider only reals r in the range $0 \le r \le 1$, and integers i in the range $0 \le i$. The argument is often presented with the aid of a picture, which motivates the name "diagonal". On row 0, we have an infinite sequence of digits. On row 1, we have another infinite sequence of digits. And so on.

```
0  →  .14159265358 ···
1  →  .14285714285 ···
2  →  .10100100010 ···
3  →  .65349764842 ···
4  →  .76436906345 ···
   ⋮
   ⋮
```

We now form an infinite sequence that is not on any row by taking its first digit different from the first digit in the first row, its second digit different from the second digit on the second row, and so on. Since our mapping from integers to reals was arbitrary, we have shown that there is no "onto" mapping from the integers to the reals. An onto mapping in the reverse direction is easy to construct, so we conclude that there are more reals than integers.

The formalist criticism begins with the observation that on row 0 we do not have an infinite sequence of digits at all; we have a finite sequence followed by three dots. How can we remove the three dots and become formal? In what sense can we have an infinite sequence? It is an ancient question. One answer is that we have an infinite sequence when we have a way of generating it. In this formalization, we must replace each row of our picture by a program, which we can do completely without ellipsis. That takes care of the horizontal dots. Now, how do we get rid of the vertical dots? How can we have an infinite sequence of programs? Again, an answer is to have a program to generate an infinite sequence of programs. Certainly we can write a program to print out all programs. What we want is a list of all programs to produce an infinite sequence of digits, *i.e.* those programs whose executions cannot halt (deadlock or livelock). If we posit a program P to produce all and only these infinite-sequence programs S_i, we obtain a contradiction by the diagonal argument, as follows. We write a new program D to simulate P, producing the S_i, and in turn simulate each S_i up to i digits, and then output a different digit. We thus create an infinite-sequence program that differs from all the S_i.

When Cantor's diagonal argument is formalized this way, it becomes a version of the halting problem (let us say the "non-halting" problem). The proper conclusion is simply that there is no program to generate all and only the infinite sequence programs. More briefly, we say that there is no sequence of all infinite sequences. We do not conclude that there are more infinite-sequence programs than natural numbers.

Another formalization of Cantor's argument comes from the theory of type constructions. It is

$$\neg\exists f \in \mathbf{N} \to \mathbf{N} \to \mathcal{T}.$$
$$\forall g \in \mathbf{N} \to \mathcal{T}.$$
$$\exists n \in \mathbf{N}.$$
$$f(n) = g$$

where $\mathbf{N}$ is the natural numbers (or integers) and $\mathcal{T}$ is any type with at least two elements. It is a beautiful theorem, but what does it say about the sizes of sets?

Two finite sets have the same size if their members can be put in one-to-one correspondence. Cantor asks us to extend this intuition to infinite sets. Doing so, we are compelled to say that there are as many even integers as integers, counter to our intuition that there are half as many. Certainly in the finite case, for any set of integers from 0 up to n, there are about half as many evens. But we are told that not all intuitions can be correctly extended from the finite to the infinite case. Next, Cantor asks us to accept that there are more reals than rationals, even though there is a rational between every two reals. Again, we are asked to reject the intuitions that do not fit. By now, we should ask ourselves why we should accept the extension of the original intuition that leads to so much trouble.

In symbols, we can define Cantor's order $A \leqslant B$ as

$$\exists f\colon B \to A. \ \forall a\colon A. \ \exists b\colon B. \ f(b)=a$$

Then Cantor's theorem says $\neg(\mathbf{N} \to \mathcal{T} \leqslant \mathbf{N})$ or if you prefer $\mathbf{N} \to \mathcal{T} > \mathbf{N}$. But we are not compelled to accept Cantor's order as a comparison of sizes.

There are good measures that provide a notion of size without violating our intuitions. One is Hölder's process. Let A be a set of natural numbers. Define rationals S_n^m as follows.

$$S_n^0 \ = \ \begin{cases} 1 \text{ if } n \in A \\ 0 \text{ if } n \notin A \end{cases}$$

$$S_n^{m+1} \ = \ \frac{\sum_{0 \leqslant i \leqslant n} S_i}{n+1}$$

Then the measure of A is the real number defined as

$$m(A) = \lim_m \lim_n S_n^m$$

This measure can be extended to sets other than the natural numbers, but it requires the type to be enumerable.

The intuitions that I refer to come from our experience of the physical world (where else?). Our experience is entirely of finite sets. The justification for inventing the infinite set of natural numbers is the same as the justification for any model: it is simpler and more understandable than what it models. In particular, it omits the usually irrelevant boundary details of a large finite set.

We may, if we like, add a value ∞ such that $\forall n: \mathbb{N}.\ n < \infty$. There is a certain elegance, and sometimes even practical reasons for doing so; the IEEE floating-point standard includes both $+\infty$ and $-\infty$. We then can decide the questions $\infty + 1 < \infty$, $\infty + 1 = \infty$, $\infty + 1 > \infty$ as we wish. In fact, we need not extend the trichotomy to these new expressions; they can all be true if we want. We can invent infinitely many infinities, extending the symbols $<$, $=$, $>$ to them however we wish. But the relevance to any intuitive notion of size is now absent. Without motivation, with diminishing elegance, the mathematics of "higher cardinalities" is of doubtful merit.

With Cantor's argument, mathematics took a bad turn from which it still has not recovered. When it does recover, the phrases "countably many" and "uncountably many" will disappear. If the word "countable" survives, its meaning will come from a formalzation of Cantor's argument. From the first formalization, it may come to mean the same as "(recursively) enumerable", or "sequenceable". Or from the second, we may decide to pronounce Cantor's order "$A \leqslant B$" as "A is as countable as B". Either way, it is not a measure of size. Cantor's informal version of the diagonal argument will seem like Zeno's version of infinite sums: a curiosity for the uneducated, but not good mathematics.

Gödel and the Unprovable

After the pioneering work of Frege, Russell, and other logicians at the beginning of this century, David Hilbert hoped it would be possible to formalize all of mathematics. But in 1931, Kurt Gödel arrived at a result which is commonly interpreted as saying that any formalism that includes axioms for the natural numbers allows us to express truths of mathematics that cannot be proven in the formalism. And with that, Hilbert's program died. I believe its death was unwarranted.

Gödel created an elaborate scheme to encode sentences and proofs as numbers. He then created a sentence which, on the surface, concerns natural numbers, but which may be viewed as code for "I am not a theorem", or "I have no proof". The "I" in that sentence is the number that encodes that very sentence. It is the Liar's Paradox in a new suit. If this sentence has a proof, then it is saying something false, so the logic is inconsistent. Assuming, as is reasonable, that the logic used by Gödel (mainly Peano's axioms via Russell and Whitehead) is consistent, we must conclude that the sentence is true and unprovable. Mustn't we?

Gödel shows how to construct his unprovable sentence, but he does not construct it. It involves immense numbers, and the encoding is so opaque that we would not be enlightened by it. In order to examine Gödel's sentence, we shall use a different, transparent encoding. Instead of numbers, we shall use character strings, a common data type in programming.

To begin, we give ourselves (first-order) predicate logic, the variables being of type string; catenation is denoted by juxtaposition. Some strings look like sentences or predicates. For example,

$$\text{"}\exists u.\ t = u\ u\text{"}$$

looks like a predicate in free variable t , true iff t is composed of two identical halves. But it is not a predicate; it is a string.

Next we need a meaning predicate M. We want it to apply to strings that look like sentences so that $M(s)$ is a theorem if s looks like a theorem, and an antitheorem if s looks like an antitheorem. (An antitheorem is a sentence whose negation is a theorem). Here are some of its properties.

$$M(\text{“}\mathbf{true}\text{”}) = \mathbf{true}$$
$$M(\text{“}\mathbf{false}\text{”}) = \mathbf{false}$$
$$\forall s.\ M(\text{“}\neg\text{”}\ s) = \neg M(s)$$

$$\forall s. \; \forall t. \; M(s \text{ “}\wedge\text{” } t) = M(s) \wedge M(t)$$

And so on. This is a denotational semantics, or interpreter, or theorem-prover, for predicate logic. Gödel showed how to express a predicate with these properties in the language of Peano arithmetic, and we could do similarly in the language of string theory. Or, as an alternative, we can add the symbol M to our language and take the above properties as axioms. The sequel can be read by viewing $M(\;)$ either as standing in place of a long expression with the indicated substitution, or as a legitimate part of the formal language.

> *Aside.* When axioms are added to the logic, we want M to apply to them also.
>
> $M(\text{“ } axiom\text{”}) = \textbf{true}$
>
> So if we take the axiomatic view of M, it may seem that we need a whole new set of axioms such as
>
> $M(\text{“}M(\text{“}\textbf{true}\text{”}) = \textbf{true}\text{”}) = \textbf{true}$
>
> and so on — a losing game. But instead, we bring M into the interpreted logic with the axiom
>
> $\forall s. \; M(\text{“}M(\text{” } s \text{ “})\text{”}) = M(s)$
>
> We make M idempotent (sort of). *End of aside.*

It is a familiar fact to computer scientists that we can write an interpreter for language L in language L, and that is just what we are doing here. Now we have our encoding function (just put quotes around), and our decoding function (M). M is the inverse of quotes: the unquoting function.

One more ingredient is needed to finish translating Gödel's work into string theory. With numbers it was called "norming"; Quine did it for strings, and Hofstadter called it "Quining". We shall call it Q. Let Q be a function from strings to strings. When applied to a string that looks like a predicate, it produces another string that looks like a predicate by replacing all occurrences of substrings that look like free variables with the entire string. For example,

$$Q(\text{“}\exists u.\ t = u\,u\text{”}) = \text{“}\exists u.\ \text{“}\exists u.\ t = u\,u\text{”} = u\,u\text{”}$$

The inner quotes are just characters in the string. Like M, Q can be completely formalized; we can write a program for it. In fact, Gödel did. And again like M, we can consider that $Q(\ )$ stands in place of a long expression, or we can add the symbol Q to our formal language. (In the latter case, we need only a single axiom, since we want to use Q only once.)

All the pieces are now in place. In particular, we have

$$Q(\text{“}\neg M(Q(s))\text{”})$$
$$= \quad \text{“}\neg M(\ Q(\text{“}\neg M(Q(s))\text{”})\ )\text{”}$$

Applying $\neg M$ to both sides of the above equation, we obtain

$$\neg M(\ Q(\text{“}\neg M(Q(s))\text{”})\ )$$
$$= \neg M(\ \text{“}\neg M(\ Q(\text{“}\neg M(Q(s))\text{”})\ )\text{”}\ )$$

which has the form $G = \neg M(\text{“}G\text{”})$. If G were a theorem, then $M(\text{“}G\text{”})$ would be also (by the design of M), hence $\neg M(\text{“}G\text{”})$ would be an antitheorem. Thus we would have a theorem equal to an antitheorem (**true=false**). If G were an antitheorem, then $M(\text{“}G\text{”})$ would be also, hence $\neg M(\text{“}G\text{”})$ would be a theorem. Thus we would have an antitheorem equal to a theorem (**false=true**). Either way, the logic would be inconsistent. Believing the logic to be consistent, we conclude that G is neither a theorem nor an antitheorem. We have constructed the famous Gödel sentence, and find that the logic is incomplete.

So far, so good, but the platonists go one step further. They ascribe to G a meaning, a truth value. And since G is not a theorem, they take $M(\text{“}G\text{”})$ to be false, hence G to be true. To a formalist, it is theoremhood that gives a sentence the meaning "true", and antitheoremhood that gives it the meaning "false". We should not read "$G = \neg M(\text{“}G\text{”})$" as "$G$ says that it is not a theorem", but as "if G says anything, then it says that it is not a theorem". Even though $G = \neg M(\text{“}G\text{”})$ is true, G is neither true nor false, and $M(\text{"}G\text{"})$ is neither true nor false. If we wish, we can consistently add either G or $\neg G$ as a new axiom, with no reason to prefer either one over the other.

Our presentation was parallel to Gödel's, but using strings instead of numbers. However, the result can be demonstrated much more simply and clearly. The heart of the argument is a transformation from one level of quotes to two levels, and back down to one, with a "not" sign appearing in the process. Let us instead go from zero to one and back. We don't take Q to be a function from strings to strings, but simply a string. We add it as a new symbol with the axiom

$$Q = \text{"}\neg M(Q)\text{"}$$

It is easy to see that by its addition we have not just made our logic incomplete: Q is a completely known 5-character string. Now let us suppose that we can completely construct (or define) an unquoting function M. Then

$$
\begin{aligned}
& M(Q) \\
= {} & M(\text{"}\neg M(Q)\text{"}) \qquad \text{replacing } Q \text{ with its equal} \\
= {} & \neg M(Q) \qquad\qquad \text{because } M \text{ unquotes}
\end{aligned}
$$

and the inconsistency is apparent.

As any programmer knows, applying interpreter M to string Q will cause an infinite execution loop, and yield no result. In programming terms, Gödel's result is once again the halting problem. In logic terms, it says that we cannot create a consistent and complete meaning function, one that gives meaning to all sentences, even those about itself. It says nothing to distinguish truth from theoremhood.

Hilbert's program lives, but perhaps not in mathematics departments. In modern terms, Hilbert's program was to reduce mathematics to computing. That is just what computer scientists are doing every day.

Note. The currently most advanced work in this direction is described in the new book *Implementing Mathematics* by R.L. Constable *et al.*, Prentice-Hall, 1986. I recommend it. *End of note.*

Heisenberg and the Unknowable

Heisenberg's "Uncertainty Principle" says that there are pairs of quantities, such as position and wavelength, that cannot be known simultaneously past a certain accuracy. The product of their "uncertainties" is of the order of Planck's constant. Thus it is claimed that our knowledge of the world is limited, not just by our imperfect measuring instruments, but in principle, a result of Quantum Mechanics. Is it a coincidence that this limitation result came at the same time as Gödel's? Heisenberg's principle is not really on the topic of these lectures, but the parallels are so strong that I shall spend a few moments on it.

In Quantum Mechanics, attributes of matter are described by wave functions, interpreted as probability distributions for observations. For certain pairs of attributes, the wave functions are related so that one is spread out, showing great "uncertainty", when the other is narrow, showing less "uncertainty". To simplify the discussion, I shall show pictures of position and wavelength more directly. These pictures should not be interpreted as probability distributions; indeed, they should not be interpreted physically at all. At one extreme, we have a sine-wave.

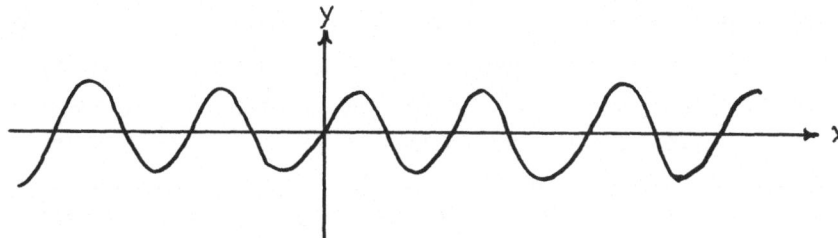

If I ask you its wavelength, you may pick up your ruler and measure. Diagrams and rulers are imprecise, so I shall give you its formula: $y = sin(x)$. Now you can calculate its wavelength to any accuracy, without limit. I also ask you its position; what is your answer? Probably you wonder what I mean, and produce no answer.

Here is the intermediate of the three pictures.

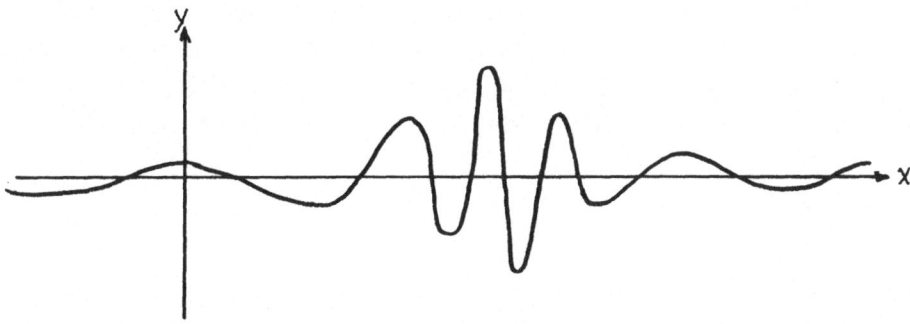

When I ask you the wavelength of this wave, you may be doubtful about what I want, but you can probably give me some sort of answer, perhaps by measuring where the amplitude is 1. When I ask you its position, you can also give an answer, perhaps by measuring to the highest peak. Your doubt is not about the wave; let us suppose I have given you its formula. Your doubt is about the meaning of "position" and "wavelength" in this case.

In the third picture, at the other extreme, the wave packet has converged to the Dirac delta function.

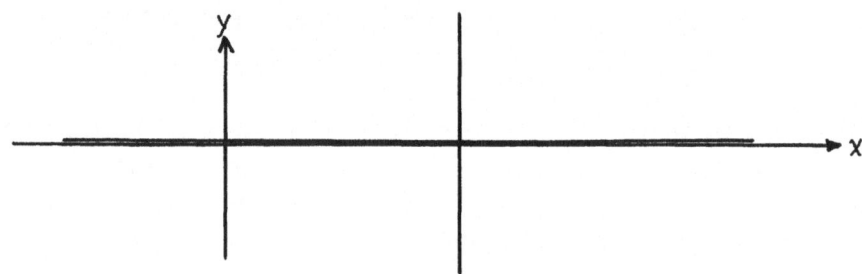

Its formula is $x \neq 3 \Rightarrow y=0$; its position is perfectly defined; its wavelength is completely undefined.

Physical quantities are defined by methods of measurement, by procedures: first do this; second do that; $\cdots$. (The procedure may include some **if**s and **loop**s, too.) The number you end with is the answer. The procedures for position and wavelength conflict with each other: one is defined to the extent that the other is not. They limit each other for the same reason that you cannot stand up and sit down at the same time. I have never considered it a limitation on my knowledge of the universe that I cannot do the self-contradictory.

Too many physicists forget that position and wavelength are procedures, that force is a fiction, that elementary particles are a model. Too often they impute to them an independent meaning, an existence of their own. They believe their models are the "truth". A toothpick bridge can be used to indicate whether a real bridge will stand, and a painting can indicate how it will look. Few of us would ask which model is the truth, or how both can be true, as physicists have done with the wave and the particle models. A variety of absurdities, including physical nondeterminism and multiple simultaneous worlds, have been proposed to explain the discrepancy between the two models. The limitation we learn about from Heisenberg is not about our possible knowledge, but about the applicability of a model.

A model that duplicates every detail of its subject does not serve its purpose. A good model must be simple in order to aid our understanding. The current state of particle physics is baroque and complex; it has wandered far from its purpose. It is not a search for the truth — just bad physics.

Mathematics is limited: it does not tell us all (any?) of the truths of this world. But that is not Gödel's theorem; it is not the kind of thing that can be proven logically. Science is also limited: we cannot know all the truths in this world because the whole cannot be comprehended by a part. Again, that result is not Heisenberg's; it is not the kind of thing that can be demonstrated by a physics experiment. To choose some particular mathematical idea and say "that is unformalizable" is just to refuse to be precise about it, to refuse to communicate it, to be non-mathematical about it. To choose some particular physical phenomenon and say "that is unknowable" is just to give up, to be non-scientific about it.

Acknowledgement. I thank Andrew Malton for many discussions, and for the universal program. Links between various kinds of logic and programming have been recognized by many pioneers, including Church, Turing, Zuse, Post, Markov, von Neumann, McCarthy, Floyd, Hoare, Scott, Strachey, Dijkstra, Colmerauer, Kowalski, Martin-Löf, and Constable.

ALGEBRAIC SPECIFICATIONS AND PROOFS FOR COMMUNICATING SEQUENTIAL PROCESSES

C.A.R. Hoare

Summary

A restricted notation is suggested for the description of communicating sequential processes. The notation is defined by algebraic equations, which permit proof of further equations describing relevant properties of the operators. Equations are also used to specify and define the behaviour of particular processes, and to prove that they meet their specifications.

The examples cover a range of simple one-way communications devices between a single sender and a single receiver. A simple theory is used at first; this is extended when its inadequacies become too obvious.

NATO ASI Series, Vol. F36
Logic of Programming and Calculi of Discrete Design
Edited by M. Broy
© Springer-Verlag Berlin Heidelberg 1987

1. Communication

We describe a process in terms of the sequence of communications in which it engages. The simplest but least useful description is one that describes all processes whatsoever. It is the predicate "true", abbreviated to

$$\top \qquad\qquad\qquad\text{(true)}$$

If P describes a process and e is an expression, then

$$!e \rightarrow P \qquad\qquad\qquad\text{(output e then P)}$$

describes a process that first outputs the value of e and then behaves as described by P. If Px describes a process whose behaviour may depend on the value of the message x, then

$$(?x \rightarrow Px) \qquad\qquad\qquad\text{(input x then P of x)}$$

describes a process which first inputs a message m, and then behaves as described by Pm. In this formula, the variable x is a bound variable, so

Axiom. $\qquad (?x \rightarrow Px) = (?y \rightarrow Py) \qquad\qquad$ (bound var)

Our first example

$$?x \rightarrow (!x \rightarrow \top)$$

describes any process whose first action is an input and whose second action is an output of the same message which it has just input. Nothing is said of its subsequent behaviour, so many different processes are described by this formula. Some of these are also described at greater length and in greater detail by the next example, which copies at least two messages

$$?x \rightarrow !x \rightarrow (?y \rightarrow !y \rightarrow \top)$$

Here, unnecessary brackets have been omitted; but they have been retained for input to indicate the scope of the bound variable.

Recursion may be used to describe the behaviour of processes into the unbounded future. For example, a process which repeatedly inputs and then outputs the same message is defined by the recursive definition

Def. $\qquad COPY \triangleq (?x \rightarrow !x \rightarrow COPY)$

The meaning of any formula in mathematics is unchanged when one replaces a defined term by the right hand side of its definition, so

Theorem. $\qquad COPY = (?x \rightarrow !x \rightarrow (?x \rightarrow !x \rightarrow COPY))$

This substitution may be carried out again and again, to reveal as much as desired of the behaviour of the process

$$COPY = ?x \to !x \to ?x \to !x \to ?x \to \ldots$$

To ensure success in definition by recursion, the right had side of a recursive definition must be *guarded,* in the sense that every recursive occurrence of the process name must be preceded by at least one input or output. Under this condition, the defining equation for the process has only one solution. This fact is formalised as the law of unique fixed points

Axiom. $\qquad P = F(P) \wedge F(Q) = Q \Rightarrow P = Q$ $\qquad\qquad$ (ufp)

$\qquad\qquad$ provided F is guarded.

For example, consider the process C, defined recursively

Def. $\qquad C \triangleq (?x \to !x \to (?y \to !y \to C))$

By substitution and change of bound variable in the definition of $COPY$, we know that

Theorem. $\qquad COPY = (?x \to !x \to (?y \to !y \to COPY))$

Thus $COPY$ and C are both solutions of the same guarded recursive equation. But there is only one solution. So these apparently different solutions are identical.

Theorem. $\qquad COPY = C$ $\qquad\qquad$ by ufp

Examples

1. A process $CPAIR$ faithfully copies messages from input to output, but batches them into pairs before delivery.

$$CPAIR \triangleq (?x \to (?y \to !x \to !y \to CPAIR))$$

2. A process $REVPR$ copies pairs of messages from input to output, but reverses the order of delivery within each pair

$$REVPR \triangleq (?x \to (?y \to !y \to !x \to REVPR))$$

3. A process $SINK$ loses every message

$$SINK \triangleq (?x \to SINK)$$

Exercises

Using only notations introduced above, describe:

1. A process *LOSEHALF* copies the first of each pair of messages and loses the second.

2. A process *K0* never inputs, and outputs only messages with value 0.

□

2. Disjunction

If P and Q are process descriptions, then their disjunction

$$P \vee Q \qquad\qquad\qquad (P \text{ or } Q)$$

describes all processes described by either P or Q. This disjunction satisfies the familiar algebraic laws of propositional logic.

Axioms. $\qquad P \vee P = P \qquad\qquad\qquad\qquad\qquad$ ($\vee$ idempotent)

$$P \vee Q = Q \vee P \qquad\qquad\qquad\qquad\quad (\vee \text{ symmetric})$$

$$P \vee (Q \vee R) = (P \vee Q) \vee R \qquad\qquad (\vee \text{ associative})$$

An operator which gives ⊤ when either of its operands is ⊤ is called *strict*. An operator which distributes both leftward and rightward through disjunction is called *disjunctive*. For example, disjunction is both strict and disjunctive.

Axiom. $\qquad P \vee \top = \top \qquad\qquad\qquad\qquad\qquad$ ($\vee$ strict)

Theorem. $\qquad P \vee (Q1 \vee Q2) = (P \vee Q1) \vee (P \vee Q2) \qquad$ ($\vee$ disjunctive)

A process which first communicates and is then described by $Q1$ or $Q2$ could also be described as a process which either communicates and then behaves as $Q1$, or performs the same communication and then behaves as $Q2$. This fact is clearly and briefly expressed as algebraic axioms

Axiom. $\qquad !e \to (Q1 \vee Q2) = (!e \to Q1) \vee (!e \to Q2) \qquad$ (! disjunctive)

Axiom. $\qquad ?x \to (Q1 \vee Q2x) = (?x \to Q1x) \vee (?x \to Q2x) \qquad$ (? disjunctive)

Disjunction is useful for describing possible transient faults in message passing systems.

Examples

1. A communications device which may sometimes duplicate a message

$$DUP \triangleq (?x \to !x \to (DUP \vee (!x \to DUP)))$$

2. A device that may sometimes lose a message

$$LOSS \triangleq (?x \rightarrow ((!x \rightarrow LOSS) \vee LOSS))$$

3. A device that may sometimes interchange the order of delivery of a pair of consecutive messages

$$SWOP2 \triangleq (?x \rightarrow ((!x \rightarrow SWOP2) \vee (?y \rightarrow !y \rightarrow !x \rightarrow SWOP2)))$$

Exercises

1. Rewrite the above processes so that they must deliver at least one message correctly after an error.

2. Prove that disjunction is disjunctive   □

A description P is as precise as Q (or more so) if everything described by P is also described by Q (but not necessarily vice-versa). In this case, we write

$$P \leq Q \text{ or } Q \geq P$$

This concept may be defined in terms of disjunction

Def. $P \leq Q$ means $(P \vee Q) = Q$

From the definition it is easy to prove that $\leq$ is an upper semilattice, in the sense that it obeys the following laws

Theorems.		
$P \leq P$		$\leq$ reflexive
$P \leq Q \wedge Q \leq P \Rightarrow P = Q$		$\leq$ antisymmetric
$P \leq Q \wedge Q \leq R \Rightarrow P \leq R$		$\leq$ transitive
$P \leq \top$		$\leq$ top $\top$
$(P \vee Q) \leq R \Leftrightarrow P \leq R \wedge Q \leq R$		$\leq$ lub $\vee$
$P \leq P \vee Q$		a fortiori

A function F is defined to be monotonic if it preserves the ordering of its operands; or in symbols

Def. $F(P) \leq F(Q)$ whenever $P \leq Q$

or $F(P1, P2) \leq F(Q1, Q2)$ whenever $P1 \leq Q1$ and $P2 \leq Q2$

and so on for functions of more than two arguments. It is easy to prove that

Theorem.   All disjunctive functions are monotonic.

Theorem.   All combinations of monotonic functions are monotonic.

A function in mathematics represents the engineering concept of an assembly, with a slot into which different components (arguments) may be plugged. A non-monotonic function would be an assembly with the peculiarity that its behaviour becomes more predictable and controllable when you plug in a less predictable and controllable component. Such assemblies are fortunately rare in engineering; because if they existed, they would be very difficult to work with. For this reason (and others which will appear later) all functions which we introduce and use for describing processes will be monotonic.

The introduction of the precision ordering $\leq$ permits a simple and useful extension of the unique fixed point law

Axiom. $\qquad P \leq F(P) \wedge F(Q) \leq Q \Rightarrow P \leq Q$ $\qquad\qquad$ (ufp)

provided F is guarded.

We use this axiom to prove that the behaviour described by COPY is also described by $LOSS$ — since $LOSS$ does not actually specify that messages *must* be lost, it could in fact describe a process which copies faithfully all the time.

Theorem. $\qquad COPY \leq LOSS$

Proof. $!x \rightarrow LOSS \leq (!x \rightarrow LOSS) \vee LOSS$ $\qquad\qquad$ (a fortiori)

(1) $\therefore$ $\quad (?x \rightarrow (!x \rightarrow LOSS)) \leq (?x \rightarrow ((!x \rightarrow LOSS) \vee LOSS))$ $\quad$ (? monotonic)

(2) $\therefore$ $\quad (?x \rightarrow !x \rightarrow LOSS) \leq LOSS$ $\qquad\qquad$ (def $LOSS$)

(3) but $\quad COPY \leq COPY$ $\qquad\qquad$ ($\leq$ refl)

(4) $\therefore$ $\quad COPY \leq (?x \rightarrow !x \rightarrow COPY)$ $\qquad\qquad$ (def $COPY$)

$\therefore$ $\qquad COPY \leq LOSS$ $\qquad\qquad$ (ufp (4) (2))

A similar proof may be given for

$SINK \leq LOSS$

and from ($\leq$ lub $\vee$) we may conclude that

$COPY \vee SINK \leq LOSS$

Exercises

Prove the following

1. $COPY \leq DUP$

2. $COPY \vee REV PR \leq SWOP2$ $\qquad\qquad$ (hint: use $\leq$ lub $\vee$)

Note that $(COPY \lor SINK)$ describes a process which may either copy or lose messages; but after the first cycle, must remain forever consistent. If the second action is an output, all subsequent messages will also be copied; otherwise they will all be lost. $LOSS$ describes these processes, as well as ones which behave differently on successive cycles. It is therefore a vaguer description.

3. Foundations

I have introduced and given some examples of a notation for description of the behaviour of communicating processes. The concept of a process can be defined more formally by a set of axioms similar to those formulated by Peano for natural numbers. Let **P** stand for the set of all processes.

1. $\top \in \mathbf{P}$

2. $(!e \to P') \in \mathbf{P} \equiv (P' \in \mathbf{P}$ and e is a message)

3. $(?x \to Px) \in \mathbf{P} \equiv (Px \in \mathbf{P}$ for all messages $x)$

4. $(P1 \lor P2) \in \mathbf{P} \equiv (P1 \in \mathbf{P}$ and $P2 \in \mathbf{P})$

5. Every process takes one of the four forms

$$\top, (!e \to P), (?x \to Px), (P1 \lor P2)$$

6. Every set of guarded recursive equations uniquely define the corresponding processes

If we were interested only in finite processes, the last two axioms would be combined into the more familiar axiom

"Everything which is a process can be proved so by application of the first four axioms."

The reason for the new formalisation of the last axiom is that we wish to include infinite processes.

In the theory of natural numbers, primitive recursion is used to define functions by showing how they apply to the two permitted forms of number, (i.e., zero and the successor of some number). Functions on processes may be similarly defined by considering all four forms which a process may take. For example, let us define a *minus* function on processes. $(-P)$ is defined as a process that behaves like P, except that whenever P would output an integer message x, $(-P)$ outputs $(-x)$ instead. The definition deals with the four cases.

1. If we don't know anything about a process, then we don't know anything about its minus.

$$-(\top) = \top$$

2. If a process behaves like P or Q, its negation behaves like the minus of P or the minus of Q.

$$\text{-}(P \vee Q) = (\text{-}P) \vee (\text{-}Q) \qquad \text{-disj.}$$

3. If a process begins with output of e, its minus begins with output of minus e, and its subsequent behaviour is also changed.

$$\text{-}(!e \rightarrow P) = !(\text{-}e) \rightarrow (\text{-}P) \qquad \text{-dist!}$$

4. If a process begins with input, its minus begins with the same input, but its subsequent behaviour is changed.

$$\text{-}(?x \rightarrow Px) = (?x \rightarrow \text{-}(Px)) \qquad \text{-dist.}$$

The definition of minus takes the form of algebraic equations which show how the function distributes through the operators used to construct a process. The intention is that any call of the function can be eliminated from any finite expression describing a process by pushing it inwards until it reaches the occurrences of $\top$ and (by 1 above) disappears; and it permits the behaviour of an infinite or recursively defined process to be explored as deeply as desired, deep enough at least to apply the theorem of unique fixed points.

Examples

1. $\text{-}(?x \rightarrow !x \rightarrow ?y \rightarrow !y \rightarrow \top)$

$$= (?x \rightarrow !(\text{-}x) \rightarrow ?y \rightarrow !(\text{-}y) \rightarrow \top)$$

2. $\text{-}COPY$

$$= (?x \rightarrow !(\text{-}x) \rightarrow (\text{-}COPY))$$

$$= NEG \qquad \text{(ufp)}$$

where $NEG \triangleq (?x \rightarrow !(\text{-}x) \rightarrow NEG)$ □

In the theory of natural numbers, the properties of functions defined by primitive recursion can be proved by mathematical induction. The corresponding technique for functions defined on other recursively defined domains is known as structural induction. It deals with all the possible structures of the induction variable, and appeals to the hypothesis that all components of the structure satisfy the theorem. Here is the proof of an obvious theorem that when you minus a process twice you get back the original process.

Theorem. $\qquad \text{-}(\text{-}P) = P$

Proof: by induction on the structure of P.

case 0: $P = \top$

$$-(\cdot\top) = (\cdot\top) = \top \qquad\qquad \text{-strict}^2$$

case 1: $P = (P1 \vee P2)$

$$-(\cdot(P1 \vee P2)) = -((\cdot P1) \vee (\cdot P2)) \qquad\qquad \text{def -}$$

$$= (-(\cdot P1)) \vee (-(\cdot P2)) \qquad\qquad \text{def -}$$

$$= P1 \vee P2 \qquad\qquad \text{by the induction hypothesis}$$

case 2: $P =!e \to P'$

$$-(\cdot P)) = -(!(\cdot e) \to (\cdot P')) \qquad\qquad \text{def -}$$

$$= !(-(\cdot e)) \to -(\cdot(P')) \qquad\qquad \text{def -}$$

$$= !e \to P' \qquad\qquad \text{induction hyp.}$$

case 3: $P = (?x \to Px)$

the proof is easier than case 2.

□

Processes differ from natural numbers in that each natural number is finite, whereas a process may be infinite. As a result, we must restrict the kinds of predicate to which structural induction is applied. They must be simple universally quantified equations, or finite disjunctions and conjunctions of such equations. Negation and infinite existential quantification are prohibited. It is this restriction that protects us from proving propositions that are true only of finite processes.

Another important restriction is necessary in the definition of functions by structural recursion. The need for it is revealed in the following example. Let f be a function which selects the first alternative of each disjunction. So

$$f(\top) = \top$$

$$f(P \vee Q) = P, \text{ etc.}$$

From the second clause we get

$$f(Q \vee P) = Q$$

But by symmetry of disjunction

$$(P \vee Q) = (Q \vee P)$$

$$\therefore \qquad P = f(P \vee Q) = f(Q \vee P) = Q \qquad\qquad \text{for } all \text{ } P \text{ and } Q$$

We have proved that all processes are equal to each other. Clearly we need to forbid definition of such disastrous functions as f. Fortunately, if the function f is defined as strict and disjunctive (which is often most reasonable anyway), the only further restriction is that the right hand sides of the definitions $f(!e \rightarrow P')$ and $f(?x \rightarrow Px)$ should be disjunctive. If the right hand sides of these equations are also guarded in $f(P)$ and $f(Px)$ respectively, then there is only one function which satisfies the recursive definition.

Exercises

1. Define a function $\sim P$ which negates each number before *input* by P.

2. Prove that $(\sim\text{-}COPY) = COPY$

□

4. Interleaving

Let P and Q be processes. Let us connect their two input channels into a single input channel in such a way that each message input on the single channel is input either by P or by Q, but for any particular input we do not know which. Similarly, let us combine their output channels so that each output message comes either from P or from Q, we know not which. As a result, all we know is that the sequence of communications performed by the pair of processes is an arbitrary interleaving of two communication sequences of each of the processes individually. The result of such a connection is called the *interleaving* of P and Q; its behaviour is denoted

$$(P|||Q)$$

and it may be represented pictorially in Figure 1.

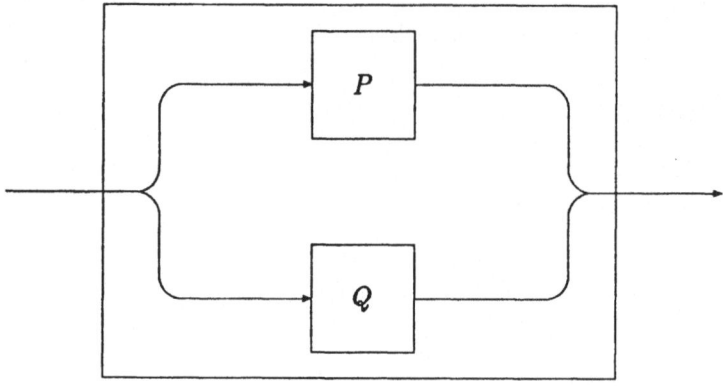

Figure 1: $P|||Q$

This informal description of the connection of two processes may be formalised in a definition by a simultaneous recursion on the structure of both operands. In principle there are sixteen cases, but fortunately they can be classified under three headings

1. If nothing is known about one of the operands of the interleaving, then nothing is known about the behaviour of their combination. This means that the interleaving operator is strict in each of its arguments

$$\top|||Q = \top = P|||\top \qquad\qquad\qquad\qquad (||| \text{ strict})$$

2. If it is not known whether one of the operands will behave like $P1$ or like $P2$, then both these possibilities are preserved in their conbination. This means that the interleaving operator is disjunctive

$$(P1 \vee P2)|||Q = (P1|||Q) \vee (P2|||Q)$$

and $\qquad P|||(Q1 \vee Q2) = (P|||Q1) \vee (P|||Q2)$

3. The two classes described above cover all cases when either operand is $\top$ or a disjunction; so in all remaining cases, both operands begin with a communication. In these cases, the first communication of the interleaving is the first communication either of the left operand or of the right operand. Whichever it is, the other operand does nothing, and its future behaviour remains unchanged. This description applies equally, whether the communication is input or output, either of which will be represented by the letters c and d.

Let $\qquad P \stackrel{\Delta}{=} c \rightarrow P'$ and $\quad Q \stackrel{\Delta}{=} d \rightarrow Q'$

$$(P|||Q) = (c \rightarrow (P'|||Q)) \vee (d \rightarrow (P|||Q')) \qquad\qquad ||| \text{ dist} \rightarrow.$$

This clause shows how interleaving distributes through the arrow.

$\square$

Example

Let $K0 \stackrel{\Delta}{=} !0 \rightarrow K0$ and $K1 \stackrel{\Delta}{=} !1 \rightarrow K1$

So $K0$ outputs only zeros and $K1$ outputs only ones.

Then $K0 ||| K1$

$= (!0 \rightarrow K0)|||(!1 \rightarrow K1)$		by def. $K0, K1$
$= (!0 \rightarrow (K0|||(!1 \rightarrow K1)))$		$|||$ dist.
$\vee (!1 \rightarrow ((!0 \rightarrow K0)|||K1))$		$|||$ dist.
$= (!0 \rightarrow (K0|||K1)) \vee (!1 \rightarrow (K0|||K1))$		by def. $K0, K1$

$= K01$ by ufp

where $K01 \triangleq (!0 \rightarrow K01) \vee (!1 \rightarrow K01)$

$K01$ outputs an arbitrary interleaving of zeros and ones.

Exercise

Prove that $SINK|||SINK = SINK$ □

An important property of the $|||$ operator is that it is symmetric. The proof follows the structure of the definition of the operator.

Theorem. $(P|||Q) = (Q|||P)$

Proof. by simultaneous induction on P and Q.

Case (1) One of the operands is $\top$

$$\top|||Q = \top = Q|||\top \qquad\qquad (||| \text{ strict})$$

Case (2) One of the operands is a disjunction

$$(P1 \vee P2)|||Q = (P1|||Q) \vee (P2|||Q) \qquad\qquad (||| \text{ disj.})$$
$$= (Q|||P1) \vee (Q|||P2) \qquad\qquad (\text{ind. hyp.})$$
$$= Q|||(P1 \vee P2) \qquad\qquad (||| \text{ disj.})$$

Case (3) Both operands begin with communication

$$P = c \rightarrow P' \quad \text{and} \quad Q = d \rightarrow Q'$$

$$P|||Q = (c \rightarrow P')|||(d \rightarrow Q')$$
$$= (c \rightarrow (P'|||Q)) \vee (d \rightarrow (P|||Q')) \qquad\qquad (||| \text{ dist. } \rightarrow)$$
$$= (c \rightarrow (Q|||P')) \vee (d \rightarrow (Q'|||P)) \qquad\qquad (\text{ind. hyp.})$$
$$= (d \rightarrow (Q'|||P)) \vee (c \rightarrow (Q|||P')) \qquad\qquad (\vee \text{ symm})$$
$$= Q|||P \qquad\qquad (||| \text{ dist. } \rightarrow)$$

Other theorems that may be similarly proved are

1. If one operand of $|||$ begins with a communication, then that communication may happen first, but maybe it doesn't

$$(c \rightarrow P)|||Q \geq c \rightarrow (P|||Q) \qquad\qquad (||| \text{ def.})$$

2. When P is interleaved with Q, we do not rule out the possibility that all communications turn out to be with P, and Q is always unfairly neglected

$$P|||Q \geq P \qquad\qquad\qquad\qquad (||| \text{ unfair})$$

3. When three processes are interleaved, it does not matter in which order they are connected

$$(P|||Q)|||R = P|||(Q|||R) \qquad\qquad\qquad (||| \text{ assoc.})$$

5. Communications Services

A simple unswitched communications service is a process that inputs messages posted in one location and delivers them at another. The most general definition of such a service is that it cannot deliver more copies of any message than have been previously posted.

A specific example of such a service is the $COPY$ process, which alternates acceptance and delivery of messages. In general, a service can accept many more messages than have been delivered, holding the balance in a buffer, often with some limit on its size. The $COPY$ process has a maximum buffer size of just one, whereas $CPAIR$ can buffer two messages. Some services, (including the letter service of the national post office) may reorder messages before delivery. For example, $REVPR$ and $SWOP2$ can reorder adjacent messages. A communications service is allowed to lose messages like $LOSS$, or even $SINK$, which avoids delivering unposted messges by the lazy expedient of not delivering any messages at all.

Suppose P and Q are communications services both connecting the same sender to the same receiver, but perhaps by different routes across the mountains which separate them. A message service of increased capacity is provided by their interleaving $P|||Q$. Each message posted may be carried by either route, and we do not know nor care which service carries a particular message. Messages sent on one route may overtake messages held in the buffer of the other route. The maximum buffer capacity of the combined service is the sum of the maxima of the individual routes.

The simplest example of a two-route service is the interleaving of two simple copying processes.

$$C|||C = (?x \to !x \to C)|||(?x \to 1x \to C) \qquad\qquad \text{def. } COPY$$

$$=?x \to ((!x \to C)|||C) \vee (?x \to (C|||(!x \to C)))$$

$$=?x \to (C|||(!x \to C)) \qquad\qquad |||\text{-symm,}$$

$$\geq ?x \to ?y \to ((!y \to C)|||(!x \to C)) \qquad\qquad |||\text{-det}$$

$$\geq ?x \to ?y \to !x \to !y \to (C|||C) \qquad\qquad |||\text{-det}^2$$

and $\quad C|||C \geq ?x \to ?y \to !y \to !x \to (C|||C) \qquad\qquad |||\text{-det}^2$

The last two lines of this calculation are in a form which permits application of the unique fixed point theorem to prove the inequations.

$$(C|||C) \geq CPAIR$$

$$(C|||C) \geq REVPR$$

from which we conclude

$$(C|||C) \geq COPY \vee CPAIR \vee REVPR \qquad\qquad (\leq \text{lub } \vee)$$

Exercise

Prove $(C|||C) \geq SWOP2$

A two-route communications-service can be extended to an n-route system thereby further increasing the buffering capacity. The definition uses normal mathematical induction on the number of routes.

$$C_1 = C$$

$$C_{n+1} = C_n|||C$$

$$= \underbrace{C|||C||| \dots |||C}_{1+n \text{ times}}$$

We now prove the existence of a reordering communication service (known as a BAG) with unbounded buffering capacity. The addition of another buffer to such a bag should not make any difference, i.e.,

$$BAG = BAG|||C$$

This equation itself cannot be used as a recursive definition because its right hand side is unguarded, and there are many solutions, including $BAG = \top$! This problem is solved by using instead the guarded definition

$$BAG \triangleq (?x \rightarrow (BAG|||(!x \rightarrow C)))$$

The essential property of an unbounded bag may now be proved as a theorem.

Theorem. $BAG|||C = BAG$

$$
\begin{aligned}
LHS \quad &= \quad (?x \rightarrow ((BAG|||(!x \rightarrow C))|||C) \\
&\qquad \vee (?x \rightarrow (BAG|||(!x \rightarrow C)))) \\
&= \quad (?x \rightarrow ((BAG|||C)|||(!x \rightarrow C))) \\
&\qquad \vee (?x \rightarrow (BAG|||(!x \rightarrow C))) \\
&= \quad ?x \rightarrow ((BAG \vee (BAG|||C))|||(!x \rightarrow C)) \\
&= \quad ?x \rightarrow ((BAG|||C)|||(!x \rightarrow C)) \\
&= \quad BAG
\end{aligned}
$$

def BAG
def C
$|||$ dist $\rightarrow$

$|||$ symm
$|||$ assoc

$\rightarrow |||$ disj
$|||$ unfair
ufp

Theorem. $\qquad BAG|||BAG = BAG$

Proof: left as an exercise.

Since we can prove $\qquad SINK \leq BAG$

we know that one of the possible behaviours of an unbounded bag is to lose all messages. But it cannot be relied upon even to do that! So for some purposes the $SINK$ is actually *better* than a bag — for example if it connects a traitor in your own camp to the tent of the enemy general. Furthermore, there is no purpose for which a BAG is reliably better than a $SINK$.

This result indicates a deficiency in the expressive power of the notation we are using to specify buffered communication services. A solution will be given in a later section.

Exercise

Define an interrupt operator $\wedge$ by recursion (on its first argument only). $P \wedge Q$ (P interrupted by Q) behaves to start with like P; but at any time (including at the start) P may stop, and Q start instead.

Prove that this operator is strict and disjunctive in both its arguments, and also associative. Show also that

$$P \vee Q \leq P \wedge Q \leq P|||Q$$

$$BAG \wedge BAG = BAG$$

6. Chaining

Let P and Q be processes. Let us connect the output channel of P directly with the input channel of Q in such a way that a message passes on the shared channel whenever P outputs it and Q inputs it simultaneously. These communications are private to the pair of processes which engage in them, and cannot be observed from their external environment. All messages input by the pair are in fact input by P, and all output in fact comes from Q, but since both processes are enclosed together in a black box, we cannot observe this fact after the connection has been made. The result of such a connection is called the chain of P and Q, and is denoted

$$P \gg Q$$

It is represented pictorially in Figure 2.

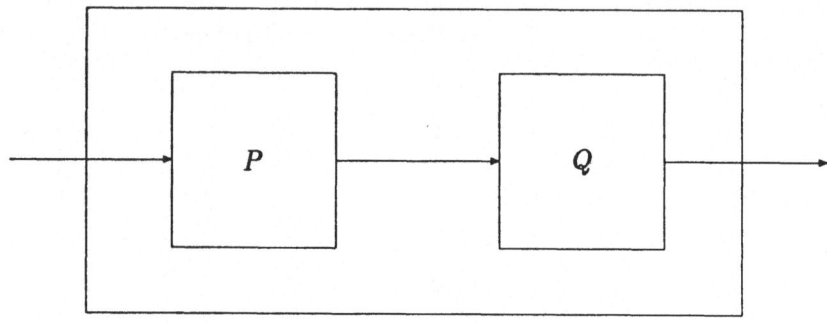

Figure 2: $(P \gg Q)$

The informal description of chaining may be formalised in a definition by simultaneous recursion on the structure of both operands.

1. As usual, chaining is both strict and disjunctive.

2. If the first action of the left operand is output, and the first action of the right operand is input, then both these actions occur immediately, simultaneously and imperceptibly; and in the subsequent behaviour of the right operand, the input variable will take the value of the mesage communicated

$$(!e \rightarrow P) \gg (?x \rightarrow Qx) = (P \gg (Qe))$$

Note that the right hand side of this definition is not guarded. This causes some problems which will be described later.

3. If the first action of both operands is output, the output by the left operand is delayed until the right operand is ready to input it. So the output by the right operand is the only possible initial action of the chain.

$$(!e \rightarrow P) \gg (!f \rightarrow Q) = !f \rightarrow ((!e \rightarrow P) \gg Q)$$

4. If the first action of both operands is input, similar reasoning applies; the first action of the chain is the input by the left operand.

$$(?x \rightarrow Px) \gg (?y \rightarrow Qy) = (?x \rightarrow (Px \gg (?y \rightarrow Qy)))$$

5. If the first action of the left operand is input and the first action of the right operand is output, then either of these actions may occur first, and the subsequent

behaviour is defined accordingly

$$(?x \to Px) \gg (!f \to Q) \quad =$$

$$(?x \to (Px \gg (!f \to Q))) \quad \lor \quad (!f \to ((?x \to Px) \gg Q))$$

From this definition it is possible to prove that chaining enjoys properties similar to those of $|||$.

Theorem.

$$(?x \to P) \gg Q \; \geq \; ?x \to (P \gg Q) \qquad \gg\text{-det}$$

$$P \gg (!f \to Q) \; \geq \; !f \to (P \gg Q) \qquad \gg\text{-det}$$

$$P \gg (Q \gg R) \; = \; (P \gg Q) \gg R \qquad \gg\text{ assoc}$$

A telegraph service is defined as a communications service with the additional useful property that it delivers messages in the same order that they were posted, though possibly after some delay. A specific example of such a service is the *COPY* process. Another example is the process *CPAIR*, which buffers up to two messages before delivery. Another less useful example is the *SINK*, which obeys the specification in its characteristically lazy way.

Suppose now that we have two telegraph services, one of which passes messages from the sender to an intermediate point in the mountains between the sender and receiver, and the other connects the intermediate point with the receiver. To complete the connection between the sender and the receiver, all that is needed is to chain together these two services. The simplest example is the chain consisting of two copying services

$$C \gg C = (?x \to ((!x \to C) \gg (?y \to !y \to C)))$$

$$= (?x \to (C \gg (!x \to C)))$$

$$= (?x \to [(!x \to (C \gg C))$$

$$\lor (?z \to ((!z \to C) \gg (!x \to C)))])$$

So $C \gg C \geq (?x \to !x \to (C \gg C))$

and $C \gg C \geq (?x \to ?z \to ((!z \to C) \gg (!x \to C)))$

$$= (?x \to ?z \to !x \to ((!z \to C) \gg C))$$

$$\geq (?x \to ?z \to !x \to !z \to (C \gg C))$$

$\therefore \; C \gg C \geq COPY \lor CPAIR$

A telegraph service with greater buffering capacity can be constructed by adding yet more copying processes to the chain. A buffer of size n is defined by induction, like a bag of size n, but with chaining rather than interleaving.

$$BUF_1 = C$$

$$BUF_{n+1} = BUF_n \gg C$$

An unbounded buffer is defined like an unbounded bag

$$BUF = (?x \rightarrow (BUF \gg (!x \rightarrow C)))$$

It is not valid to assume from its appearance that the right hand side of this equation is guarded: nevertheless, we will make this assumption without proof.

It is now easy to prove that chaining another buffer (bounded or unbounded) at either end of an unbounded buffer makes no difference.

Theorem. $\qquad BUF = BUF \gg C = C \gg BUF$

$$= BUF \gg BUF$$

Clearly, to behave like a buffer is one of the possibilities for a bag.

Theorem. $\qquad BUF \leq BAG$

Furthermore, chaining or interleaving buffers or bags to a bag makes no difference. These facts are summarised in the series of equations

Theorem. $\quad BAG = BUF \gg BAG = BAG \gg BUF = BAG \gg BAG$

$$= BUF |||BAG = BUF \vee BAG = BAG|||BAG$$

Thus any combination of bags and buffers (including at least one bag) will be a bag, for example

$$(BAG \gg ((BUF \vee BAG)|||BUF))|||(BAG \gg BUF) = BAG$$

Since all the operators are monotonic, any component of this expression can be replaced by a more precisely described component, and the only result is to increase the precision of the whole expression. For example,

$$(B_7 \gg ((C_{12} \vee SWOP2)|||CPAIR))|||(LOSS \gg C) \leq BAG$$

The left hand side of this inequality describes the structure of a simple unswitched store-and-forward message passing system consisting of a number of nodes connected in series or in parallel. If each node acts as a mail service, we have proved that the whole network does so too. A theorem of this kind explains the success of message services like the *ARPANET*. The significance of this particular version of the theorem is much diminished by the fact that a *SINK* meets the same specification.

7. Divergence

The time has come to describe some of the problems arising from the fact that one of the clauses in the definition of the chaining operator is unguarded. Consider the process

$$K0 \gg SINK = (!0 \to K0) \gg (?x \to SINK) \qquad \text{def. } K0,\ SINK$$

$$= K0 \gg SINK \qquad \gg \text{dist.} \to$$

$$= (!0 \to K0) \gg (?x \to SINK) \qquad \text{def } K0,\ SINK$$

$$= \ldots$$

It is clearly impossible either for man or machine ever to discover what is the first action of this process. Such an ill-defined process is said to *diverge*. We may believe that it will never perform any action at all but we cannot prove this, or even describe this behaviour in our restricted notations. The only description we could validly give of it is the vacuous description $\top$.

Consider now the result of chaining this divergent process to $K0$

$$(K0 \gg SINK) \gg K0$$

Since there is no way of discovering the first action of the left operand of the chain, it is not possible to use any of the distribution laws for chaining to calculate the first action of this triple chain. We may believe that the first action can only be (or even must be) the output of a zero, but the axioms do not permit a proof of this, or of any other non-trivial fact about this process.

The same phenomenon of divergence arises if we permit unguarded expressions on the right hand side of a recursive definition. Consider for example

$$DIV \triangleq DIV \vee (!0 \to DIV)$$

$$= (DIV \vee (!0 \to DIV)) \vee (!0 \to (DIV \vee (!0 \to DIV)))$$

$$= DIV \vee (!0 \to DIV) \vee (!0 \to (!0 \to DIV)) \vee \ldots$$

Again, it is not possible to discover by substitution (any number of times) what the possible initial actions of this process might be. We do not know whether the first action of DIV will or will not be output, or indeed whether it diverges without performing any action at all. Because it is unguarded, the recursive equation which was supposed to define DIV has many solutions, including $K0$, $SINK|||K0$, $K0|||K1$, and even $\top$, which is the vaguest of all process descriptions.

If this is regarded as a problem, one widely accepted solution is to identify all processes which may diverge with the process $\top$. This extreme measure can be justified both on practical and on theoretical grounds.

1. A potentially divergent process is no use to man or machine. So its occurrence in a specification can only be a mistake. Its occurrence in a program submitted for execution on a computer is an even worse mistake. There is no point in making subtle distinctions between different kinds of mistake; it is much simpler to lump them all together and call them $\top$.

2. The simplest and most widely accepted theory of recursion is that proposed by Dana Scott.

A very simple introduction is as follows.

A *finite* process is one which can be described as a single expression without using recursion, so the ultimate components of the expression can only be $\top$. An infinite process is determined by the set of all finite processes (called approximations) which are equal or less precise than it. The set of approximations which determine a recursively defined process

$$R = F(R)$$

is generated by iterating or unfolding the function of F

$$R = \bigcup_{n \geq 0} \{X | X \text{is finite and} X \geq F^n(\top)\}$$

where $F^o(X) = X$

$$F^{n+1}(X) = F(F^n(X))$$

For example, the approximations of $K0$ are

$$\{\top, (!0 \to \top), (!0 \to !0 \to \top), \ldots\}$$

and those of $SINK$ are

$$\{\top, (?x \to \top), (?x \to ?x \to \top), \ldots\}$$

In the case of a guarded recursion, each successive approximation reveals more and more of the initial behaviour of the process. However, for an unguarded recursion like DIV, *all* the approximations are equal to $\top$; and hence DIV also is equal to $\top$, which is the most general and least precise of all solutions of its defining equation.

The finite approximations of a process described by an introduced operator like interleaving are obtained by applying the operator to the approximations of its operands. For example, a typical approximation of

$$K0 \gg SINK$$

involves n outputs by $K0$ and m inputs by $SINK$

$$(!0 \to !0 \to \ldots \to \top) \gg (?x \to ?x \to \ldots \top)$$

By the laws which define chaining, all such approximations are equal to $\top$, and so is the chain.

8. Choice

Suppose I have the opportunity of using a process described by the disjunction

$$P = P1 \vee P2,$$

where $P1 = \,!e \rightarrow P1$ and $P2 = (?x \rightarrow P2x)$

The process P may start with either output or input; and I cannot predict or control which the first action will be. If I want the process to input it may actually output; and if I want it to output, it may input. In the first case, I would have preferred to use a process described by the stronger specification $P1$; and in the second case, I would have preferred one satisfying the stronger specification $P2$. Their disjunction P is adequate only in cases when I really don't care which the first action is, and in which I would be equally satisfied with $P1$ or $P2$. So $P1$ is always as good as P, and sometimes better.

Thus we can interpret the ordering

$$P1 \leq P$$

to mean that a process with specification $P1$ is (in general) more predictable than P, more controllable, and more useful in all circumstances than a process of which the strongest thing we know is that it may behave like $P1$ or like $P2$.

This reasoning shows that alternative behaviours are never a desirable possibility in a delivered product. The value of disjunction lies in the specification: it abstracts from detail, and allows alternative implementations. So as a *specification* $(P1 \vee P2)$ can actually be *better* than $P1$, if it is easier or cheaper to implement.

Now I want to specify a new kind of process whose first action is either input output; but I also specify that *I myself* wish to choose between these alternatives *after* the process has been made and delivered to me. Thus the process must initially be *ready* to input (if thats what I eventually choose); and it must be initially ready to output (if that's what I choose instead). It is not permitted for the implementor to make this choice before delivery. To express this new requirement a new operator $\square$ is introduced into our notation.

$$(!e \rightarrow P) \,\square\, (?x \rightarrow Qx)$$

describes a process that initially offers a choice of input or output. Only one of these actions will actually occur. If the first action is input, the subsequent behaviour of the process will be described by P; and if the first action is input of a message value m, the subsequent behaviour will be (Qm).

The meaning of the new operator is made more precise by the following axioms.

1. Like most other operators, $\square$ is strict and disjunctive.

2. A choice between input and output is the same as a choice between output and

input

$$(!e \rightarrow P) \; \Box \; (?x \rightarrow Px) = (?x \rightarrow Px) \; \Box \; (!e \rightarrow P)$$

This law is not guarded, and gives no way to eliminate the $\Box$ operator, even from finite processes.

3. A choice between input and input is impossible for me to make. However, both alternatives remain possible, so the effect of $\Box$ is the same as that of disjunction.

$$(?x \rightarrow Px) \; \Box \; (?y \rightarrow Qy) = (?x \rightarrow Px) \vee (?y \rightarrow Qy)$$

4. Choice between outputs is also impossible. I am not allowed to look at the message about to be delivered before making my choice

$$(!e \rightarrow P) \; \Box \; (!f \rightarrow Q) = (!e \rightarrow P) \vee (!f \rightarrow Q)$$

5. Finally, a process which offers a choice can never be worse than one which may make that choice arbitrarily

$$P \; \Box \; Q \leq P \vee Q$$

This axiom may seem strange; it could be replaced (if you prefer) by postulating idempotence of $\Box$, which is more obvious, and from which it can be proved.

These laws are adequate for proof of the most obvious properties of choice.

Theorem. $\Box$ is idempotent, symmetric, and associative. Furthermore, $\vee$ distributes through $\Box$.

The introduction of a new primitive operator to describe a new feature of the behaviour of processes now requires that all previous definitions of operators be extended to deal with this new case, and all theorems should also be re-examined. Instead of doing this, we will give definitions of two completely new operators $\gg\!\!\!\gg$ and $\widehat{\|\|}$, which are very similar to $\gg$ and $|||$ except that, whenever there are alternative actions, the user is offered a choice between them. Both operators are strict and disjunctive.

Axiom. Let $P = (c1 \rightarrow P1) \; \Box \; (c2 \rightarrow P2)$

$\qquad\quad Q \quad = (d1 \rightarrow Q1) \; \Box \; (d2 \rightarrow Q2)$

Then $\quad P\widehat{\|\|}Q \; = \; (c1 \rightarrow (P1\widehat{\|\|}Q)) \; \Box \; (c2 \rightarrow (P2\widehat{\|\|}Q)$

$\qquad\qquad\qquad\quad \Box(d1 \rightarrow (P\widehat{\|\|}Q1)) \; \Box \; (d2 \rightarrow (P\widehat{\|\|}Q2))$

The relevant equation when P or Q do not initially offer choice can be deduced from this by idempotence of $\Box$.

The distribution law for $\gg\!\!\!\gg$ is more complicated

$$
\begin{aligned}
\text{Let} \quad P \quad &= \quad (?x \rightarrow P1x) \,\square\, (!e \rightarrow P2) \\
Q \quad &= \quad (?y \rightarrow Q1y) \,\square\, (!f \rightarrow Q2) \\
P \ggg Q \quad &= \quad (R \,\square\, S) \vee R
\end{aligned}
$$

$$
\text{where} \quad R \quad = \quad P2 \ggg (Q1e)
$$

$$
\text{and} \quad S \quad = \quad (?x \rightarrow (P1x \gg Q)) \,\square\, (!f \rightarrow (P \gg Q2))
$$

The process R describes what happens when the internal concealed communication occurs first; and this may happen autonomously and outside the control or knowledge of the user. The process S describes what happens if the user engages in a communication before the internal communication has occurred. The asymmetric combination of R and S by $\square$ and $\vee$ is necessary: $(R \,\square\, S)$ offers the user too much choice, and $(R \vee S)$ too little.

Using these improved operators, we can define improved versions of the bounded and unbounded buffers and bags.

$$
\begin{aligned}
\widehat{B}_1 \quad &\triangleq \quad \widehat{C}_1 \triangleq C \\
\widehat{B}_{n+1} \quad &\triangleq \quad \widehat{B}_n \,\widehat{\|\|}\, C \\
\widehat{C}_{n+1} \quad &\triangleq \quad \widehat{C}_n \ggg C \\
B\widehat{A}G \quad &\triangleq \quad (?x \rightarrow (B\widehat{A}G \,\widehat{\|\|}\, (!x \rightarrow C))) \\
B\widehat{U}F \quad &\triangleq \quad (?x \rightarrow (B\widehat{U}F \ggg (!x \rightarrow C)))
\end{aligned}
$$

For these processes one can no longer prove such undesirable properties as

$$
\begin{aligned}
&\widehat{B}_n \leq \widehat{B}_{n+1} \leq B\widehat{A}G \\
&\widehat{C}_n \leq \widehat{C}_{n+1} \leq B\widehat{U}F \\
&SINK \leq B\widehat{A}G \\
&SINK \leq B\widehat{U}F
\end{aligned}
$$

It is useful also to define buffers and bags in a way which allows *any* finite buffer size, either with a limit n or without.

$$BB_1 \quad \triangleq \quad BC_1 = C$$

$$BB_{n+1} \quad \triangleq \quad \hat{B}_{n+1} \vee BB_n$$

$$BC_{n+1} \quad \triangleq \quad \hat{C}_{n+1} \vee BC_n$$

$$BBAG \quad \triangleq \quad (?x \rightarrow ((!x \rightarrow C) \vee (BBAG \widehat{\|}(!x \rightarrow C))))$$

$$BBUF \quad \triangleq \quad (?x \rightarrow ((!x \rightarrow C) \vee (BBUF \gg (!x \rightarrow C))))$$

It would be interesting to see whether these processes can be composed into arbitrary serial and parallel networks, in the same way as the mail services defined in section 6.

9. Acknowledgements

The technical substance of this paper is due primarily to A.W. Roscoe and He Jifeng. The idea of defining the concept of a process by its algebra is due to Robin Milner, and the application of algebra to the specification and proof of properties of protocols has been developed in a series of papers by Bergstra, Baeten, and Klop.

G. Huet

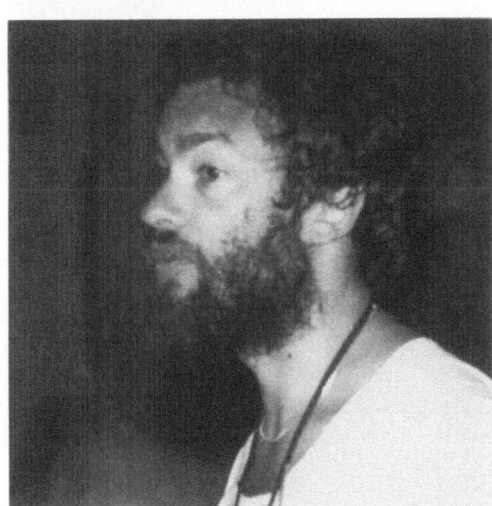

G. Winskel

M. Sintzoff

Part III

Design and Construction Calculi

For the specification, the verification, and the design of programs, calculi are of major importance. Intractable calculi are not helpful. Formalization has to aim at elegant and adequate, tractable calculi that can be supported by tools of thought as well as technical tools. Finally, however, not only proof, derivation, and evaluation calculi are needed, but also calculi that can express, document, and manipulate design and proof descriptions as well as their properties.

Part III

Design and Construction Phase

Deduction and Computation

Gérard Huet

INRIA

Abstract

We present in a unified framework the basic syntactic notions of deduction and computation.

A preliminary version of these course notes was presented at the Advanced Course in Artificial Intelligence held in Vignieu (France) in July 1985, and appeared in "Fundamentals in Artificial Intelligence", Eds. W. Bibel and Ph. Jorrand, Springer-Verlag Lecture Notes in Computer Science vol. 232.

1 Terms and types

1.1 General notations

We assume known elementary set theory and algebra. $\mathcal{N}$ is the set $\{0, 1, ...\}$ of natural numbers, $\mathcal{N}_+$ the set of positive natural numbers. We shall identify the natural n with the set $\{0, ..., n-1\}$, and thus 0 is also the empty set $\emptyset$. Every finite set S is isomorphic to n, with n the cardinal of S, denoted $n = |S|$. If A and B are sets, we write $A \to B$, or sometimes B^A, for the set of functions with domain A and codomain B.

1.2 Languages, concrete syntax

Let Σ be a finite alphabet. A *string* u of *length* n is a function in $n \to \Sigma$. The set of all strings over Σ is

$$\Sigma^* = \bigcup_{n \in \mathcal{N}} \Sigma^n.$$

We write $|u|$ for the length n of u. We write u_i for $u(i-1)$, when $i \leq n$. The null string, unique element of Σ^0, is denoted Λ. The unit string mapping 1 to $a \in \Sigma$ is denoted 'a'. The concatenation of strings u and v, defined in the usual fashion, is denoted $u \hat{\ } v$, and when there is no ambiguity we write e.g. 'abc' for 'a' $\hat{\ }$ 'b' $\hat{\ }$ 'c'. When $u \in \Sigma^*$ and $a \in \Sigma$, we write $u \cdot a$ for $u \hat{\ }$ 'a'. We define an ordering $\leq$ on Σ^*, called the *prefix* ordering, by

$$u \leq v \Leftrightarrow \exists w \quad v = u \hat{\ } w.$$

If $u \leq v$, the residual w is unique, and we write $w = v/u$. We say that strings u and v are *disjoint*, and we write $u|v$, iff u and v are unrelated by the partial ordering $\leq$. Finally we let $u < v$ iff $u \leq v$ with $u \neq v$.

The set Σ^* has the structure of a monoïd, that is:

$$Ass : (u \hat{\ } v) \hat{\ } w = u \hat{\ } (v \hat{\ } w)$$

$$IdL : \Lambda \hat{\ } u = u$$

NATO ASI Series, Vol. F36
Logic of Programming and Calculi of Discrete Design
Edited by M. Broy
© Springer-Verlag Berlin Heidelberg 1987

$$IdR : u \,\hat{}\, \Lambda \,=\, u.$$

Actually, Σ^* is the *free* monoïd generated by Σ.

Examples.

1. $\Sigma = 0$. We get $\Sigma^* = 1$.

2. $\Sigma = 1$. We get $\Sigma^* = \mathcal{N}$. Strings are here natural numbers in unary notation, and concatenation corresponds to addition.

3. $\Sigma = 2 = \{0,1\}$ (the Booleans). The set Σ^* is the set of all binary words.

4. $\Sigma = \mathcal{N}_+$. We call the elements of Σ^* *occurrences*. When $u = w \cdot m$ and $v = w \cdot n$, with $m < n$, we say that u is *left* of v, and write $u <_L v$.

1.3 Terms: abstract syntax

We first define a *tree domain* as a subset D of $\mathcal{N}_+^*$ closed under $<$ and $<_L$:

$$u \in D \,\wedge\, v < u \;\Rightarrow\; v \in D$$

$$u \in D \,\wedge\, v <_L u \;\Rightarrow\; v \in D.$$

We say that M is a Σ-tree iff $M \in D \to \Sigma$, for some tree domain D. We define $D(M)$ as D, and we say that $D(M)$ is the *set of occurrences* in M. M is said to be *finite* whenever $D(M)$ is, which we shall assume in the following.

We shall now use occurrences to designate nodes of a tree, and the subtree starting at that node. If $u \in D(M)$, we define the Σ-tree M/u as mapping occurrence v to $M(u \,\hat{}\, v)$. We say that M/u is the sl subtree of M at occurrence u. If N is also a Σ-tree, we define the *graft* $M[u \leftarrow N]$ as the Σ-tree mapping v to $N(w)$ whenever $v = u \,\hat{}\, w$ with $w \in D(N)$, and to $M(v)$ if $v \in D(M)$ and not $u \leq v$.

We need one auxiliary notion, that of *width* of a tree. If $M \in \Sigma^*$, we define the (top) width of M as

$$\|M\| \,=\, \max\{n \mid {}^\backprime n^\backprime \in D(M)\}.$$

We shall now consider Σ a *graded* alphabet, that is given with an arity function α in $\Sigma \to \mathcal{N}$. We then say that M is a Σ-*term* iff M is a Σ-tree verifying the supplementary consistency condition:

$$\forall u \in D(M) \;\; \|M/u\| \,=\, \alpha(M(u)).$$

That is, every subtree of M is of the form $F(M_1, M_2, ..., M_n)$, with $n = \alpha(F)$. We write $T(\Sigma)$ for the set of Σ-terms. If $M_1, M_2, ...M_n \in T(\Sigma)$ and $F \in \Sigma$, with $\alpha(F) = n$, then $M = F(M_1, M_2, ...M_n)$ is easily defined as a Σ-term. This gives $T(\Sigma)$ the structure of a Σ-algebra. Since conversely the decomposition of M is uniquely determined, we call $T(\Sigma)$ the *completely free* Σ-algebra.

Example

With $\Sigma = \{+, S, 0\}$, $\alpha(+) = 2$, $\alpha(S) = 1$, $\alpha(0) = 0$, the following structure represents a Σ-term:

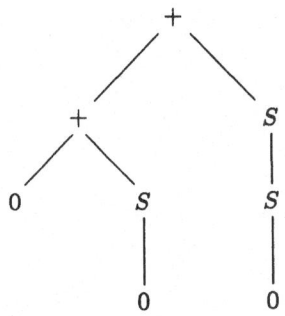

The following proposition is easy to prove by induction. All occurrences are supposed to be universally quantified in the relevant tree domain.

Proposition 1.

$$Embedding: \quad M[u \leftarrow N]/(u \,\hat{}\, v) \;=\; N/v$$

$$Associativity: M[u \leftarrow N][u \,\hat{}\, v \leftarrow P] \;=\; M[u \leftarrow N[v \leftarrow P]]$$

$$Persistence: M[u \leftarrow N]/v \;=\; M/v \quad (u|v)$$

$$Commutativity: M[u \leftarrow N][v \leftarrow P] \;=\; M[v \leftarrow P][u \leftarrow N] \quad (u|v)$$

$$Distributivity: M[u \leftarrow N]/v \;=\; (M/v)[u/v \leftarrow N] \quad (v \le u)$$

$$Dominance: M[u \leftarrow N][v \leftarrow P] \;=\; M[v \leftarrow P] \quad (v \le u).$$

We define the *length* $|M|$ of a (finite) term M recursively by:

$$|F(M_1, ..., M_2)| \;=\; 1 + \Sigma_{i=1}^n |M_i|.$$

1.4 Parsing

It is well-known that the term in the example above can be represented unambiguously as a Σ-string, for instance in *prefix polish notation*, that is here: $++0S0SS0$. This result is not very interesting: such strings are neither good notations for humans, nor good representations for computers, since the graft operation necessitates unnecessary copying. We shall discuss later better machine representations, using binary graphs. As far as human readibility is concerned, we assume known parsing techniques. This permits to represent terms, on an extended alphabet with parentheses and commas, which is closer to standard mathematical practice. Also, infix notation and indentation permit to keep in the string some of the tree structure more apparent. We shall not make explicit the exact representation grammar, and allow ourselves to write freely for instance $(0 + S(0)) + S(S(0))$. Note that we avoid explicit quotes as well, which permits us to mix freely meta-variables with object structures, like in $S(M)$, where M is a meta-variable denoting a Σ-term.

1.5 Terms with variables, substitution

The idea is to internalize the notation $S(M)$ above as a term $S(x)$ over an extended alphabet containing special symbols of arity 0 called *variables*. Such terms with variables are thus polynomial expressions, in the case of completely free operators.

Let V be a denumerable set disjoint from Σ. We define the set of terms with variables, $T(\Sigma, V)$, in exactly the same way as $T(\Sigma \cup V)$, extending the arity function so that $\alpha(x) = 0$ for every x in V. The only difference between the variables and the constants (symbol of arity 0) is that a constant has an existential import: it denotes a value in the domain we are modelling with our term language, whereas a variable denotes a term. The difference is important only when there are no constants in Σ, since then $T(\Sigma)$ is empty.

All of the notions defined for terms extend to terms with variables. We define the set $V(M)$ of *variables* occurring in M as:

$$V(M) = \{x \in V \mid \exists u \in D(M) \quad M(u) = x\},$$

and we define the number of distinct variables in M as $\nu(M) = |V(M)|$.

We shall now formalize the notion of substitution of terms for variables in a term containing variables. From now on, the sets Σ and V are fixed, and we use T to denote $T(\Sigma, V)$. A *substitution* σ is a function in $V \to T$, identity almost everywhere. That is, the set $D(\sigma) = \{x \in V \mid \sigma(x) \neq x\}$ is finite. We call it the *domain* of σ. Substitutions are extended to Σ-morphisms over T by

$$\sigma(F(M_1, ..., M_n)) = F(\sigma(M_1), ..., \sigma(M_n)).$$

Bijective substitutions are called *permutations*. When $U \subseteq V$, we write σ_U for the restriction of substitution σ to U. It is easy to show that, for all σ, M and U:

$$V(M) \subseteq U \;\Rightarrow\; \sigma(M) = \sigma_U(M).$$

Alternatively, we can define the replacement $M[x \leftarrow N]$ as

$$M[u_1 \leftarrow N]...[u_n \leftarrow N],$$

where $\{u_1, ..., u_n\} = \{u \mid M(u) = x\}$ and then

$$\sigma(M) = M[x \leftarrow \sigma(x) \mid x \in V(M)]$$

with an obvious notation.

We now define the quasi-ordering $\leq$ of *matching* in T by:

$$M \leq N \;\Leftrightarrow\; \exists \sigma \quad N = \sigma(M).$$

It is easy to show that if such a σ exists, $\sigma_{V(M)}$ is unique. We shall call it the *match of N by M*, and denote it by N/M.

We define $M \equiv N \;\Leftrightarrow\; M \leq N \;\wedge\; N \leq M$. When $M \equiv N$, we say that M and N are *isomorphic*. This is equivalent to say that $M = \sigma(N)$ for some permutation σ. Note that $M \equiv N$ implies $|M| = |N|$. Finally, we define

$$M > N \;\Leftrightarrow\; N \leq M \;\wedge\; \neg M \leq N.$$

Proposition. $>$ is a well-ordering on T.

Proof. We show that $M > N$ implies $\mu(M) > \mu(N)$, with $\mu(M) = |M| - \nu(M)$.

Let φ be any bijection between $T \times T$ and V. We define a binary operation $\cap$ in T by:

$$F(M_1, ..., M_n) \cap F(N_1, ..., N_n) = F(M_1 \cap N_1, ..., M_n \cap N_n)$$

$$M \cap N = \varphi(M, N) \quad \text{in all other cases.}$$

$M \cap N$ is uniquely determined from φ and, for distinct φ's, is unique up to $\equiv$.

Proposition. $M \cap N$ is a g.l.b. of M and N under the match quasi-ordering.

Let **T** be the quotient poset $T/\equiv$, completed with a maximum element $\top$. From the propositions above we conclude:

Theorem. **T** is a complete lattice.

Corollary. If two terms M and N have an upper bound, i.e. a common instance $\sigma(M) = \sigma'(N)$, they have a l.u.b. $M \cup N$, which is a most general such instance; that is, $\sigma = \sigma_0 \circ \tau$, and $\sigma' = \sigma'_0 \circ \tau$, for some substitution τ called the *principal unifier* of M and N. The term $M \cup N$ is unique modulo $\equiv$ and may be found by the *unification* algorithm [144].

Proposition.

$$D(\sigma(M)) = D(M) \cup \bigcup_{\{u \mid M(u) \in V\}} \{u \hat{\ } v \mid v \in D(\sigma(M(u)))\}$$

$$\forall u \in D(M) \quad M(u) = x \in V \Rightarrow \forall v \in D(\sigma(x)) \ \sigma(M)/(u \hat{\ } v) = \sigma(x)/v$$

$$\forall u \in D(M) \ \sigma(M)/u = \sigma(M/u)$$

$$\forall u \in D(M) \ \sigma(M)[u \leftarrow \sigma(N)] = \sigma(M[u \leftarrow N]).$$

1.6 Graph representations, dags

It is usual to represent trees in computers by binary graphs implemented as pairs of machine words. In the simplest scheme, a word is partitioned into one tag bit, and one field interpreted either as an address in the graph memory, or as a natural number, according to the value of the tag. In this last case, some natural (say 0) is reserved for *nil*, the empty list of trees. Symbols from Σ are then coded up as positive naturals. If tree M is represented by the word W and the list L is represented by the word W', then the list $M \cdot L$ is represented by the address of a graph node implemented as the pair (W, W'). Similarly, if symbol F is coded up as the word W and the list L is represented by the word W', then the tree $F(L)$ is represented by the address of a graph node implemented as the pair (W, W').

Thus every tree is mapped into a graph, and this representation allows sharing of common subtrees. Assignment to fields may implement grafting without copying, but this method is not usually compatible with sharing. This is the standard way of representing trees and lists in symbol-manipulation languages such as LISP [111]. The principal problem to be solved in such languages is to keep track dynamically of which areas of the storage are used to represent actively used subtrees. Garbage-collection algorithms have been proposed to solve this problem, but this method is becoming problematic with the current technology of very large virtual memories. A precise description of such memory allocation issues is beyond the scope of these notes.

Terms are of course represented as trees. A global table holds the arity function. There are several possibilities for the representation of variables. They may be represented as symbols. But then the scope structure must be computed by an algorithm, rather than being implicit in the structure. Also a global scanning of the term is necessary to determine its set of variables, and substitution involves copying of the substituted term. For these reasons, variables are often represented rather as integer offsets in stacks of bindings. Such "structure sharing" representations are now standard for PROLOG implementations.

A precise account of the various representations schemes for term structures, and of the accompanying algorithms, is out of the scope of these notes. It should be born in mind that the crucial problem is memory utilization: the trade-off between copying and sharing is often the deciding factor for an implementation. Languages with garbage-collected structures, such as LISP, are ideal for programming "quick and dirty" prototypes. But serious implementation efforts should aim at good algorithmic performance on realistic size applications.

The crucial algorithms in formula and proof manipulation are matching, unification, substitution and grafting. First-order unification has been specially well studied. A linear algorithm is known [127,22], but in practice quasi-linear algorithms based on congruence classes operations are preferred [103,104]. Furthermore, these algorithms extend without modification to unification of infinite rational terms represented by finite graphs [68].

Implementation methods may be partitioned into two families. Some depend on logical properties (e.g. sharing subterms in dags arising from substitution to a term containing several occurrences of the same variable). Some are purely statistical (e.g. sharing structures globally through hash-coding techniques). Particular applications require a careful analysis of the optimal trade-off between logical and statistical techniques.

There is no comprehensive survey on implementation issues. Some partial aspects are described in [8,145,105,103,169,164,120,44,1,36,46,19,49,150,165].

2 Inference rules

We shall now study *inference systems*, defined by inference rules. The general form of an inference rule is:

$$IR : \frac{P_1 \; P_2 \; ... \; P_n}{Q},$$

where the P_i's and Q are *propositions* belonging to some formal language. We shall here regard these propositions as *types*, and the inference rule as the description of the signature of IR considered as a typed operator. More precisely, IR has arity n, P_i is the type of its i-th argument, and Q is the type of its result. Well-typed terms composed of inference operators are called the *proofs* defined by the inference system. Let us now examine a few familiar inference systems.

2.1 The trivial homogeneous case: Arities

A graded alphabet Σ may be considered as the simplest inference systems, where types are reduced to arities. I.e., the set of propositions is 1, and an operator F of arity n is an inference rule

$$F : \frac{0 \; 0 \; ... \; 0}{0}$$

(with n zero's in the numerator). A Σ-proof corresponds to our Σ-terms above.

2.2 Finite systems of types: Sorts

The next level of inference systems consist in choosing a finite set S of elementary propositions, usually called *sorts*. For instance, let $S = \{int, bool\}$, and Σ be defined by:

$$0 : int \quad S : int \to int \quad true : bool \quad false : bool \quad if : bool, int, int \to int,$$

where we use the alternative syntax $P_1, ..., P_n \to Q$ for an inference rule. The term $if(true, 0, S(0))$ is of sort *int*, i.e. it is a proof of proposition *int*.

As another example, consider the puzzle "Missionaries and Cannibals". We call *configuration* any triple $\langle b, m, c \rangle \in 2 \times 4 \times 4$. The boolean b indicates the position of the boat, m (resp. c) is the number of missionaries (resp. cannibals) on the left bank. The set of states S is the set of *legal* configurations, that obey the condition

$$P(m, c) \equiv m = c \text{ or } m = 0 \text{ or } m = 3.$$

There are thus 10 distinct states or sorts. The rules of inference comprise first a constant denoting the starting configuration:

$$s_0 : \langle 0, 3, 3 \rangle$$

then the transitions carrying p missionaries and q cannibals from left to right:

$$L_{m,c,p,q} : \langle 0, m, c \rangle \rightarrow \langle 1, m - p, c - q \rangle \quad (m \geq p, c \geq q, P(m, c), P(m - p, c - q), 1 \leq p + q \leq 2)$$

and finally the transitions $R_{m,c,p,q}$, which are inverses of $L_{m,c,p,q}$. The game consists in finding a proof of $\langle 1, 0, 0 \rangle$.

This simple example of a finite group of transformations applies to more complex tasks, such as Rubik's cube. All state transition systems can be described in a similar fashion. Examples of such proofs are parse-trees of regular grammars, where the inference rules signatures correspond to a finite automaton transition graph. Slightly more complicated formalisms allow subsorts, i.e. containment relationships between the sorts. That is, we postulate primitive implications between the elementary propositions. These systems reduce to simple sorts by considering dummy transitions corresponding to the implicit coercions.

2.3 Types as terms: standard proof trees

We shall here describe our types as terms formed over an alphabet Φ of type operators, which we shall call *functors*. For the moment, we shall assume that we have just one category of such propositions, i.e. the functors have just an arity. The alphabet Σ of inference rules determines the legal proof trees.

Example: Combinatory logic.

We take as functors a set Φ of constants Φ_0, plus a binary operator $\rightarrow$, which we shall write in infix notation. We call *functionality* a term in $T(\Phi)$. We have three families of rules in Σ. In the following, the meta-variables A, B, C denote arbitrary functionalities. The operators of the K and S families are of arity 0, the operators of the *App* family are binary.

$$K_{A,B} : A \rightarrow (B \rightarrow A)$$

$$S_{A,B,C} : (A \rightarrow (B \rightarrow C)) \rightarrow ((A \rightarrow B) \rightarrow (A \rightarrow C))$$

$$App_{A,B} : \frac{A \rightarrow B \quad A}{B}.$$

Here is an example of a proof. Let A and B be any functionalities, $C = B \rightarrow A$, $D = A \rightarrow C$, $E = A \rightarrow A$, $F = A \rightarrow (C \rightarrow A)$, $G = D \rightarrow E$. The term

$$App_{D,E}(App_{F,G}(S_{A,C,A}, K_{A,C}), K_{A,B})$$

has type E, i.e. it gives a proof of the proposition $A \rightarrow A$.

We express formally that proof M proves proposition P in the inference system Σ as: $\Sigma \models M : P$. That is, we think of a theorem as the type of its proof tree. Proof-checking is identified with type-checking. Here this is a simple consistency check; that is, if operator F is declared in Σ as: $F : P_1, ..., P_n \rightarrow Q$ and if $\Sigma \models M_i : P_i$ for $1 \leq i \leq n$, then $\Sigma \models F(M_1, ..., M_n) : Q$.

2.4 Polymorphism: Rule schemes

This next level of generality consists in allowing variables in the propositional terms. This is very natural, since it internalizes the meta-variables used to index families of inference rules as propositional variables. The rules of inference become thus polymorphic operators, whose types are expressions containing free variables. This is the traditional notion of schematic inference rule from mathematical logic.

Example. The example from the previous section is more naturally expressed in this polymorphic formalism. We replace the set Φ_0 by a set of variables V, and now we have just 3 rules of inference: K, S and *App*. The types can be completely dispensed with, since a well typed term possesses a most general type, called its *principal type*. For instance, in the example above, the proof $App(App(S,K),K)$ has the principal type $A \to A$, with $A \in V$. This term is usually written $I = SKK$ in combinatory logic, where the concrete syntax convention is to write combinator strings to represent sequences of applications associated to the left.

The notion of principal type, first discovered by Hindley in the combinatory logic context, and independently by Milner for ML type-checking [115], is actually completely general:

Theorem. Let Σ be any signature of polymorphic operators over a functor signature Φ. Let M be a legal proof term. Then M possesses a principal type $\tau \in T(\Phi,V)$. That is, $\Sigma \models M : \tau$, and for all $\tau' \in T(\Phi,V)$, $\Sigma \models M : \tau'$ implies $\tau \leq \tau'$.

Proof. This is an easy application of the unification theorem.

By now we have developed enough formalism to make sense out of our "propositions as types" paradigm. Actually, the example we have discussed above is the fragment of propositional logic known as "minimal logic". When regarding the functor $\to$ as (intuitionistic) implication, and *App* as the usual inference rule of Modus ponens, K and S are the two axioms of minimal logic presented as a Hilbert calculus. Combinatory logic is thus the calculus of proofs in minimal logic [41].

Actually combinators don't just have a type, they have a value. They can be *defined* with definition equations in terms of application. Using the concrete syntax mentioned above, we get for instance K and S defined by the following equations:

$$Def_K :\ K\,x\,y\ =\ x$$

$$Def_S :\ S\,x\,y\,z\ =\ x\,z\,(y\,z).$$

Exercise. Verify that the two equations above, when seen as unification constraints, define the expected principal types for K and S.

This point of view of considering equality axiomatizations of the proof structures corresponds to what the proof-theorists call *cut elimination*. That is, the two equations above can be used as rewrite rules in order to eliminate redundancies corresponding to useless detours in the proofs. We shall develop more completely this point of view of *computation as proof normalization* in section 4.4 below.

The current formalism of inference rules typed by terms with variables corresponds to intuitionistic sequents in proof theory, and to Horn clauses in automated reasoning. For instance, a PROLOG [25] interpreter may be seen in this framework as a proof synthesis method. Given an alphabet Σ of polymorphic inference rules (usually called definite clauses), and a proposition τ over functor alphabet Φ, it returns (when possible) a proof term M such that M is a legal Σ-proof term of principal type τ' instance of τ:

$$\Sigma \models M : \tau' \geq \tau.$$

With $\sigma = \tau'/\tau$, we say that σ is a PROLOG answer to the query τ. Of course this explanation is incomplete; we have to explain that PROLOG finds all such instances by a backtrack procedure constructing proofs in a bottom-up left-to-right fashion, using operators from Σ in a specific order (the order in which clauses are declared); this last requirement leads to incompleteness, since PROLOG may loop with recursively composable operators, whereas a different order might lead to termination of the procedure. Also, PROLOG may be presented several goals together, and they may share certain variables, but this may be explained by a simple extension of the above proof-synthesis explanation.

We claim that this explanation of PROLOG is more faithful to reality than the usual one with Horn clauses. In particular, our explanation is completely constructive, and we do not have to explain the processes of conjunctive normalization and Skolemization. Furthermore, there is no distinction in Φ between predicate and function symbols, consistently with most PROLOG implementations. Actually, we even allow polymorphic signatures which would not be accepted as definite clauses, since some of the types may be reduced to single variables, like for *App* above.

2.5 Proof terms with variables, natural deduction.

The example above demonstrated the difficulty of proofs presented in a Hilbert style. The completely trivial theorem $\forall A \cdot A \to A$ had a complicated proof using three axioms and two applications of modus ponens. Of course one could consider adding combinator I as an axiom, but this is only begging the question since other trivial natural theorems would present similar difficulties. And of course there is no easy way to decide which combinators are well-typed. For instance, Peirce's law:

$$Peirce: \ ((A \to B) \to A) \to A,$$

although a propositional tautology easily checkable by the truth-table method, is *not* intuitionistically valid.

The natural proof of $A \to A$ consists in, given a proof x of A, returning merely x as a proof of A. that is, the *natural* proof of $A \to A$ is the (polymorphic) identity algorithm. This method of proof usually proceeds through the deduction theorem below.

Deduction theorem. Let Γ be any set of propositions, A and B be two propositions. We have $\Gamma, A \vdash B$ iff $\Gamma \vdash A \to B$.

The deduction theorem holds in any reasonable system of logic. It can be proved easily in minimal logic, by induction on the size of proofs. Unfortunately, the deduction theorem is a *meta* theorem, i.e. a mathematical theorem of the meta-theory analyzing the proof system, as opposed to the theorems, or well-typed proof terms inside the proof system.

We shall see in section 4 that it is easy to internalize *deductions* as proof terms with variables, called *sequents*. This point of view will lead to logic presented in *natural deduction* style, that is to λ-calculus formalisms. Before investigating this next level of expressive power, we consider in the next section a particularly important inference system Σ, that of *equational logic*.

3 Rewriting inference and equational logic

3.1 The classical presentation

Equational logic is classically presented as a restriction of first-order logic, where the only predicate symbol is =, and the only non-logical axioms are universal equalities between terms containing free variables. For instance, the theory of groups is classically presented over the functor alphabet

$$\Phi = \{*, {}^{-1}, 1\}$$

by the equations:

$$Idl : \quad 1 * x = x$$

$$Invl : \quad x^{-1} * x = 1$$

$$Ass : \quad (x * y) * z = x * (y * z)$$

and the class of all first order models of these equations is called the *variety* of groups. The well known completeness theorem of Birkhoff states that a universally quantified equation between terms over Φ is valid in the variety iff it can be deduced from the axioms using the rules of substitution and of replacement of equal for equal.

3.2 The proof-theoretic formalization

Here we ignore the abstract notion of model and concentrate on the rules of inference. We assume given a functor alphabet Φ given with arity function α, in which we distinguish an atom $\rightarrow$ given with arity 2. The substitution inference rule disappears, since it is implicit from the polymorphism of other rules. The replacement of equals for equals is decomposed into elementary steps of term replacement rules:

$$Id_A : \quad A \rightarrow A \qquad\qquad\qquad Reflexivity$$

$$; : \quad \frac{A \rightarrow B \quad B \rightarrow C}{A \rightarrow C} \qquad\qquad Transitivity$$

which specify that the rewriting arrow $\rightarrow$ is a quasi-ordering. Now we must state that $\rightarrow$ is compatible with the rest of the Φ-structure. That is, for every functor F in $\Phi - \{\rightarrow\}$ of arity n and for every $i \leq n$ we take a congruence rule:

$$Funct_{F,i} : \quad \frac{A \rightarrow B}{F(A_1, ..., A_{i-1}, A, A_{i+1}, ..., A_n) \rightarrow F(A_1, ..., A_{i-1}, B, A_{i+1}, ..., A_n)} \qquad Congruence$$

If we add the rule of symmetry we get the theory of equality, where we usually use symbol = instead of $\rightarrow$:

$$Op : \quad \frac{A = B}{B = A} \qquad\qquad\qquad Symmetry$$

The non-logical axioms of the variety are then added as so many constants. For instance, over groups, we obtain a proof of proposition $y = x^{-1} * (x * y)$ by the term

$$Op(Funct_{*,1}(Invl); Idl); Ass : \quad y = x^{-1} * (x * y)$$

Exercise: Show a proof of $x * 1 = x$ using the inference system Σ above.

The conclusion we may draw from the example above is that, beyond its apparent simplicity, equational reasoning may indeed be quite complicated. The rule of symmetry is specially hard to use since it expresses a commutativity of $\rightarrow$, harder to visualize than the easier monoïd structure implicit from the rules Id and ";". It is then natural to ask:

1) Can we eliminate Op

2) More generally, can we normalize equational proofs?

3.3 The categorical viewpoint

This viewpoint gives a prominent role to the monoïd structure of the quasi-ordering $\rightarrow$. Simplifying the presentation, we may present a *category* as presented by a set of *objects Obj*, which we shall here confuse with the set of (closed) terms over some functor alphabet Φ, and by a set of *arrows* (or morphisms) which we shall here confuse with the set of (closed) proofs generated from some inference system Σ containing initially the two rules:

$$Id_A \; : \; A \rightarrow A \qquad\qquad \textit{Identity}$$

$$; \; : \; \frac{A \rightarrow B \quad B \rightarrow C}{A \rightarrow C} \qquad\qquad \textit{Composition}$$

Whenever $f : A \rightarrow B$, we say that arrow f has *domain A* and *codomain B*. Furthermore, it is specified that the proofs are quotiented by a congruence $=$ verifying:

$$Idl : \; Id; f \; = \; f$$

$$Idr : \; f; Id \; = \; f$$

$$Ass : \; (f; g); h \; = \; f; (g; h).$$

So we see that a category is a structure obtained as a hybrid of quasi-ordering and of monoïd, to which it reduces in the two degenerate cases (i.e. respectively $|f : A \rightarrow B| \leq 1$ and $|Obj| = 1$). Note that we have given the same name to axiom Idl as for the axiomatization of groups above, although here the operator ";" is a Σ-operator, and not just a Φ-operator like "*". However the unification theorem allows us to make implicit the type of variable f above, and the overloading of "*Idl*" may be seen as a reflection principle.

If **A** and **B** are two categories, a functor F from **A** to **B** associates to every object A of **A** an object $F(A)$ of **B**, and to every arrow $f : A \rightarrow B$ an arrow $F(f) : F(A) \rightarrow F(B)$ such that the following functorial conditions hold:

$$F(Id) \; = \; Id$$

$$F(f; g) \; = \; F(f); F(g).$$

We see a great analogy between the notion of rewriting inference system and the main categorical notions. Actually, the categorical viewpoint is richer in that the functors have sorts themselves (i.e., the categories), and poorer in that they do not yet have arities (i.e. we just have monadic functors so far). In order to build-in arities we shall need products, and a full categorical account of minimal logic is obtained by a further adjunction, namely exponentiation. But we shall defer this explanation until we develop natural deduction in section 4. We have given this elementary development of category theory essentially to justify our terminology. The congruence rule of term formation explains a functoriality condition on the object part, and the functoriality condition on the arrow part of the functor expresses the congruence property for rewriting. Substitutivity in rewrite rules is expressed by defining them as natural transformations between the functors denoted by the two sides of the rule. That is, a *natural transformation* τ between functors F and

G (both from category **A** to category **B**) is a mapping associating to every object A of **A** an arrow $\tau_A : F(A) \to G(A)$ such that

$$\tau_A ; G(f) = F(f) ; \tau_B.$$

And if we consider equations rather than simply rewrite rules, the symmetry inference rule is interpreted as the existence of inverses to arrows. Equations are thus defined as natural isomorphisms.

Category theory is explained in Mac Lane [98]. The categorical viewpoint for algebra has been developed by Lawvere and others [101]. Its application to proof theory is explained (in a somewhat complicated form) in Szabo [157].

3.4 Confluence and Termination

We come back to the problem of eliminating the symmetry rule. Let now $\to$ be any binary relation over some set S, $\to^*$ be its reflexive-transitive closure, $\leftrightarrow^*$ be its equivalence closure. We say that $\to$ verifies the *Church-Rosser property* iff

$$x \leftrightarrow^* y \Leftrightarrow \exists z \ \ x \to^* z \wedge y \to^* z.$$

It is easy to show that this condition is equivalent to *confluence*, i.e.

$$u \to^* x \wedge u \to^* y \Leftrightarrow \exists z \ \ x \to^* z \wedge y \to^* z$$

that is, diagrammatically:

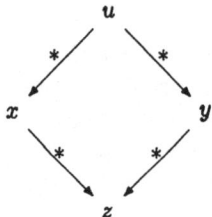

When $\to$ is a confluent relation, normal forms (i.e. terminal elements) are unique whenever they exist, and equality (i.e. $\leftrightarrow^*$) may be decided by rewriting. That is, deduction may be replaced by computation, and symmetry is eliminated in all but one instance.

For instance, the following set of 10 rewrite rules defines a confluent term rewriting system for group theory:

$$1 * x \ \to \ x$$
$$x^{-1} * x \ \to \ 1$$
$$(x * y) * z \ \to \ x * (y * z)$$
$$x * 1 \ \to \ x$$
$$x * x^{-1} \ \to \ 1$$
$$(x^{-1})^{-1} \ \to \ x$$
$$1^{-1} \ \to \ 1$$
$$x * (x^{-1} * y) \ \to \ y$$

$$x^{-1} * (x * y) \rightarrow y$$
$$(x * y)^{-1} \rightarrow y^{-1} * x^{-1}.$$

The rewrite relation associated with such a term rewriting system R is defined by $M \rightarrow_R N$ iff there exists a rule $\alpha \rightarrow \beta$ in R and an occurrence u in $D(M)$ such that $M/u = \sigma(\alpha)$ for some substitution σ, and $N = M[u \leftarrow \sigma(\beta)]$. It is clear that the group axioms are decided by the system R above. Conversely all rewrite rules in R may be shown to be valid equations in group theory (see the exercise above). What is less obvious is to decide the confluence of R. We shall see in the next section that is is easy to show that it is *locally confluent*, in the sense that:

$$u \rightarrow x \wedge u \rightarrow y \Leftrightarrow \exists z \quad x \rightarrow^* z \wedge y \rightarrow^* z$$

that is, diagrammatically:

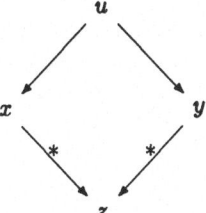

However, local confluence is not enough to prove confluence, as shown by the following counter-examples, due respectively to Newman and Hindley:

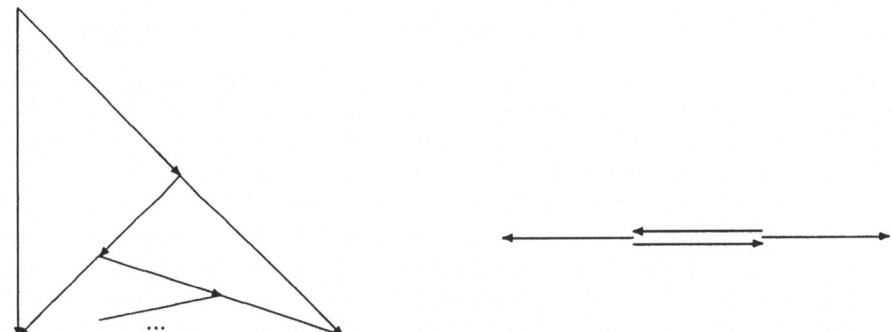

3.5 The Nœtherian case: Knuth and Bendix

The problem encountered with the above counter-examples is that the rewriting relation possessed infinite chains. Let us say that relation $\rightarrow$ is *Nœtherian* iff there is no infinite chain $x_1 \rightarrow x_2 \rightarrow \dots$ (Then, its transitive closure $\rightarrow^+$ is a well-founded ordering). We remark that $\rightarrow$ is Nœtherian over S iff every non-empty subset of S admits a minimal element with respect to $\rightarrow^+$.

Now let us say that a predicate P over S is $\rightarrow$-*hereditary* iff

$$\forall x \in S \quad [\forall y \quad x \rightarrow^+ y \Rightarrow P(y)] \Rightarrow P(x).$$

Now we may state an important induction principle.

Principle of Nœtherian Induction: Let $\rightarrow$ be a Nœtherian relation over S. Then for every $\rightarrow$-hereditary predicate P we have $\forall x \in S \; P(x)$.

It is easy to validate this induction principle using the above remark, by considering the set of all x's such that $\neg P(x)$. And now we may show that local confluence implies confluence for Nœtherian relations.

Newman's lemma. A Nœtherian relation is confluent iff it is locally confluent.

Proof: Nœtherian induction on predicate P defined as:

$$P(u) \;=\; \forall x, y \quad u \rightarrow^* x \wedge u \rightarrow^* y \;\Rightarrow\; \exists z \quad x \rightarrow^* z \wedge y \rightarrow^* z.$$

We now explain the Knuth-Bendix decision procedure for the confluence of Nœtherian term rewriting systems. First let us give an algorithm.

Superposition algorithm. Let $\alpha_1 \rightarrow \beta_1$ and $\alpha_2 \rightarrow \beta_2$ be two rewrite rules in R, let $u \in D(\alpha_1)$ and $M = \alpha_1/u$ be such that M is a non-variable term unifiable with α_2. Let $N = \sigma_1(M) = \sigma_2(\alpha_2)$ be a principal instance, with $V(N) \cap V(\alpha_1) = \emptyset$. We say that the *superposition* of $\alpha_2 \rightarrow \beta_2$ on $\alpha_1 \rightarrow \beta_1$ at u determines the *critical pair* $\langle P, Q \rangle$, with $P = \sigma_1(\alpha_1)[u \leftarrow \sigma_2(\beta_2)]$ and $Q = \sigma_1(\beta_1)$.

Examples.
- $G(B, x) \rightarrow K(x)$ superposes on $F(x, G(x, A)) \rightarrow H(x)$ at '2' to give $P = F(B, K(A))$ and $Q = H(B)$.
- $H(H(x)) \rightarrow K(x)$ superposes on itself at '1' to give $P = H(K(y))$ and $Q = K(H(y))$.

The Knuth-Bendix theorem. The relation $\rightarrow_R$ is locally confluent iff for every critical pair $\langle P, Q \rangle$ there exists N such that $P \rightarrow_R^* N$ and $Q \rightarrow_R^* N$.

Corollary. If R is a Nœtherian term rewriting system, its confluence is decidable.

The above theorem may be used to check the local confluence of the 10 group rewrite rules above. Assuming termination, this shows that any group equality may be decided by mere rewriting.

Actually, the method may be extended to systems of rules that fail the test. If for some critical pair $\langle P, Q \rangle$ we reduce P and Q to two distinct irreducible terms P' and Q', we have generated an interesting lemma $P' = Q'$, which is an equational consequence of the rules considered as equations. It may be possible to give an orientation to this new equality for forming an extended term rewriting system, while preserving the finite termination property. This is the basis of the Knuth-Bendix completion method, which attempts to complete a term rewriting system to a confluent one. This method may be considered a way of compiling a canonical form algorithm from an equational specification.

We cannot describe the method fully here. The main ideas are that unresolved critical pairs are kept as new rewrite rules, and that all rules are kept inter-reduced. The procedure may stop with a canonical system, it may fail because termination is impossible to establish, or it may loop. Whenever it does not fail, it gives a semi-decision procedure for the original equational theory, as explained in Huet [70]. More detailed expositions of the method may be found in [88,69,76].

Failure may result from some permutative consequence such as commutativity. The method has been extended in various ways in order to consider rewritings modulo such permutative axioms. For instance, Peterson and Stickel [132] have shown that it was possible to extend the method to complete equational presentations, where one or several functors were assumed to be associative and commutative, using Stickel's associative-commutative unification algorithm [156,47]. This method has been extended by Jouannaud and Kirchner [78].

Various other extensions of the Knuth-Bendix procedure have been proposed, for handling constructors (free functors) [74] and for solving word problems in finitely presented algebras [94]. The Knuth-Bendix completion procedure and its extensions give a general framework to simplification techniques.

As example of canonical term rewriting system we give distributive lattices. Here $\cap$ and $\cup$ are assumed to be associative and commutative. The canonical set consists in the following four rules:

$$x \cap (x \cup y) \rightarrow x$$

$$x \cup (y \cap z) \rightarrow (x \cup y) \cap (x \cup z)$$

$$x \cup x \rightarrow x$$

$$x \cap x \rightarrow x.$$

Exercise. Show that the other distributivity law is a consequence of the above rules.

Finally, we show the canonical system for Boolean algebras. Now the connectives $\wedge$ and $\oplus$ (exclusive or) are assumed to be associative and commutative, and we axiomatize Boolean algebras as Boolean rings:

$$x \wedge 1 \rightarrow x$$

$$x \wedge 0 \rightarrow 0$$

$$x \wedge x \rightarrow x$$

$$x \oplus 0 \rightarrow x$$

$$x \oplus x \rightarrow 0$$

$$(x \oplus y) \wedge z \rightarrow (x \wedge z) \oplus (y \wedge z).$$

This canonical set can be used to decide propositional calculus, using the following translations:

$$\neg x \rightarrow x \oplus 1$$

$$x \vee y \rightarrow x \oplus y \oplus (x \wedge y)$$

$$x \Rightarrow y \rightarrow x \oplus (x \wedge y) \oplus 1.$$

The resulting decision method is basically the method of Venn's diagrams, as the following example demonstrates. With three propositional letters a, b and c, the proposition

$$(a \wedge \neg b) \vee (b \wedge \neg c) \vee (c \wedge \neg a)$$

reduces to its canonical form:

$$a \oplus b \oplus c \oplus a \wedge b \oplus b \wedge c \oplus c \wedge a,$$

which can easily be "seen" as a disjoint union of regions in the following Venn diagram:

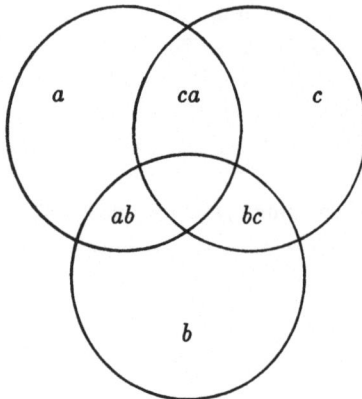

This example also shows that disjunctive normal form is *not* a canonical form, since the above proposition possesses another d.n.f.

$$(b \wedge \neg a) \ \vee \ (c \wedge \neg b) \ \vee \ (a \wedge \neg c)$$

or, as Quine puts it, a formula may have distinct minimal sets of prime implicants [137].

A dual canonical system is obtained by axiomatizing disjunction $\vee$ and equivalence $\equiv$, both assumed to be associative and commutative:

$$x \vee 0 \ \rightarrow \ x$$

$$x \vee 1 \ \rightarrow \ 1$$

$$x \vee x \ \rightarrow \ x$$

$$x \equiv 1 \ \rightarrow \ x$$

$$x \equiv x \ \rightarrow \ 1$$

$$(x \equiv y) \vee z \ \rightarrow \ (x \vee z) \equiv (y \vee z).$$

The canonical forms obtained by this system are of the form:

$$\pm [X_1 \equiv X_2 \cdots \equiv X_n] \qquad (n \geq 0)$$

where the X_i's are *distinct* expressions which are disjunctions of *distinct* letters:

$$X_i \ = \ x_i^1 \vee x_i^2 \vee \cdots \vee x_i^{p_i} \qquad (p_i \geq 1).$$

3.6   Sequential computations

We now consider term rewriting systems with two constraints:

(a) left linearity: for every $\alpha \rightarrow \beta$ in R, every variable of α occurs exactly once

(b) non ambiguity: there are no critical pairs

As we shall see, these systems are always confluent, their termination is unnecessary. Functional programming languages, and more generally operational semantics rules can usually be expressed as such systems of rewrite rules [62]. As a very simple example, consider the system of two rules Def_K and Def_S defining the combinators S and K.

We shall here define the main notions of computation using rewrite rules. The full theory is given in Huet-Lévy [75]. We call *redex* in term M an occurrence $u \in D(M)$ such that $\alpha \leq M/u$ for some left-hand side α of a rule in R. We define the reduction relation $\to_R$ associated with R in the same way as in the preceding section. We shall assume R fixed from now on, and write simply $\to$ for reduction. Let $M \to N$ at redex occurrence $u \in D(M)$, using rule $\alpha \to \beta \in R$. Let now v be any redex in M. We define the set $v\backslash u$ of *residuals* of v as a set of redexes in N defined as follows. If $v = u$, $v\backslash u = \emptyset$. If $v < u$ or $v|u$, then $v\backslash u = \{v\}$. Finally, if $v > u$, this means, by non-overlapping, that v is below some variable x of α. By linearity, x has a unique occurrence in α, which we shall denote by x as well. That is, $v = u \hat{\ } x \hat{\ } w$ for some w. Now let X be the set of occurrences of variable x in β. We define $v\backslash u = \{u \hat{\ } y \hat{\ } w \mid y \in X\}$.

Thus redex v may have zero, one or several residuals in N. Intuitively, these residuals are the places where one must reduce in N in order to effect the computation step consisting in reducing at redex v in M. Actually, on the natural dag implementation all the occurrences of $v\backslash u$ denote the same shared node of the dag representing N. Symmetrically the same holds of $u\backslash v$. And as expected we have a local confluence diagram, where the single steps u and v confluate using all the steps in $v\backslash u$ (resp. $u\backslash v$).

This is not enough to conclude that the system is confluent, since we do not want to require $\to$ to be Nœtherian. However, it is easy to notice that all the redexes in $v\backslash u$ are mutually disjoint, and that any residual of some redex is always disjoint from any residual of some other disjoint redex. Thus it is natural to extend the reduction relation $\to$ to parallel reduction of a set of mutually disjoint redexes, a relation we shall write $\rightarrowtail\!\!\!\!+$. If $M \rightarrowtail\!\!\!\!+ N$ using set of redexes U, then for every set V of mutually disjoint redexes in M, we define the residuals of V by U as: $V\backslash U = \{w \in v\backslash u \mid u \in U \ \wedge \ v \in V\}$. And now we have a strong confluence property:

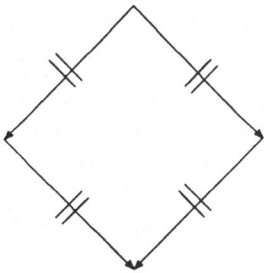

which extends easily to multi-steps derivations A and B, yielding:

The parallel moves theorem. Let A and B be two co-initial derivations. Define $A \cup B$ as $A; B\backslash A$. Then $A \cup B \equiv B \cup A$, in the sense that these two derivations are co-final, and preserve residuals.

The categorical formulation. The category whose objects are terms, and whose arrows from M to N are parallel derivations, quotiented by the equivalence $\equiv$, admits pushouts.

Corollary. The reduction relation $\to$ has the Church-Rosser property.

Caution! The lattice structure given by the parallel moves theorem is on *derivations*, and *not* on terms. For instance, if we consider the system R consisting solely of the rules $I(x) \to x$ and $J(x) \to x$, the following derivations diagram shows that the terms $I(J(K))$ and $J(I(K))$ do not possess a l.u.b.

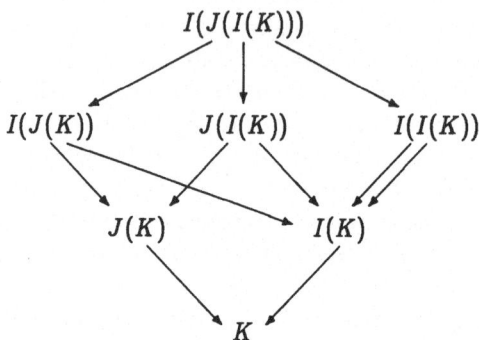

Note that this phenomenon may be traced to the existence of two non-equivalent derivations between $I(I(K))$ and $I(K)$. This shows that the categorical viewpoint is the right one here: we need to talk in terms of arrows, not just relations between terms.

The standardization theorem. It is always possible to compute in an outside-in manner.

We do not have the space here to explain in a rigorous manner what *outside-in* exactly means. We just remark that this may be more complicated than merely reducing the leftmost-outermost redex, i.e. the redex minimum in the total ordering on occurrences defined by $u <_{LO} v$ iff either $u < v$, or else there exist $u' \leq u$ and $v' \leq v$ with $u' <_L v'$. For instance, with R consisting of $F(x, D) \to C$, $B \to D$ and $\bot \to \bot$, the standard derivation going from $F(\bot, B)$ to its canonical form C is:

$$F(\bot, B) \;\to\; F(\bot, D) \;\to\; C$$

whereas the leftmost-outermost rule leads to a non-terminating loop.

This theorem suggests it can be used to define a *computation rule*, usable to drive an interpreter computing "lazily". However, this is not true, since the standard derivation in a derivation class is not simply a function of the starting term. For instance, consider Gustave's function, an example due to G.G. Berry; with R consisting of the 3 rules $F(0, 1, x) \to A$, $F(x, 0, 1) \to A$ and $F(1, x, 0) \to A$, nothing tells us where to compute next in a term $F(M_1, M_2, M_3)$. This example is just as bad as the classical "parallel-or" definition, an obviously non-sequential example ruled out here because we do not admit critical pairs.

Thus it is clear that we do not have strong enough syntactic restrictions on the left-hand sides of our rewrite rules to be able to define sequential computation rules. The key to such restrictions is to adapt the Kahn-Plotkin sequentiality theory [81] to define a notion of "needed" redex. This leads to the notion of sequential term rewriting system. A further refinement, strong sequentiality, gives a decidable criterion which may be used to drive efficient interpreters which look for a needed redex in linear time, using a generalization to trees of the Knuth-Morris-Pratt string-matching algorithm [89]. This theory is completely explained in Huet-Lévy [75].

In practice, we obtain easy criterions for strong sequentiality in the particular cases of systems with constructors, and "left" systems such as systems of combinators definitions.

4 Natural deduction and λ-calculus

4.1 Proofs with variables: sequents

We now come back to the general theory of proof structures. We saw earlier that the Hilbert presentation of minimal logic was not very natural, in that the trivial theorem $A \to A$ necessitated a complex proof $S\,K\,K$. The problem is that in practice one does not use just proof terms, but *deductions* of the form

$$\Gamma \vdash A$$

where Γ is a set of (hypothetic) propositions.

Deductions are exactly proof terms *with variables*. Naming these hypothesis variables and the proof term, we write:

$$\{\dots[x_i : A_i]\dots \mid i \leq n\} \vdash M : A$$

with $V(M) \subseteq \{x_1, \dots, x_n\}$. Such formulas are called *sequents*. Since this point of view is not very well-known, let us emphasize this constatation:

Sequents represent proof terms with variables.

Note that so far our notion of proof construction has not changed:
$\Gamma \vdash_\Sigma M : A$ iff $\vdash_{\Sigma \cup \Gamma} M : A$, i.e. the hypotheses from Γ are used as supplementary axioms, in the same way that in the very beginning we have defined $T(\Sigma, V)$ as $T(\Sigma \cup V)$.

4.2 The deduction theorem

This theorem, fundamental for doing proofs in practice, gives an equivalence between proof terms with variables and functional proof terms:

$$\Gamma \cup \{A\} \vdash B \;\Leftrightarrow\; \Gamma \vdash A \to B.$$

That is, in our notations:
a) $\Gamma \vdash M : A \to B \;\Rightarrow\; \Gamma \cup \{x : A\} \vdash (M\,x) : B$
This direction is immediate, using App, i.e. Modus Ponens.
b) $\Gamma \cup \{x : A\} \vdash M : B \;\Rightarrow\; \Gamma \vdash [x]M : A \to B$
where the term $[x]M$ is given by the following algorithm.

Schönfinkel's abstraction algorithm:

$$
\begin{aligned}
[x]x &= I & (&= S\,K\,K) \\
[x]y &= K\,y & (&y \neq x) \\
[x](M\,N) &= S\,[x]M\,[x]N.
\end{aligned}
$$

Note that this algorithm motivates the choice of combinators S and K (and optionally I). Again we stress a basic observation:

Schönfinkel's algorithm is the essence of the proof of the deduction theorem.

Now let us consider the rewriting system R defined by the rules Def_K and Def_S, optionally supplemented by:

$$Def_I : I\,x\ =\ x$$

and let us write $\rhd$ for the corresponding reduction relation.

Fact. $([x]M\ \ N)\ \ \rhd^*\ \ M[x \leftarrow N]$.

We leave the proof of this very important property to the reader. The important point is that the abstraction operation, together with the application operator and the reduction $\rhd$, define a *substitution* machinery. We shall now use this idea more generally, in order to internalize the deduction theorem in a basic calculus of functionality. That is, we forget the specific combinators S and K, in favor of abstraction seen now as a new term constructor.

4.3 λ calculus.

Here we give up Σ-terms in general, in favor of λ-terms constructed by 3 elementary operations:

$$x \qquad\qquad\qquad\qquad\qquad \textit{variable}$$

$$(M\ N) \qquad\qquad\qquad\qquad \textit{application}$$

$$[x]M \qquad\qquad\qquad\qquad \textit{abstraction}$$

This last case is usually written $\lambda x \cdot M$, whence the name λ-notation. The λ-notation is first a non-ambiguous notation for expressions denoting functions. For instance, the function of two arguments which computes sin of its first argument and adds it to cos of its second is written

$$[x]\,[y]\,sin(x) + cos(y).$$

The variables x and y are *bound* variables, that is they are dummies and their name does not matter, as long as there are no clashes. This defines a congruence of renaming of bound variables usually called α-conversion. Another method is to adopt de Bruijn's indexes, where variable names disappear in favor of positive natural numbers [15]. We define recursively the sets λ_n of λ-expressions valid in a context of length $n \geq 0$ as follows:

$$
\begin{aligned}
\lambda_n\ =\ \ &k & &(1 \leq k \leq n)\\
\mid\ &(M\ N) & &(M, N \in \lambda_n)\\
\mid\ &[\,]M & &M \in \lambda_{n+1}.
\end{aligned}
$$

Thus integer n refers to the variable bound by the n-th abstraction above it. For instance, the expression $[\,](1\ [\,](1\ 2))$ corresponds to $[x](x\ [y](y\ x))$. This example shows that, although more rigorous from a formal point of view, the de Bruijn naming scheme is not fit for human understanding, and we shall now come back to the more usual concrete notation with variable names.

The fact observed above is now edicted as a computation rule, usually called β-*reduction*. Let $\rhd$ be the smallest relation on λ-expressions compatible with application and abstraction and such that:

$$([x]M\ \ N)\ \ \rhd\ \ M[x \leftarrow N].$$

We call λ-calculus the λ-notation equipped with the β-reduction computation rule ▷. λ-calculus is the basic calculus of substitution, and β-reduction is the basic computation mechanism of functional programming languages. Here is an example of computation:

$$([x][y](x\,(y\,x))\,[u](u\,u)\,[v][w]v)$$

$$\triangleright ([y]([u](u\,u)\,(y\,[u](u\,u)))\,[v][w]v)$$

$$\triangleright^2 ([u](u\,u)\,[w][u](u\,u))$$

$$\triangleright ([w][u](u\,u)\,[w][u](u\,u))\ \triangleright\ [u](u\,u)$$

We briefly sketch here the syntactic properties of λ-calculus. Similarly to the theory developed above, the notion of residual can be defined. However, the residuals of a redex may not always be disjoint, and thus the theory of derivations is more complex. However the parallel moves lemma still holds, and thus the Church-Rosser property is also true. Finally, the standardization theorem holds, and here it means that it is possible to compute in a leftmost-outermost fashion. These results, and more details, in particular the precise conditions under which β-reduction simulates combinatory logic calculus, are precisely stated in Barendregt [4].

We finally remark that λ-calculus computations may not always terminate. For instance, with $\Delta = [u](u\,u)$ and $\bot = (\Delta\,\Delta)$, we get $\bot \triangleright \bot \triangleright \ldots$ A more interesting example is given by

$$Y = [f]([u](f\,(u\,u))\,[u](f\,(u\,u)))$$

since $(Y\,f)\ \triangleright^* (f\,(Y\,f))$ shows that Y defines a general fixpoint operator. This shows that (full) λ-calculus is inconsistent with logic. What could $(Y\,\neg)$ mean? As usual with such paradoxical situations, it is necessary to introduce *types* in order to stratify the definable notions in a logically meaningful way. Thus, the basic inconsistency of Church's λ-calculus, shown by Rosser, led to Church's theory of types [23]. On the other hand, λ-calculus as a pure computation mechanism is perfectly meaningful, and C. Strachey prompted D. Scott to develop the theory of reflexive domains as a model theory for full λ-calculus. This topic is out of the scope of these notes, and we refer the interested reader to [4]. We now return to the typed universe.

4.4   Gentzen's system N of natural deduction

The idea of λ-notation proofs underlies Gentzen's natural deduction inference rules [52], where *App* is called →-elim and *Abs* is called →-intro. The role of variables is taken by the base sequents:

$$Axiom_A\ :\ A \vdash A$$

together with the structural *thinning* rule:

$$Thinning\ :\ \frac{\Gamma \vdash B}{\Gamma \cup \{A\} \vdash B}$$

which expresses that a proof may not use all of the hypotheses. Gentzen's remaining rules give types to proofs according to propositions built as functor terms, each functor corresponding to a propositional connective. The main idea of his system is that inference rules should not be arbitrary, but should follow the functor structure, in explaining in a uniform fashion how to *introduce* a functor, and how to *eliminate* it. For instance, mininal logic is obtained with $\Phi = \{\to\}$, and the rules of $\to -intro$ and $\to -elim$, that is:

$$Abs\ :\ \frac{\Gamma \cup \{A\} \vdash B}{\Gamma \vdash A \to B}$$

$$App \quad : \quad \frac{\Gamma \vdash A \to B \quad \Delta \vdash A}{\Gamma \cup \Delta \vdash B}.$$

Now, the β-reduction of λ-calculus corresponds to cut-elimination, i.e. to proof-simplification. Reducing a redex corresponds to eliminating a detour in the demonstration, using an intermediate lemma. But now we have termination of this normalization process, that is the relation $\to$ is Nœtherian on valid proofs. This result is usually called *strong normalization* in proof theory. A full account of this theory is given in Stenlund [155].

Minimal logic can then be extended by adding more functors and corresponding inference rules. For instance, conjunction $\wedge$ is taken into account by the intro rule:

$$Pair \quad : \quad \frac{\Gamma \vdash A \quad \Delta \vdash B}{\Gamma \cup \Delta \vdash A \wedge B}$$

which, from the types point of view, may be considered as product formation, and by the two elim rules:

$$Fst \quad : \quad \frac{\Gamma \vdash A \wedge B}{\Gamma \vdash A}$$

$$Snd \quad : \quad \frac{\Gamma \vdash A \wedge B}{\Gamma \vdash B}$$

corresponding to the two projection functions. This corresponds to building-in a λ-calculus with pairing. Generalizing the notion of redex (cut) to the configuration of a connective intro, immediately followed by elim of the same connective, we get new computation rules:

$$Fst(Pair(x,y)) \quad \triangleright \quad x$$

$$Snd(Pair(x,y)) \quad \triangleright \quad y$$

and the Nœtherian property of $\triangleright$ still holds. We shall not develop further Gentzen's system. We just remark:

(a) More connectives, such as disjunction, can be added in a similar fashion. It is also possible to give rules for quantifiers, although we prefer to differ this topic until we consider dependent bindings.

(b) Gentzen originally considered natural deduction systems for meta-mathematical reasons, namely to prove their consistency. He considered another presentation of sequent inference rules, the L system, which possesses the subformula property (i.e. the result type of every operator is formed of subterms of the argument types), and is thus trivially consistent. Strong normalization in this context was the essential technical tool to establish the equivalence of the L and the N systems. Of course, according to Gödel's theorem, this does not establish *absolute* consistency of the logic, but relativizes it to a carefully identified troublesome point, the proof of termination of some reduction relation. This has the additional advantage of providing a hierarchy of strengths of inference systems, classified according to the ordinal necessary to consider for the termination proof. We refer the interested reader to standard books on proof theory, such as Schütte's [146].

(c) All this development concerns the so called *intuitionistic* logic, where operators (inference rules) are deterministic. It is possible to generalize the inference systems to *classical* logic, using a generalized notion of sequent $\Gamma \vdash \Delta$, where the right part Δ is also a set of propositions. It is possible to explain the composition of such non-deterministic operators, which leads to Gentzen's systems NK and LK (Klassical logic!). Remark that the analogue of the unification theorem above gives then precisely Robinson's resolution principle for general clauses [144].

(d) The categorical viewpoint fits nicely these developments. This point of view is completely developed in Szabo [157]. The specially important connections between λ-calculus, natural deduction proofs and cartesian closed categories are investigated in [102,126,91,148,39,72]. Further readings on natural deduction proof theory are Prawitz [135] and Dummett [45]. The connection with recursion theory is developed in Kleene [85] and an algebraic treatment of these matters is given in Rasiowa-Sikorski [138].

4.5 Programming languages, recursion

The design of programming languages such as ALGOL 60 was greatly influenced by λ-calculus. In 1966 Peter Landin wrote a landmark article setting the stage for the consistent design of powerful functional languages in the λ-calculus tradition [93]. The core language of his proposal, ISWIM (If you see what I mean!) meant λ-calculus, with syntactically sugared versions of the β-redex ($[x]M\,N$), namely *let $x = N$ in M* and *M where $x = N$* respectively. His language followed the static binding rules of λ-calculus. For instance, after the declarations:

$$let\ f\ x\ =\ x + y\ where\ y = 1;$$

$$let\ y\ =\ 2;$$

the evaluation (reduction) of expression ($f\ 1$) leads to value 2, as expected. Note that in contrast languages such as LISP [111], although bearing some similarity with the λ-notation, implement rather *dynamic* binding, which would result in the example above in the incorrect result 3. This discrepancy has led to heated debates which we want to avoid here, but we remark that static binding is generally considered safer and leads to more efficient implementations where compilation is consistent with interpretation. However, ISWIM is not completely faithful to λ-calculus in one respect: its implementation does not follow the outside-in normal order of evaluation corresponding to the standardization theorem. Instead it follows the inside-out applicative order of evaluation demanding the arguments to be evaluated before a procedure is called. In the ALGOL terminology, ISWIM follows *call by value* instead of *call by name*.

The development of natural deduction as typed λ-calculus fits the design of an ISWIM-based language with a type discipline. We shall call this language ML, which stands for "meta-language", in the spirit of LCF's ML [58,57]. For instance, we get a core ML_0 by considering minimal logic, with → interpreted as functionality, and further constant functors added for basic types such as *triv, bool, int* and *string*.

Adding products we get a language ML_1 where types reflect an intuitionistic predicate calculus with → and ∧. We may define functions on a pattern argument formed by pairing, such as:

$$let\ fst(x, y)\ =\ x$$

and the categorical analogue are the so-called *cartesian closed categories* (CCCs). Adding sums lead to Bi-CCC's with co-product. The corresponding ML_2 primitives are inl, inr, outl, outr and isl, with obvious meaning. So far all computations terminate, since the corresponding reduction relations are Nœtherian.

However such a programming language is too weak for practical use, since recursion is missing. Adding recursion operators may be done in a stratified manner, as presented in Gödel's system T [55], or in a completely general way in ML_3, where we allow a "rec" construct permitting arbitrary recursive definitions, such as:

$$let\ rec\ fact\ n\ =\ if\ n = 0\ then\ 1\ else\ n * (fact\ (n - 1))$$

But then we loose the termination of computations, since it is possible to write un-founded definitions such as

$$let\ rec\ absurd\ x\ =\ absurd\ x.$$

Furthermore, because ML follows the applicative order of evaluation we may get looping computations in cases where a λ-calculus normal form exists, such as for

$$let\ f\ x\ =\ 0\ in\ f\ (absurd\ x).$$

4.6 Polymorphism

We have polymorphic operators (inference rules) at the meta level. It seems a good idea to push polymorphism to the object level, for functions defined by the user as λ-expressions. To this end, we introduce bindings for type variables. This idea of type quantification corresponds to allowing proposition quantifiers in our propositional logic. First we allow a universal quantifier in prenex position. That is, with $T_0 = T(\Phi, V)$, we now introduce *type schemas* in $T_1 = T_0 \cup \forall \alpha\ T_1, \alpha \in V$. A (type) term in T_1 has thus both free and bound variables, and we write $FV(M)$ and $BV(M)$ for the sets of free (respectively bound) variables.

We now define *generic instantiation*.
Let $\tau = \forall \alpha_1...\alpha_m \cdot \tau_0 \in T_1$ and $\tau' = \forall \beta_1...\beta_n \cdot \tau'_0 \in T_1$. We define $\tau' \geq_G \tau$ iff $\tau'_0 = \sigma(\tau_0)$ with $D(\sigma) \subseteq \{\alpha_1, ..., \alpha_m\}$ and $\beta_1 \notin FV(\tau)$ $(1 \leq i \leq n)$. Remark that $\geq$ acts on FV whereas $\geq_G$ acts on BV. Also note

$$\tau' \geq_G \tau \ \Rightarrow \ \sigma(\tau') \geq_G \sigma(\tau).$$

We now present the Damas-Milner inference system for polymorphic λ-calculus [43]. In what follows, a sequent hypothesis A is assumed to be a list of specifications $x_i : \tau_i$, with $\tau_i \in T_1$, and we write $FV(A) = \bigcup_i FV(\tau_i)$.

$$TAUT\ :\ A \vdash x\ :\ \alpha\ \ (x : \alpha \in A)$$

$$INST\ :\ \frac{A \vdash M\ :\ \alpha}{A \vdash M\ :\ \beta}\ \ \alpha \leq_G \beta)$$

$$GEN\ :\ \frac{A \vdash M\ :\ \tau}{A \vdash M\ :\ \forall \alpha \cdot \tau}\ \ (\alpha \notin FV(A))$$

$$APP\ :\ \frac{A \vdash M\ :\ \tau' \to \tau \quad A \vdash N\ :\ \tau'}{A \vdash (M\ N)\ :\ \tau}$$

$$ABS\ :\ \frac{A \cup \{x : \tau'\} \vdash M\ :\ \tau}{A \vdash [x] M\ :\ \tau' \to \tau}$$

$$LET\ :\ \frac{A \vdash M\ :\ \tau' \quad A \cup \{x : \tau'\} \vdash N\ :\ \tau}{A \vdash let\ x = M\ in\ N\ :\ \tau}.$$

For instance, it is an easy exercise to show that

$$\vdash let\ i\ =\ [x] x\ in\ (i\ i)\ :\ \alpha \to \alpha.$$

The above system may be extended without difficulty by other functors such as product, and by other ML contructions such as rec. Actually every ML compiler contains a typechecker implementing implicitly the above inference system. For instance, with the unary functor *list* and the following ML primitives: [] : $(list\ \alpha)$, $cons : \alpha \times (list\ \alpha)$ (written infix as a dot), $hd : (list\ \alpha) \to \alpha$ and $tl : (list\ \alpha) \to (list\ \alpha)$, we may define recursively the map functional as:

$$let\ rec\ map\ f\ l\ =\ if\ l = []\ then\ []\ else\ (f\ (hd\ l))\ \cdot\ map\ f\ (tl\ l)$$

and we get as its type:

$$\vdash\ map : (\alpha \to \beta) \to (list\ \alpha) \to (list\ \beta).$$

Of course the ML compiler does not implement directly the inference system above, which is non-deterministic because of rules $INST$ and GEN. It uses unification instead, and thus computes deterministically a principal type, which is minimum with respect to $\leq_G$:

Milner's Theorem. Every typable expression of the polymorphic λ-calculus possesses a principal type, minimum with respect to generic instantiation.

We obtain ML$_4$ by restricting ML$_3$ to the type system above. ML$_4$ is a strongly typed programming language, where type inference is possible because of the above theorem: the user need not write type specifications. The compiler of the language does more than typechecking, since it actually performs a proof synthesis. Types disappear at run time, but because of the type analysis no dynamic checks are needed to inforce the consistency of data operations, and this allows fast execution of ML programs. ML is a generic name for languages of the ML family. For instance, by adding to ML$_4$ exceptions, abstract data types (permitting in particular user-defined functors) and references, one gets approximately the meta-language of the LCF proof assistant [58]. By adding record type declarations (i.e. labeled sums and products) one gets L. Cardelli's ML [20]. By adding constructor types, pattern-matching and concrete syntax, we get the CAML language under development at Inria in the Formel project [37]. A more complete language, including modules, is under design as Standard ML [116]. It is to be hoped than less than 700 iterations of the language design will be necessary before the ultimate ML is agreed upon [93]! Current research topics on the design of ML-like languages are incorporation of object-oriented features allowing subtypes, remanent data structures and bitmap operations [21], and "lazy evaluation" permitting streams and ZF expressions [167,123].

Note on the relationship between ML and λ-calculus. First, ML uses so-called call by value implementation of procedure call, corresponding to innermost reduction, as opposed to the outermost regime of the standard reduction. Lazy evaluation permits standard reductions, but closures (i.e. objects of a functional type $\alpha \to \beta$) are *not* evaluated. Finally, types in ML serve for insuring the integrity of data operations, but still allow infinite computations by non-terminating recursions.

4.7 The limits of ML's polymorphism

Consider the following ML definition:

$$let\ rec\ power\ n\ f\ u\ =\ if\ n = 0\ then\ u\ else\ f\ (power\ (n-1)\ f\ u),$$

of type $nat \to (\alpha \to \alpha) \to (\alpha \to \alpha)$. This function, which associates to natural n the polymorphic iterator mapping function f to the n-th power of f, may be considered a coercion operator between ML's internal naturals and Church's representation of naturals in pure λ-calculus [24]. Let us recall briefly this representation. Integer 0 is represented as the projection term $[f][u]u$. Integer 1 is $[f][u](f\ u)$. More generally, n is represented as the functional $\bar{n}$ iterating a function f to its n-th power:

$$\bar{n}\ =\ [f][u](f\ (f\ ...(f\ u)...))$$

and the arithmetic operators may be coded respectively as:

$$n + m = [f][u](n\ f\ (m\ f\ u))$$

$$n \times m = [f](n\ (m\ f))$$

$$n^m = (m\ n).$$

For instance, with $\bar{2} = [f][u](f\ (f\ u))$, we check that $\bar{2} \times \bar{2}$ converts to its normal form $\bar{4}$.
We would like to consider a type

$$NAT = \forall \alpha \cdot (\alpha \to \alpha) \to (\alpha \to \alpha)$$

and be able to type the operations above as functions of type $NAT \to NAT \to NAT$. However the
notion of polymorphism found in ML does not support such a type, it allows only to write

$$\forall \alpha \cdot ((\alpha \to \alpha) \to (\alpha \to \alpha)) \to ((\alpha \to \alpha) \to (\alpha \to \alpha)) \to ((\alpha \to \alpha) \to (\alpha \to \alpha))$$

which is inadequate, since it forces the *same* generic instantiation of NAT in the two arguments.

4.8 Girard's second order λ-calculus.

The example above suggests using the universal type quantifier *inside* type formulas. We thus
consider a functor alphabet based on one binary $\to$ constructor and one quantifier $\forall$. We shall now
consider a λ-calculus with such types, which we shall call *second-order λ-calculus*, owing to the
fact that the type language is now a second-order propositional logic, with propositional variables
explicitly quantified. Such a calculus was proposed by J.Y. Girard [53,54], and independently
discovered by J. Reynolds [140].

4.8.1 The inference system

We now have two kinds of variables, the variables bound by λ-abstraction, and the propositional
variables. Each kind will have its own indexing scheme, but we put both kinds of bindings in one
context sequence, in order to ensure that in a λ-binding $[x : P]$ the free propositional variables
of P are correctly scoped. A *context* Γ is thus a sequence of bindings $[x : P]$ and of bindings
$[A : Prop]$.

We now have two binding operations: *functional abstraction* $[x : P]M$ where P is a proposition,
and *type quantification* $\forall A \cdot P$ for propositional variables. Finally an operation $\Lambda A \cdot M$ binds a
propositional variable in a term.

A context Γ is said to be *valid* if it binds variables with well-formed propositions. Thus the
empty context is valid, if Γ is valid and does not bind A then $\Gamma[A : Prop]$ is valid, and finally if
Γ is valid and does not bind x then $\Gamma[x : P]$ is valid provided $\Gamma \vdash P : Prop$. This last judgement
(propositional formation) is defined recursively as follows:

$$\frac{[A : Prop] \in \Gamma}{\Gamma \vdash A : Prop}$$

$$\frac{\Gamma \vdash P : Prop \qquad \Gamma \vdash Q : Prop}{\Gamma \vdash P \Rightarrow Q : Prop}$$

$$\frac{\Gamma[A : Prop] \vdash P : Prop}{\Gamma \vdash \forall A \cdot P : Prop}.$$

Let us now give the term-formation rules. We have two more constructors: $\Lambda A \cdot M$ which makes a term polymorphic, by $\forall$-introduction, and $< M\ P >$, which instantiates the polymorphic term M over the type corresponding to proposition P, by $\forall$-elimination.

$$Var \quad : \quad \frac{[x:P] \in \Gamma}{\Gamma \vdash x : P}$$

$$Abstr \quad : \quad \frac{\Gamma \vdash P : Prop \qquad \Gamma[x:P] \vdash M : Q}{\Gamma \vdash [x:P]M : P \Rightarrow Q}$$

$$Appl \quad : \quad \frac{\Gamma \vdash M : P \Rightarrow Q \qquad \Gamma \vdash N : P}{\Gamma \vdash (M\ N) : Q}$$

$$Gen \quad : \quad \frac{\Gamma[A:Prop] \vdash M : P}{\Gamma \vdash \Lambda A \cdot M : \forall A \cdot P}$$

$$Inst \quad : \quad \frac{\Gamma \vdash M : \forall A \cdot P \qquad \Gamma \vdash Q : Prop}{\Gamma \vdash < M\ Q >: P[A \leftarrow Q]}.$$

Proposition 1. If Γ is valid, then $\Gamma \vdash M : P$ implies $\Gamma \vdash P : Prop$.

Let us now give an example of a derivation. Let $Id := \Lambda A \cdot [x:A]x$. Id is the polymorphic identity algorithm, and we check easily that $\vdash Id : One$, where $One := \forall A \cdot A \Rightarrow A$. Note that indeed One is well-formed in the empty context. Now we may instantiate Id over its own type One, yielding: $\vdash< Id\ One >: One \Rightarrow One$. The resulting term may thus be applied to Id, yielding: $\vdash (< Id\ One >\ Id) : One$.

4.8.2 The conversion rules

The calculus admits two conversion rules. The first one is just β:

$$\beta \quad : \quad \frac{}{\Gamma \vdash ([x:P]M\ N) \rhd M[x \leftarrow N]}.$$

The second one eliminates the cut formed by introducing and eliminating a quantification:

$$\beta' \quad : \quad \frac{}{\Gamma \vdash< \Lambda A \cdot M\ P > \rhd M[A \leftarrow P]}.$$

Of course, we assume all other rules extending $\rhd$ as a term congruence, as before.

Proposition 2. If Γ is valid, $\Gamma \vdash M : P$ and $\Gamma \vdash M \rhd N$ then $\Gamma \vdash N : P$.

4.8.3 Basic meta-mathematical properties

Girard's theorem. The conversion $\rhd$ on typed terms is Nœtherian.

Corollary. There is no term M which proves $\nabla = \forall A \cdot A$.

This last result may be used as a soundness theorem, ∇ playing logically the rôle of falsity. Girard used it to show the consistency of second-order logic, i.e. analysis.

Second-order λ-calculus is a very powerful language. Most usual data structures may be represented as types. Furthermore, it captures a large class of total recursive functions (precisely, all the functions *provably* total in second-order arithmetic). It may seriously be considered as a candidate for the foundations of powerful programming languages, where *recursion* is replaced by *iteration*.

But the price we pay by extending polymorphism in this drastic fashion is that the notion of principal type is lost. Type synthesis is possible only in easy cases, and thus in general the programmer has to specify the types of its data.

Further discussions on the second-order λ-calculus may be found in [112,50,95,7].

5 Type theory

5.1 Quantification

So far we have dealt only with types as propositions of some (intuitionistic) propositional logic. We shall now consider stronger logics, where it is possible to have statements depending upon variables that are λ-bound. We shall continue our identification of propositions and types, and thus consider a first-order statement such as $\forall x \in E \cdot P(x)$ as a product-forming type $\Pi_{x \in E} P(x)$.

We shall call such types *dependent*, in that it is now possible to declare a variable of a type which depends on the binding of some previously bound variable. Let us first of all remark that such types are absolutely necessary for practical programming purposes. For instance, a matrix manipulation procedure should have a declaration prefix of the type:

$$[n : nat]\,[matrix : array(n)]$$

where the second type *depends* on the dimension parameter. PASCAL programmers know that the lack of such declarations in the language is a serious hindrance.

We shall not develop first-order notions here, and shall rather jump directly to calculi based on higher-order logic. For lack of space we cannot give detailed presentations of the many formalisms which have been proposed for the formalization of constructive mathematics, and thus limit ourselves to a brief survey of this very active research area. See [34] for a selected bibliography of this area.

5.2 Martin-Löf's Intuitionistic Theory of Types

P. Martin-Löf has been developing for the last 10 years a higher-order intuitionist logic based on a theory of types, allowing dependent sums and products [108,109,110]. His theory is not explicitly based on λ-calculus, but it is formulated in the spirit of natural deduction, with introduction and elimination rules for the various type constructors. Consistency is inferred from semantic considerations, with a model theory giving an analysis of the normal forms of elements of a type, and of the equality predicate for each type.

Martin-Löf's system has been advocated as a good candidate for the description and validation of computer programs, and is an active topic of research by the Göteborg Programming Methodology group [122,124,125]. A particularly ambitious implementation of Martin-Löf's system and extensions is under way at Cornell University, under the direction of R. Constable [26,27,28].

5.3 de Bruijn's AUTOMATH languages

The mathematical language AUTOMATH has been developed and implemented by the Eindhoven group, under the direction of prof. N.G. de Bruijn [14,16,18]. AUTOMATH is a λ-calculus with types that are themselves λ-expressions. It is based on the natural idea that λ-binding and universal instantiation are similar substitution operations. Thus in AUTOMATH there is only one binding operation, used both for parameter abstraction and product instantiation. The meta-theory of the various languages of the AUTOMATH family are investigated in [118,42,80]. The most notable success of the AUTOMATH effort has been the translation and mechanical validation of Landau's Grundlagen [79].

5.4   A Calculus of Constructions.

AUTOMATH established the correct linguistic foundations for higher-order natural deduction. Unfortunately, it did not allow Girard's second-order types, and probably for this reason was never considered under the programming language aspect. Th. Coquand showed that a slight extension of the notation allowed the incorporation of Girard's types to AUTOMATH in a natural manner [29]. Coquand showed by a strong normalization theorem that the formalism is consistent. Experiments with an implementation of the calculus showed that it is well adapted to expressing naturally and concisely mathematical proofs and computer algorithms [32]. Variations on this calculus are under development [33,35,30,117].

Conclusion

We have presented in these notes a uniform account of logic and computation theory, based on proof theory notions, and most importantly on the Curry-Howard correspondance between propositions and types [41,63].

These notes are based on a course given at the Advanced School of Artificial Intelligence, Vigneu, France, in July 1985, and on a course given at the International Summer School on Logic of Programming and Calculi of Discrete Design, Marktoberdorf, Germany, in August 1986. An extended version, completely formalized in the ML language, is in preparation [73].

References

[1] A. Aho, J. Hopcroft, J. Ullman. "The Design and Analysis of Computer Algorithms." Addison-Wesley (1974).

[2] P. B. Andrews. "Resolution in Type Theory." Journal of Symbolic Logic **36,3** (1971), 414–432.

[3] P. B. Andrews, D. A. Miller, E. L. Cohen, F. Pfenning. "Automating higher-order logic." Dept of Math, University Carnegie-Mellon, (Jan. 1983).

[4] H. Barendregt. "The Lambda-Calculus: Its Syntax and Semantics." North-Holland (1980).

[5] E. Bishop. "Foundations of Constructive Analysis." McGraw-Hill, New-York (1967).

[6] E. Bishop. "Mathematics as a numerical language." Intuitionism and Proof Theory, Eds. J. Myhill, A.Kino and R.E.Vesley, North-Holland, Amsterdam, (1970) 53–71.

[7] C. Böhm, A. Berarducci. "Automatic Synthesis of Typed Lambda-Programs on Term Algebras." Unpublished manuscript, (June 1984).

[8] R.S. Boyer, J Moore. "The sharing of structure in theorem proving programs." Machine Intelligence 7 (1972) Edinburgh U. Press, 101–116.

[9] R. Boyer, J Moore. "A Lemma Driven Automatic Theorem Prover for Recursive Function Theory." 5th International Joint Conference on Artificial Intelligence, (1977) 511–519.

[10] R. Boyer, J Moore. "A Computational Logic." Academic Press (1979).

[11] R. Boyer, J Moore. "A mechanical proof of the unsolvability of the halting problem." Report ICSCA-CMP-28, Institute for Computing Science, University of Texas at Austin (July 1982).

[12] R. Boyer, J Moore. "Proof Checking the RSA Public Key Encryption Algorithm." Report ICSCA-CMP-33, Institute for Computing Science, University of Texas at Austin (Sept. 1982).

[13] R. Boyer, J Moore. "Proof checking theorem proving and program verification." Report ICSCA-CMP-35, Institute for Computing Science, University of Texas at Austin (Jan. 1983).

[14] N.G. de Bruijn. "The mathematical language AUTOMATH, its usage and some of its extensions." Symposium on Automatic Demonstration, IRIA, Versailles, 1968. Printed as Springer-Verlag Lecture Notes in Mathematics 125, (1970) 29–61.

[15] N.G. de Bruijn. "Lambda-Calculus Notation with Nameless Dummies, a Tool for Automatic Formula Manipulation, with Application to the Church-Rosser Theorem." Indag. Math. 34,5 (1972), 381–392.

[16] N.G. de Bruijn. "Automath a language for mathematics." Les Presses de l'Université de Montréal, (1973).

[17] N.G. de Bruijn. "Some extensions of Automath: the AUT-4 family." Internal Automath memo M10 (Jan. 1974).

[18] N.G. de Bruijn. "A survey of the project Automath." (1980) in to H. B. Curry: Essays on Combinatory Logic, Lambda Calculus and Formalism, Eds Seldin J. P. and Hindley J. R., Academic Press (1980).

[19] M. Bruynooghe. "The Memory Management of PROLOG implementations." Logic Programming Workshop. Ed. Tarnlund S.A (July 1980).

[20] L. Cardelli. "ML under UNIX." Bell Laboratories, Murray Hill, New Jersey (1982).

[21] L. Cardelli. "Amber." Bell Laboratories, Murray Hill, New Jersey (1985).

[22] D. de Champeaux. "About the Paterson-Wegman Linear Unification Algorithm." J. of Comp. and System Sciences 32 (1986) 79–90.

[23] A. Church. "A formulation of the simple theory of types." Journal of Symbolic Logic 5,1 (1940) 56–68.

[24] A. Church. "The Calculi of Lambda-Conversion." Princeton U. Press, Princeton N.J. (1941).

[25] A. Colmerauer, H. Kanoui, R. Pasero, Ph. Roussel. "Un système de communication homme-machine en francais." Rapport de recherche, Groupe Intelligence Artificielle, Faculté des Sciences de Luminy, Marseille (1973).

[26] R.L. Constable, J.L. Bates. "Proofs as Programs." Dept. of Computer Science, Cornell University. (Feb. 1983).

[27] R.L. Constable, J.L. Bates. "The Nearly Ultimate Pearl." Dept. of Computer Science, Cornell University. (Dec. 1983).

[28] R.L. Constable et al. "Implementing Mathematics in the NuPrl System." Prentice-Hall (1986).

[29] Th. Coquand. "Une théorie des constructions." Thèse de troisième cycle, Université Paris VII (Jan. 85).

[30] Th. Coquand. "An analysis of Girard's paradox." First Conference on Logic in Computer Science, Boston (June 1986).

[31] Th. Coquand, G. Huet. "A Theory of Constructions." Preliminary version, presented at the International Symposium on Semantics of Data Types, Sophia-Antipolis (June 84).

[32] Th. Coquand, G. Huet. "Constructions: A Higher Order Proof System for Mechanizing Mathematics." EUROCAL85, Linz, Springer-Verlag LNCS 203 (1985).

[33] Th. Coquand, G. Huet. "Concepts Mathématiques et Informatiques Formalisés dans le Calcul des Constructions." Colloque de Logique, Orsay (Juil. 1985).

[34] Th. Coquand, G. Huet. "A Selected Bibliography on Constructive Mathematics, Intuitionistic Type Theory and Higher Order Deduction." J. Symbolic Computation (1985) **1** 323–328.

[35] Th. Coquand, G. Huet. "The Calculus of Constructions." To appear, JCSS (1986).

[36] J. Corbin, M. Bidoit. "A Rehabilitation of Robinson's Unification Algorithm." IFIP 83, Elsevier Science (1983) 909–914.

[37] G. Cousineau, P.L. Curien and M. Mauny. "The Categorical Abstract Machine." In Functional Programming Languages and Computer Architecture, Ed. J. P. Jouannaud, Springer-Verlag LNCS 201 (1985) 50–64.

[38] P.L. Curien. "Combinateurs catégoriques, algorithmes séquentiels et programmation applicative." Thèse de Doctorat d'Etat, Université Paris VII (Dec. 1983).

[39] P. L. Curien. "Categorical Combinatory Logic." ICALP 85, Nafplion, Springer-Verlag LNCS 194 (1985).

[40] P.L. Curien. "Categorical Combinators, Sequential Algorithms and Functional Programming." Pitman (1986).

[41] H. B. Curry, R. Feys. "Combinatory Logic Vol. I." North-Holland, Amsterdam (1958).

[42] D. Van Daalen. "The language theory of Automath." Ph. D. Dissertation, Technological Univ. Eindhoven (1980).

[43] Luis Damas, Robin Milner. "Principal type-schemas for functional programs." Edinburgh University (1982).

[44] P.J. Downey, R. Sethi, R. Tarjan. "Variations on the common subexpression problem." JACM **27,4** (1980) 758–771.

[45] M. Dummett. "Elements of Intuitionism." Clarendon Press, Oxford (1977).

[46] F. Fages. "Formes canoniques dans les algèbres booléennes et application à la démonstration automatique en logique de premier ordre." Thèse de 3ème cycle, Univ. de Paris VI (Juin 1983).

[47] F. Fages. "Associative-Commutative Unification." Submitted for publication (1985).

[48] F. Fages, G. Huet. "Unification and Matching in Equational Theories." CAAP 83, l'Aquila, Italy. In Springer-Verlag LNCS **159** (1983).

[49] P. Flajolet, J.M. Steyaert. "On the Analysis of Tree-Matching Algorithms." in Automata, Languages and Programming 7th Int. Coll., Lecture Notes in Computer Science **85** Springer Verlag (1980) 208–219.

[50] S. Fortune, D. Leivant, M. O'Donnell. "The Expressiveness of Simple and Second-Order Type Structures." Journal of the Assoc. for Comp. Mach., **30,1**, (Jan. 1983) 151–185.

[51] G. Frege. "Begriffschrift, a formula language, modeled upon that of arithmetic, for pure thought." (1879). Reprinted in From Frege to Gödel, J. van Heijenoort, Harvard University Press, 1967.

[52] G. Gentzen. "The Collected Papers of Gerhard Gentzen." Ed. E. Szabo, North-Holland, Amsterdam (1969).

[53] J.Y. Girard. "Une extension de l'interprétation de Gödel à l'analyse, et son application à l'élimination des coupures dans l'analyse et la théorie des types. Proceedings of the Second Scandinavian Logic Symposium, Ed. J.E. Fenstad, North Holland (1970) 63–92.

[54] J.Y. Girard. "Interprétation fonctionnelle et élimination des coupures dans l'arithmétique d'ordre supérieure." Thèse d'Etat, Université Paris VII (1972).

[55] K. Gödel. "Uber eine bisher noch nicht benutze Erweitrung des finiten Standpunktes." Dialectica, **12** (1958).

[56] W. D. Goldfarb. "The Undecidability of the Second-order Unification Problem." Theoretical Computer Science, **13**, (1981) 225–230.

[57] M. Gordon, R. Milner, C. Wadsworth. "A Metalanguage for Interactive Proof in LCF." Internal Report CSR-16-77, Department of Computer Science, University of Edinburgh (Sept. 1977).

[58] M. J. Gordon, A. J. Milner, C. P. Wadsworth. "Edinburgh LCF" Springer-Verlag LNCS **78** (1979).

[59] W. E. Gould. "A Matching Procedure for Omega Order Logic." Scientific Report 1, AFCRL 66-781, contract AF19 (628)-3250 (1966).

[60] J. Guard. "Automated Logic for Semi-Automated Mathematics." Scientific Report 1, AFCRL (1964).

[61] J. Herbrand. "Recherches sur la théorie de la démonstration." Thèse, U. de Paris (1930). In: Ecrits logiques de Jacques Herbrand, PUF Paris (1968).

[62] C. M. Hoffmann, M. J. O'Donnell. "Programming with Equations." ACM Transactions on Programming Languages and Systems, **4,1** (1982) 83–112.

[63] W. A. Howard. "The formulæ-as-types notion of construction." Unpublished manuscript (1969). Reprinted in to H. B. Curry: Essays on Combinatory Logic, Lambda Calculus and Formalism, Eds Seldin J. P. and Hindley J. R., Academic Press (1980).

[64] G. Huet. "Constrained Resolution: a Complete Method for Type Theory." Ph.D. Thesis, Jennings Computing Center Report 1117, Case Western Reserve University (1972).

[65] G. Huet. "A Mechanization of Type Theory." Proceedings, 3rd IJCAI, Stanford (Aug. 1973).

[66] G. Huet. "The Undecidability of Unification in Third Order Logic." Information and Control **22** (1973) 257–267.

[67] G. Huet. "A Unification Algorithm for Typed Lambda Calculus." Theoretical Computer Science, **1.1** (1975) 27–57.

[68] G. Huet. "Résolution d'équations dans des langages d'ordre 1,2, ... ω." Thèse d'Etat, Université Paris VII (1976).

[69] G. Huet. "Confluent Reductions: Abstract Properties and Applications to Term Rewriting Systems." J. Assoc. Comp. Mach. **27,4** (1980) 797–821.

[70] G. Huet. "A Complete Proof of Correctness of the Knuth-Bendix Completion Algorithm." JCSS **23,1** (1981) 11-21.

[71] G. Huet. "Initiation à la Théorie des Catégories." Polycopié de cours de DEA, Université Paris VII (Nov. 1985).

[72] G. Huet. "Cartesian Closed Categories and Lambda-Calculus." Category Theory Seminar, Carnegie-Mellon University (Dec. 1985).

[73] G. Huet. "Formal Structures for Computation and Deduction." In preparation.

[74] G. Huet, J.M. Hullot. "Proofs by Induction in Equational Theories With Constructors." JCSS **25,2** (1982) 239–266.

[75] G. Huet, J.J. Lévy "Call by Need Computations in Non-Ambiguous Linear Term Rewriting Systems." Rapport Laboria 359, IRIA (Aug. 1979).

[76] G. Huet, D. Oppen. "Equations and Rewrite Rules: a Survey." In Formal Languages: Perspectives and Open Problems, Ed. Book R., Academic Press (1980).

[77] J.M. Hullot "Compilation de Formes Canoniques dans les Théories Equationnelles." Thèse de 3ème cycle, U. de Paris Sud (Nov. 80).

[78] Jean Pierre Jouannaud, Helene Kirchner. "Completion of a set of rules modulo a set of equations." CSL Technical Note, SRI International (April 1984). To appear, SIAM Journal on Computing.

[79] L.S. Jutting. "A translation of Landau's "Grundlagen" in AUTOMATH." Eindhoven University of Technology, Dept of Mathematics (Oct. 1976).

[80] L.S. van Benthem Jutting. "The language theory of Λ_∞, a typed λ-calculus where terms are types." Unpublished manuscript (1984).

[81] G. Kahn, G. Plotkin. "Domaines concrets." Rapport Laboria 336, IRIA (Déc. 1978).

[82] J. Ketonen, J. S. Weening. "The language of an interactive proof checker." Stanford University (1984).

[83] J. Ketonen. "EKL-A Mathematically Oriented Proof Checker." 7th International Conference on Automated Deduction, Napa, California (May 1984). Springer-Verlag LNCS **170**.

[84] J. Ketonen. "A mechanical proof of Ramsey theorem." Stanford Univ. (1983).

[85] S.C. Kleene. "On the interpretation of intuitionistic number theory." J. Symbolic Logic **10** (1945).

[86] S.C. Kleene. "Introduction to Meta-mathematics." North Holland (1952).

[87] J.W. Klop. "Combinatory Reduction Systems." Ph. D. Thesis, Mathematisch Centrum Amsterdam (1980).

[88] D. Knuth, P. Bendix. "Simple word problems in universal algebras". In: Computational Problems in Abstract Algebra, J. Leech Ed., Pergamon (1970) 263–297.

[89] D.E. Knuth, J. Morris, V. Pratt. "Fast Pattern Matching in Strings." SIAM Journal on Computing **6,2** (1977) 323–350.

[90] G. Kreisel. "On the interpretation of nonfinitist proofs, Part I, II." JSL **16,17** (1952, 1953).

[91] J. Lambek. "From Lambda-calculus to Cartesian Closed Categories." in To H. B. Curry: Essays on Combinatory Logic, Lambda-calculus and Formalism, Eds. J. P. Seldin and J. R. Hindley, Academic Press (1980).

[92] J. Lambek and P. J. Scott. "Aspects of Higher Order Categorical Logic." Contemporary Mathematics **30** (1984) 145–174.

[93] P. J. Landin. "The next 700 programming languages." Comm. ACM **9,3** (1966) 157–166.

[94] Philippe Le Chenadec. "Formes canoniques dans les algèbres finiment présentées." Thèse de 3ème cycle, Univ. d'Orsay (Juin 1983).

[95] D. Leivant. "Polymorphic type inference." 10th ACM Symposium on Principles of Programming Languages (1983).

[96] D. Leivant. "Structural semantics for polymorphic data types." 10th ACM Conference on Principles of Programming Languages (1983).

[97] J.J. Lévy. "Réductions correctes et optimales dans le λ-calcul." Thèse d'Etat, U. Paris VII (1978).

[98] S. MacLane. "Categories for the Working Mathematician." Springer-Verlag (1971).

[99] D. MacQueen, G. Plotkin, R. Sethi. "An ideal model for recursive polymorphic types." Proceedings, Principles of Programming Languages Symposium, Jan. 1984, 165–174.

[100] D. B. MacQueen, R. Sethi. "A semantic model of types for applicative languages." ACM Symposium on Lisp and Functional Programming (Aug. 1982).

[101] E.G. Manes. "Algebraic Theories." Springer-Verlag (1976).

[102] C. Mann. "The Connection between Equivalence of Proofs and Cartesian Closed Categories." Proc. London Math. Soc. **31** (1975) 289–310.

[103] A. Martelli, U. Montanari. "Theorem proving with structure sharing and efficient unification." Proc. 5th IJCAI, Boston, (1977) p 543.

[104] A. Martelli, U. Montanari. "An Efficient Unification Algorithm." ACM Trans. on Prog. Lang. and Syst. **4,2** (1982) 258–282.

[105] William A. Martin. "Determining the equivalence of algebraic expressions by hash coding." JACM **18,4** (1971) 549–558.

[106] P. Martin-Löf. "A theory of types." Report 71-3, Dept. of Mathematics, University of Stockholm, Feb. 1971, revised (Oct. 1971).

[107] P. Martin-Löf. "About models for intuitionistic type theories and the notion of definitional equality." Paper read at the Orléans Logic Conference (1972).

[108] P. Martin-Löf. "An intuitionistic Theory of Types: predicative part." Logic Colloquium 73, Eds. H. Rose and J. Sepherdson, North-Holland, (1974) 73–118.

[109] P. Martin-Löf. "Constructive Mathematics and Computer Programming." In Logic, Methodology and Philosophy of Science **6** (1980) 153–175, North-Holland.

[110] P. Martin-Löf. "Intuitionistic Type Theory." Studies in Proof Theory, Bibliopolis (1984).

[111] J. Mc Carthy. "Recursive functions of symbolic expressions and their computation by machine." CACM **3,4** (1960) 184–195.

[112] N. McCracken. "An investigation of a programming language with a polymorphic type structure." Ph.D. Dissertation, Syracuse University (1979).

[113] D.A. Miller. "Proofs in Higher-order Logic." Ph. D. Dissertation, Carnegie-Mellon University (Aug. 1983).

[114] D.A. Miller. "Expansion tree proofs and their conversion to natural deduction proofs." Technical report MS-CIS-84-6, University of Pennsylvania (Feb. 1984).

[115] R. Milner. "A Theory of Type Polymorphism in Programming." Journal of Computer and System Sciences **17** (1978) 348–375.

[116] R. Milner. "A proposal for Standard ML." Report CSR-157-83, Computer Science Dept., University of Edinburgh (1983).

[117] C. Mohring. "Algorithm Development in the Calculus of Constructions." IEEE Symposium on Logic in Computer Science, Cambridge, Mass. (June 1986).

[118] R.P. Nederpelt. "Strong normalization in a typed λ calculus with λ structured types." Ph. D. Thesis, Eindhoven University of Technology (1973).

[119] R.P. Nederpelt. "An approach to theorem proving on the basis of a typed λ-calculus." 5th Conference on Automated Deduction, Les Arcs, France. Springer-Verlag LNCS **87** (1980).

[120] G. Nelson, D.C. Oppen. "Fast decision procedures based on congruence closure." JACM **27,2** (1980) 356–364.

[121] M.H.A. Newman. "On Theories with a Combinatorial Definition of "Equivalence"." Annals of Math. **43,2** (1942) 223–243.

[122] B. Nordström. "Programming in Constructive Set Theory: Some Examples." Proceedings of the ACM Conference on Functional Programming Languages and Computer Architecture, Portmouth, New Hampshire (Oct. 1981) 141–154.

[123] B. Nordström. "Description of a Simple Programming Language." Report 1, Programming Methodology Group, University of Goteborg (Apr. 1984).

[124] B. Nordström, K. Petersson. "Types and Specifications." Information Processing 83, Ed. R. Mason, North-Holland, (1983) 915–920.

[125] B. Nordström, J. Smith. "Propositions and Specifications of Programs in Martin-Löf's Type Theory." BIT **24**, (1984) 288–301.

[126] A. Obtulowicz. "The Logic of Categories of Partial Functions and its Applications." Dissertationes Mathematicae 241 (1982).

[127] M.S. Paterson, M.N. Wegman. "Linear Unification." J. of Computer and Systems Sciences **16** (1978) 158–167.

[128] L. Paulson. "Recent Developments in LCF : Examples of structural induction." Technical Report No 34, Computer Laboratory, University of Cambridge (Jan. 1983).

[129] L. Paulson. "Tactics and Tacticals in Cambridge LCF." Technical Report No 39, Computer Laboratory, University of Cambridge (July 1983).

[130] L. Paulson. "Verifying the unification algorithm in LCF." Technical report No 50, Computer Laboratory, University of Cambridge (March 1984).

[131] L. C. Paulson. "Constructing Recursion Operators in Intuitionistic Type Theory." Tech. Report 57, Computer Laboratory, University of Cambridge (Oct. 1984).

[132] G.E. Peterson, M.E. Stickel. "Complete Sets of Reduction for Equational Theories with Complete Unification Algorithms." JACM **28,2** (1981) 233–264.

[133] T. Pietrzykowski, D.C. Jensen. "A complete mechanization of ω-order type theory." Proceedings of ACM Annual Conference (1972).

[134] T. Pietrzykowski. "A Complete Mechanization of Second-Order Type Theory." JACM **20** (1973) 333–364.

[135] D. Prawitz. "Natural Deduction." Almqist and Wiskell, Stockolm (1965).

[136] D. Prawitz. "Ideas and results in proof theory." Proceedings of the Second Scandinavian Logic Symposium (1971).

[137] W. V. Quine. "The problem of simplifying truth functions." Amer. Math. Monthly bf 59,8 (1952) 521–531.

[138] H. Rasiowa, R. Sikorski "The Mathematics of Metamathematics." Monografie Matematyczne tom **41**, PWN, Polish Scientific Publishers, Warszawa (1963).

[139] J. C. Reynolds. "Definitional Interpreters for Higher Order Programming Languages." Proc. ACM National Conference, Boston, (Aug. 72) 717–740.

[140] J. C. Reynolds. "Towards a Theory of Type Structure." Programming Symposium, Paris. Springer Verlag LNCS **19** (1974) 408–425.

[141] J. C. Reynolds. "Types, abstraction, and parametric polymorphism." IFIP Congress'83, Paris (Sept. 1983).

[142] J. C. Reynolds. "Polymorphism is not set-theoretic." International Symposium on Semantics of Data Types, Sophia-Antipolis (June 1984).

[143] J. C. Reynolds. "Three approaches to type structure." TAPSOFT Advanced Seminar on the Role of Semantics in Software Development, Berlin (March 1985).

[144] J. A. Robinson. "A Machine-Oriented Logic Based on the Resolution Principle." JACM **12** (1965) 32–41.

[145] J. A. Robinson. "Computational Logic: the Unification Computation." Machine Intelligence **6** Eds B. Meltzer and D.Michie, American Elsevier, New-York (1971).

[146] K. Schütte. "Proof theory." Springer-Verlag (1977).

[147] D. Scott. "Constructive validity." Symposium on Automatic Demonstration, Springer-Verlag Lecture Notes in Mathematics, **125** (1970).

[148] D. Scott. "Relating Theories of the Lambda-Calculus." in To H. B. Curry: Essays on Combinatory Logic, Lambda-calculus and Formalism, Eds. J. P. Seldin and J. R. Hindley, Academic Press (1980).

[149] J.R. Shoenfield. "Mathematical Logic." Addison-Wesley (1967).

[150] R.E. Shostak "Deciding Combinations of Theories." JACM **31,1** (1985) 1–12.

[151] J. Smith. "Course-of-values recursion on lists in intuitionistic type theory." Unpublished notes, Göteborg University (Sept. 1981).

[152] J. Smith. "The identification of propositions and types in Martin-Lof's type theory : a programming example." International Conference on Foundations of Computation Theory, Borgholm, Sweden, (Aug. 1983) Springer-Verlag LNCS **158**.

[153] R. Statman. "Intuitionistic Propositional Logic is Polynomial-space Complete." Theoretical Computer Science **9** (1979) 67–72, North-Holland.

[154] R. Statman. "The typed Lambda-Calculus is not Elementary Recursive." Theoretical Computer Science **9** (1979) 73–81.

[155] S. Stenlund. "Combinators λ-terms, and proof theory." Reidel (1972).

[156] M.E. Stickel "A Complete Unification Algorithm for Associative-Commutative Functions." JACM **28,3** (1981) 423–434.

[157] M.E. Szabo. "Algebra of Proofs." North-Holland (1978).

[158] W. Tait. "A non constructive proof of Gentzen's Hauptsatz for second order predicate logic." Bull. Amer. Math. Soc. **72** (1966).

[159] W. Tait. "Intensional interpretations of functionals of finite type I." J. of Symbolic Logic **32** (1967) 198–212.

[160] W. Tait. "A Realizability Interpretation of the Theory of Species." Logic Colloquium, Ed. R. Parikh, Springer Verlag Lecture Notes **453** (1975).

[161] M. Takahashi. "A proof of cut-elimination theorem in simple type theory." J. Math. Soc. Japan **19** (1967).

[162] G. Takeuti. "On a generalized logic calculus." Japan J. Math. **23** (1953).

[163] G. Takeuti. "Proof theory." Studies in Logic **81** Amsterdam (1975).

[164] R. E. Tarjan. "Efficiency of a good but non linear set union algorithm." JACM **22,2** (1975) 215–225.

[165] R. E. Tarjan, J. van Leeuwen. "Worst-case Analysis of Set Union Algorithms." JACM **31,2** (1985) 245–281.

[166] A. Tarski. "A lattice-theoretical fixpoint theorem and its applications." Pacific J. Math. **5** (1955) 285–309.

[167] D.A. Turner. "Miranda: A non-strict functional language with polymorphic types." In Functional Programming Languages and Computer Architecture, Ed. J. P. Jouannaud, Springer-Verlag LNCS 201 (1985) 1–16.

[168] R. de Vrijer "Big Trees in a λ-calculus with λ-expressions as types." Conference on λ-calculus and Computer Science Theory, Rome, Springer-Verlag LNCS **37** (1975) 252–271.

[169] D. Warren "Applied Logic - Its use and implementation as a programming tool." Ph.D. Thesis, University of Edinburgh (1977).

Expressing program developments in a design calculus

Michel Sintzoff

Unité d'Informatique
Université Catholique de Louvain
place Sainte-Barbe 2
B-1348 Louvain-la-Neuve, Belgium

Introduction

The present paper describes a step in the study of means to express software developments. This study is also related to approaches where programs are extracted from proofs, and it is influenced by the spirit and the techniques of constructive logic.

The first priority is given to the style in which to express developments. Development schemes, not only isolated rules, and properties of developments, not only their construction, must be expressible. Other essential topics, such as mathematical foundations and computer support, are complementary. The work described here is to program development what the work on Pebble [Burstall and Lampson] is to module interconnection; it tries to be a brick in a bridge between the research on program design and the elaboration of logic frameworks such as those developed on the basis of [Curry and Feys, §9E]; significant such bricks already exist in [Abrial], [Bauer, Pepper], [Constable et al.], [Coquand and Huet], [Hanna and Daeche], [Milner], [Nordström]. Compared to the latter approaches, the present work has been primarily guided by needs which were progressively identified in attempts to understand and to express software developments and development methods. The use of constructive logic and higher-order functions is a by-product of this progressive identification.

The paper is organized as follows. First, the current status of the definition of the calculus used is described. Then a few small exercises illustrate how this calculus can be applied in various contexts. The last section presents more or less developed expressions of typical development schemes.

On the whole, this paper must be seen as a progress report rather than as a complete synthesis; it serves as an additional contribution to a research on a development language [de Groote and al.].

1 Working definition of the design calculus

We present here the current version of the definition of the design calculus. The driving forces are the following:

NATO ASI Series, Vol. F36
Logic of Programming and Calculi of Discrete Design
Edited by M. Broy
© Springer-Verlag Berlin Heidelberg 1987

1. Continuity from algorithms to logic: constructions and their properties are expressed uniformly; there is no frozen boundary between them. This also holds for properties of various strength, such as so-called strong types.

2. Higher order: developments, development schemes, and their own derivations, should all be expressed by terms of the calculus. As far as reasonable, activities initially described outside the calculus are made expressible within the calculus.

3. Reexpression, rather than invention: the aim is merely to express already available development techniques, and not to propose new ones or to reinvent known ones.

4. Communication, not only deduction: although deduction, computation, and edition are important similar activities, communication between human beings is given priority; concrete syntax is important.

The current definition is not final: there is a continued interplay between the experiments with case studies and the adaptations of the definition. The version presented here is a *post facto* reconstruction; it consists in extending constructive logic with terms expressing demonstrations or, alternatively, in extending a functional language with sentences expressing properties. This extension is not intended to provide a theoretically minimal basis, but rather a practically usable linguistic system. In comparison with Automath [deBruijn80] and its derivatives, the present design-calculus allows to treat proofs and developments as first-class citizens; this is also achieved a.o. in [Constable] and [Hanna and Daeche]; moreover, the same notations are used for expressing properties, viz. predicates or types, and constructions, viz. functions or programs.

For the time being, the current version of the design calculus is nicknamed *d-calculus*, in consonance with the p-calculus [Goad]; this must not be confused with the D-calculus [Novikov], equivalent to Gödel's B-calculus.

The definition given below includes a concrete context-free syntax, context-conditions, and rules for deducing or reducing forms; the latter rules are mostly expressed within the calculus itself. Alternative definition techniques of course can be used, for instance in terms of abstract data types [Hanna and Daeche].

1.1 Formation of syntactically correct formulas

We give a context-free syntax, context-conditions, notational conventions, and auxiliary syntactical predicates.

1.1.1 Context-free syntax

A BNF context-free rule such as

$$\langle \, expression \, \rangle ::= \langle \, variable \, \rangle \mid + \langle \, expression \, \rangle \langle \, expression \, \rangle$$

will be written as

$$expression : variable \mid \text{``+''} \; expression \, , \, expression.$$

Below, an *identifier* is a sequence of symbols taken among the lower- or upper-case letters and the digits; such an identifier may not begin with a digit, and may not be a single upper-case letter; single upper-case letters will be used as metavariables for variables; *form* abbreviates "d-formulas".

form : *constant* | *variable* | *cform, operator, cform* | *abstraction* | *instantiation*
| *application* | *substitution* | *certification* | *reduction.*

cform : "(" *form* ")".

constant : *ko. ko* : "⊥".
variable : *identifier.*
operator : *and* | *or* | *then* | *equiv.*
and : ",". *or* : "|". *then* : "⊢". *equiv* : "≡".

abstraction : *quantifier, cform.*
quantifier : *some* | *all.*
some : *variables* ".". *all* : "[" *variables* "]".
variables : *variable* | *variables* "," *variable.*

instantiation : "[" *definitions* "]" *cform.*
definitions : *definition* | *definitions* "," *definition.*
definition : *variable* ":=" *cform.*

application : *cform* ";" *cform.*
substitution : *definitions* ";" *cform.*

certification : *cform* "√".

reduction : "▷" *cform.*

The only predefined constant is the failure element ⊥; other constants can be defined as identifiers for 0-ary functions or predicates; predicates are considered as propositional functions. Instantiations amount to definitions of actual parameters or witnesses. Certifications correspond to valid formulas in the case of predicates, and to correct constructs in the case of functions. Reductions are formulas with which specific deduction rules are associated; applications and substitutions are such formulas used in reductions.

For optical reasons, parentheses can be removed by using conventional precedence rules with common sense, and as far as no harmful ambiguities are introduced; benign ambiguities are for instance those which apply properties of associativity and commutativity. The operators √ and ▷ have the lowest priority. The notations for the junctors and the quantifiers are based on those used in logic languages and in programming languages; thus $(a|b)$, (a, b), $(a \vdash b)$, $[x]a$, $x.a$, may respectively correspond to $(a \lor b)$, $(a \land b)$, $(a \Rightarrow b)$, $\forall x.a$, $\exists x.a$, if predicates are intended; if constructions are intended, such expressions may correspond to $[a|b]$, (a, b), $[a \rightarrow b]$, $\lambda x.a$, let x in a. An instantiation such as $[x := b][x]a$ can be viewed as a function closure; the corresponding substitution $x := b; a$ specifies the actual replacement of x by b in a; these two examples differ only in their computational properties, viz. they play the same logical role.

Conventions:

" ;" in *applications* is left-associative ;
$A, B, \ldots, Z$ are metavariables for *variables* ;
$\alpha, \beta, \ldots, \omega$ are metavariables for *formulas* ;
$\simeq$ denotes meta-equivalence;
$\oplus$ denotes any of the three *operators and* ",", *or* "|", *then* "⊢";
$(\mathcal{Q}A)$ denotes any of the two *quantifiers* "A." or "$[A]$".

1.1.2 Context conditions

"Static", Algol-like scope rules are used. Binding relations, between defining and applied occurrences of variables, are defined independently of the concrete identifiers used as variables; this can be achieved by using squares and lines [Bourbaki], or integers for scope levels [de Bruijn 72]. For instance, let us assume that variables at a given scope level are numbered according to their alphabetical order, and that $3\uparrow 2$ and $5\downarrow 7$ respectively refer to *the third variable two levels up* and to *the fifth variable seven levels down*; then we have

$$[Y, X][Z](Y, Z) \simeq [2, 1][1](2\uparrow 1 , 1\uparrow 0)$$

and

$$[Y := \beta][X, Z][X, Y]\alpha \simeq [2\downarrow 1 := \beta][1, 2][1, 2]\alpha$$

The latter instantiation can be reduced to an equivalent form where the corresponding substitution appears:

$$[X, Z][X](Y := \beta; \alpha) \simeq [1, 2][1](2\downarrow 0 := \beta ; \alpha)$$

From now on, variables will always be treated in their concrete form; this is not completely rigorous but simplifies the presentation.

Observe how bindings can be put in factor :

$$[Y := \beta] ([X, Y]\alpha 1, [X, Y, Z]\alpha 2) \equiv ([Y := \beta][X, Y]\alpha 1, [Y := \beta][X, Y, Z]\alpha 2)$$

The scope of a variable defined in some *definitions* $\mathcal{D}$ does not include the formulas occurring in $\mathcal{D}$: in this section, it is assumed that definitions are not recursive. A variable may not be defined more than once at the same scope level; a variable occurring as definiendum in an instantiation is an alias for its occurrence in the corresponding quantifier.

The ordering within *variables* and *definitions* is immaterial; they are taken in parallel. This can be summarised as follows:

$$X, Y \simeq Y, X \qquad X := \alpha, Y := \beta \simeq Y := \beta, X := \alpha$$

1.1.3 Notational extensions

These extensions are merely suggested, rather than defined formally, because this is a secondary issue in the current study. The principle is the freedom of choice of concrete syntax.

Graphical notations:

$$\alpha, \beta \quad \simeq \quad \alpha\,\beta \quad \simeq \quad \begin{matrix} \alpha \\ \beta \end{matrix} \qquad\qquad\qquad \alpha|\beta \quad \simeq \quad \begin{matrix} \alpha \\ |\beta \end{matrix}$$

$$\alpha \vdash \beta \quad \simeq \quad \beta \dashv \alpha \quad \simeq \quad \left|\begin{matrix} \alpha \\ \hline \beta \end{matrix}\right. \qquad\qquad \alpha \equiv \beta \quad \simeq \quad \frac{\alpha}{\beta}$$

$$(\alpha) \quad \simeq \quad \textbf{begin}\ \alpha\ \textbf{end} \quad \simeq \quad |\alpha| \quad \simeq \quad \boxed{\alpha}$$

$$X, Y \quad \simeq \quad \begin{matrix} X \\ Y \end{matrix} \qquad\qquad\qquad X := \alpha, Y := \beta \quad \simeq \quad \begin{matrix} X := \alpha \\ Y := \beta \end{matrix}$$

Harmful ambiguities are avoided by using such displays with good taste.

Notations for functions and operations:

After a definition such as

$$f := [X_1, X_2]\alpha$$

we may use

$$f(\beta_1, \beta_2) \simeq [X_1 := \beta_1, X_2 := \beta_2]f$$

This allows to use conventional notations, such as $f(a, b)$, and $p(u, b)$, for formulas corresponding to terms and to atomic formulas. Ambiguities are prevented e.g. by identifying the textual ordering of variables with their alphabetical one, in case the correspondence shown in §1.1.2 is used.

Mixfix notations for operators can be introduced in a similar way: after a definition such as

$$[X]\mathbf{f}[Y]\mathbf{g}[Z] := \alpha$$

we may use

$$\beta \, \mathbf{f} \, \gamma \, \mathbf{g} \, \delta \; \simeq \; [X := \beta, Y := \gamma, Z := \delta]\alpha$$

The corresponding operator symbol is denoted $[] \, \mathbf{f} \, [] \, \mathbf{g} \, []$. This can be generalized to two-dimensional operators; concatenation has then a vertical axis, in addition to the horizontal one. Fine arts could be used as well.

1.1.4 Auxiliary syntactical predicates

The following syntactical predicates will be used:

> $HasUse(X,a)$: X does occur free in a,
> $NoUse(X,a)$: X does not occur free in a,
> $HasDef(X,a)$: a quantification on X occurs in a,
> $NoDef(X,a)$: no quantification on X occurs in a.
> $X = Y$: X and Y denote syntactically identical objects.

Axiom schemes defining these concepts can be writtten on the basis of calculi of free occurrence and of its negation [Hermes]:

$$NoUse(X, \bot), \quad NoDef(X, \bot)$$

$$HasUse(X, X), \quad \frac{X \neq Y}{NoUse(X, Y)}, \quad NoDef(X, Y)$$

$$[a, b] \left| \frac{\begin{array}{l} HasUse(X, a) \\ |HasUse(X, b) \end{array}}{HasUse(X, a \oplus b)} \right. , \quad [a, b] \left| \frac{\begin{array}{l} HasDef(X, a) \\ |HasDef(X, b) \end{array}}{HasDef(X, a \oplus b)} \right.$$

$$[a, b] \left| \frac{\begin{array}{l} NoUse(X, a) \\ NoUse(X, b) \end{array}}{NoUse(X, a \oplus b)} \right. , \quad [a, b] \left| \frac{\begin{array}{l} NoDef(X, a) \\ NoDef(X, b) \end{array}}{NoDef(X, a \oplus b)} \right.$$

$$[a] \left| \frac{\begin{array}{l} HasUse(X, a) \\ X \neq Y \end{array}}{HasUse(X, (\mathcal{Q}Y)a)} \right. , \quad [a] \left| \frac{\begin{array}{l} HasDef(X, a) \\ |X = Y \end{array}}{HasDef(X, (\mathcal{Q}Y)a)} \right.$$

$$[a]\left|\frac{\begin{array}{c}NoUse(X,a)\\ |X=Y\end{array}}{NoUse(X,(\mathcal{Q}Y)a)}\right., \qquad [a]\left|\frac{\begin{array}{c}NoDef(X,a)\\ X\neq Y\end{array}}{NoDef(X,(\mathcal{Q}Y)a)}\right.$$

Syntactical predicates such as $HasDef(X,a)$ are not d-formulas, because quotation is not formally included yet. They must be seen as metalinguistic statements, where e.g. X and a respectively denote a quoted variable and a quoted formula; to internalize these rules completely within the d-calculus requires the capability to tansform formulas into data structures and conversely. Syntactical predicates are usually defined by induction on the syntactical structure of formulas.

1.2 Deduction of well-deduced formulas

Well-deduced formulas are the valid, sound, admissible ones; they are intended to express theorems or semantically acceptable expressions. The axioms are well-deduced formulas from which or by which all the other ones can be produced. Note that most of these axioms take the form of formulas of the calculus. The axioms given here are chosen so as to define a reasonably convenient basic library; thus they do not at all constitute a minimal set.

1.2.1 Compositional axioms

$$ExPreAnd[i] := [a_1,a_2]\left|\frac{a_1,a_2}{a_{[i]}}\right., \quad InPostOr[i] := [a_1,a_2]\left|\frac{a_{[i]}}{a_1\mid a_2}\right. \tag{1}$$

where $[i]$ is a meta-variable denoting 1 or 2.

$$PostAnd := [a_1,a_2,b]\frac{\left|\dfrac{b}{a_1}\right.\ \left|\dfrac{b}{a_2}\right.}{\left|\dfrac{b}{a_1,a_2}\right.}, \quad PreOr := [a_1,a_2,b]\frac{\left|\dfrac{a_1}{b}\right.\ \left|\dfrac{a_2}{b}\right.}{\left|\dfrac{a_1\mid a_2}{b}\right.} \tag{2}$$

The laws below are given as axiom schemes, where X stands for any variable. These axiom schemes can be generalized to the case of multiple variables. $NoUse$ is defined in §1.1.3.

$$ExPreAll := [a,b]\left|\frac{[X]a}{X:=b;\ a}\right., \quad InPostSome := [a,b]\left|\frac{X:=b;\ a}{X.a}\right. \tag{3}$$

$$PostAll := [a,b]\left(NoUse(X,b)\ \vdash\ \frac{[X]\left|\dfrac{b}{a}\right.}{\left|\dfrac{b}{[X]a}\right.}\right) \tag{4}$$

$$PreSome := [a,b]\left(NoUse(X,b)\ \vdash\ \frac{[X]\left|\dfrac{a}{b}\right.}{\left|\dfrac{X.a}{b}\right.}\right) \tag{5}$$

1.2.2 Basic axioms

$$Identity := [a]\left|\frac{a}{a}\right., \quad ExFalso := [a]\left|\frac{\perp}{a}\right. \tag{6}$$

$$InPostThen := [a,b]\left|\frac{a}{b \vdash a}\right., \quad ExPreThen := [a,b]\left|\frac{a,\left|\frac{a}{b}\right.}{b}\right. \tag{7}$$

$$DistrThenThen := [a,b,c]\left|\frac{a \vdash \left|\frac{b}{c}\right.}{\left|\frac{a \vdash b}{a \vdash c}\right.}\right., \quad TransThen := [a,b,c]\left|\frac{\left|\frac{a}{b}\right., \left|\frac{b}{c}\right.}{\left|\frac{a}{c}\right.}\right. \tag{8}$$

$$PropEquiv := [a,b]\left(\frac{\left|\frac{a}{b}\right., \left|\frac{b}{a}\right.}{a \equiv b}, \frac{a \equiv b}{\left|\frac{a}{b}\right., \left|\frac{b}{a}\right.}\right), \quad Curry := [a,b,c]\frac{a \vdash (b \vdash c)}{(a,b) \vdash c} \tag{9}$$

$$Monotonicity := [a,b,c]\frac{[X]\left|\frac{a}{b}\right.}{[X]\left|\frac{c \oplus a}{c \oplus b}\right., [X]\left|\frac{b \vdash c}{a \vdash c}\right., \left|\frac{(\varrho X)a}{(\varrho X)b}\right.} \tag{10}$$

The axioms and inference rules of intuitionistic predicate logic [Novikov] are obtained from axioms 1 to 9. Other properties of associativity, commutativity, reflexivity, distributivity, transitivity, are not included explicitly; they can be derived [Kleene] from the axioms given.

1.2.3 Structural axioms

Let us first introduce two syntactical predicates (in the sense of §1.1.4):

$IsIncr(X,a)$: there is exactly one occurrence of X in a, and a is monotonically increasing w.r.t. X,

$IsDecr(X,a)$: there is exactly one occurrence of X in a, and a is monotonically decreasing w.r.t. X.

A formula is monotonically increasing (resp. decreasing) w.r.t. the free occurrence X if any formula occurring in place of X can be replaced by a weaker (resp. stronger) one [Novikov]. This can be defined constructively as done for positive and negative parts [Schütte], since a positive (resp. negative) form is monotonically increasing (resp. decreasing):

$$IsIncr(X,X), \quad [a,b]\left|\frac{NoUse(X,a)}{IsIncr(X,b)}\right., \quad [a]\left|\frac{IsIncr(X,a)}{X \neq Y}\right.$$

$$[a,b]\left|\frac{IsIncr(X,(a,b))}{IsIncr(X,(b,a))}\right., \quad [a,b]\left|\frac{IsIncr(X,(a|b))}{IsIncr(X,(b|a))}\right., \quad [a,b]\left|\frac{IsIncr(X,(a \vdash b))}{IsDecr(X,(b \vdash a))}\right.$$

$$[a,b] \frac{\begin{array}{cc} IsIncr(X,a) & NoUse(Y,a) \\ NoUse(X,b) & IsIncr(Y,b) \end{array}}{IsIncr(X,(Y:=a;\ b))} \tag{11}$$

The remaining laws are defined by duality: in the above rules, *IsIncr* and *IsDecr* respectively become *IsDecr* and *IsIncr*, except that *IsIncr*(X, X) has no such dual. An amusing concrete syntax is to use green and red colours for increasing and decreasing places when they are displayed graphically.

With these auxiliary predicates, the structural axioms can now be given:

$$Inc := [a,b,c] \frac{\dfrac{IsIncr(X,c)}{a \vdash b}}{(X:=a;\ c) \vdash (X:=b;\ c)}, \ Dec := [a,b,c] \frac{\dfrac{IsDecr(X,c)}{b \vdash a}}{(X:=a;\ c) \vdash (X:=b;\ c)} \tag{12}$$

$$Equate := [a,b,c] \frac{a \equiv b}{(X:=a;\ c) \equiv (X:=b;\ c)} \tag{13}$$

The concepts of increasing and decreasing formulas, or of positive and negative forms, can be traced back to the evenly and oddly enclosed existential graphs [Peirce]; in [Schütte], positive and negative forms are presented as a generalization of succedent and antecedent formulas in Gentzen's natural deduction rules. Such structural axioms provide a macroscopic deduction mechanism; they are also used intensively in [Sowa], and their power is theoretically analysed in [de Groote]. They play a significant role in various proof techniques [Delsarte and al., Manna and Waldinger, Miller and Felty, Murray, Traugott].

Let us consider the first-order case. Then the axioms 1 - 13 are axioms or theorems of intuitionistic logic in [Kleene, Novikov]. In other words these axioms, restricted to the first-order case, are admissible in intuitionistic predicate logic.

1.2.4 Deduction laws

Well-deduced formulas are inductively generated by applying the following meta-rules of inference:

1. An axiom is a well-deduced formula.

2. If α and $\alpha \vdash \beta$ are well-deduced formulas, then β is a well-deduced formula.

3. If $[X]\alpha$ is a well-deduced formula and β is a formula, then $(X := \beta;\ \alpha)$ is a well-deduced formula.

Using certification-formulas such as

$$\alpha\sqrt{} \quad \simeq \quad \alpha \text{ is a well deduced formula,}$$

the above inductive definition can be presented as follows, but still outside the d-calculus itself:

1. $a\checkmark$,   for each axiom a

2. $[a,b]\left\|\dfrac{\left\|\dfrac{a}{b}\checkmark\right.}{\left\|\dfrac{a\checkmark}{b\checkmark}\right.}\right.\checkmark$, i.e. $[a,b]\left\|\dfrac{a\checkmark,\ \ \left\|\dfrac{a}{b}\checkmark\right.}{b\checkmark}\right.\checkmark$

3. $[X,a,b]\left|\dfrac{[X]a\checkmark,\ \ b}{X:=b;\ a\ \checkmark}\right.\checkmark$

Law2 has the same structure as that of *DistrThenThen* (Axiom 8), and is related to a predicative definition proposed [Martin-Löf] for an Automath-like metalanguage . Law3 corresponds, in classical formal systems, to the generation of axioms by instantiation of axiom schemes.

1.3   Controlled reduction of admissible formulas

Certain formulas, such as $(c; (c \vdash d))$, express proofs. Consider such a proof-formula $(\alpha; \varrho)$, and let β be the formula resulting from the reduction of $(\triangleright \alpha; \varrho)$. If α and ϱ are well derived, then β is well derived too. Thus, deductions and reductions respectively correspond to transformations and evaluations of programs.

1.3.1   Reductions as deductions

Reductions amount to specific, controlled deductions:

$$[a,b]\left(\left\|\dfrac{\triangleright a}{\triangleright b}\right.\ \vdash\ \left|\dfrac{a}{b}\right.\right),\qquad [a,b]\left|\dfrac{a;b}{a,b}\right.$$

$$[a,b]\left|\dfrac{a;b}{\triangleright a;b}\right.,\qquad [a,b]\dfrac{[X:=b]a}{\triangleright [X:=b]a},\qquad [a,b]\dfrac{X:=b;a}{\triangleright X:=b;a}$$

We use $\triangleright$ as a unary operator of reduction, rather than as a binary one, in order to keep "$\vdash$" as a unique derivation operator.

1.3.2   Reduction axioms

For application:

$$[a,b]\left|\dfrac{\triangleright a;\left|\dfrac{a}{b}\right.}{\triangleright b}\right.$$

More reduction axioms can be defined for application, by considering various other useful deduction rules, e.g. those based on resolution principles.

For instantiations and substitutions:

$$[a]\frac{\begin{array}{c} NoDef(X,a) \\ \hline \rhd[X:=b]a \end{array}}{\rhd a}, \qquad [a]\frac{\begin{array}{c} NoUse(X,a) \\ \hline \rhd X:=b;a \end{array}}{\rhd a}$$

$$[a,b,c]\frac{\begin{array}{c} HasDef(X,a\oplus b) \\ \hline \rhd\,[X:=c](a\oplus b) \end{array}}{(\rhd[X:=c]a)\oplus(\rhd[X:=c]b)}, \qquad [a,b,c]\frac{\begin{array}{c} HasUse(X,a\oplus b) \\ \hline \rhd\,X:=c;\ (a\oplus b) \end{array}}{(\rhd X:=c;\ a)\oplus(\rhd X:=c;\ b)}$$

$$[a,b]\frac{\begin{array}{c} HasDef(X,a) \\ X\neq Y \\ NoUse(Y,b) \\ \hline \rhd\,[X:=b](QY)a \end{array}}{(QY)(\rhd[X:=b]a)}, \qquad [a,b]\frac{\begin{array}{c} HasUse(X,a) \\ X\neq Y \\ NoUse(Y,b) \\ \hline \rhd\,X:=b;(QY)a \end{array}}{(QY)(\rhd X:=b;a)}$$

$$[a,b]\frac{\rhd[X:=b](QX)a}{\rhd\,X:=b\,;\,a}, \qquad [b]\frac{\rhd X:=b;X}{\rhd b} \tag{14}$$

To reduce an instantiation $[x:=b]a$ requires to find within a the binding occurrences of x, and then to apply the substitution $(x:=b;\ldots)$ within the scope of these occurrences. To apply a substitution $(x:=b;a)$ requires to find within a the free occurrences of x, and to replace these occurrences by b. Here is an illustration, written in a linear style:

$$\begin{aligned} &\rhd\,[x:=c]\ (\,[x](a,x)\mid[x](b|x)\,) \\ \vdash\ &\rhd\,[x:=c][x](a,x)\mid[x:=c][x](b|x) \\ \vdash\ &\rhd\,(x:=c;(a,x))\mid(x:=c;(b|x)) \\ \vdash\ &\rhd\,(a,c)|(b|c) \end{aligned}$$

Most of the above reduction axioms are presented as equivalences. In order to orient reductions, a reasonable and simple strategy is to ensure that each reduction step strictly decreases the maximum of the lengths of the formulas occurring in the scope of a reduction symbol $\rhd$. However this does not ensure confluence: as it stands, the reduction system is non-deterministic, and reductions can be inner-, outer-, left- or right-most.

1.4 Extensions to the current definition of the d-calculus

The examples presented in §§2,3 below use constructs which are not yet integrated within the working definition presented above. These constructs are among the following ones.

Recursive definitions are made available by relaxing the context conditions in §1.1.2: the scope of a variable defined in some definitions $\mathcal{D}$ now includes the formulas occurring in $\mathcal{D}$. For the time being, it is prudent to require that each recursive schema be monotone. The evaluation of recursive definitions is defined by the following generalization of axiom 14:

$$[a,b]\frac{\rhd\,[X:=b](QX)a}{\rhd\,[X:=b](\,\rhd X:=b;a)}$$

The instantiation $[X := b]$ is applied to the result of a first reduction of the substitution $(X := b; a)$, and this can be repeated until a reduct is obtained which contains no binding occurrence of X anymore.

Ordered tuples may be used. For instance, pairs are defined as usual and are noted $< a, b >$. Application is extended to pairs:

$$[a, b, c, d] \left| \frac{\triangleright \ < a, b > \ ; \ < c, d >}{< \ (\triangleright \ a; c) \ , \ (\triangleright \ b; d) \ >} \right.$$

Typed quantifications are described as follows:

$$[X : \alpha]\beta \ \simeq \ [X]\left|\frac{\alpha}{\beta}\right., \qquad X : \alpha : \ \beta \ \simeq \ X. \left| \begin{array}{c} \alpha \\ \beta \end{array} \right|$$

Quotation and antiquotation are defined and noted as in [Milner]:

If X is "abcd"
then $\uparrow X$ is abcd

Definitions can be used as formulas and be imported. In the scope of

$$Z := (X := \alpha, \ Y := \beta),$$

we have by convention

$$\textbf{use } Z. \ \gamma \ \simeq \ (X := \alpha, \ Y := \beta; \ \gamma)$$

Pattern matching is expressed by

$$\alpha :: \beta$$

which yields $\top$ if the formula α has the same syntactical structure as the formula β. The constant $\top$ is such that

$$\top \equiv \left|\frac{\perp}{\perp}\right., \qquad [a]\frac{\top \vdash a}{a}$$

Quantifiers can be constrained by pattern conditions:

$$[X :: \alpha]\beta \ \simeq \ [X]\left|\frac{X :: \alpha}{\beta}\right., \qquad X :: \alpha : \ \beta \ \simeq \ X. \left| \begin{array}{c} X :: \alpha \\ \beta \end{array} \right|$$

Sequences of deduction steps are expressed by formulas such as

$$a \vdash b \ \cdot \vdash c \ \cdot \vdash d \qquad \text{or} \qquad \begin{array}{c} a \\ \vdash b \\ \cdot \vdash c \\ \cdot \vdash d \end{array}$$

which are equivalent to

$$\left|\frac{a}{b}\right., \left|\frac{b}{c}\right., \left|\frac{c}{d}\right.$$

The integration of the above extensions with the working definition of §§1.1-1.3 needs care and should be guided by results in the area of logico-functional languages [Hindley and Seldin].

2 Examples

They serve to illustrate typical uses of the d-calculus. The first examples follow the working definition of §1 more strictly than the later ones, in which the extensions of §1.4 are applied.

2.1 Elementary reductions

In the scope of

$$g := [x](IsInt(x) \vdash x + 2),$$

we have

$$
\begin{array}{llll}
\triangleright g(3) & \simeq & \triangleright[x := 3]g & \cdot \vdash \quad \triangleright \; IsInt(3) \vdash 3 + 2 \\
& \vdash & \triangleright[x := 3][x](IsInt(x) \vdash x + 2) & \cdot \vdash \quad \triangleright \; \top \vdash 5 \\
& \cdot \vdash & \triangleright \; x := 3; (IsInt(x) \vdash x + 2) & \cdot \vdash \quad \triangleright \; 5
\end{array}
$$

The replacement of $IsInt(3)$ by $\top$ results from an application of axiom 13 using the formula $IsInt(3) \equiv \top$, which in turn is deduced from an auxiliary set of axioms defining integers; this subsidiary deduction is not detailed, but it is obtained in a similar way.

From now on, we shall usually leave out the reduction operator $\triangleright$ since it only affects the control, not the logic.

2.2 A deduction

In the context of §1.2.2, if we define

$$Syllogism := TransThen,$$

we may deduce

$$
\begin{array}{l}
[a := (p|q), b := (p,q), c := q] \; Syllogism \\
\vdash \; [a := (p|q), b := (p,q), c := q] \; TransThen
\end{array}
$$

$$
\cdot \vdash \; [a := (p|q), b := (p,q), c := q] \; [a, b, c]
\left.
\begin{array}{|l|l}
\dfrac{\big|\, a}{\big|\, b} & \dfrac{\big|\, b}{\big|\, c} \\
\hline
\multicolumn{2}{c}{\dfrac{\big|\, a}{\big|\, c}}
\end{array}
\right.
$$

$$
\cdot \vdash \; a := (p|q), b := (p,q), c := q;
\left.
\begin{array}{|l|l}
\dfrac{\big|\, a}{\big|\, b} & \dfrac{\big|\, b}{\big|\, c} \\
\hline
\multicolumn{2}{c}{\dfrac{\big|\, a}{\big|\, c}}
\end{array}
\right.
$$

$$
\cdot \vdash
\left.
\begin{array}{|l|l}
\dfrac{\big|\, p|q}{\big|\, p,q} & \dfrac{\big|\, p,q}{\big|\, q} \\
\hline
\multicolumn{2}{c}{\dfrac{\big|\, p|q}{\big|\, q}}
\end{array}
\right.
$$

This instantiation of an axiom yields a valid, but not helpful, formula.

2.3   A constructive function

If we define

$$Fib := [x] \begin{array}{|l} \quad\quad IsInt(x) \\ \hline \begin{array}{l|l} x = 0 | x = 1 & \quad x \geq 2 \\ \hline \quad\quad 1 & Fib(x-1) + Fib(x-2) \end{array} \end{array}$$

then a deduction with the following main steps can be obtained:

$$Fib(2) \quad \vdash \begin{array}{|c} \quad\quad \top \\ \hline \begin{array}{c|c} \bot & \quad \top \\ \hline 1 & Fib(1) + Fib(0) \end{array} \end{array}$$

$$\cdot \vdash Fib(1) + Fib(0) \quad\quad \cdot \vdash 1 + 1 \quad \cdot \vdash 2$$

The equivalences $(2 = 0|2 = 1) \equiv \bot$ and $(2 \geq 2) \equiv \top$ are derived by using an auxiliary set of axioms about integers.

2.4   A relational equivalent

Consider

$$IsFib := [x, y] \begin{array}{|l} \quad\quad\quad IsInt(x) \\ \hline \begin{array}{l|l} x = 0 | x = 1 & \quad\quad x \geq 2 \\ \hline \quad y = 1 & \begin{array}{l} IsFib(x-1, y1) \\ IsFib(x-2, y2) \\ \hline IsSum(y1, y2, y) \end{array} \end{array} \end{array}$$

Then the following property can be deduced if an adequate induction principle is available:

$$[m, n] \dfrac{IsFib(m, n)}{Fib(m) \vdash n}$$

2.5   A simple induction principle

$$NatInduc := [p] \begin{array}{|l} \quad IsIntPredicate(p) \\ \quad HasUse(X, p) \\ \hline \begin{array}{l|l} X := 0; p \quad, & \begin{array}{c} p \\ \hline X := X + 1; p \end{array} \\ \hline \quad\quad\quad [X]p \end{array} \end{array}$$

The syntactical constraints mentioned on the first line are usually left implicit.

2.6   A formal language

This example shows that the d-calculus also allows to express higher-order production systems. The concatenation operator is denoted by $\odot$, and strings are indicated between the symbols ⟨

and). Let us introduce the following definitions:

$$f := [n] \ (g(n)|f(n+1))$$

$$g := [n] \ h(\langle a \rangle, n) \ \odot \ h(\langle b \rangle, n) \ \odot \ h(\langle a \rangle, n)$$

$$h := [x, n] \left(\begin{array}{l} n = 1 \vdash x \\ n > 1 \vdash x \odot h(x, n-1) \end{array} \right)$$

Then we can deduce

$$h(a, 2) \ \vdash \ \langle aa \rangle$$
$$g(2) \ \vdash \ \langle aabbaa \rangle, \ \text{viz.} \ \langle a^2 b^2 a^2 \rangle$$
$$f(1) \ \vdash \ (\ \langle aba \rangle \ | \ \langle a^2 b^2 a^2 \rangle \ | \ldots | \ \langle a^n b^n a^n \rangle \ | f(n+1))$$

2.7 A proof-formula

Object theories, e.g. classical propositional calculus, can be defined in the d-calculus, and theorems in such theories can be derived from proofs expressed as d-terms. For example, we define as follows a subset of the classical propositional calculus, where only the connectors $\vee, \rightarrow, \neg$, are used, and we derive the commutativity of disjunction:

$$LittleTheory := \ \neg[], \ \ []\vee[], \ \ []\rightarrow[] \ .$$

$$
\boxed{
\begin{array}{ll}
ExDisj := [a, b, c] \dfrac{\begin{array}{c|c} a & b \\ \hline c & c \end{array}}{\begin{array}{c} a \vee b \\ \hline c \end{array}}, & TerNonDat := [a](\neg a \vee a) \\[2em]
InDisjL := [a, b] \dfrac{a}{a \vee b} & InDisjR := [a, b] \dfrac{b}{a \vee b} \\[1.5em]
InImpl := [a, b] \dfrac{\begin{array}{c} \vdash a \\ \hline b \end{array}}{a \rightarrow b} & PropImpl := [a] \dfrac{a \rightarrow b}{\neg a \vee b}
\end{array}
} \ \checkmark
$$

The above formula can be seen as a little theory defining $\neg, \vee, \rightarrow$. In this context, the following formula is valid, i.e. well deduced:

$$
Proof := [a, b] \ \boxed{
\begin{array}{l}
[a := b, b := a] \ (InDisjR, InDisjL); \\
[c := b \vee a] \ ExDisj; \\
[a := a \vee b, b := b \vee a] \ InImpl
\end{array}
} \ \checkmark
$$

The formula on the first line of the definiens is well deduced because of the following known property:

$$[u, v] \dfrac{[X]u, \ [X]v}{[X](u, v)}$$

which entails

$$[u, v, c] \dfrac{[X := c] \ ([X]u, [X]v)}{[X := c][X](u, v)}$$

The well-deduced formula *Proof* can be reduced as follows:

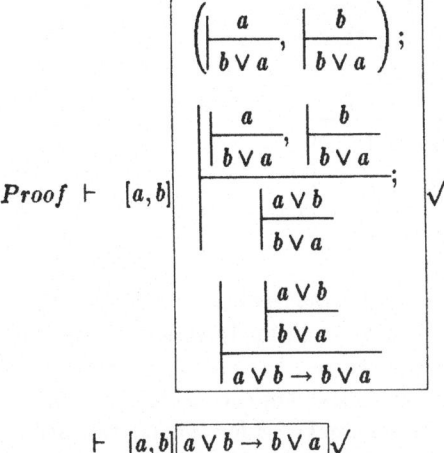

$$Proof \vdash [a,b]$$

$$\vdash [a,b]\boxed{a \vee b \rightarrow b \vee a}\surd$$

Hence the following definition can be added to the little theory above:

$$CommutDisj := [a,b](a \vee b \rightarrow b \vee a)\surd$$

This fact can be summarised by

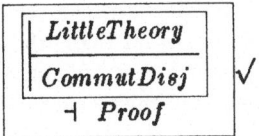

or by

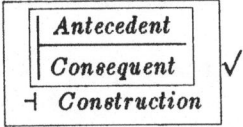

The important result is the validity of *CommutDisj*. The *Proof* is an auxiliary, albeit indispensable, information; it must be possible to show it or to hide it at will, in the same way as in the case of the implementation of a software module. The general pattern [Sintzoff 80,84a] is

$$\begin{array}{|l}\hline Antecedent \\ \hline Consequent \\ \hline \end{array}$$
$$\dashv\ Construction \quad \surd$$

and it occurs at many levels [Sintzoff 84b,85]: constructions can be programs, or development of programs, or derivations of development schemes, or proofs of useful theorems in a specific theory.

2.8 More or less constructive specifications of a function

The above examples illustrate the use of the d-calculus to express predicates, functions and production systems. Let us now show the continuity between expressions for constructions and for properties.

$$SortD := [s] \left| \begin{array}{l} \dfrac{IsSeq(s)}{t. \left| \begin{array}{l} IsOrdSeq(t) \\ IsPermut(t,s) \end{array} \right.} \end{array} \right.$$

$$SortF := [s] \left| \dfrac{IsSeq(s)}{\left| \dfrac{length(s) = 1}{s} \right., \left| \dfrac{length(s) > 1}{t.s1, s2 . \left| \begin{array}{l} t = merge(SortD(s1), SortD(s2)) \\ s = concat(s1, s2) \end{array} \right.} \right.} \right.$$

The more constructive *SortF* "calls" the less constructive *SortD*. Thus, it is possible to design a recursive sorting function which would apply various strategies at various recursion levels. The functions *concat* and *merge* can also be more or less constructive. The definition of *SortF* becomes fully constructive when all its components are. We could give inference rules to define well-constructible formulas, as done in §1.2.4 for defining well-deduced formulas.

The transition between forms denoting predicates and forms denoting expressions is carried out by using the following equivalence:

$$\begin{array}{l} y.\ y = f(x.p) \\ \equiv \quad y.x.\ ((y = f(x), p) \end{array}$$

3 Schemes of program development

The aim is to reexpress in the d-calculus known development schemes. Such expressions are tentative since the d-calculus is defined only partially; their role is precisely to guide this definition. As far as possible, no development scheme or method is given privileges; in particular, the fact that the d-calculus is related to intuitionistic logic does not imply that program derivation by proof pruning is a technique more important than other ones.

Design schemes usually include preconditions of applicability. If such preconditions are not provably met, the corresponding schemes of course cannot be applied.

3.1 Derivation of a modelling rule for data types

One of the main concepts used in [Jones] is a proof technique for modelling operations of data types. This proof technique is justified informally. We show here how it can itself be proved formally. The following well-deduced formula can be derived from axioms 2 and 6:

$$InPostAnd := [a, b] \left| \dfrac{a \vdash b}{a \vdash (a, b)} \right.$$

Consider then the well-deduced proof-formula

$$ProofMR := [\ p :: \left| \dfrac{c}{a} \right., \quad q :: \left| \dfrac{a}{b} \right., \quad r :: \left| \dfrac{c, b}{d} \right.\ ] \left| \begin{array}{l} ((p, q); \\ ([a := c, b := a, c := b]\ Syllogism; \\ [a := c, b := b]\ InPostAnd \quad),\ r); \\ [a := c,\ b := (c, b),\ c := d]\ Syllogism \end{array} \right.$$

We may apply it as follows:

$$[\,p:=\left|\frac{c}{a}\right., \quad q:=\left|\frac{a}{b}\right., \quad r:=\left|\frac{c,b}{d}\right.\,]\ ProofMR$$

$$\vdash\left(\left(\left|\frac{c}{b}\right.;\ [a:=c,b:=b]\ InPostAnd\right),\left|\frac{c,b}{d}\right.\right);\ [a:=c,b:=(c,b),c:=d]\ Syllogism$$

$$\cdot\vdash\left(\left|\frac{c}{c,b}\right.,\left|\frac{c,b}{d}\right.\right);\ [a:=c,b:=(c,b),c:=d]\ Syllogism$$

$$\cdot\vdash\left|\frac{c}{d}\right.$$

Hence, by the second axiom in (9),

$$ProofMR\ \vdash\ \left|\frac{\left|\frac{c}{a}\right.,\ \left|\frac{a}{b}\right.,\ \left|\frac{c,b}{d}\right.}{\left|\frac{c}{d}\right.}\right.\quad\cdot\vdash\ \left|\frac{\left|\frac{c}{a}\right.,\ c\vdash\left|\frac{b}{d}\right.}{\left|\frac{a}{b}\right.\vdash\left|\frac{c}{d}\right.}\right.$$

Let us now define

$$[f]\ \textbf{fits}\ [g]:=a,b,c,d.\left(\begin{array}{c} f::\left|\frac{a}{b}\right.\ ,\ g::\left|\frac{c}{d}\right. \\ c\vdash a\ ,\ c\vdash\left|\frac{b}{d}\right. \end{array}\right)$$

and

$$ModelRule:=[f,g]\left|\frac{f\ \textbf{fits}\ g}{f\vdash g}\right.$$

This *ModelRule* is well deduced because of the above well-deduced deductions; formally:

$$\left|\frac{\left|\frac{Axioms}{ModelRule}\right.}{\dashv\ ProofMR}\right.\quad\checkmark$$

3.2 Divide and conquer

We reexpress the scheme elaborated a.o. in [Smith], and show how to instantiate it in various examples of program design. This case study is worked out in [Nguyen 85]. As it is well known, the scheme for divide-and-conquer has a wide range of applicability.

3.2.1 General scheme

It can be defined as follows:

$$DivCon := [Spec, IsEl, ElSol, Comp, DeComp, CompSol]$$

$$
\frac{\begin{array}{l} [a]\left(\begin{array}{l} IsEl(a) \vdash Spec(a) = ElSol(a) \\ \neg IsEl(a) \vdash Comp(DeComp(a)) = a \end{array}\right) \\[2ex] [a,b]\left(\begin{array}{l} Spec(Comp(a,b)) \\ \quad = CompSol(Spec \textbf{ thru } (a,b)) \end{array}\right) \end{array}}{Prog := [a]\left(\begin{array}{l} IsEl(a) \vdash ElSol(a) \\ \neg IsEl(a) \vdash CompSol(Prog \textbf{ thru } (DeComp(a))) \end{array}\right)} \quad \checkmark
$$

By convention

$$f \textbf{ thru } (a,b) \equiv (f(a), f(b))$$

This scheme could itself be validated, thanks to a proof of $Prog \vdash Spec$.

3.2.2 Derivation of a mergesort-like program

We assume the context contains the definition of $SortD$ given in §2.8.

$$
SortProps := \left|\begin{array}{l} [a]\left(\begin{array}{l} LgthOne(a) \vdash SortD(a) = a \\ \neg LgthOne(a) \vdash concat(split(a)) = a \end{array}\right) \\[2ex] [a,b]\left(\begin{array}{l} SortD(concat(a,b)) \\ \quad = merge(SortD \textbf{ thru } (a,b)) \end{array}\right) \end{array}\right| \checkmark \ ;
$$

$$
DivConM := \left[\begin{array}{l} Spec := SortD, \ IsEl := LgthOne, \ ElSol := identity, \\ Comp := concat, \ DeComp := split, \ CompSol := merge \end{array}\right] DivCon \ \checkmark \ ;
$$

$$
DerivM := (\ SortProps \ ; \ DivConM \ ) \ \checkmark \ ;
$$

$$
SortM := [a]\left|\begin{array}{l} LgthOne(a) \vdash a \\ \neg LgthOne(a) \vdash merge(SortM \textbf{ thru } split(a)) \end{array}\right| ;
$$

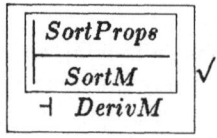

The result $SortM$ of this well-deduced derivation is well deduced provided the validity of $SortProps$ is ensured; here, the latter is assumed; an adequate theory of $split, concat, merge,$ should be referred to. Efficiency can be ensured by adding criteria for balanced decomposition in the definition of $DivCon$.

3.2.3 Remarks

In order to derive quicksort-like programs, the following instantiations should be used:

$$DeComp := orderedsplit, \quad CompSol := concat$$

In comparison with the merge-like sort above, there is more reordering during the problem decomposition but less during the solution composition.

The preconditions in the scheme $DivCon$ can be seen as the specification of an abstract type of decomposable problems. In this light, $DivConM$ defines a particular model of this abstract type. This view is related to the treatment of data types in a.o. [Mitchell].

A similar presentation can be made for a dynamic programming scheme. This allows for instance to derive in a straightforward way the general parsing algorithm, of cubic complexity, for context-free grammars.

3.3 Invariant-driven design

We show how to express techniques à la Dijkstra [Gries]. More substantial examples have been worked out in [Nguyen 86]. The main scheme is the following one:

$$IterDesign := [pre, post, X, init, invar, f, []\succ[]]$$

$$IsWellOrder([]\succ[])$$
$$pre \Rightarrow [X := init]invar$$
$$itercond \wedge invar \Rightarrow [X := f(X)]invar \wedge (X \succ f(X))$$
$$\neg itercond \wedge invar \Rightarrow post$$

$$X := init; \ \textbf{do} \ itercond \rightarrow X := f(X) \ \textbf{od}$$

The context must provide a theory of logical assertions and a theory of weakest preconditions for **do-od** programs; it is recognized that the d-calculus could have much in common with those object theories; this may justify the overloading of notations such as :=. The well-ordering $\succ$ is to be defined on the space of program states. To validate $IterDesign$ is to express a proof of

$$\begin{array}{|c|}
\hline
pre \\
\hline
post \\
\hline
\dashv \ p \\
\end{array} \ \checkmark$$

for any program p resulting from an application of $IterDesign$.

The use of the above scheme is facilitated by auxiliary, more specific rules such as the following one:

$$RangeInvar := [pre, post, X, r, a, b]$$

$$(X = a) \wedge r \Rightarrow post$$
$$pre \Rightarrow b \geq X \geq a$$

$$invar := (b \geq X \geq a) \wedge r$$
$$itercond := X > a$$
$$f := [X]X - 1$$
$$init := b$$
$$[x] \succ [y] := x - a > y - a$$

The composition of *RangeInvar* and *IterDesign* allows to derive linear-search programs.

Invariant-driven development can be seen as an instance of induction-based design, which also underlies the Burstall-Darlington transformational techniques and the derivation of programs from constructive proofs. These connections are not yet formally expressed by d-terms, but the expression of such transformational techniques has been investigated in [Jähnichen].

3.4 Type-driven design

The treatment of the modelling rule, in §3.1, is a first example of this topic. As another example, we express the gist of the strategy proposed in [Ehrich] for deriving representations of abstract data types:

$$ReprE := [abstr, concr, inverse, enricha, enrichc, mid] .$$

$$
\begin{array}{l}
enricha \vdash \dfrac{abstr}{mid} \\[2mm]
enrichc \vdash \dfrac{concr}{mid} \\[2mm]
\hline
enricha;\ inverse(enrichc)
\end{array}
$$

Additional preconditions are left implicit: $abstr, concr, mid$ are types; $enricha, enrichc$ are type transformers; $inverse$ is a functional on type transformers. The context must provide a theory of abstract data types, of enrichments, and of inversions. To validate the above scheme is to prove

$$
[a, c, i] \left| \begin{array}{c} \left| \dfrac{a}{c} \right. \\ \dashv\ ReprE(a,c,i) \end{array} \right. \quad \checkmark
$$

This can be done by showing that

$$(\triangleright a;\ ReprE(a,c,i)) \vdash \triangleright c$$

This example, admittedly very sketchy, illustrates the goal of expressing large development schemes by small d-formulas.

Specifications of abstract data types in the d-calculus should follow the idea of expressing them as higher-order existential formulas [Cardelli, Mitchell, Nait Abdallah]. Thus, a given abstract data type is to be defined according to the following pattern:

$$ADT := Opns, Obj.Laws$$

An example is the *LittleTheory* in §2.7.

The representation of an abstract data type by a concrete one is desribed as an instantiation:

$$
\begin{array}{l}
Rep := \quad (Opns := ConcOpns, Obj := ConcObj) \\
CDT := [Rep]ADT
\end{array}
$$

To prove the validity of the representation is to verify the validity of the instantiated laws. Then, the existence of a valid instance, i.e. the concrete data type, entails the validity of the abstract data type: a valid witness of the existential form has been constructed.

This can be extended to the case of parametrised abstract data types:

$$PADT := [Params]Opns, Obj.Laws$$
$$PRep := (Params := ConcParams)$$
$$ORep := (Opns := ConcOpns, Obj := ConcObj)$$
$$PCDT := [PRep][ORep]PADT$$

The technical elaboration of these simple-minded views requires an auxiliary calculus of *definitions*, and an adequate expression of relations between theories.

Last but not least, some form of typing scheme could be necessary in the d-calculus itself in order to prove consistency.

Acknowledgement. The above work has much benefitted from cooperation with Ph. de Groote, D. Dzierzgowski, R. Jacquart, T.T. Nguyen, P.-Y. Schobbens and colleagues of the ToolUse project.

4 References

Abrial, J.R., Programming as a mathematical exercise, in: C.A.R. Hoare and J.C. Shepherdson (eds.), *Mathematical Logic and Programming languages*, Prentice-Hall, 1985.

Bauer, F., et al., *The Munich Project CIP, Vol. I*, LNCS183, Springer, 1985.

Bourbaki, N., *Théorie des Ensembles*, Hermann, Paris, 1970.

Burstall, R.M., and J.A. Darlington, A transformation system for developing recursive programs, *JACM* **24**,1(1977)44-67.

Burstall, R.M., and B.Lampson, A kernel language for abstract data types and modules, *Proc. Symp. on Semantics of Data Types*, LNCS173, Springer, 1984.

Cardelli, L., A polymorphic λ-calculus with type: type, R10, Digital Systems Research Center, Palo Alto CA, 1986.

Coquand, Th., and G.Huet, Constructions: a higher order proof system, *EURO-CAL85*, LNCS203, Springer, 1985.

Constable, R.L., and al., *Implementing Mathematics with the Nuprl Proof Development System*, Prentice Hall, 1986.

Curry, H.B., and R.Feys, *Combinatory Logic Vol. I*, North-Holland, 1958.

de Bruijn, N.G., Lambda-calculus notation with nameless dummies, *Indag. Math.* **34**, 5(1972),381-392.

de Bruijn, N.G., A survey of the project Automath, in: J.P.Seldin and J.R.Hindley (eds.), *To H.B.Curry: Essays in Combinatory Logic, Lambda Calculus and Formalism*, Academic Press, 1980.

de Groote, Ph., Peirce-like formalization of intuitionistic propositional logic, RR86-12, Unité d'Informatique, University of Louvain, 1986.

de Groote, Ph., Fatima A. Hussain, R. Jacquart, S. Jähnichen, T.T. Nguyen, M. Sintzoff, and M. Weber, Requirements and feasibility studies for a development language, Esprit510(ToolUse)-T32, RR86-06, Unité d'Informatique, University of Louvain, 1986.

Delsarte, Ph., D.Snyers and A.Thayse, Preuves de théorèmes basées sur des propositions de la logique de Boole, *C.R. 5ème Congrès Reconnaissance des Formes et Intelligence Artificielle*, AFCET, Paris, 1985, 869-879.

Ehrich, H.D., On the theory of specification, implementation, and parametrization of abstract data types, *JACM* **29**,1(1982), 206-227.

Goad, Ch.A., *Computational uses of the manipulation of formal proofs*, Ph.D. thesis, Computer Sci. Dept, Stanford University, 1980.

Gries, D., *The Science of Programming*, Springer, 1981.

Hanna, F.K., and N. Daeche, Purely functional implementation of a logic, *Proc. 8th Intern. Conf. on Automated Deduction*, Springer LNCS 230, 1986, 598-607.

Hermes, H., *Introduction to Mathematical Logic*, Springer, 1973.

Hindley, J.R., and J.P. Seldin, *Introduction to Combinators and λ-Calculus*, Cambridge University Press, 1986.

Jähnichen S., Fatima A. Hussain, and M.Weber, Program development using a design calculus, *Proc. ESPRIT Technical Week 86*, North-Holland, 1986.

Jones, C.B., *Systematic Software development using VDM*, Prentice-Hall, 1986.

Kleene, S.C., *Introduction to Metamathematics*, North-Holland, 1952.

Manna, Z., and R.Waldinger, Special relations in automated deduction, *JACM* **33**,1 (1986), 1-59.

Martin-Löf, P., Amendment and addition to the intuitionistic theory of types, Lecture, University of Louvain, April 1986.

Miller, D., and A. Felty, An integration of resolution and natural deduction theorem proving, *Proc. 5th Natl Conf. on Artif. Intelligence AAAI86*, Morgan Kaufmann, Los Altos CA, 1986, 198-202.

Milner, R., The use of machines to assist in rigorous proof, in: C.A.R. Hoare and J.C. Shepherdson (eds.), *Mathematical Logic and Programming languages*, Prentice-Hall, 1985.

Mitchell, J.C., Representation independence and data abstraction, *Proc. 13th Conf. on Principles of Progr. Languages*, ACM, 1986.

Murray, N., Completely non-clausal theorem proving, *J. Artif. Intelligence* **18**(1982), 67-85.

Nait Abdallah, M.A., Procedures in Horn-clause programming, *3rd Intern. Conf. on Logic Programming*, Springer LNCS225, 1986, 433-447.

Nguyen, T.T., Divide and conquer strategy, RR85-11, Unité d'Informatique, University of Louvain, 1985.

Nguyen, T.T., Development of iterative programs, RR86-10, Unité d'Informatique, University of Louvain, 1986.

Nordström, B., Programming in constructive set theory: some examples, *Proc. Conf. on Functional Programming Languages and Computer Architecture*, ACM, 1981.

Novikov, P.S., *Konstruktivnaya Matematicheskaya Logika s Tochki Zreniya Klassicheskoi*, Nauka, 1977.

Peirce, Ch.S., Existential Graphs, in: Ch.Hartshorne and P.Weiss (eds.), *Collected Papers of Charles Saunders Peirce*, Vol. IV, Harvard University Press, 4th ed., 1974.

Pepper, P., A simple calculus for program transformations, Institut für Informatik, Technical University of Munich, 1984.

Schütte, K., *Proof Theory*, Springer, 1977.

Sintzoff, M., Suggestions for composing and specifying program design decisions, *Proc. 4th Symp. on Programming*, LNCS70, Springer, 1980.

Sintzoff, M., Proof-oriented and applicative valuations in definitions of algorithms, *Proc. Conf. on Functional Languages and Computer Architecture*, ACM, 1981.

Sintzoff, M., Understanding and expressing software construction, in: P.Pepper (ed.), *Program Transformation and Programming Environments*, Springer, 1984.

Sintzoff, M., Exploratory proposals for a calculus of software development, RR84-2,

Unité d'Informatique, University of Louvain; Workshop on Combining Specification Methods, Denmark, 1984.

Sintzoff, M., Desiderata for a design calculus, RR85-13, Unité d'Informatique, University of Louvain; Workshop on Specification and Derivation of Programs, Sweden, 1985.

Smith, D.R., Top-down synthesis of divide-and-conquer algorithms, *J. Artif. Intelligence* **27**,1(1985).

Sowa, J.F., *Conceptual Structures*, Addison Wesley, 1984.

Traugott, J., Nested resolution, *Proc. 8th Intern. Conf. Automated Deduction*, Springer LNCS 230, 1986, 394-402.

Models and logic of MOS circuits

by
Glynn Winskel
University of Cambridge,
Computer Laboratory,
Corn Exchange Street,
Cambridge CB2 3QG.

Abstract

Various models of hardware have been proposed though virtually all of them do not model circuits adequately enough to support and provide a formal basis for many of the informal arguments used by designers of MOS circuits. Such arguments use rather crude discrete notions of strength—designers cannot be too finicky about precise resistances and capacitances when building a chip—as well as subtle derived notions of information flow between points in the circuit. One model, that of R.E.Bryant, tackles such issues in reasonable generality and has been used as the basis of several hardware simulators. However Bryant's model is not compositional. These lectures introduce Bryant's ideas and present a compositional model for the behaviour of MOS circuits when the input is steady, show how this leads to a logic, and indicate the difficulties in providing a full and accurate treatment for circuits with changing inputs.

0. Introduction.

There are some tricky issues in the verification of hardware. We all know that verification of any device can only be done in terms of a model for its behaviour. However it is very easy to forget that verification depends crucially on the accuracy of the model. The verification of hardware has been very successful when the model assumes there are basic trusted functional devices out of which all other devices are built (see *e.g.* [Gor1, She, Mos] and the classical work on implementing Boolean functions). The mathematics of functions and functional programs is well–understood so it makes good sense to translate hardware into functions; they can be reasoned about or even run as functional programs to simulate the behaviour of the hardware. Fortunately this kind of model is often appropriate and proofs of properties of hardware amount to large but essentially trivial manipulations of expressions for functions or relations. Sometimes, however, the physical nature of the device intrudes. Designers, generally indifferent to slick proofs of correctness, use their knowledge of the physics of devices to improve performance or layout. Designers in metal oxide semiconductor (MOS) technology can use a variety of techniques. They exploit bidirectionality and the fact that signals do not have uniform strengths to improve their designs. Most approaches model such designs in an *ad hoc* way; directionality is often imposed, rather than derived, and effects due to signal strength are fudged. In what sense can a verification, based on such a model be trusted? After all directions can only be assigned correctly when the circuit behaviour is understood thoroughly and an incorrect assignment can easily lead to an incorrect prediction about the circuit's behaviour. As a last resort there are the precise models of

NATO ASI Series, Vol. F36
Logic of Programming and Calculi of Discrete Design
Edited by M. Broy
© Springer-Verlag Berlin Heidelberg 1987

physics but, even aside from whether these are tractable or not, they are often far too detailed. A designer cannot be finicky about the precise resistance or capacitance to be realised in a VLSI chip; designs should be fairly robust in order to tolerate variations in manufacture. There is a need for a model and proof system for circuits which while close to the logical behaviour of hardware devices also captures the effects used by designers.

In these lectures we shall look at the most striking problems with many of the models in use and attempt to remedy their faults. In addressing these problems we shall make use of the ideas in R.E.Bryant's model of MOS circuits. Bryant's ideas have been developed chiefly with the aim of accurate simulation in mind and they are not directly suitable as a basis for a proof system for circuits. We shall work towards achieving this. Firstly, we illustrate some of the problems that arise in other approaches to modelling circuits.

1. Relational models and their problems.

Modelling circuits as functions can often impose an unnatural directionality and lead to inaccurate models which predict the wrong behaviour. Instead we might try to model circuits as some form of relation. This is the course followed in [Gor] and less explicitly in [Mos]. It should be mentioned that although we base our criticism on the work [Gor] this is largely because it is there the problems are shown–up clearly, in their basic form. Essentially the same difficulties arise in the treatments [Mos, Mi]. Incidentally, all the approaches [Gor, Mi, Mos, Sh] seem to cope well at higher levels of abstraction.

Consider a CMOS inverter:

The effect of the inverter is to output at β the inverse of the value input at γ. We illustrate for this simple example how one expresses and argues in the framework of [Gor2,3] that the circuit drawn meets this specification.

The circuit is built out of two kinds of transistors. A p-type transistor $ptran(\alpha, \beta, \gamma)$, generally drawn as

is a device which, when the voltage value at the gate is low, $i.e.$ $V\gamma = L$, connects α and β, so $V\alpha = V\beta$. When the value at γ is high, $V\gamma = H$, the points α and β are disconnected so we cannot say what the relation is between α and β—it all depends on what they are connected to. The other kind of transistor, an n–type transistor $ntran(\beta, \delta, \gamma)$, drawn

behaves in a converse fashion; when $V\gamma = H$, β and δ are connected and $V\beta = V\delta$, and when $V\gamma = L$ they are disconnected. In approaches like [Gor2,3, Mos] a circuit (and hardware in general) is modelled by a relation between values at the significant points of the circuit. This is expressed as an assertion. So in the work [Gor2,3] the assertions associated with the two transistors are

$$ptran(\alpha, \beta, \gamma) \equiv (V\gamma = L \rightarrow V\alpha = V\beta),$$
$$ntran(\beta, \delta, \gamma) \equiv (V\gamma = H \rightarrow V\beta = V\delta).$$

(We use $\equiv$ to mean definitional equality; the left–hand side stands for the right–hand side.)

Two kinds of sources are used in the CMOS inverter. *Power* connected at α is regarded as maintaining the voltage value as high at α and *ground* (or *earth*) at δ maintains the value at low. The corresponding assertions are:

$$Pow\ \alpha \equiv (V\alpha = H),$$
$$Gnd\ \delta \equiv (V\delta = L).$$

So each component is described by an assertion about values at the points with which it is associated. Their composition, got by joining points in common, meets all the relations of the components, and so satisfies the conjunction:

$$ptran(\alpha, \beta, \gamma) \wedge ntran(\beta, \delta, \gamma) \wedge Pow\ \alpha \wedge Gnd\ \delta$$

For the inverter we wish to hide the points α and δ from the environment. This is achieved by existential quantification to give the following assertion for the CMOS inverter:

$$\text{Inv}(\gamma, \beta) \equiv \exists V\alpha \exists V\delta.\ ptran(\alpha, \beta, \gamma) \wedge ntran(\beta, \delta, \gamma) \wedge Pow\ \alpha \wedge Gnd\ \delta$$

The CMOS inverter is intended to implement the specification:

$$\text{Spec}(\gamma, \beta) \equiv (V\gamma = H \rightarrow V\beta = L) \wedge (V\gamma = L \rightarrow V\beta = H)$$

A simple proof using well-known rules of logic shows

$$\text{Inv}(\gamma, \beta) \rightarrow \text{Spec}(\gamma, \beta).$$

We can prove the assertion $\text{Inv}(\gamma, \beta)$ implies $\text{Spec}(\gamma, \beta)$. In this sense we can prove $\text{Inv}(\gamma, \beta)$ implements $\text{Spec}(\gamma, \beta)$. To recap: We have described the behaviour of circuits by assertions, their composition by conjunction, hiding of points by existential quantification and taken implementation as implication between the assertions for the circuit and its specification.

This general scheme can be followed equally well for dynamically changing circuits subject to voltages which change over time [Gor2, 3]. The only change is to model a circuit as a relation between histories of voltage values at the points of interest (histories are functions from time $0, 1, \cdots, t, \cdots$ to $\{H, L\}$) taking *e.g.* the assertion for a p–type transistor to be

$$ptran(\alpha, \beta, \gamma) \equiv \forall t. \ V(\gamma, t) = L \rightarrow V(\alpha, t) = V(\beta, t).$$

The approach is noteworthy because it does not impose an unrealistic directionality on devices as would for example be forced in the approach [Sh] were it to tackle such low–level circuits. The model and logic are also compositional; one can reason about the behaviour of circuits in terms of the behaviour of their components. A similar scheme is followed in [Mos], but there assertions in a temporal logic are used instead.

Unfortunately, there is a major deficiency in this approach—natural and useful as it is in many examples. According to this scheme a "short circuit" implements any specification! A short circuit, achieved most simply, by joining power and ground together at a point α is described by the assertion

$$Pow \ \alpha \land Gnd \ \alpha$$

But $Pow \ \alpha \land Gnd \ \alpha$ is equivalent to $V\alpha = H \land V\alpha = L$, and because H and L are assumed unequal, this is equivalent to ff, the logical value false. Thus $Pow \ \alpha \land Gnd \ \alpha$, like ff, implies every assertion and so "implements" any specification whatsoever.

Several ways have been suggested to get around this undesirable situation. Sticking with the above method of modelling circuits by assertions, the only course is to use some other notion of implementation. In some contexts it appears reasonable to say a circuit implements a specification if the associated assertions are equivalent (see [Gor2]). But following that line would, in general, lead to unnecessarily detailed specifications. Another suggestion, discussed in [CGM], is to say a circuit $circ(\iota, o)$ with input values $V\iota$ and output values Vo, correctly implements a specification $spec(\iota, o)$ iff

$$(\forall V\iota, \ Vo. \ circ(\iota, o) \rightarrow spec(\iota, o)) \ \land \ (\forall V\iota \exists Vo. \ circ(\iota, o)).$$

A circuit meeting such a requirement cannot be equivalent to ff for any particular input value. But this solution depends on having clearly defined input and output points. It is hard to see, if this were so at every stage in constructing a design, how the method of construction could allow short–circuits to be formed, and any method which bans short–circuits outright is too restrictive to provide a general model. Another possibility, suggested in [F], is to use the power of higher order logic and make specifications of higher type than circuit behaviours. This proposal has promise but has not yet led a calculus for reasoning about circuits. Most significant of all, each of these suggestions fails to face the fact that voltage values other than high and low can appear in designs, often quite innocently, without trivialising their behaviour.

We look for a model of circuits which can handle voltage values other than just high and low, and in particular treat short circuits. When a source of power and ground are connected together they give rise to a voltage which has an indeterminate effect when applied to the gates of transistors. We can take a voltage to have value X when it lies in a region between those corresponding to H and L. Similarly we can take a voltage at a point to have a value $\emptyset$ when the point is not connected to any significant sources of charge. It will be useful to order the values $H, L, X, \emptyset$ as

$$\bullet X$$

$$H\bullet \qquad\qquad \bullet L$$

$$\bullet \emptyset$$

(Note this order is not directly related to the underlying order on voltages, measured as reals.) A point connected just to power takes the value H, just to ground the value L, to both the value X and to no sources the value $\emptyset$. Can our earlier ideas be adapted to cope with these extra values? For the composition of assertions to be conjunction we now require

$$Pow\ \alpha \equiv V\alpha \geq H,$$
$$Gnd\ \alpha \equiv V\alpha \geq L.$$

In this way we allow for the effect of the environment on the value at α. Then the conjunction $Pow\ \alpha \wedge Gnd\ \alpha$ is equivalent to $V\alpha = X$, as required, and not to ff. Unfortunately hiding can no longer be treated as simple $\exists$–quantification. For example, connecting and hiding a power source to the gate γ of an n-type transistor $ntran(\alpha, \beta, \gamma)$ should yield a circuit equivalent in behaviour to a wire between α and β. However $ntran(\alpha, \beta, \gamma)$ is still described by

$$ntran(\beta, \delta, \gamma) \equiv (V\gamma = H \rightarrow V\beta = V\delta),$$

for the same reasons as before, so using $\exists$-quantification to hide we obtain

$$\exists V\gamma.\ Pow\ \gamma \wedge ntran(\alpha, \beta, \gamma)$$

which is

$$\exists V\gamma.\ V\gamma \geq H \wedge (V\gamma = H \rightarrow V\alpha = V\beta).$$

This does not imply $V\alpha = V\beta$, the assertion we would like, because of the possibility that $V\gamma = X$.

The above example might suggest that when we hide a node the value associated with the node should be the least possible—to rule out the possibility that $V\gamma = X$ in the example above. However, there are examples where this does not work. Consider hiding γ in the following circuit:

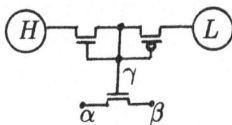

It is unclear whether we should hide γ with $V\gamma$ taking the value H, L, X or $\emptyset$—all are possible.

One way to manage the new value X and still treat hiding by $\exists$–quantification is to impose enough directionality on devices so they can be modelled as functions. Again, this suffers the drawback of leading to an unrealistic model. There is no easy fix without complicating the relational model. We need somehow to express the fact that the values associated with a hidden point are precisely those which are maintained by connections to sources. We shall address this problem and the related one of providing a model which deals correctly with signal strengths.

2. Signal strengths.

In NMOS technology p–type transitors are not available so inverters are constructed in a different way. An NMOS inverter has the following design

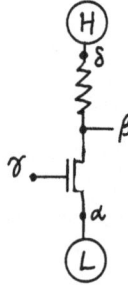

The design uses a strong resistance

$$\beta \cdot\!\!\text{\Large www}\!\!\cdot \delta$$

connected to power. In NMOS this is implemented as a pull–up transistor. The behaviour of the inverter is remarkably subtle for its size (see [MC, MD]). In those environments where the point β is not connected to any other sources, the inverse of the value $V\gamma$, input at γ, is output as $V\beta$ at β, so as a makeshift description of its behaviour we can take:

$$V\gamma = L \rightarrow V\beta = H \,\wedge$$
$$V\gamma = H \rightarrow V\beta = L.$$

Later in section 4, after we have given the semantics of circuits and enriched the class of assertions, we can provide a complete description of its behaviour and, in particular, see what value $V\beta$ takes for input $V\gamma = X$. The informal English description of how the inverter works is sometimes given as follows:

> When γ is low the n–type transistor disconnects so the only voltage contribution to β is from the power source so β is high.

> When γ is high the transistor connects so there is a voltage contribution of low from ground and a voltage contribution of high from power, weakened however by the large resistor, so the contribution from ground dominates and the net effect is to make β low.

Though this argument is perhaps not convincing at first, it can be justified by a simple application of Ohm's law. Suppose γ is high. Then α and β are connected with a very small resistance r relative to the large resistance R between β and δ. Let $v_\alpha, v_\beta, v_\delta$ be the voltage values (real numbers) at the corresponding points. By Ohm's law we see

$$\frac{v_\beta - v_\alpha}{v_\delta - v_\beta} = \frac{Ir}{IR} = \frac{r}{R}$$

which we have assumed is very small. Because v_α is safely inside the half–open interval qualifying as high, taking R large enough ensures v_β is high too.

It is often convenient to use the inverse notion of conductance instead of resistance. In the literature (*e.g.* [B, Hay]), sources are pictured as transmitting signals to points of a circuit. The signals not only have a value—$H, L, X, \emptyset$—but also a strength depending on the conductance strength of the path along which the signal has travelled. These ideas generalise when signals from capacitance, another source of charge, are considered.

The NMOS inverter illustrates a principle used in circuit design:

A signal from power or ground via a strong conductance overrides a signal via a relatively weak conductance.

It is not unusual for designs to use three ranks of conductance strengths, a signal via a conductance in one rank is overridden by a signal via a conductance in a rank strictly above it.

Extra signal strengths arise from capacitance. A simple dynamic register takes the form

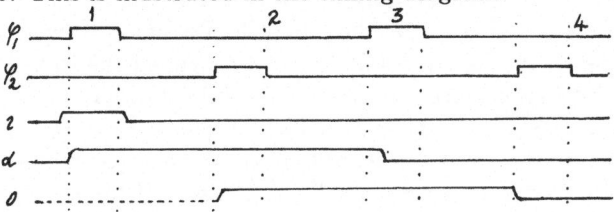

in which use is made of the high capacitance cap^α at the node α. The points ϕ_1 and ϕ_2 are connected to clocks which alternately send pulses of high and low voltage. They are out of phase as shown in the timing diagram below. If a signal, say from power, is present at a pulse of ϕ_1, then the left transistor connects and the right transistor disconnects and whatever charge was stored at cap^α is overridden by the current supplied from ι. This assumes the clock pulse of ϕ_1 is long enough for the opposite charge stored in cap^α to drain away. Then when ϕ_1 goes low both transistors are disconnecting and cap^α stores a high voltage. This is delivered at o at the next rise of the clock ϕ_2. Assuming node α has a very high capacitance relative to o, the net effect is to produce a high voltage at o. This is illustrated in the timing diagram.

More succinctly we can describe the behaviour by

$$\forall t.\ V(o, t+1) = V(\iota, t)$$

where we take a discrete model of time with the high pulses of ϕ_1 and ϕ_2 corresponding to alternate numbers.

We used two principles to explain the behaviour of the dynamic register:

A signal from power or ground overrides a signal from a capacitance.

A signal from a large capacitance overrides a signal from a relatively weak capacitance.

A circuit design may involve a range of signal strengths which give a discrete measure of the current driving capability in the analogue circuit. The strength order is derived from a deliberately crude ranking of resistances and capacitances. Two resistances R and R' are assigned conductance strengths g, g' respectively, with $g < g'$, if the ratio R/R' is *very large*. Then, arguing by Ohm's law, as we did before, if two resistances R and R' of strength g and g' are connected in series the resulting resistance $R + R'$ should be assigned conductance strength $g \cdot g'$, the *minimum* of g and g'. This is because, for example, if R/R' is very large then so is $(R + R')/R'$. Connected in parallel their resulting resistance, $RR'/(R + R')$, should be assigned strength $g + g'$, the *maximum* of g and g'. We would like to conclude that whenever we encounter a chain of resistances, of strengths $g_1, g_2, \ldots, g_n$, in series then we can regard it as equivalent to a single resistance of strength $\Pi\{g_1, \ldots, g_n\}$, the minimum strength along the chain. We cannot quite do this because "very large" is a vague concept; even though R/R' is very large R/nR' need not be. The point is that with respect to a particular design a very large number L can be chosen (to stand for "very large") so that the number of times resistances are placed in series or parallel *in the design* has no significant effect. Still, we should bear in mind that such problems can arise through our choosing to work with an abstract strength order, and that without care they can lead to inaccuracies in the model.

In a similar way capacitances are ranked in a total order of capacitance strengths. The signal stored by a capacitance of strength k is overridden by one from a capacitance of strength k' with $k < k'$. As we have observed, signals from sources override those due to capacitance so we arrive at the concept of a *strength order* as consisting of two finite sets $K = \{k_1, \ldots, k_m\}$ and and $G = \{g_1, \ldots, g_n\}$ in a total order

$$0 < k_1 < \cdots < k_m < g_1 < \cdots < g_n < \infty.$$

We use 0, zero strength, to stand for a strength of a negligible signal, from zero capacitance or a non–conductance, and ∞ to be the strength of a signal from a source via a perfect conductance. The restriction $\mathbf{K} = (K \cup \{0\}, \leq)$, is called the *capacitance order* and its elements are called *capacitance strengths*. The restriction $\mathbf{G} = (G \cup \{0, \infty\}, \leq)$ is called the *conductance order*, with elements called *conductance strengths*. Often we shall write a strength order as $\mathbf{S}$, and sometimes, when we wish to emphasise the conductance and capacitance strengths as $\mathbf{S}_{K,G}$. We shall use $s \cdot s'$ for the minimum and

$s + s'$ for the maximum of two strengths s and s'. We can write the minimum of a set of strengths A as ΠA and their maximum as ΣA.

Recall the lattice of values:

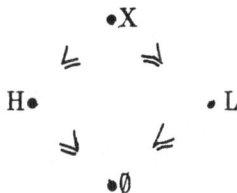

The value $\emptyset$ is associated with points which are at 0 strength so they are not connected to any significant sources of current or charge. Sometimes it is said that such points "float" because they adopt, or float to, the value of whatever they are connected to. We can call the $\emptyset$ value *floating*, though sometimes we use it in contexts where the intuition suggesting this name is not appropriate. Values now form a finite lattice. We use $U + U'$ for the join (or least upper bound) of two values U, U', $U \cdot U'$ for their meet, and ΣA, and ΠA, for the join, respectively meet, of a set of values A. (Our notation is thus consistent with that for the strength order considered as a lattice.)

Consider how signals are transmitted through a resistance between α and β of strength g. Suppose a signal of strength g', a conductance strength, and value $V \in \{H, L\}$ is applied to one end α of the resistance. By our earlier observation concerning resistances in series, the resulting signal at β has strength $g \cdot g'$ and value V.

If instead a signal of strength k, a capacitance strength, and value V is applied at α, assuming the resistance has negligible capacitance, the resulting signal at β is the same, with strength still k and value V.

In both situations a signal of strength s and value V, applied at α gives rise to a signal of strength $s \cdot g$ and value V at β. A signal of strength $s > g$ is cut–down to a signal of strength g while a signal of strength $s \leq g$ is unchanged.

Notice that these assumptions are dependent on connections lasting long enough for the charges in capacitances to reach stable levels. We shall have cause to examine this assumption more carefully later in the conclusion.

We have said that directionality in circuits should be derived rather than imposed. Where is this directionality to come from? It comes from the effects of resistance. Consider a resistance of conductance strength g between points α and β in some environment in which the strength of the signal at α is $S\alpha$ and that at β is $S\beta$. Assume too that the associated values are $V\alpha$ and $V\beta$ in $\{H, L, X, \emptyset\}$. We know from the behaviour of resistances, considering the transmission of signals from α to β that

$$S\alpha \cdot g \leq S\beta$$

(and similarly that $S\beta \cdot g \leq S\alpha$).

In the case when $S\alpha \cdot g < S\beta$ the signal from α is overridden and so has no effect on that at β. On the other hand, if $S\alpha \cdot g = S\beta$ then the signal from α is not overridden and has an effect on that at β. Values "flow" from α to β and so $V\alpha \leq V\beta$. In particular if $V\alpha = H$ then $V\beta = H$, or X if β happens also to be connected to ground. There is a connection, possibly one–way, between α and β, and we can write this suggestively as $\alpha \rightsquigarrow \beta$. We have $\beta \rightsquigarrow \alpha$ as well only if $S\beta \cdot g = S\alpha$. It is easy to check that elements of this "flow relation" compose, so if $\alpha \rightsquigarrow \beta$ and $\beta \rightsquigarrow \gamma$ then $\alpha \rightsquigarrow \gamma$. For this more general understanding of the flow relation we still have

$$\alpha \rightsquigarrow \beta \rightarrow V\alpha \leq V\beta.$$

It is helpful to think of the strength function S as giving a "height" of each point, and indeed

$$\alpha \rightsquigarrow \beta \rightarrow S\beta \leq S\alpha,$$

so flow is never "uphill". This understanding accounts for the following assignment of flows, strengths and values:

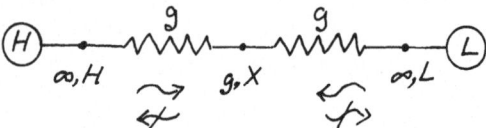

It is the flow relation, rather than the graph of conductances, which plays the central control in analysing the behaviour of circuits.

This exposition has been based largely on Bryant's work (see [B]). The paper [Hay] deals with similar ideas but the model it presents seems only to apply in situations where the components can be understood as functions with definite input and output ports. Our "flow relation" corresponds to Bryant's idea of "unblocked path" in a steady state. Note our subsequent presentation will be markedly different than Bryant's. This is because we shall develop a compositional model, one on which we can base a proof system structured by the way circuits are built–up.

3. States of circuits—static configurations.

Assume a particular strength order $\mathbf{S} = \mathbf{S}_{K,G}$.

We explain the intuition behind the definition of static configuration. Imagine a circuit connected to some environment via points Λ. Assume that in this environment the circuit has settled into a steady state. The definition of static configuration is intended to formalise this notion, picking out those features essential for the compositional account of circuit behaviour that follows. Note here we ignore the possibility that a circuit may never settle into a steady state in an environment. This model of circuits can be seen as analogous to those models of programs which only capture their partial correctness.

In a static configuration each point of a circuit is associated with a signal with a certain strength and value. So each point α is associated with with a strength $S\alpha \in \mathbf{S}$ and a resultant value $V\alpha \in \mathbf{V}$. Some of this signal may be contributed by sources inside the circuit; the internal contribution at α can be recorded by a value $I\alpha \in \mathbf{V}$.

Of course points are connected to each other according to the state of transistors and the connections have certain conductance strengths. This gives rise to a flow relation $\rightsquigarrow$ between points, though in the rather indirect way we saw in the last section. It is this relation, derived from the more basic and detailed conductance relation between points, which plays the central role in our model of the behaviour of circuits. Intuitively, the relation $\rightsquigarrow$ captures the flow of information in a circuit; it expresses how the values of signals flow (or are transmitted) from points at high strength to points at lower or equal strength along flows of conductance.

3.1 Definition. Let Λ be a set of points. A *static configuration* of sort Λ is a 4-tuple

$$\langle S, V, I, \rightsquigarrow \rangle$$

where

$\qquad S : \Lambda \to \mathbf{S}$ (the *strength function*),
$\qquad V : \Lambda \to \mathbf{V}$ (the *value function*),
$\qquad I : \Lambda \to \mathbf{V}$ (the *internal* value function) and
$\qquad \rightsquigarrow$ is a reflexive, transitive relation on Λ (the *flow relation*),

which satisfy

(i) $\quad \alpha \rightsquigarrow \beta \to S\alpha \geq S\beta$,
(ii) $\quad \alpha \rightsquigarrow \beta \wedge S\alpha = S\beta \to \beta \rightsquigarrow \alpha$,
(iii) $\quad \alpha \rightsquigarrow \beta \wedge S\beta \in K \to S\alpha = S\beta$,
(iv) $\quad S\alpha = 0 \leftrightarrow V\alpha = \emptyset$,
(v) $\quad I\alpha \leq V\alpha$,
(vi) $\quad \alpha \rightsquigarrow \beta \to I\alpha \leq I\beta \wedge V\alpha \leq V\beta$.

Write sort(σ) for the sort of a configuration σ. Write $\mathrm{Sta}_S[\Lambda]$ for the set of static configurations of sort Λ. We say a static configuration is *finite* when it has finite sort.

Property (i) says a signal cannot flow from a point at weaker strength to a point at stronger strength. Property (ii) expresses the fact that if $\alpha \rightsquigarrow \beta$, so information can flow from α to β, and α and β are at the same strength then $\beta \rightsquigarrow \alpha$, so information can flow in the other direction too. To justify (ii) assume that $\alpha \rightsquigarrow \beta$ and $S\alpha = S\beta$. Then, according to the last section, $\alpha \rightsquigarrow \beta$ arises iff there is a conductance, of strength g say, between α and β so that $S\alpha \cdot g = S\beta$. Hence $S\beta \cdot g = S\alpha$ too making $\beta \rightsquigarrow \alpha$. Property (iii) states that if $\alpha \rightsquigarrow \beta$ and $S\beta$ is a capacitance strength then $S\alpha$ is the same strength. This follows capacitance strengths are always ranked below those of conductance in the strength order. Assume $\alpha \rightsquigarrow \beta$ and $S\beta \in K$. Then $S\alpha \cdot g = S\beta$ for some conductance strength g for which $S\beta \le g$. This can only occur with $S\alpha = S\beta$. Property (iv) says a signal of no strength has no content and *vice versa*. Naturally the internal contribution cannot exceed the resultant value—property (v). The final property (vi) formalises the intention that $\rightsquigarrow$ should represent the direction in which information is transmitted through the circuit.

The strength and value functions are used later to specify when two static configurations can sensibly be linked together in parallel. It is necessary to keep track of the internal contribution to the value function and flow relation to give a satisfactory treatment of hiding. They determine when a point may be insulated from the environment without changing its resultant signal.

To make these somewhat abstract ideas a little clearer we present some static configurations of basic devices.

3.2 Example. *A source:*

A source Pow^{α} supplies an internal contribution of strength ∞ and value H to a point α which may well receive a contribution of L from the environment to yield a resultant value $V\alpha = X$.

$$S\alpha = \infty \wedge V\alpha = X \wedge I\alpha = H$$

3.3 Example. *A wire:*

A resistance of perfect conductance $res^{\alpha,\beta}_{\infty}$ can be regarded as a wire between α and β in which signals flow unimpaired between the two points. There are no internal sources.

$$S\alpha = S\beta = s \wedge V\alpha = V\beta = U \wedge I\alpha = I\beta = \emptyset \wedge \alpha \rightsquigarrow \beta \wedge \beta \rightsquigarrow \alpha$$

3.4 Example. *A resistance:*

A resistance of strength g contains no internal sources. If (in the environment) power and no other source is applied at α and β is connected to ground via conductance g then the static configuration shown would result.

$$Sα = \infty \wedge Sβ = g \wedge$$
$$Vα = H \wedge Vβ = X \wedge$$
$$Iα = Iβ = \emptyset \wedge$$
$$α \rightsquigarrow β \wedge \neg β \rightsquigarrow α.$$

3.5 Example. *A transistor:*

If an n–type transistor $ntran^{α,β,γ}$ is placed in an environment in which positive charge is applied to the gate $γ$ then $α$ and $β$ are connected and behave like a wire.

$$Sα = k \wedge Sα = Sβ = s \wedge$$
$$Vα = Vβ = U \wedge$$
$$Iα = Iβ = Iγ = \emptyset \wedge$$
$$α \rightsquigarrow β \wedge β \rightsquigarrow α \wedge$$
$$\neg(α \rightsquigarrow γ \vee γ \rightsquigarrow α) \wedge \neg(β \rightsquigarrow γ \vee γ \rightsquigarrow β).$$

In a static configuration, two points α and β may be both in the relation $\alpha \rightsquigarrow \beta$ and $\beta \rightsquigarrow \alpha$. In this case the points α and β receive the same signals both in value and strength. Sometimes neither $\alpha \rightsquigarrow \beta$ nor $\beta \rightsquigarrow \alpha$—the two points are incomparable— with respect to the flow relation $\rightsquigarrow$. Intuitively this means that the signal at one point does not affect the signal at the other. We introduce notation to describe these circumstances.

3.6 Definition. Let $\sigma = \langle S, V, I, \rightsquigarrow \rangle$ be a static configuration of sort Λ. For $\alpha, \beta \in \Lambda$ define

$$α \sim β \equiv α \rightsquigarrow β \wedge β \rightsquigarrow α$$
$$α \parallel β \equiv \neg(α \rightsquigarrow β) \wedge \neg(β \rightsquigarrow α).$$

In the special case where the effects of resistance are negligible there is only only one positive conductance strength ∞, corresponding to perfect conductance, the flow relation ⤳ coincides with the equivalence relation ∼. The proof is a little exercise in using the axioms which define a static configuration.

3.7 Proposition. *Assume there are only the two conductance strengths $0 < \infty$. Then for any static configuration σ the relation ⤳ is symmetric and so an equivalence relation on points with $x ⤳ y$ iff $x \sim y$ for all points x, y of σ.*

Proof. Suppose $\alpha ⤳ \beta$.

Assume $S\beta = 0$. Then $S\alpha = 0$ by (iv) and (vi). Assume $S\beta \in K$. Then $S\alpha = S\beta$ by (iii). Assume the remaining case that $S\beta = \infty$. Then $S\alpha = \infty$ by (i). Therefore, as in all cases $S\alpha = S\beta$, we see $\beta ⤳ \alpha$ by (ii).

Thus $\alpha ⤳ \beta$ implies $\beta ⤳ \alpha$, making ⤳ symmetric. By definition ⤳ is reflexive and transitive, so ⤳ is an equivalence relation. Hence the relations ⤳ and ∼ are equal. ∎

Proposition 3.7 may increase our level of confidence in the axioms proposed for a static configuration. Still there are sufficiently many axioms, and the idea of static configuration sufficiently complicated, to raise the question of their completeness. We have used arguments from physics for the soundness of the axioms. To show completeness we need an argument showing that there are no properties shared by all static configurations of real (or buildable) circuits which do not follow from those written down in the definition? Afterall, axiom (ii) does not spring to mind immediately from idea of static configuration or the examples we have considered. Later in proposition 4.4 we shall show that every structure $\langle S, V, I, ⤳ \rangle$ on a finite set of points which satisfies all the axioms of 3.1 can be realised as the static configuration of a circuit built-up from resistances and sources connected to those points. Then any property of structures $\langle S, V, I, ⤳ \rangle$ which holds of all static configurations of circuits must also hold of all finite structures in 3.1.

We make the static configurations with sorts Λ a subset of some universe of points Π into a partial algebra with operations associated with composition and hiding.

3.8 Notation. Let L be a complete lattice ordered by $\leq$ with binary join $+$ and arbitrary join Σ. Let M and Λ be sets. Let $f : M \to L$ and $g : \Lambda \to L$ be functions to the lattice. We define their join $f + g : M \cup \Lambda \to L$ by

$$(f + g)(x) = \begin{cases} f(x) & \text{if } x \in M \setminus \Lambda \\ g(x) & \text{if } x \in \Lambda \setminus M \\ f(x) + g(x) & \text{if } x \in M \cap \Lambda. \end{cases}$$

for $x \in M \cup \Lambda$.

If $f : M \to L$ we write $f \restriction \Lambda$ for the restriction of f to the subset $M \cap \Lambda$. If R is a binary relation on M we write $R \restriction \Lambda = R \cap (\Lambda \times \Lambda)$ for its restriction.

Let R be a binary relation on M. Let $f : \Lambda \to L$ be a function from $\Lambda \subseteq M$ to the lattice L. Define the *application* of relation R to f to be the function $(R \, . \, f) : M \to L$ given by

$$(R \, . \, f)(x) = \Sigma\{f(z) \mid z \in \Lambda \ \& \ (z, x) \in R\}.$$

We shall use this operation to transmit the values at a subset of points in a static configuration to other points in accord with the flow relation $\rightsquigarrow$.

Assume σ_0 is a static configuration of a circuit c_0 and σ_1 is a static configuration of a circuit c_1. When can σ_0 and σ_1 be composed to give a static configuration of c_0 and c_1? When their strengths and values agree at common points; only then do σ_0 and σ_1 make consistent assumptions about the environment. Then the resulting flow relation should be the transitive closure of the flow relations in the components and the internal contribution should be spread out accordingly.

3.9 Definition. Let $\sigma_0 = \langle S_0, V_0, I_0, \rightsquigarrow_0 \rangle$ be a static configuration of sort Λ_0 and $\sigma_1 = \langle S_1, V_1, I_1, \rightsquigarrow_1 \rangle$ be a static configuration of sort Λ_1. Define their *composition* to be

$$\sigma_0 \bullet \sigma_1 = \begin{cases} \langle S, V, I, \rightsquigarrow \rangle & \text{if } S_0 \lceil \Lambda_1 = S_1 \lceil \Lambda_0 \text{ and} \\ & \qquad V_0 \lceil \Lambda_1 = V_1 \lceil \Lambda_0 \\ \text{undefined} & \text{otherwise} \end{cases}$$

where

$$S = S_0 + S_1,$$
$$V = V_0 + V_1,$$
$$\rightsquigarrow = (\rightsquigarrow_0 \cup \rightsquigarrow_1)^* \quad \text{and}$$
$$I = \rightsquigarrow . (I_0 + I_1).$$

Suppose σ is a static configuration of a circuit c. When does σ restrict to a configuration of a circuit like c but in which all points but those in Λ are hidden? When all the points to be hidden have values (and strengths) which result from the combined effect of internal sources and the contribution from unhidden points Λ. More precisely when for all points α to be hidden we have $V\alpha = I\alpha + (\rightsquigarrow . V\lceil\Lambda)\alpha$. Then the hiding of points not in Λ will make no difference.

3.10 Definition. Let $\sigma = \langle S, V, I, \rightsquigarrow \rangle$ be a static configuration of sort M and Λ a set of points. Define the *restriction* of σ to Λ to be

$$\sigma\lceil\Lambda = \begin{cases} \langle S\lceil\Lambda, V\lceil\Lambda, I\lceil\Lambda, \rightsquigarrow\lceil\Lambda \rangle & \text{if } V = I + (\rightsquigarrow . V\lceil\Lambda) \\ \text{undefined} & \text{otherwise.} \end{cases}$$

3.11 Notation. We indicate $\sigma_0 \bullet \sigma_1$ and $\sigma\lceil\Lambda$ are defined by writing $\sigma_0 \bullet \sigma_1 \downarrow$ and $\sigma\lceil\Lambda \downarrow$.

4. The semantics of static circuits.

Assume the strength order is $\mathbf{S} = \mathbf{S}_{K,G}$. Also assume a countably infinite set of *point names* Π.

4.1 Definition.   A little language for static circuits—**circ**.
The syntax of **circ** is given by:

$$c ::= Pow\ \alpha \mid Gnd\ \alpha \mid cap_{kU}\alpha \mid res_g(\alpha,\beta) \mid ntran(\alpha,\beta,\gamma) \mid ptran(\alpha,\beta,\gamma) \mid c \bullet c \mid c\lceil\Lambda$$

where $k \in K$, $\emptyset \neq U \in \mathbf{V}$, $g \in G \cup \{\infty\}$ and α,β,γ are distinct point names in Π and $\Lambda \subseteq \Pi$.

The constant terms $Pow\ \alpha$ and $Gnd\ \alpha$ stand for sources providing a signal of strength ∞ at point α with values H and L respectively. Another kind of source arises through charge storage, when the strength s is an element of K. A term $cap_{kU}\alpha$ represents a capacitance of strength k, charged up with value U. The constant term $res_g(\alpha,\beta)$ stands for a resistance connecting points α and β with conductance $g \in G$. The constant $ntran(\alpha,\beta,\gamma)$ stands for an n–type transistor with a gate γ which when it is high connects points α and β with perfect conductance. The constant term $ptran(\alpha,\beta,\gamma)$ stands for a p–type transistor with a gate γ which connects points α and β, again with perfect conductance, when the gate γ is low. Of course, should the effect of resistance be significant we can insert a suitable resistance between α and β.

We take the behaviour of a circuit in **circ** to be the set of possible static configurations it can settle into in some static environment. For compactness, in the following definition we assume that a static configuration σ is $\langle S, V, I, \twoheadrightarrow \rangle$.

4.2 Definition.   The semantics of **circ**.
Let $\mathrm{Sta} = \bigcup_{\Lambda \subseteq \Pi} \mathrm{Sta}[\Lambda]$, the set of static configurations with sorts which are subsets of Π.

Define the semantic function $[\![\ ]\!] : \mathbf{circ} \to P(\mathrm{Sta})$ to be the map defined by the structural induction

$$[\![Pow\ \alpha]\!] = \{\sigma \in \mathrm{Sta}[\alpha] \mid S\alpha = \infty \wedge I\alpha = \mathrm{H}\}$$

$$[\![Gnd\ \alpha]\!] = \{\sigma \in \mathrm{Sta}[\alpha] \mid S\alpha = \infty \wedge I\alpha = \mathrm{L}\}$$

$$[\![cap_{kU}\alpha]\!] = \{\sigma \in \mathrm{Sta}[\alpha] \mid S\alpha \geq k \wedge$$
$$(S\alpha = k \to I\alpha = U) \wedge (S\alpha > k \to I\alpha = \emptyset)\}$$

$$[\![res_g(\alpha,\beta)]\!] = \{\sigma \in \mathrm{Sta}[\alpha,\beta] \mid I\alpha = \emptyset \wedge I\beta = \emptyset \wedge$$
$$S\alpha{\cdot}g \le S\beta \wedge S\beta{\cdot}g \le S\alpha \wedge$$
$$(S\alpha{\cdot}g = S\beta \leftrightarrow \alpha \rightsquigarrow \beta) \wedge (S\beta{\cdot}g = S\alpha \leftrightarrow \beta \rightsquigarrow \alpha)\}$$

$$[\![ntran(\alpha,\beta,\gamma)]\!] = \{\sigma \in \mathrm{Sta}[\alpha,\beta,\gamma] \mid I\alpha = \emptyset \wedge I\beta = \emptyset \wedge I\gamma = \emptyset \wedge$$
$$\gamma \parallel \alpha \wedge \gamma \parallel \beta \wedge (\alpha \parallel \beta \vee \alpha \sim \beta) \wedge$$
$$(V\gamma = \mathrm{H} \to \alpha \sim \beta) \wedge (V\gamma = \mathrm{L} \to \alpha \parallel \beta)\}$$

$$[\![ptran(\alpha,\beta,\gamma)]\!] = \{\sigma \in \mathrm{Sta}[\alpha,\beta,\gamma] \mid I\alpha = \emptyset \wedge I\beta = \emptyset \wedge I\gamma = \emptyset \wedge$$
$$\gamma \parallel \alpha \wedge \gamma \parallel \beta \wedge (\alpha \parallel \beta \vee \alpha \sim \beta) \wedge$$
$$(V\gamma = \mathrm{L} \to \alpha \sim \beta) \wedge (V\gamma = \mathrm{H} \to \alpha \parallel \beta)\}$$

$$[\![c \bullet d]\!] = \{\sigma \bullet \rho \mid \sigma \in [\![c]\!] \ \& \ \rho \in [\![d]\!] \ \& \ \sigma \bullet \rho \downarrow\}$$

$$[\![c\lceil\Lambda]\!] = \{\sigma\lceil\Lambda \mid \sigma \in [\![c]\!] \ \& \ \sigma\lceil\Lambda \downarrow\}.$$

Further terms can be defined. For example, we can define a wire $wre(\alpha,\beta)$ between α and β, with denotation

$$[\![wre(\alpha,\beta)]\!] = \{\sigma \in \mathrm{Sta}[\alpha,\beta] \mid I\alpha = \emptyset \wedge I\beta = \emptyset \wedge \alpha \sim \beta\},$$

which can be realised by a resistance with perfect conductance, *i.e.*

$$[\![wre(\alpha,\beta)]\!] = [\![res_\infty(\alpha,\beta)]\!].$$

More interestingly, We can define a general source $sce_{sU}\alpha$, at α, of strength s and value $U \in \mathbf{V}$, to have denotation

$$[\![sce_{sU}\alpha]\!] = \{\sigma \in \mathrm{Sta}[\alpha] \mid S\alpha \ge s \wedge$$
$$(S\alpha = s \to I\alpha = U) \wedge (S\alpha > s \to I\alpha = \emptyset)\}$$

Such a source only makes a contribution at α if the strength of α is exactly s. We only consider sources $sce_{sU}\alpha$ for which $s = 0 \Leftrightarrow U = \emptyset$—any others could have no static configurations. If s is a capacitance strength k then such a weakened source can be realised by the charged capacitance cap^α_{kU}. If s is a conductance strength g it can be realised by passing signals from ground or power through a resistance of strength g. For example, if $U = H$, we have

$$[\![sce_{gH}\alpha]\!] = [\![(Pow\ \beta \bullet res_g(\beta,\alpha))\lceil\alpha]\!].$$

The one remaining case, $sce_{0\emptyset}\alpha$ can be realised as a single connection point standing alone, and this can be made by hiding one end of a resistance, *i.e.*

$$[\![sce_{0\emptyset}\alpha]\!] = [\![res_g(\alpha,\beta)\lceil\alpha]\!].$$

It is helpful to explain the ways sources combine using an ordering between pairs sU, where $s \in \mathbf{S}$ and $U \in \mathbf{V}$ and $s = 0$ iff $U = \emptyset$. On such pairs define

$$sU \leq s'U' \text{ iff } s < s' \text{ or } (s = s' \ \& \ U \leq U').$$

This forms a finite distributive lattice (meet $\cdot$ and join $+$), mentioned in [B1] and [Hay], which may be drawn as:

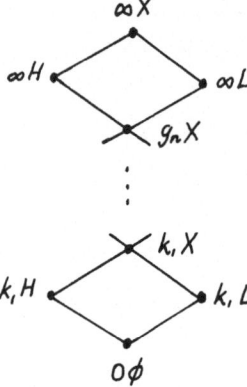

Now we can list some basic equivalences between circuit terms, which can be proved from the denotational semantics.

4.3 Proposition. *Some equivalences on circuits*
   Write $c = c'$ iff $[\![c]\!] = [\![c']\!]$, for circuit terms c, c'.
Realising sources: If k is a capacitance strength and g a conductance strength then

$$sce_{0\emptyset}\alpha = res_g(\alpha, \beta)\lceil \alpha,$$
$$sce_{kU}\alpha = cap_{kU}\alpha,$$
$$sce_{gH}\alpha = (Pow\ \beta \bullet res_g(\beta, \alpha))\lceil \alpha,$$
$$sce_{gL}\alpha = (Gnd\ \beta \bullet res_g(\beta, \alpha))\lceil \alpha,$$
$$sce_{gX}\alpha = sce_{gH}\alpha \bullet sce_{gL}\alpha.$$

Composing sources: $sce_{sU}\alpha \bullet sce_{s'U'}\alpha = sce_{sU+s'U'}\alpha.$
Resistances in series and parallel:
   $(res_g(\alpha, \beta) \bullet res_{g'}(\beta, \gamma))\lceil\{\alpha, \gamma\} = res_{g \cdot g'}(\alpha, \gamma).$
   $(res_g(\alpha, \beta) \bullet res_{g'}(\alpha, \beta)) = res_{g+g'}(\alpha, \beta).$
Wires, resistances and transistors:

$$wre(\alpha, \beta) = res_\infty(\alpha, \beta)$$
$$= (Pow\ \alpha \bullet ntran(\alpha, \beta, \gamma))\lceil\{\alpha, \beta\}$$
$$= (Gnd\ \alpha \bullet ptran(\alpha, \beta, \gamma))\lceil\{\alpha, \beta\}.$$

Earlier we pointed out the problem of knowing whether or not we had written down sufficient axioms for static configurations. From the remarks in the last section it is sufficient to show every finite static configuration can be realised as a static configuration of a circuit term. This is established in the following proposition.

4.4 Proposition. *Any static configuration σ of sort Λ a finite subset of Π is the static configuration of some circuit c i.e. $\sigma \in [\![c]\!]$.*

Proof. We sketch the proof. Given σ, we define the required circuit to be the composition of the following finite set of components:

$$\{sce_{S\alpha U}\alpha \mid \alpha \in \Lambda \ \& \ I\alpha = U \neq \emptyset\} \cup$$
$$\{res_g(\alpha, \beta) \mid \alpha \rightsquigarrow \beta \ \& \ g \text{ is the minimum conductance strength s.t. } S\alpha \cdot S\beta \leq g\}.$$

This uses our knowledge of how to build all sources $sce_{sU}\alpha$ as circuits. From the definition of sources, resistances and composition, it can be seen $\sigma \in [\![c]\!]$. ∎

Now we can see how to give a more accurate specification of the NMOS inverter of section 2. Its circuit is constructed by the term

$$c \equiv (ntran(\alpha, \beta, \gamma) \bullet res_g(\beta, \delta) \bullet Pow \ \delta \bullet Gnd \ \alpha) \lceil \{\alpha, \beta\}.$$

Informally, its output β behaves like a direct connection to ground when its input γ is high and like a weakened power source when γ is low. Formally, if we define

$$Sce_{sU}x \equiv Sx \geq s \ \wedge$$
$$Sx = s \rightarrow Ix = U \ \wedge$$
$$Sx = s \rightarrow Ix = U,$$

then we can say c satisfies the assertion

$$V\gamma = H \rightarrow Sce_{\infty L}\beta \ \wedge$$
$$V\gamma = L \rightarrow Sce_{gH}\beta.$$

This illustrates how the model is closely associated with assertions for specifying the behaviour of circuits. Of course we should give a more rigorous treatment of their syntax and semantics. This is done in the next section where a complete proof system is presented for proving a circuit satisfies an assertion.

Technically, it will be simpler to work with more basic predicates than Vx and Ix. Say σ satisfies $H\alpha$ if $H \leq V\alpha$, meaning α is connected to a source of positive charge (either in the environment or internal). Similarly, say σ satisfies $L\alpha$ if $L \leq V\alpha$. The assertion $V\alpha = H$ can then be expressed equivalently by $H\alpha \wedge \neg L\alpha$, while $V\alpha = X$ is equivalent to $H\alpha \wedge L\alpha$. For internal signals say σ satisfies $h\alpha$ if $H \leq I\alpha$ and $l\alpha$ if $L \leq V\alpha$. Then, for instance, σ satisfies $h\alpha$ if α is connected to an internal source of positive charge.

To conclude this section, we note we have not completely eliminated the kind of problems raised in the section 1. Certainly we now have an adequate treatment of short circuits. In particular

$$[\![Pow \ \alpha \bullet Gnd \ \alpha]\!] \neq \emptyset,$$

and so, when we come to the logic, the circuit $Pow \ \alpha \bullet Gnd \ \alpha$ will not satisfy ff. However, there are other circuit terms which do denote $\emptyset$ and so will satisfy ff. Roughly speaking, these are terms which represent circuits whose only possible behaviour is to oscillate. For example the term

$$c \equiv (ntran(\alpha, \beta, \gamma) \bullet res_g(\beta, \delta) \bullet Pow\ \delta \bullet Gnd\ \alpha \bullet wre(\gamma, \beta)) \lceil \emptyset,$$

with g a conductance strength strictly between 0 and ∞, "ties–back" the output of an NMOS inverter to its input, and then insulates all points from the environment. It can be drawn as:

The circuit c denotes the emptyset, $[\![c]\!] = \emptyset$. (The circuit is a little peculiar in that it has an empty sort. A trivial modification—connecting the wire to the gate of another transistor—produces a term with nonempty sort and empty denotation.) The logic of circuits will thus be akin to the logic of partial correctness assertions (Hoare logic); a purely oscillating circuit will satisfy any assertion just as a diverging program satisfies all partial correctness assertions.

5. A proof system.

We show how to construct a proof system for circuits. In this section we highlight its main features, and refer to the appendix for the full syntax, semantics and proof rules. The proof system consists of a complete set of rules to prove formally that a circuit, described by a term c, satisfies a property described by an assertion A. It is compositional in that proving an assertion holds of a compound circuit of the form $c\lceil\Lambda$ or $c_0 \bullet c_1$ reduces to proving assertions about the components, c of $c\lceil\Lambda$, and c_0 and c_1 of $c_0 \bullet c_1$. Assertions describe the possible static configurations the circuit can settle into. We have seen several examples where a static configuration satisfies some particular logical assertion. Of course, an assertion determines all those configurations which satisfy it, and in the formal treatment we take the meaning, or denotation, of an assertion A, written $[\![A]\!]$, to be the set of all those static configurations which satisfy it. Thus we seek a way to prove relations $[\![c]\!] \subseteq [\![A]\!]$, which we write as $c \models A$, hold between circuit terms c and assertions A. In order to establish such relations it is useful to treat circuit terms as just another kind of assertion in our semantics and proof rules. We write $\sigma \models c$ to mean σ is a static configuration of the circuit c, just as we do for more usual assertions. We make use of relations $\Gamma \models A$ between a set Γ and A where Γ and A are *circuit-assertions* (see L.1 in the appendix) which may include, or be built out of circuit terms. The relation $\Gamma \models A$ means any static configuration σ which satisfies all of Γ satisfies A too. Such relations have their syntactic counterpart in the proof system. The proof rules are written in a natural-deduction style, keeping track of the assumptions in sequents of the form $\Gamma \vdash A$.

We settle on a countably infinite set of point names Π, with typical members $\alpha, \beta, \cdots$, and a fixed strength order $\mathbf{S}$. It is simplest to assume that point names are in 1–1 correspondence with points, so two distinct names cannot be associated with the same point (we shall axiomatise the equality relation between points accordingly). Our previous work suggests the form assertions should take. A static configuration σ, with sort $\Lambda \subseteq \Pi$, is a structure $\langle S, V, I, \rightarrowtail \rangle$ over individuals Λ. We could treat σ as a structure for a first order logic with function symbols S, V, I and relation symbols $\rightarrowtail$ and $=$. We do not quite follow this course. There is first of all the problem that the sorts are not all the same, and in particular we allow the trivial empty static configuration—a source of trouble should we follow a traditional treatment where it is usual to ban empty structures. We could use a family of logics, one for each sort, but instead it is much more convenient and much less messy to use a *free logic* in which it is not necessary that terms are defined, or denote existing things. In the free logic a static configuration σ satisfies $\forall x.A$ when $A[\alpha/x]$ holds for all points α in sort(σ), and similarly σ satisfies $\exists x.A$ if for some α in sort(σ) the assertion $A[\alpha/x]$ is satisfied by σ; quantification is only taken to be over existing, or defined, elements. On the other hand, all variables are understood to range over all potential individuals Π. Our style of free logic is based on [S] and includes an existence predicate E; $E\alpha$ holds in a static configuration precisely when $\alpha \in$ sort(σ). We have constant symbols from Π, a function symbol S, as well as relations $\rightarrowtail$ and $=$ in the logical language. Instead of using functions V and I we use the predicates Hx, Lx and hx, lx mentioned in the last section 4.

The *point relations, prel,* have the form

$$H\pi \mid L\pi \mid h\pi \mid l\pi \mid \pi_0 = \pi_1 \mid \pi_0 \rightarrowtail \pi_1 \mid E\pi$$

where π, π_0, π_1 range over points and variables.

To reason formally about strengths we need *strength expressions* of the form

$$s \mid S\pi \mid e_0 \cdot e_1 \mid e_0 + e_1$$

where $s \in S$, π is a point or variable and e_0, e_1 are strength expressions. Note we need an existence predicate for strength expressions as well as points. This is because $S\alpha$ only makes sense, with respect to a static configuration σ, if $\alpha \in \mathrm{sort}(\sigma)$. Define the *strength relations*, *srel*, to have the form

$$Ee \mid e_0 \leq e_1 \mid e_0 = e_1$$

where e, e_0 and e_1 are strength expressions.

Now the *first order assertions* of our free logic are:

$$A ::= prel \mid srel \mid \mathrm{t\!t} \mid \mathrm{f\!f} \mid A \wedge A \mid A \vee A \mid A \rightarrow A \mid \exists x.A \mid \forall x.A$$

with atoms which are point and strength relations. The full semantics and proof system can be seen in the appendix (for the moment ignore the second order assertions and rules). Notable, special to a free logic, are the quantifier rules which must take account of existence and the rule (refl) the axiom for existence—the equality $\alpha = \alpha$ only holds of an existing point α. The paper [S] gives an excellent discussion of the axioms and rules.

5.1 Theorem. *A first–order assertion is provable using the proof system in the appendix iff it is satisfied by all static configurations.*

Proof. The proof is omitted. Unfortunately, I do not know an adequate reference for a completeness result in the form we want it, though completeness can be proved rather indirectly from results in [FS] and [Gr]. More direct proofs can be got by following the lines of Henkin's completeness proof for the predicate calculus. ∎

It is as well to get a basic fact about strength relations out of the way. It will be useful to observe that any strength relation can be reduced to ones of a special form, described in the following.

5.2 Proposition. *Let R be a strength relation. There is a propositional assertion A which includes strength assertions solely of the form $S\pi = s$ such that $\vdash R \leftrightarrow A$.*

Proof.

By structural induction,

$$\vdash Ee \leftrightarrow \bigwedge_{\pi \ in \ e} E\pi$$

for any strength expression e, where π ranges over the variables or points mentioned in e. This establishes the proposition for strength relations of the form Ee.

By structural induction,
$$\vdash Ee \leftrightarrow \bigvee_{s \in S} e = s$$

for any strength expression e. It follows from the axioms that

$$\vdash e_0 \cdot e_1 = s \leftrightarrow \bigvee_{s_0, s_1 \in S}(e_0 = s_0 \wedge e_1 = s_1 \wedge s_0 \cdot s_1 = s)$$

$$\vdash e_0 + e_1 = s \leftrightarrow \bigvee_{s_0, s_1 \in S}(e_0 = s_0 \wedge e_1 = s_1 \wedge s_0 + s_1 = s)$$

$$\vdash e_0 \leq e_1 \leftrightarrow \bigvee_{s_0, s_1 \in S}(e_0 = s_0 \wedge e_1 = s_1 \wedge s_0 \leq s_1)$$

$$\vdash e_0 = e_1 \leftrightarrow \bigvee_{s_0, s_1 \in S}(e_0 = s_0 \wedge e_1 = s_1 \wedge s_0 = s_1).$$

Whence, by structural induction on expressions, any strength relation of the form $e_0 \leq e_1$ or $e_0 = e_1$ is provably equivalent to a propositional assertion of the required form.
∎

We are still left with the major problem of how to incorporate rules for reasoning about circuit terms in the logic. As mentioned we can include them in the logic, treating them much the same way as assertions. They are built–up using restrictions $\lceil \Lambda$ and composition • from atoms like $Pow\ \alpha$ and $ntran(\alpha, \beta, \gamma)$. It is a simple matter to incorporate atoms. For example, the rules (L.10) include an elimination rule of the form

$$(Pow\ E) \qquad Pow\ \alpha \vdash S\alpha = \infty \wedge h\alpha \wedge \neg l\alpha \wedge \forall x.x = \alpha$$

whose role is to replace proving a property of a power source $Pow\ \alpha$ to proving a consequence of an assertion expressing its behaviour. But how are we to treat compound terms? Our approach is to associate modal operations, analogous to weakest liberal preconditions, with the operators $\lceil \Lambda$ and •. This line was inspired by the general treatment in [A], though, of course, their specific use in the semantics of imperative programming language is well known, largely due to [D]. We also extend the logic to include second–order quantifiers, to obtain the following syntactic category of second–order assertions:

$$A ::= prel \mid srel \mid \mathrm{tt} \mid \mathrm{ff} \mid A \wedge A \mid A \vee A \mid A \rightarrow A \mid \exists x.A \mid \forall x.A$$
$$\{x : A\}\pi \mid P\pi \mid \exists P.A \mid \forall P.A \mid$$

Though the reason for this will not become clear until we deal with the preconditions for composition.

The treatment of the restriction operator $\lceil \Lambda$, for a finite subset Λ of Π, is easier to explain first. The use of preconditions arises naturally from the requirement that the proof system be compositional. The requirement of compositionality begs the question:

> What has to be true of a circuit c in order to be guaranteed that $c\lceil \Lambda$ satisfies an assertion A?

And this question amounts to:

> What must be true of a static configuration σ so that if $\sigma\lceil \Lambda$ is defined then $\sigma\lceil \Lambda$ satisfies A?

Rather tautologously, we can answer that σ must satisfy the $\lceil\Lambda$–precondition of A, written $^\Lambda A$, which has the denotation

$$[\![^\Lambda A]\!] = \{\sigma \mid \sigma\lceil\Lambda \downarrow \Rightarrow \sigma\lceil\Lambda \models A\}.$$

We might instead of $^\Lambda A$ write $[\lceil\Lambda]A$ because $[\![^\Lambda A]\!]$ could have been written equally well as

$$\{\sigma \mid \forall\sigma'.\ \sigma\lceil\Lambda = \sigma' \Rightarrow \sigma' \models A\},$$

making the precondition look even more like a modal operator of the kind used in dynamic logic [Ha]. This precondition is analogous to weakest liberal preconditions because if $\sigma\lceil\Lambda$ is undefined then σ satisfies $^\Lambda A$. We could have worked instead with the analogue of weakest precondition. We temporarily introduce it as $\langle\lceil\Lambda\rangle A$ with the meaning

$$[\![\langle\lceil\Lambda\rangle A]\!] = \{\sigma \mid \exists\sigma'.\ \sigma\lceil\Lambda = \sigma'\ \&\ \sigma' \models A\},$$

but do not make any further use of it. It turns out to be definable in terms of $^\Lambda A$, and is not quite as directly useful. For $^\Lambda A$ we have the following fact:

5.3 Proposition.

Let c be a circuit term and A a second–order assertion. Then

$$c\lceil\Lambda \models A \text{ iff } c \models {}^\Lambda A.$$

Proof.

$$
\begin{aligned}
c\lceil\Lambda \models A \text{ iff } & [\![c\lceil\Lambda]\!] \subseteq [\![A]\!]\\
\text{iff } & \forall\sigma'.\ \sigma' \models c\lceil\Lambda \Rightarrow \sigma' \models A\\
\text{iff } & \forall\sigma.\ (\sigma \models c\ \&\ \sigma\lceil\Lambda \downarrow) \Rightarrow \sigma\lceil\Lambda \models A\\
\text{iff } & \forall\sigma.\ \sigma \models c \Rightarrow (\sigma\lceil\Lambda \downarrow \Rightarrow \sigma\lceil\Lambda \models A)\\
\text{iff } & \forall\sigma.\ \sigma \models c \Rightarrow \sigma \models {}^\Lambda A\\
\text{iff } & [\![c]\!] \subseteq [\![^\Lambda A]\!]\\
\text{iff } & c \models {}^\Lambda A.
\end{aligned}
$$

∎

We extend the second–order assertions by preconditions and call the resulting syntactic category simply *assertions*. Proposition 5.3 suggests an obvious elimination rule for preconditions:

$$\frac{c \vdash {}^\Lambda A}{c\lceil\Lambda \vdash A}$$

in which the semantic relation of satisfaction has been replaced by the syntactic one of entailment in a sequent calculus. Standing alone this proof rule would not get us very far. True we can eliminate an occurrence of the restriction operator, but only at the expense of introducing a precondition. Fortunately it is a purely mechanical process, captured mainly in the distribution laws for $^\Lambda(\ )$, listed in L.6, to eliminate all occurrences of $\lceil\Lambda$–preconditions; an assertion containing them can be proved equivalent to an assertion without any.

We explain the rules for $^\Lambda(\ )$, leaving the detailed proofs of soundness to the reader. Regarding preconditions as modal operators suggests the introduction rule

$$\frac{\vdash A}{\vdash {}^\Lambda A}$$

familiar from proof systems with modal operators. The other introduction rule for such preconditions accompanies the fact that if $\sigma\lceil\Lambda$ is undefined then $\sigma \models {}^\Lambda A$. Take

$$G \equiv \forall x.\ \neg \Lambda x \to \left[\text{H}x \to hx \lor (\exists y : \Lambda.\ \text{H}y \land y \rightarrowtail x)\right] \land$$
$$\left[\text{L}x \to lx \lor (\exists y : \Lambda.\ \text{L}y \land y \rightarrowtail x)\right].$$

The assertion G expresses definedness in the sense that

$$\sigma \models G \text{ iff } \sigma\lceil\Lambda \downarrow.$$

The other introduction rule for preconditions is

$$\neg G \vdash {}^\Lambda A.$$

The remaining $^\Lambda(\ )$ rules say how the operator distributes over logical operators. Their role is to enable preconditions to be pushed through and finally eliminated from assertions. Using them we can for instance derive the rule

$$\frac{\Gamma \vdash A}{{}^\Lambda \Gamma \vdash {}^\Lambda A}$$

where by $^\Lambda\Gamma$ we mean $\{{}^\Lambda B \mid B \in \Gamma\}$, for a finite set of assumptions Γ. From $\Gamma \vdash A$ we derive $\vdash \bigwedge\Gamma \to A$ and hence $\vdash {}^\Lambda(\bigwedge\Gamma \to A)$. Using the distribution rules we deduce $G \vdash \bigwedge{}^\Lambda\Gamma \to {}^\Lambda A$. This gives $G, \bigwedge{}^\Lambda\Gamma \vdash {}^\Lambda A$ which combined with $\neg G \vdash {}^\Lambda A$ yields $\bigwedge{}^\Lambda\Gamma \vdash {}^\Lambda A$, and finally $^\Lambda\Gamma \vdash {}^\Lambda A$. In particular using this we can for instance show $\vdash {}^\Lambda A \leftrightarrow {}^\Lambda B$ if $\vdash A \leftrightarrow B$; equivalent assertions have equivalent preconditions. This means that preconditions of strength relations can be replaced by preconditions of assertions of the form given in proposition 5.2 from which all preconditions can be eliminated using the distribution rules.

5.4 Theorem.

Let A be an assertion, which may include restriction preconditions. There is an assertion B, which does not contain any preconditions, such that $\vdash A \leftrightarrow B$.

Proof. By the remarks above, using the distribution laws, we obtain

$$G \vdash {}^\Lambda A \leftrightarrow C$$

where C contains no preconditions. But $\neg G \vdash {}^\Lambda A$. Therefore $\vdash {}^\Lambda A \leftrightarrow (G \to C)$, with $B \equiv (G \to C)$ an assertion of the required form. ∎

Proving $c\lceil\Lambda \models A$ reduces to proving $c \models {}^\Lambda A$ which, by the metatheorem and modus ponens, reduces to proving $c \models B$ where B contains no preconditions—and this can be done formally in the proof system. We have reduced the problem of proving an assertion A holds of $c \lceil \Lambda$ to proving an assertion B holds of c. We have achieved compositionality for restriction.

The term c may well contain compositions using $\bullet$. For our proof system to be compositional we must "decompose" the proof that an assertion A is satisfied by a composition $c_0 \bullet c_1$ to proofs that assertions A_0 and A_1, are satisfied by the components c_0 and c_1, respectively. Problems like this have received a great deal of attention recently (see *e.g.* [deR, OH, St, W]) and our approach throws some light on the problem of obtaining compositional proof systems for parallel processes, and even suggests a general approach. Again the use of a modal operator plays a central role, this time associated with composition. Composition $\bullet$ is a binary operator so the $\bullet$–precondition of an assertion A is satisfied' by those pairs of static configurations (σ, ρ) whose composition $\sigma \bullet \rho$, when defined, satisfies A , *i.e.*

$$\llbracket {}^\bullet A \rrbracket = \{ (\sigma, \rho) \mid \sigma \bullet \rho \downarrow \Rightarrow \sigma \bullet \rho \models A \}.$$

Thus the assertion ${}^\bullet A$ is of a different type than those we have encountered previously. It is satisfied by *pairs* of static configurations. To emphasise that it has a different type we call it, and other assertions satisfied by pairs of configurations, product assertions. It is useful to define another operator for forming atomic product assertions. For assertions A and B, take $A \times B$ to be satisfied by those pairs (σ, ρ) where σ satisfies A and ρ satisfies B, *i.e.* so

$$\llbracket A \times B \rrbracket = \llbracket A \rrbracket \times \llbracket B \rrbracket.$$

The full syntactic category of *product assertions* is:

$$D ::= A \times B \mid {}^\bullet A \mid E\pi \mid \pi_0 = \pi_1$$
$$\text{tt} \mid \text{ff} \mid D_0 \wedge D_1 \mid D_0 \vee D_1 \mid D_0 \to D_1 \mid \exists x.D \mid \forall x.D \mid$$
$$\{x : D\}\pi \mid \exists P.D \mid \forall P.D$$

which includes the apparatus of first and second order free logic with equality.

We can treat circuit terms similarly, and with the obvious definition of $\models$ between product assertions, obtain the following proposition relating the $\bullet$–precondition to composition.

5.5 Proposition.

Let c_0 and c_1 be circuit terms and A an assertion. Then

$$c_0 \bullet c_1 \models A \text{ iff } c_0 \times c_1 \models {}^\bullet A.$$

Proof.

$$
\begin{aligned}
c_0 \bullet c_1 \models A \text{ iff } & \llbracket c_0 \bullet c_1 \rrbracket \subseteq \llbracket A \rrbracket \\
\text{iff } & \forall \sigma'.\ \sigma' \models c_0 \bullet c_1 \Rightarrow \sigma' \models A \\
\text{iff } & \forall \sigma, \rho.\ (\sigma \models c_0 \ \& \ \rho \models c_1 \ \& \ \sigma \bullet \rho \downarrow) \Rightarrow \sigma \bullet \rho \models A \\
\text{iff } & \forall \sigma, \rho.\ \sigma \models c_0 \ \& \ \rho \models c_1 \Rightarrow (\sigma \bullet \rho \downarrow \Rightarrow \sigma \bullet \rho \models A) \\
\text{iff } & \forall \sigma, \rho.\ (\sigma, \rho) \models c_0 \times c_1 \Rightarrow (\sigma, \rho) \models {}^\bullet A \\
\text{iff } & \llbracket c_0 \times c_1 \rrbracket \subseteq \llbracket {}^\bullet A \rrbracket \\
\text{iff } & c_0 \times c_1 \models {}^\bullet A. \quad \blacksquare
\end{aligned}
$$

The proposition asserts the soundness of the elimination rule for composition:

$$\frac{c_0 \times c_1 \vdash {}^{\bullet}A}{c_0 \bullet c_1 \vdash A}$$

We want the proof of $c_0 \times c_1 \models {}^{\bullet}A$ to "factor" into proving

$$c_0 \models A_0 \ \& \ c_1 \models A_1 \ \& \ A_0 \times A_1 \models {}^{\bullet}A.$$

The key to a compositional proof system for $\bullet$ is to obtain such assertions so that we can prove formally the relation between assertions, that $A_0 \times A_1 \vdash {}^{\bullet}A$. Then we have reduced proving a property holds of a composition $c_0 \bullet c_1$ to proving properties hold of its components c_0 and c_1: If there are such assertions then by the rules $(\times \vdash)$ and (tran), and provided $c_0 \vdash A_0$ and $c_1 \vdash A_1$, we can deduce $c_0 \times c_1 \vdash {}^{\bullet}A$ and so $c_0 \bullet c_1 \vdash A$. Obtaining suitable assertions A_0 and A_1 is quite involved.

The rules for $\bullet$–preconditions are like those for $\lceil \Lambda$–preconditions and are presented in L.9. There are two introduction rules, one of which makes use of a definedness assertion D, with

$$D \equiv \forall x. \, ([Ex \times \mathbb{t}] \wedge [\mathbb{t} \times Ex]) \rightarrow$$
$$([Hx \times \mathbb{t}] \leftrightarrow [\mathbb{t} \times Hx] \wedge$$
$$[Lx \times \mathbb{t}] \leftrightarrow [\mathbb{t} \times Lx] \wedge$$
$$\mathbb{W}_{s \in S}[Sx = s \times Sx = s]),$$

so $(\sigma, \rho) \models D$ iff $\sigma \bullet \rho \downarrow$. This is where the cost of making assertions second-order pays-off. Because we can quantify over subsets (or properties), we can reduce ${}^{\bullet}A$ to a provably equivalent product assertion which contains no preconditions. The quantification over sets is used to express the fact that the flow relation in a composition $\sigma \bullet \rho$, assumed defined, is the transitive closure of the flow relations contributed by the components σ and ρ. This is the role of axiom $(d^{\bullet} \rightsquigarrow)$. Suppose $\sigma \bullet \rho$ is defined. Then $(\sigma, \rho) \models$ ${}^{\bullet}(\alpha \rightsquigarrow \beta)$ means simply that $\sigma \bullet \rho \models \alpha \rightsquigarrow \beta$ for $\alpha, \beta \in \mathrm{sort}(\sigma \bullet \rho)$. Let $\Lambda \subseteq \mathrm{sort}(\sigma \bullet \rho)$. Note we can represent the set Λ as the term Λ which is $\{x : \mathbb{W}_{\lambda \in \Lambda} x = \lambda\}$ in the logic. Say Λ is *closed*, with respect to σ, ρ, if

$$\sigma \bullet \rho \models \Lambda\gamma \ \& \ (\sigma \models \gamma \rightsquigarrow \delta \ \text{or} \ \rho \models \gamma \rightsquigarrow \delta) \Rightarrow \sigma \bullet \rho \models \Lambda\delta$$

for all $\gamma, \delta \in \mathrm{sort}(\sigma \bullet \rho)$. Now, the flow relation in $\sigma \bullet \rho$ is characterised as being the transitive closure of the flow relations of the components, and this is expressed by the property that

$$\Lambda\alpha \ \& \ \Lambda \text{ is closed} \ \Rightarrow \Lambda\beta$$

for all $\alpha, \beta \in \mathrm{sort}(\sigma \bullet \rho)$ and for any Λ. This gives the gist of axiom $(d^{\bullet} \rightsquigarrow)$. Notice it depends on quantifying over subsets. Once we have gone second-order, the distribution axioms for ${}^{\bullet}(\ )$ enable us to eliminate occurrences of $\bullet$–preconditions from product assertions.

5.6 Theorem.

Let A be a product assertion which may include composition preconditions. There is a product assertion B, which does not contain any preconditions such that $\vdash A \leftrightarrow B$.

Proof. The proof follows the same lines as for restriction preconditions. ∎

But, of course, this was at the expense of making our logic second–order and it is well-known that there is no complete effective axiomatisation of second–order logic. Fortunately we can use the fact that circuits are finite to get around this difficulty. In contexts where it is assumed that all points lie within some finite set we can reduce second-order assertions to provably equivalent first-order or even propositional assertions. (An assertion is *propositional* if it contains no quantifiers or preconditions.)

It is easy to define the sort of circuit term by structural induction:

$$\text{sort}(Pow\ \alpha) = \text{sort}(Gnd\ \alpha) = \{\alpha\}$$
$$\text{sort}(res_g(\alpha, \beta)) = \{\alpha, \beta\}$$
$$\text{sort}(ntran(\alpha, \beta, \gamma)) = \text{sort}(ptran(\alpha, \beta, \gamma)) = \{\alpha, \beta, \gamma\}$$
$$\text{sort}(c \bullet d) = \text{sort}(c) \cup \text{sort}(d)$$
$$\text{sort}(c \lceil \Lambda) = \text{sort}(c) \cap \Lambda.$$

In the logic, the fact that a circuit term c has sort Λ, a finite set, is expressed by

$$c \models \bigwedge\nolimits_{\lambda \in \Lambda} E\lambda \wedge \forall x.\Lambda x$$

where Λx abbreviates $\{y : \bigvee_{\lambda \in \Lambda} y = \lambda\}x$ and so is equivalent to $\bigvee_{\lambda \in \Lambda} x = \lambda$. This can be proved in the formal system, though all we need to show completeness is the following.

5.7 Proposition.

(i)   Let c be a circuit term of sort Λ. Then $c \vdash \forall x.\Lambda x$.

(ii)   Let c_0, c_1 be circuit terms of sort Λ_0 and Λ_1 respectively. Then $c_0 \times c_1 \vdash \forall x. (\Lambda_0 \cup \Lambda_1)x.$

Proof. The proof of (i) is by structural induction on circuit terms.

For basic components, like transistors the sorts are specified in their associated assertions so for a basic component c we have $c \vdash \forall x. (\text{sort}(c))x$.

Assume we already know $c \vdash \forall x.Mx$ where M is the sort of c. Then $c \vdash Ex \to Mx$. Hence $c \vdash \Lambda x \to \Lambda x \wedge Mx$. But this yields $c \vdash {}^\Lambda(Ex \to (\Lambda \cap M)x)$ from which we derive $c \lceil \Lambda \vdash Ex \to (\Lambda \cap M)x$. Therefore $c \lceil \Lambda \vdash \forall x.(\Lambda \cap M)x$ and, of course, $\Lambda \cap M$ is the sort of $c \lceil \Lambda$.

Suppose we already know $c_0 \vdash \forall x.\Lambda_0 x$ and $c_1 \vdash \forall x.\Lambda_1 x$ where Λ_0 and Λ_1 are the sorts of c_0 and c_1. Thus

$$c_0 \vdash Ex \to \Lambda_0 x \text{ and } c_1 \vdash Ex \to \Lambda_1 x.$$

By the $(\times \vdash)$ rule, $c_0 \times c_1 \vdash [(Ex \rightarrow \Lambda_0 x) \times (Ex \rightarrow \Lambda_1 x)]$. From the rule $(\times E)$ for product assertions we derive

$$c_0 \times c_1 \vdash Ex \rightarrow ([\Lambda_0 x \times \mathrm{t\!t}] \vee [\mathrm{t\!t} \times \Lambda_1 x])$$

from which

$$c_0 \times c_1 \vdash Ex \rightarrow (\Lambda_0 \cup \Lambda_1) x$$

follows. We get

$$c_0 \times c_1 \vdash \forall x.(\Lambda_0 \cup \Lambda_1) x$$

directly, and from the $^\bullet(\ )$ rules we obtain

$$c_0 \times c_1 \vdash {}^\bullet(\forall x.(\Lambda_0 \cup \Lambda_1) x).$$

Now we see $c_0 \bullet c_1 \vdash \forall x.(\Lambda_0 \cup \Lambda_1) x$, as required.

This completes the structural induction, to show (i). It also makes clear how (ii) follows. ∎

In contexts where we know every point belongs to some finite set we can eliminate all quantifiers, both first and second order, to obtain an equivalent propositional assertion (without any quantifiers).

5.8 Proposition. *Let Λ be a finite set of points.*
  (ia) $\forall x.\Lambda x \vdash \exists x.A \leftrightarrow \bigvee_{\lambda \in \Lambda}(E\lambda \wedge A[\lambda/x])$.
  (ib) $\forall x.\Lambda x \vdash \forall x.A \leftrightarrow \bigwedge_{\lambda \in \Lambda}(E\lambda \rightarrow A[\lambda/x])$.
  (iia) $\forall x.\Lambda x \vdash \exists P.A \leftrightarrow \bigvee_{M \subseteq \Lambda} A[M/P]$.
  (iib) $\forall x.\Lambda x \vdash \forall P.A \leftrightarrow \bigwedge_{M \subseteq \Lambda} A[M/P]$.

Proof.

(ia) Clearly

$$\vdash \bigvee_{\lambda \in \Lambda}(E\lambda \wedge A[\lambda/x]) \rightarrow \exists x.A. \qquad (1)$$

As $\quad \forall x.\Lambda x \vdash \bigvee_{\lambda \in \Lambda} x = \lambda,$

$$\exists x.A, \forall x.\Lambda x \vdash (Ex \wedge A) \wedge \bigvee_{\lambda \in \Lambda} x = \lambda.$$

Hence

$$\exists x.A, \forall x.\Lambda x \vdash \bigvee_{\lambda \in \Lambda}(Ex \wedge A \wedge x = \lambda).$$

Now, using (eq),

$$\exists x.A, \forall x.\Lambda x \vdash \bigvee_{\lambda \in \Lambda}(E\lambda \wedge A[\lambda/x]).$$

Thus

$$\forall x.\Lambda x \vdash \exists x.A \rightarrow \bigvee_{\lambda \in \Lambda}(E\lambda \wedge A[\lambda/x]). \qquad (2)$$

Combining (1) and (2) we obtain (ia).

(ib) The proof is similar to that of (ia), but using $\forall$ in place of $\exists$ rules.

(iia) Let $P = Q$ abbreviate $\forall x.Px \leftrightarrow Qx$, where P and Q are second–order variables or terms. By structural induction on A the following substitution property for second–order terms:

$$\vdash P = Q \wedge A[P/R] \rightarrow A[Q/R].$$

For any finite set Λ, we know

$$\vdash \bigwedge\nolimits_{\lambda \in \Lambda} (P\lambda \wedge \neg P\lambda).$$

By the distribution of $\bigwedge$ over $\vee$ (a metaresult about the proof system),

$$\vdash \bigvee\nolimits_{M \subseteq \Lambda} ([\bigwedge\nolimits_{\lambda \in M} P\lambda] \wedge [\bigwedge\nolimits_{\lambda \in \Lambda \setminus M} \neg P\lambda]),$$

or better,

$$\vdash \bigvee\nolimits_{M \subseteq \Lambda} \bigwedge\nolimits_{\lambda \in \Lambda} (P\lambda \leftrightarrow M\lambda).$$

Hence by part (i),

$$\forall x.\Lambda x \vdash \bigvee\nolimits_{M \subseteq \Lambda} P = M.$$

Now (iia) and (iib) follow by proofs on the same lines as in part (i). ∎

It now follows that for a circuit term c and possibly second-order assertion A that

$$c \vdash A \leftrightarrow B$$

where B is purely first–order. The second–order quantifiers may be useful but they are not essential, and can be provably eliminated. Indeed, this is also true for the first order quantifiers, but having already a complete proof system for the underlying first–order free logic there is no need to eliminate them in our earlier work on restriction. However at present obtaining a complete system of proof rules for composition seems to require a stronger elimination for product assertions.

5.9 Corollary. *Let Λ be a finite set of points. Let A be an assertion. There is a propositional assertion p such that*

$$\forall x.\Lambda x \vdash A \leftrightarrow p.$$

Let c be a circuit term, and A an assertion. There is a propositional assertion p such that

$$c \vdash A \leftrightarrow p$$

Proof. By theorem 5.4 we can eliminate preconditions. Then the first part is proved by successively applying the results above. The second part, for circuits, follows by 5.7(i) because entailment is transitive. ∎

It follows from corollary 5.9 that product assertions of interest can be reduced to provably equivalent propositional assertions, in the context of reasoning about circuits. Just as before we can eliminate first–order quantifiers, and second–order quantifiers can be eliminated at least for the product assertions of concern, those of the form $^\bullet A$.

5.10 Proposition. *Let Λ be a finite set of points.*
For product assertions C,

(a) $\quad \forall x.\Lambda x \vdash \exists x.C \leftrightarrow \bigvee_{\lambda \in \Lambda}(E\lambda \wedge C[\lambda/x])$.

(b) $\quad \forall x.\Lambda x \vdash \forall x.C \leftrightarrow \bigwedge_{\lambda \in \Lambda}(E\lambda \rightarrow C[\lambda/x])$.

For an assertion A,

$\qquad \forall x.\Lambda x \vdash {}^{\bullet}A \leftrightarrow p$ *where p is a propositional product assertion* .

Proof.

Parts (a) and (b) follow as earlier.

Arguing in the same way as we did for restriction preconditions, we can derive the rule

$$\frac{\Gamma \vdash A}{{}^{\bullet}\Gamma \vdash {}^{\bullet}A},$$

from which we observe it follows that if $\Gamma \vdash A \leftrightarrow B$ then ${}^{\bullet}\Gamma \vdash {}^{\bullet}A \leftrightarrow {}^{\bullet}B$. By corollary 5.9, $\forall x.\Lambda x \vdash A \leftrightarrow r$ where r is a propositional assertion. By the observation, we see

$$ {}^{\bullet}\forall x.\Lambda x \vdash {}^{\bullet}A \leftrightarrow {}^{\bullet}r. $$

From the distribution rules for ${}^{\bullet}(\ )$,

$$ D, {}^{\bullet}\forall x.\Lambda x \vdash {}^{\bullet}A \leftrightarrow q, $$

where q is propositional. Hence

$$ \forall x.\Lambda x \vdash {}^{\bullet}A \leftrightarrow (D \rightarrow q), $$

and now by (a) we can eliminate all the quantifiers in D to obtain the required propositional product assertion p. ∎

5.11 Corollary. *Let c_0 and c_1 be circuit terms. Let A be a second order assertion. Then there is a propositional product assertion p such that*

$$ c_0 \times c_1 \vdash {}^{\bullet}A \leftrightarrow p. $$

Proof. By the transitivity of entailment using 5.7(ii). ∎

Product assertions which are propositional can be put into a useful normal form. The purpose of the distribution rules for product (L.8) is to enable this to be done formally in the proof system.

5.12 Proposition. *Let A be a product assertion which is propositional. Then*

$$ \vdash A \leftrightarrow \bigvee_{i \in I} B_i \times C_i $$

where I is a finite set, indexing assertions B_i and C_i.

Proof.

Firstly the logic is classical so $\vdash (A \to B) \leftrightarrow (\neg A \vee B)$ and so we can eliminate occurrences of $\to$ in favour of $\neg$ and $\vee$. Thus without loss of generality we can assume that A is built up solely using $\wedge, \vee, \neg$. The proposition now follows by structural induction on A using basic distributivity properties of the logical connectives. For example, to deal with the hardest case of the induction, we show if we assume the proposition holds for assertion D then it holds for assertion $\neg D$.

Suppose $\vdash D \leftrightarrow \bigvee_{i \in I} B_i \times C_i$. Then

$$\vdash \neg D \leftrightarrow \bigwedge_{i \in I} \neg[B_i \times C_i],$$

and so

$$\vdash \neg D \leftrightarrow \bigwedge_{i \in I}([\neg B_i \times \mathbb{t}] \vee [\mathbb{t} \times \neg C_i]).$$

But then $\vdash \neg D \leftrightarrow \bigvee W$ where W is the set of product assertions

$$\{[\bigwedge_{i \in I} B_i^* \times \bigwedge_{i \in I} C_i^*] |$$
$$(B_i^* \equiv \neg B_i \ \& \ C_i^* \equiv \mathbb{t}) \ \text{or} \ (B_i^* \equiv \mathbb{t} \ \& \ C_i^* \equiv \neg C_i), \text{ all } i \in I\},$$

making D provably equivalent to an assertion of the right form. ∎

Now the problem of proving $c_0 \bullet c_1 \models A$ has reduced to proving $c_0 \times c_1 \models \bigvee_{i \in I} B_i \times C_i$. To achieve compositionality we would like to reduce this further, to proving assertions hold of c_0 and c_1. We need to show:

5.13 Lemma. *Let c_0 and c_1 be circuit terms such that*

$$c_0 \times c_1 \models \bigvee_{i \in I} B_i \times C_i$$

for indexed assertions B_i, C_i. Then there are assertions A_0 and A_1 for which

$$c_0 \models A_0 \ \& \ c_1 \models A_1 \ \& \ A_0 \times A_1 \vdash \bigvee_{i \in I} B_i \times C_i.$$

Proof. It is simpler to argue that A_0 and A_1 exist in a nonconstructive way which shows there exists a proof, so $A_0 \times A_1 \vdash \bigvee_{i \in I} B_i \times C_i$, without giving it explicitly. Of course, this is all that is needed to show completeness. We know $c_0 \times c_1 \models \bigvee_{i \in I} B_i \times C_i$. Hence there is a function $i[\ , \ ]$ so that for any $\sigma \models c_0$ and $\rho \models c_1$ there is $i[\sigma, \rho] \in I$ such that

$$\sigma \models B_{i[\sigma,\rho]} \ \& \ \rho \models C_{i[\sigma,\rho]}.$$

(Note this does not determine $i[\ , \ ]$ uniquely).
Now

$$\sigma \models \bigwedge_{\rho \models c_1} B_{i[\sigma,\rho]} \ \& \ \rho \models \bigwedge_{\sigma \models c_0} C_{i[\sigma,\rho]}$$

for any $\sigma \models c_0$ and $\rho \models c_1$. We use *e.g.* $\bigwedge_{\rho \models c_1} B_{i[\sigma,\rho]}$ to mean the finite conjunction

$$\bigwedge \{B_{i[\sigma,\rho]} \mid \rho \models c_1\}.$$

Clearly

$$\text{\Large\bigwedge}_{\rho \models c_1} B_{i[\sigma,\rho]} \vdash B_{i[\sigma,\rho]} \text{ for } \sigma \models c_0 \text{ and } \rho \models c_1, \text{ and}$$

$$\text{\Large\bigwedge}_{\sigma \models c_0} C_{i[\sigma,\rho]} \vdash C_{i[\sigma,\rho]} \text{ for } \sigma \models c_0 \text{ and } \rho \models c_1,$$

as *e.g.* the conjunction $\text{\Large\bigwedge}_{\rho \models c_1} B_{i[\sigma,\rho]}$ contains $B_{i[\sigma,\rho]}$ as a conjunct. Thus

$$\text{\Large\bigwedge}_{\rho \models c_1} B_{i[\sigma,\rho]} \times \text{\Large\bigwedge}_{\sigma \models c_0} C_{i[\sigma,\rho]} \vdash B_{i[\sigma,\rho]} \times C_{i[\sigma,\rho]}$$

for any $\sigma \models c_0$ and $\rho \models c_1$. Write

$$A_0 \equiv \text{\Large\bigvee}_{\sigma \models c_0} \text{\Large\bigwedge}_{\rho \models c_1} B_{i[\sigma,\rho]} \quad \text{and} \quad A_1 \equiv \text{\Large\bigvee}_{\rho \models c_1} \text{\Large\bigwedge}_{\sigma \models c_0} C_{i[\sigma,\rho]}.$$

By $(\times \vee)$,

$$A_0 \times A_1 \vdash \text{\Large\bigvee}_{(\sigma,\rho) \models c_0 \times c_1} [\text{\Large\bigwedge}_{\rho \models c_1} B_{i[\sigma,\rho]} \times \text{\Large\bigwedge}_{\sigma \models c_0} C_{i[\sigma,\rho]}].$$

Also, obviously,

$$\text{\Large\bigvee}_{(\sigma,\rho) \models c_0 \times c_1} [\text{\Large\bigwedge}_{\rho \models c_1} B_{i[\sigma,\rho]} \times \text{\Large\bigwedge}_{\sigma \models c_0} C_{i[\sigma,\rho]}] \vdash \text{\Large\bigvee}_{i \in I} B_i \times C_i.$$

Therefore $A_0 \times A_1 \vdash \text{\Large\bigvee}_{i \in I} B_i \times C_i$. Clearly $c_0 \models A_0$ and $c_1 \models A_1$. ∎

Now we can tidy up all the loose ends and prove soundness and completeness.

5.14 Theorem. *The proof system is sound i.e.*

$$\Gamma \vdash A \Rightarrow \Gamma \models A$$

for a finite set Γ of circuit–assertions and circuit–assertion A. It is complete in the restricted sense that

$$c \models A \Rightarrow c \vdash A$$

for a circuit term c and assertion A.

Proof. We omit the proof of soundness which is routine if tedious. The proof of completeness follows by structural induction on c.

Suppose the case where c is an atomic circuit term, so suppose for example $c \equiv ntran(\alpha, \beta, \gamma)$. The rule $(ntran \text{ E})$ has the form $ntran(\alpha, \beta, \gamma) \vdash NT$, where NT is a first order assertion describing the behaviour of $ntran(\alpha, \beta, \gamma)$. In fact $[\![ntran(\alpha, \beta, \gamma)]\!] = [\![NT]\!]$. Suppose $ntran(\alpha, \beta, \gamma) \models A$ for an assertion A. Then, as we have shown, $ntran(\alpha, \beta, \gamma) \vdash A \leftrightarrow B$ where B is a first–order assertion. Thus $NT \models B$, so by the completeness theorem 5.1, $NT \vdash B$. Hence $ntran(\alpha, \beta, \gamma) \vdash A$. The other atomic cases are similar.

In the case of restriction suppose $c \lceil \Lambda \models A$ and inductively assume that $c \models B$ iff $c \vdash B$ for any assertion B. Then $c \models {}^\Lambda A$. By the metatheorem 5.4, we can eliminate all preconditions to obtain

$$\vdash {}^\Lambda A \leftrightarrow B$$

for some assertion B. But $c \models B$ and by the inductive assumption $c \vdash B$. This gives $c \vdash {}^\wedge A$ so $c \lceil \Lambda \vdash A$, as required in this case.

In the case of composition, suppose $c_0 \bullet c_1 \models A$ and inductively assume $c_0 \models A_0$ iff $c_0 \vdash A_0$ and $c_1 \models A_1$ iff $c_1 \vdash A_1$ for any assertions A_0 and A_1. Then $c_0 \times c_1 \models {}^\bullet A$. Our earlier results show that

$$c_0 \times c_1 \vdash {}^\bullet A \leftrightarrow \bigvee\nolimits_{i \in I} B_i \times C_i,$$

and, the above lemma, that in such a case there are A_0 and A_1 with

$$c_0 \models A_0 \ \& \ c_1 \models A_1 \ \& \ A_0 \times A_1 \vdash \bigvee\nolimits_{i \in I} B_i \times C_i,$$

precisely what is needed to conclude $c_0 \times c_1 \vdash {}^\bullet A$ and hence $c_0 \bullet c_1 \vdash A$. ∎

6. Conclusion.

We have presented a compositional model for the behaviour of MOS circuits in a static environment. Certainly such a model is necessary for a satisfactory treatment of dynamically changing circuits. Their behaviour can often be viewed as going through a sequence of static configurations as data changes in synchrony with one or several clocks. The data and the clock pulses are held long enough for the circuit to settle into a static configuration. It seems natural therefore to represent a possible history for such a circuit as a sequence of static configurations. Copying the approach in [Gor2,3] we could try to extend our work to the dynamic case by simply including a time parameter $t \in \omega$, and associating devices with assertions expressing time dependencies between static configurations at different times. For example, then we could express facts like a capacitance would contribute a charge at time $t + 1$ if it was precharged at time t. Although it is not hard to push through this programme, it is disappointing that there are difficulties in making the model accurate. A main problem it seems is that short–term capacitance effects influence the physical behaviour but are not captured easily in any extension of our model. The strength orders we use assume that the environment is stable long enough for sources of current to override charges stored by capacitance. This assumption breaks down in some stages needed to explain the behaviour of devices like the following register:

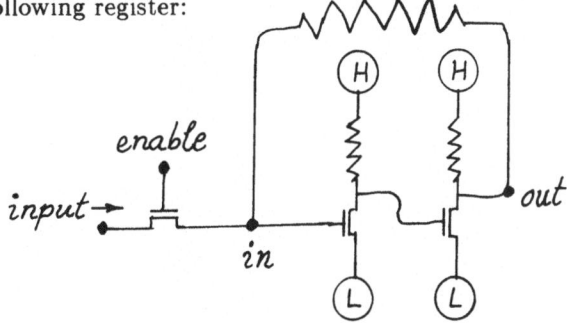

When *enable* is high, a strong signal at *in* overrides that already present, and its value is established, after two inversions, at *out*. When *enable* becomes low the value is preserved at *out* (the input value is stored). Speaking loosely, the latter stage relies on capacitance to maintain the value at *in* until the feedback loop takes over. This occurs over a very short time when the assumptions behind the strength order are violated. I cannot, at present, see how to extend the model to account for effects over such a short time. Through failing to cope adequately with such short–term effects, the models I have developed allow more possibilities than are physically possible. By the way, the work of Bryant does not address this problem; a simulator need only generate one possible course of behaviour and Bryant does this by making a unit–delay assumption. (In his simulators all transistors switch with the same delay after their gates change.)

It is unfortunate that the logic is so complicated even for static circuits. This may be in the nature of things. If so it makes even more pressing the task of relating models of the kind here to the models and logic like [Gor2,3] which are relatively simple to work with. There must be "correspondence principles" which express how and when one model reduces to another. In general relations between models may be quite complex. A physical model implements a discrete model only provided certain conditions are met.

So far there have been several successful attempts at relating the physical and the logical levels for specific pieces of hardware, *e.g.* [GH, HD], and carrying through the thesis proposal [Me] should lay bare some of the key issues.

Acknowledgements

I am grateful to many people for help at various times. I owe a debt to the thesis work of Luca Cardelli [Car]; there Luca attempted to give a semantics to circuits on roughly similar lines to section 4 though his model was not sufficiently detailed to support a satisfactory treatment of hiding. His approach and mine were guided by work on CCS and CSP. Mike Gordon's course on hardware verification exposed the problems which led to this work. I would like to thank him and members of the hardware verification group here for help and encouragement on many occasions in an area where I'm still finding my feet. Special thanks are due to Inder Dhingra, Edmund Ronald and Edmund Robinson, all of whom contributed ideas. The work [A] of Samson Abramsky provided a vital hint on how to make the proof system, and the work in [S] and [P] gave useful leads. Many thanks to Mogens Nielsen for his patient reading of this and his constructive criticism. Thanks too to Randy Bryant for encouragement.

Appendix. The logic of static circuits .

L.1 The assertion language for circuits.

Assume a particular strength order $\mathbf{S}$ (with typical members $s, s', \cdots$), a countably infinite set of point names Π (with typical members $\alpha, \beta, \gamma, \cdots$) and Var a set of variables, ranging over points (with typical members $x, y, z, \cdots$) and Pvar a set of second order variables ranging over sets (or properties) of points (with typical members $P, Q, R, \cdots$).

Define a *strength expression*, by induction, to have the form

$$s \mid S\pi \mid e_0 \cdot e_1 \mid e_0 + e_1$$

where $s \in \mathbf{S}$, $\pi \in \Pi \cup \text{Var}$ and e_0, e_1 are strength expressions.

Define a *point relation* to have the form

$$H\pi \mid L\pi \mid h\pi \mid l\pi \mid \pi_0 = \pi_1 \mid \pi_0 \rightsquigarrow \pi_1 \mid E\pi$$

where $\pi, \pi_0, \pi_1 \in \Pi \cup \text{Var}$.

Define a *strength relation* to have the form

$$Ee \mid e_0 \le e_1 \mid e_0 = e_1$$

where e, e_0 and e_1 are strength expressions.

Define a *circuit-assertion*, by induction, to have the form

$$
\begin{aligned}
&circ \mid srel \mid prel \mid \\
&\text{tt} \mid \text{ff} \mid A \wedge B \mid A \vee B \mid A \rightarrow B \mid \exists x.A \mid \forall x.A \mid \\
&\{x : A\}\pi \mid P\pi \mid \exists P.A \mid \forall P.A \mid \\
&{}^{\Lambda}A
\end{aligned}
$$

where *srel* is a strength relation, *prel* is a point relation, *circ* is a circuit term, and Λ is a finite subset of ports with $x \in \text{Var}$ and $P \in \text{Pvar}$.

L.2 Notation.

We shall take the treatment of free and bound variables, and open and closed strength expressions and assertions as understood. Write $FV(A)$ for the set of free variables (first and second order) of an assertion A. We write $A[\pi/x]$ for the result of substituting π for all free occurrences of the variable x in A, and similarly $A[T/P]$ for the result of substituting a term denoting a property for the second order variable P—we assume changes are made in the naming of bound variables to avoid the binding of free variables in the substituted terms.

Take $\neg A$ to abbreviate the assertion $A \rightarrow \text{ff}$, for an assertion A. Take $A \leftrightarrow B$ to abbreviate $A \rightarrow B \wedge B \rightarrow A$.

Let $\Gamma = \{A_0, \cdots, A_n\}$ be a finite set of assertions. We use $\bigwedge\Gamma$ to abbreviate their conjunction $A_0 \wedge \cdots \wedge A_n$ and $\bigvee\Gamma$ to abbreviate their disjunction $A_0 \vee \cdots \vee A_n$. We identify $\bigwedge\emptyset$ with $\mathbb{t}$ and $\bigvee\emptyset$ with $\mathbb{f}$.

We use $\forall x : Q.\ A$ to abbreviate $\forall x.\ Qx \to A$ and $\exists x : Q.\ A$ to abbreviate $\exists x.\ Qx \wedge A$. If Λ is a finite set we use Λ in the logic to abbreviate the term $\{x : \bigvee_{\lambda \in \Lambda} x = \lambda\}$.

L.3 Semantics of the assertion language

We take the set of points to be Π, and static configurations to have sorts a subset of these. A point name α is thus associated with a corresponding point.

Semantics of strength expressions

Define $[\![\ ]\!]$ from closed strength expressions to subsets of pairs of static configurations and strengths by the following induction, with the understanding that static configurations σ have the form $\sigma = \langle S, V, I, \rightsquigarrow \rangle$.

$$[\![s]\!] = \{(\sigma, s) \mid \sigma \in \mathrm{Sta}\}$$
$$[\![S\alpha]\!] = \{(\sigma, s) \mid \alpha \in \mathrm{sort}(\sigma)\ \&\ S\alpha = s\}$$
$$[\![e_0 \cdot e_1]\!] = \{(\sigma, s_0 \cdot s_1) \mid (\sigma, s_0) \in [\![e_0]\!]\ \&\ (\sigma, s_1) \in [\![e_1]\!]\}$$
$$[\![e_0 + e_1]\!] = \{(\sigma, s_0 + s_1) \mid (\sigma, s_0) \in [\![e_0]\!]\ \&\ (\sigma, s_1) \in [\![e_1]\!]\}$$

Semantics of circuit assertions

We firstly define the semantics of point relations, with the understanding that static configurations σ have the form $\sigma = \langle S, V, I, \rightsquigarrow \rangle$. Define $[\![\ ]\!]$ from closed point relations to the subsets of static configurations which satisfy them by

$$[\![H\alpha]\!] = \{\sigma \mid \alpha \in \mathrm{sort}(\sigma)\ \&\ H \leq V\alpha\}$$
$$[\![L\alpha]\!] = \{\sigma \mid \alpha \in \mathrm{sort}(\sigma)\ \&\ L \leq V\alpha\}$$
$$[\![h\alpha]\!] = \{\sigma \mid \alpha \in \mathrm{sort}(\sigma)\ \&\ H \leq I\alpha\}$$
$$[\![l\alpha]\!] = \{\sigma \mid \alpha \in \mathrm{sort}(\sigma)\ \&\ L \leq I\alpha\}$$
$$[\![\alpha = \beta]\!] = \{\sigma \mid \alpha = \beta \in \mathrm{sort}(\sigma)\}$$
$$[\![\alpha \rightsquigarrow \beta]\!] = \{\sigma \mid \alpha, \beta \in \mathrm{sort}(\sigma)\ \&\ \alpha \rightsquigarrow \beta\}$$
$$[\![E\alpha]\!] = \{\sigma \mid \alpha \in \mathrm{sort}(\sigma)\}.$$

Now we define the semantics of strength relations:

$$[\![Ee]\!] = \{\sigma \mid \exists s.\ (\sigma, s) \in [\![e]\!]\}$$
$$[\![e_0 \leq e_1]\!] = \{\sigma \mid \exists s_0, s_1.\ (\sigma, s_0) \in [\![e_0]\!]\ \&\ (\sigma, s_1) \in [\![e_1]\!]\ \&\ s_0 \leq s_1\}$$
$$[\![e_0 = e_1]\!] = \{\sigma \mid \exists s_0, s_1.\ (\sigma, s_0) \in [\![e_0]\!]\ \&\ (\sigma, s_1) \in [\![e_1]\!]\ \&\ s_0 = s_1\}$$

Now we have defined the semantics of point and strength relations, we extend the semantics to all closed assertions by the following induction on the length of assertions:

$$[\![\mathbf{tt}]\!] = \mathrm{Sta}$$
$$[\![\mathbf{ff}]\!] = \emptyset$$
$$[\![A \wedge B]\!] = [\![A]\!] \cap [\![B]\!]$$
$$[\![A \vee B]\!] = [\![A]\!] \cup [\![B]\!]$$
$$[\![A \rightarrow B]\!] = (\mathrm{Sta} \setminus [\![A]\!]) \cup [\![B]\!]$$
$$[\![\exists x.A]\!] = \{ \sigma \mid \exists \alpha \in \mathrm{sort}(\sigma).\ \sigma \in [\![A[\alpha/x]]\!] \}$$
$$[\![\forall x.A]\!] = \{ \sigma \mid \forall \alpha \in \mathrm{sort}(\sigma).\ \sigma \in [\![A[\alpha/x]]\!] \}$$
$$[\![\{x : A\}\alpha]\!] = [\![E\alpha\ \&\ A[\alpha/x]]\!]$$
$$[\![\exists P.A]\!] = \{ \sigma \mid \exists \Lambda \subseteq \mathrm{sort}(\sigma).\ \sigma \in [\![A[\Lambda/P]]\!] \}$$
$$[\![\forall P.A]\!] = \{ \sigma \mid \forall \Lambda \subseteq \mathrm{sort}(\sigma).\ \sigma \in [\![A[\Lambda/P]]\!] \},$$
$$[\![{}^{\Lambda}A]\!] = \{ \sigma \mid \sigma \lceil \Lambda \downarrow \Rightarrow \sigma \lceil \Lambda \in [\![A]\!] \}.$$

We have already seen how to define the denotations of circuit terms in section 4.

L.4 Satisfaction, validity and entailment

For a closed circuit assertion A we write

$$\sigma \models A \text{ iff } \sigma \in [\![A]\!],$$

and say σ *satisfies* A.

Let A be an assertion with free variables $x_0, \ldots, P_0, \ldots$. Define

$$\models A \quad \text{iff} \quad \sigma \models A[\alpha_0/x_0, \ldots, \Lambda_0/P_0, \ldots] \text{ for all } \sigma \in \mathrm{Sta}$$

for any substitution with $\alpha_0, \ldots \in \Pi$ and $\Lambda_0, \ldots \subseteq \Pi$. When $\models A$ we say A is *valid*.

More generally, letting Γ be a set of assertions and A an assertion, define $\Gamma \models A$ iff for every substitution ϑ of the free variables in Γ and A every static configuration which satisfies each assertion $B[\vartheta]$, for B in Γ, also satisfies $A[\vartheta]$.

L.5 Proof rules for circuit assertions

The proof rules follow a natural deduction style [Pr], with extra axioms special to static configurations and circuits.

Structural rules

(refl) $\Gamma \vdash A$ if $A \in \Gamma$ (tran) $\dfrac{\Gamma \vdash A \quad \Delta, A \vdash B}{\Gamma, \Delta \vdash B}$

Propositional logic

($\wedge$I) $\dfrac{\Gamma \vdash A \quad \Gamma \vdash B}{\Gamma \vdash A \wedge B}$ ($\wedge$E) $\dfrac{\Gamma \vdash A \wedge B}{\Gamma \vdash A} \quad \dfrac{\Gamma \vdash A \wedge B}{\Gamma \vdash B}$

($\vee$I) $\dfrac{\Gamma \vdash A}{\Gamma \vdash A \vee B} \quad \dfrac{\Gamma \vdash B}{\Gamma \vdash A \vee B}$ ($\vee$E) $\dfrac{\Gamma \vdash A \vee B \quad \Gamma, A \vdash C \quad \Gamma, B \vdash C}{\Gamma \vdash C}$

($\rightarrow$ I) $\dfrac{\Gamma, A \vdash B}{\Gamma \vdash A \rightarrow B}$ ($\rightarrow$ E) $\dfrac{\Gamma \vdash A \rightarrow B \quad \Gamma \vdash A}{\Gamma \vdash B}$

(tt) $\Gamma \vdash \text{tt}$ (ff) $\dfrac{\Gamma, \neg A \vdash \text{ff}}{\Gamma \vdash A}$

First-order rules

(sub) $\dfrac{\Gamma \vdash A}{\Gamma \vdash A[\pi/x]}$ $(x \notin \mathrm{FV}(\Gamma))$

($\forall$I) $\dfrac{\Gamma \vdash Ex \rightarrow A}{\Gamma \vdash \forall x.\, A}$ $(x \notin \mathrm{FV}(\Gamma))$ ($\forall$E) $\dfrac{\Gamma \vdash \forall x.\, A}{\Gamma \vdash Et \rightarrow A[t/x]}$

($\exists$I) $\dfrac{\Gamma \vdash Et \wedge A[t/x]}{\Gamma \vdash \exists x.\, A}$ ($\exists$E) $\dfrac{\Gamma \vdash \exists x.\, A \quad \Gamma, Ex \wedge A \vdash B}{\Gamma \vdash B}$ $(x \notin \mathrm{FV}(\Gamma, B$

Rules for second-order quantifiers and abstraction

(sub²) $\dfrac{\Gamma \vdash A}{\Gamma \vdash A[T/P]}$ $(P \notin \mathrm{FV}(\Gamma))$

($\forall^2$I) $\dfrac{\Gamma \vdash A}{\Gamma \vdash \forall P.\, A}$ $(P \notin \mathrm{FV}(\Gamma))$ ($\forall^2$E) $\dfrac{\Gamma \vdash \forall P.\, A}{\Gamma \vdash A[T/P]}$

($\exists^2$I) $\dfrac{\Gamma \vdash A[T/P]}{\Gamma \vdash \exists P.\, A}$ ($\exists^2$E) $\dfrac{\Gamma \vdash \exists P.\, A \quad \Gamma, A \vdash B}{\Gamma \vdash B}$ $(P \notin \mathrm{FV}(\Gamma, B))$

(ab I) $\dfrac{\Gamma \vdash Ey \wedge A[y/x]}{\Gamma \vdash \{x : A\}y}$ (ab E) $\dfrac{\Gamma \vdash \{x : A\}y}{\Gamma \vdash Ey \wedge A[y/x]}$

(strict) $\Gamma \vdash Px \rightarrow Ex$

Remark. A word on the second–order logic: The idea is that in a particular static configuration σ, $\{x : A\}$ denotes the set of points in sort(σ) which satisfy A. So unlike first–order terms for points or strengths, set abstractions are always defined, and the second–order rules do not need to invoke an existence predicate. Although set abstractions only appear within assertions in the form $\{x : A\}\pi$, their use enable a simpler account of the rules for second–order quantifiers—*e.g.* try writing the ($\exists^2 I$) rule without!

Proof rules for point relations

We assume that point names are in 1–1 correspondence with points, so we have the following basic axioms.

$\vdash \alpha = \beta$ iff $\models \alpha = \beta$ (*i.e.* α and β are the same point name).

$\vdash \neg\alpha = \beta$ iff $\models \neg\alpha = \beta$ (*i.e.* α and β are different point names).

The following axioms are essentially a reformulation of the axioms for static configurations which we have seen earlier.

(refl) $\vdash Ex \leftrightarrow x = x$
(eq) $\vdash x = y \wedge A[x/z] \rightarrow A[y/z]$

(str) $\vdash Hx \rightarrow Ex$

$\vdash Lx \rightarrow Ex$

$\vdash hx \rightarrow Ex$

$\vdash lx \rightarrow Ex$

$\vdash x \rightsquigarrow y \rightarrow Ex \wedge Ey$

$\vdash Ex \rightarrow x \rightsquigarrow x$

$\vdash x \rightsquigarrow y \wedge y \rightsquigarrow z \rightarrow x \rightsquigarrow z$

$\vdash x \rightsquigarrow y \rightarrow Sx \geq Sy$

$\vdash x \rightsquigarrow y \wedge Sx = Sy \rightarrow y \rightsquigarrow x$

$\vdash x \rightsquigarrow y \wedge \bigvee_{k \in K} Sy = k \rightarrow Sx = Sy$

$\vdash Sx = 0 \leftrightarrow \neg Hx \wedge \neg Lx$

$\vdash hx \rightarrow Hx \wedge lx \rightarrow Lx$

$\vdash Hx \wedge x \rightsquigarrow y \rightarrow Hy$

$\vdash Lx \wedge x \rightsquigarrow y \rightarrow Ly$

$\vdash hx \wedge x \rightsquigarrow y \rightarrow hy$

$\vdash lx \wedge x \rightsquigarrow y \rightarrow ly$

Proof rules for strength relations

$\vdash s \leq s'$ if $\models s \leq s'$ $\vdash \neg s \leq s'$ if $\models \neg s \leq s'$
$\vdash s = s'$ if $\models s = s'$ $\vdash \neg s = s'$ if $\models \neg s = s'$
$\vdash s_0 \cdot s_1 = s$ if $\models s_0 \cdot s_1 = s$ $\vdash \neg s_0 \cdot s_1 = s$ if $\models \neg s_0 \cdot s_1 = s$
$\vdash s_0 + s_1 = s$ if $\models s_0 + s_1 = s$ $\vdash \neg s_0 + s_1 = s$ if $\models \neg s_0 + s_1 = s$

$\vdash Ee \leftrightarrow e = e$

$\vdash e = e' \rightarrow e' = e$

$$\vdash e = e' \wedge e' = e'' \to e = e''$$

$$\vdash Ex \to \bigvee_{s \in S} Sx = s$$
$$\vdash E(Sx) \to Ex$$
$$\vdash E(e_0 \cdot e_1) \leftrightarrow Ee_0 \wedge Ee_1$$
$$\vdash E(e_0 + e_1) \leftrightarrow Ee_0 \wedge Ee_1$$
$$\vdash e_0 \le e_1 \to Ee_0 \wedge Ee_1$$

$$\vdash e_0 = e_0' \wedge e_1 = e_1' \to e_0 \cdot e_1 = e_0' \cdot e_1'$$
$$\vdash e_0 = e_0' \wedge e_1 = e_1' \to e_0 + e_1 = e_0' + e_1'$$
$$\vdash e_0 = e_0' \wedge e_1 = e_1' \wedge e_0 \le e_1 \to e_0' \le e_1'$$

L.6 Rules for restriction preconditions

Let

$$G \equiv \forall x. \, \neg \Lambda x \to [Hx \to hx \vee (\exists y : \Lambda. \, Hy \wedge y \rightsquigarrow x)] \wedge$$
$$[Lx \to lx \vee (\exists y : \Lambda. \, Ly \wedge y \rightsquigarrow x)]$$

Introduction rules for $^\Lambda(\ )$:

$$\frac{\vdash A}{\vdash {}^\Lambda A} \qquad\qquad \neg G \vdash {}^\Lambda A$$

Distribution rules for $^\Lambda(\ )$:

$$G \vdash {}^\Lambda(Sx = s) \leftrightarrow (Sx = s \wedge \Lambda x)$$
$$G \vdash {}^\Lambda(Hx) \leftrightarrow (Hx \wedge \Lambda x) \qquad\qquad G \vdash {}^\Lambda(Lx) \leftrightarrow (Lx \wedge \Lambda x)$$
$$G \vdash {}^\Lambda(hx) \leftrightarrow (hx \wedge \Lambda x) \qquad\qquad G \vdash {}^\Lambda(lx) \leftrightarrow (lx \wedge \Lambda x)$$
$$G \vdash {}^\Lambda(x \rightsquigarrow y) \leftrightarrow (x \rightsquigarrow y \wedge \Lambda x \wedge \Lambda y) \qquad G \vdash {}^\Lambda(x = y) \leftrightarrow (x = y \wedge \Lambda x \wedge \Lambda y)$$
$$G \vdash {}^\Lambda(Ex) \leftrightarrow \Lambda x$$
$$G \vdash {}^\Lambda \mathrm{tt} \leftrightarrow \mathrm{tt} \qquad\qquad G \vdash {}^\Lambda \mathrm{ff} \leftrightarrow \mathrm{ff}$$
$$G \vdash {}^\Lambda(A \wedge B) \leftrightarrow ({}^\Lambda A \wedge {}^\Lambda B) \qquad G \vdash {}^\Lambda(A \vee B) \leftrightarrow ({}^\Lambda A \vee {}^\Lambda B)$$
$$G \vdash {}^\Lambda(A \to B) \leftrightarrow ({}^\Lambda A \to {}^\Lambda B)$$
$$G \vdash {}^\Lambda(\forall x.A) \leftrightarrow (\forall x : \Lambda. \, {}^\Lambda A) \qquad G \vdash {}^\Lambda(\exists x.A) \leftrightarrow (\exists x : \Lambda. \, {}^\Lambda A)$$
$$G \vdash {}^\Lambda(\{x : A\}y) \leftrightarrow (\{x : {}^\Lambda A\}y \wedge \Lambda y) \qquad G \vdash {}^\Lambda(Px) \leftrightarrow (Px \wedge \Lambda x)$$
$$G \vdash {}^\Lambda(\forall P.A) \leftrightarrow \forall P. \, {}^\Lambda A \qquad G \vdash {}^\Lambda(\exists P.A) \leftrightarrow \exists P. \, {}^\Lambda A$$

L.7 Product circuit–assertions

Product circuit–assertions are defined inductively to have the form

$$A \times B \mid {}^{\bullet}A \mid E\pi \mid \pi_0 = \pi_1$$
$$\mathbf{tt} \mid \mathbf{ff} \mid D_0 \wedge D_1 \mid D_0 \vee D_1 \mid D_0 \rightarrow D_1 \mid \exists x.D \mid \forall x.D \mid$$
$$\{x : D\}\pi \mid \exists P.D \mid \forall P.D$$

where A, B are circuit–assertions and D, D_0, D_1 are product assertions.

L.8 Semantics of product assertions:

$$[\![A \times B]\!] = [\![A]\!] \times [\![B]\!]$$
$$[\![{}^{\bullet}A]\!] = \{(\sigma, \rho) \mid \sigma \bullet \rho \downarrow \Rightarrow \sigma \bullet \rho \in [\![A]\!]\}$$
$$[\![E\alpha]\!] = \{(\sigma, \rho) \mid \alpha \in \mathrm{sort}(\sigma) \cup \mathrm{sort}(\rho)\}$$
$$[\![\alpha = \beta]\!] = \{(\sigma, \rho) \mid \alpha = \beta \in \mathrm{sort}(\sigma) \cup \mathrm{sort}(\rho)\}$$
$$[\![\{x : D\}\alpha]\!] = [\![E\alpha \wedge D[\alpha/x]]\!]$$
$$[\![\exists P.D]\!] = \{(\sigma, \rho) \mid \exists \Lambda \subseteq \mathrm{sort}(\sigma) \cup \mathrm{sort}(\rho). (\sigma, \rho) \in [\![D[\Lambda/P]]\!]\}$$
$$[\![\forall P.D]\!] = \{(\sigma, \rho) \mid \forall \Lambda \subseteq \mathrm{sort}(\sigma) \cup \rho. (\sigma, \rho) \in [\![D[\Lambda/P]]\!]\}$$

The semantics for the remaining clauses follow those for circuit assertions. The proof rules for product assertions include those for for second order logic, with the understanding that terms T substituted in the second order quantifier rules are first–order set abstractions, *i.e.* of the form $\{x : A\}$ with A first–order. We include, in addition, the following.

Proof rules for product assertions:

$(\times \vdash)$

$$\frac{A \vdash A' \quad B \vdash B'}{A \times B \vdash A' \times B'}$$

$(\times E)$ $\vdash Ex \leftrightarrow ([Ex \times \mathbf{tt}] \vee [\mathbf{tt} \times Ex])$

$(\times =)$ $\vdash x = y \leftrightarrow ([x = y \times \mathbf{tt}] \vee [\mathbf{tt} \times x = y])$

(eq) $\vdash x = y \wedge C[x/z] \rightarrow C[y/z]$

$(\times \mathbf{tt})$ $\vdash \mathbf{tt} \leftrightarrow [\mathbf{tt} \times \mathbf{tt}]$

$(\times \mathbf{ff})$ $\vdash \mathbf{ff} \leftrightarrow ([\mathbf{ff} \times \mathbf{tt}] \vee [\mathbf{tt} \times \mathbf{ff}])$

$(\times \wedge)$ $\vdash ([A \times B] \wedge [A' \times B']) \leftrightarrow ([A \wedge A'] \times [B \wedge B'])$

$(\times \vee)$ $\vdash [(A \vee A') \times B] \leftrightarrow ([A \times B] \vee [A' \times B])$

                         $\vdash [A \times (B \vee B')] \leftrightarrow ([A \times B] \vee [A \times B'])$

$(\times \neg)$ $\vdash \neg[A \times B] \leftrightarrow ([\neg A \times \mathbf{tt}] \vee [\mathbf{tt} \times \neg B])$

L.9. Rules for composition precondition

Let

$$D \equiv \forall x.\ ([Ex \times \mathfrak{t}] \wedge [\mathfrak{t} \times Ex]) \rightarrow$$

$$([Hx \times \mathfrak{t}] \leftrightarrow [\mathfrak{t} \times Hx] \wedge$$
$$[Lx \times \mathfrak{t}] \leftrightarrow [\mathfrak{t} \times Lx] \wedge$$
$$\bigvee_{s \in S}[Sx = s \times Sx = s])$$

Introduction rules for $^{\bullet}(\ )$:

$(^{\bullet}I)$
$$\dfrac{\vdash A}{\vdash {}^{\bullet}A}$$
$$\neg D \vdash {}^{\bullet}A$$

Distribution rules for $^{\bullet}(\ )$:

$(d\ ^{\bullet}S)$ $D \vdash {}^{\bullet}(Sx = s) \leftrightarrow ([Sx = s \times \mathfrak{t}] \vee [\mathfrak{t} \times Sx = s])$

$(d\ ^{\bullet}H)$ $D \vdash {}^{\bullet}(Hx) \leftrightarrow ([Hx \times \mathfrak{t}] \vee [\mathfrak{t} \times Hx])$

$(d\ ^{\bullet}L)$ $D \vdash {}^{\bullet}(Lx) \leftrightarrow ([Lx \times \mathfrak{t}] \vee [\mathfrak{t} \times Lx])$

$(d\ ^{\bullet}h)$ $D \vdash {}^{\bullet}(hx) \leftrightarrow (\exists y.\ ([hy \times \mathfrak{t}] \vee [\mathfrak{t} \times hy]) \wedge {}^{\bullet}y \rightsquigarrow x)$

$(d\ ^{\bullet}l)$ $D \vdash {}^{\bullet}(lx) \leftrightarrow (\exists y.\ ([ly \times \mathfrak{t}] \vee [\mathfrak{t} \times ly]) \wedge {}^{\bullet}y \rightsquigarrow x)$

$(d\ ^{\bullet}\rightsquigarrow)$ $D \vdash {}^{\bullet}(x \rightsquigarrow y) \leftrightarrow$

$\qquad [\forall P.\ {}^{\bullet}Px \wedge$

$\qquad\qquad (\forall v, w.\ {}^{\bullet}Pv \wedge ([v \rightsquigarrow w \times \mathfrak{t}] \vee [\mathfrak{t} \times v \rightsquigarrow w]) \rightarrow {}^{\bullet}Pw) \rightarrow {}^{\bullet}Py]$

$(d\ ^{\bullet}=)$ $D \vdash {}^{\bullet}(x = y) \leftrightarrow ([x = y \times \mathfrak{t}] \vee [\mathfrak{t} \times x = y])$

$(d\ ^{\bullet}E)$ $D \vdash {}^{\bullet}(Ex) \leftrightarrow Ex$

$(d\ ^{\bullet}\mathfrak{t})$ $D \vdash {}^{\bullet}\mathfrak{t} \leftrightarrow \mathfrak{t}$

$(d\ ^{\bullet}\mathfrak{f})$ $D \vdash {}^{\bullet}\mathfrak{f} \leftrightarrow \mathfrak{f}$

$(d\ ^{\bullet}\wedge)$ $D \vdash {}^{\bullet}(A \wedge B) \leftrightarrow ({}^{\bullet}A \wedge {}^{\bullet}B)$

$(d\ ^{\bullet}\vee)$ $D \vdash {}^{\bullet}(A \vee B) \leftrightarrow ({}^{\bullet}A \vee {}^{\bullet}B)$

$(d\ ^{\bullet}\rightarrow)$ $D \vdash {}^{\bullet}(A \rightarrow B) \leftrightarrow ({}^{\bullet}A \rightarrow {}^{\bullet}B)$

$(d\ ^{\bullet}\forall)$ $D \vdash {}^{\bullet}(\forall x.A) \leftrightarrow \forall x.\ {}^{\bullet}A$

$(d\ ^{\bullet}\exists)$ $D \vdash {}^{\bullet}(\exists x.A) \leftrightarrow \exists x.\ {}^{\bullet}A$

$(d\ ^{\bullet}ab)$ $D \vdash {}^{\bullet}(\{x : A\}y) \leftrightarrow \{x : {}^{\bullet}A\}y$

$(d\ ^{\bullet}\forall^2)$ $D \vdash {}^{\bullet}(\forall P.A) \leftrightarrow \forall P.\ {}^{\bullet}A$

$(d\ ^{\bullet}\exists^2)$ $D \vdash {}^{\bullet}(\exists P.A) \leftrightarrow \exists P.\ {}^{\bullet}A$

L.10. Elimination rules for circuit terms

$$\frac{c \vdash {}^{\wedge}A}{c\lceil \Lambda \vdash A}$$

$$\frac{c_0 \times c_1 \vdash {}^{\bullet}A}{c_0 \bullet c_1 \vdash A}$$

The elimination rules for the basic components obtained directly from their semantics in 4.2, with equations such as $I\alpha = H$ being understood as abbreviating assertions in the logic, in this case $hx \wedge \neg lx$. For example, the elimination rule for a resistance $res_g(\alpha, \beta)$ takes the form:

$$res_g(\alpha, \beta) \vdash E\alpha \wedge E\beta \wedge (\forall x.\ x = \alpha \vee x = \beta) \wedge$$
$$\forall x.\ (\neg hx \wedge \neg lx) \wedge$$
$$S\alpha{\cdot}g \leq S\beta \wedge S\beta{\cdot}g \leq S\alpha \wedge$$
$$(S\alpha{\cdot}g = S\beta \leftrightarrow \alpha \rightsquigarrow \beta) \wedge (S\beta{\cdot}g = S\alpha \leftrightarrow \beta \rightsquigarrow \alpha)\}$$

References

[A] Abramsky, S., An intuitionistic logic of computable functions. Copy of slides 1984.

[B1] Bryant, R.E., A switch–level model of MOS circuits. In VLSI '81, Ed. J. Gray, Academic Press 1981.

[B] Bryant, R.E., A switch–level model and simulator for MOS digital systems. IEEE Transactions on Computers C–33 (2) pp. 160–177, February 1984.

[C] Cardelli, L., An algebraic approach to hardware description and verification. Ph.D. thesis, Comp.Sc.Dept., University of Edinburgh (1982).

[CGM] Camilleri, A., Gordon, M., and Melham, T., Hardware verification using higher order logic. To appear in the proceedings of the IFIP International working conference, Grenoble, France, September 1986. Also available as a report 91 of the Computer Laboratory, University of Cambridge (1986).

[D] Dijkstra, E.W., A discipline of programming. Prentice–Hall (1976).

[F] Fourman, M.P., Verification using higher–order specifications and transformations. Department of Electrical Engineering, Brunel University (1986).

[FS] Fourman, M.P., and Scott, D.S., Sheaves and logic. In proc. of Durham conference on Applications of Sheaves 1977, Lecture notes in Math., Springer–Verlag 1979.

[Gor1] Gordon, M.J.C., LCF–LSM. Report no. 41 of the Computer Laboratory, University of Cambridge (1983).

[Gor2] Gordon, M.J.C., How to specify and verify hardware using higher order logic. Lecture notes, Computer Laboratory, University of Cambridge (1984).

[Gor3] Gordon, M.J.C., Why higher order logic is a good formalism for specifying and verifying hardware. Report no.77 of the Computer Laboratory, Cambridge University 1985.

[GH] Gordon, M.J.C., and Herbert, J., A formal methodology and its approach to a network interface chip. Report no.84 of the Computer Laboratory, Cambridge University 1985.

[Gra] Grayson, R., Heyting–valued semantics. Proc. logic colloquium '82, North–Holland (1984).

[Ha] Harel, D., First–order dynamic logic. Springer Verlag Lecture Notes in Comp.Sc., vol. 68 (1979).

[HD] Hanna, F.K., and Daeche, N., Specification and verification using higher–order logic. Proc. IFIP WG 10.2, 7th. international conference on computer hardware description languages and their applications, Tokyo, Japan 1985, Koomen & Moto-oka (eds.), North–Holland (1985)

[Hay] Hayes, J., A unified switching theory with applications to VLSI design. Proc. IEEE 70 (10) pp. 1140–1155 Oct. 1982.

[KB] Bergstra, J.A., and Klop, J.W., A proof rule for restoring logic circuits. Integration 1 pp.161–178 (1983).

[MC] Mead, C., and Conway, L., Introduction to VLSI systems. Addison–Wesley (1980).

[MD] Mavor, J., and Denyer, P.B., Introduction to MOS design. Addison Wesley 1983.

[Me] Melham, T., Abstraction in hardware verification. Progress report and thesis proposal, Computer Laboratory, University of Cambridge (1985).

[Mi] Milne, G., CIRCAL, TOPLAS April 1985.

[Mos] Moszkowski, B., Executing temporal logic programs. Report no.71 of the Computer Laboratory, Cambridge University 1985.

[OH] Olderog, E., and Hoare, C.A.R., Specification–oriented semantics for communicating processes. ICALP 83, Springer Lecture Notes in Comp. Sc. vol. 154 (1983).

[P] Plotkin, G.D., Types and partial functions. Lecture notes, Computer Science Dept., University of Edinburgh 1985.

[Pr] Prawitz, D., Natural deduction. Almqvist and Wiksell 1985.

[deR] de Roever, W.P., The quest for compositionality. In the proceedings of the IFIP working conference, January 1985, North–Holland (1985).

[S] Scott, D.S., Identity and existence in intuitionistic logic. In proc. of Durham conference on Applications of Sheaves 1977, Lecture notes in Math., Springer–Verlag 1979.

[She] Sheeran, M., μFP an algebraic VLSI description language. D.Phil. thesis, Oxford 1983.

[St] Stirling, C., Modal logics for communicating systems. Report CSR–193–85 of the Computer Science Dept., Univ. of Edinburgh (1985).

[W] Winskel, G., A complete proof system for SCCS with modal assertions. In the proceedings of Foundations of Software Technology, Springer lecture notes in Comp.Sc. (1985).

List of Lecturers

Richard S. Bird , Oxford University Computing Lab., Programming Research Group
8-11 Keble Road, Oxford OX1 3QD, United Kingdom

Manfred Broy, Fakultät für Mathematik und Informatik, Universität Passau
Postfach 2540, 8390 Passau, Germany

Edsger W. Dijkstra, Dept. of Computer Sciences, The University of Texas at Austin
Austin, Texas 78712-1188, USA

Eric C.R. Hehner, Computer Systems Research Institute, University of Toronto
Sandford Fleming Building, 10 King´s College Road, Toronto, Canada M5S 1A4

C.A.R. Hoare, Oxford University Computing Lab., Programming Research Group
8-11 Keble Road, Oxford OX1 3QD, United Kingdom

Gérard Huet, INRIA, Domaine de Voluceau - Rocquencourt
B.P. 105, 78153 Le Chesnay Cedex, France

Cliff B. Jones, Department of Computer Science, The Manchester University
Manchester M 13 9PL, United Kingdom

J. Alan Robinson, Syracruse University
607 Bird Library, Syracruse N.Y. 13210, USA

Michel Sintzoff,Unité d'Informatique,Université Catholique de Louvain
place Sainte-Barbe 2, 1348 Louvain-la-Neuve, Belgium

Glynn Winskel, University of Cambridge, Computer Laboratory
Corn Exchange Street, Cambridge CB2 3QG, England

NATO ASI Series F

NATO ASI Series F